Rare Diseases
Challenges and Opportunities
for Social Entrepreneurs

RARE DISEASES

Challenges and Opportunities for Social Entrepreneurs

Edited by
Nicolas Sireau

Greenleaf
PUBLISHING

© 2013 Greenleaf Publishing Limited

Published by Greenleaf Publishing Limited
Aizlewood's Mill
Nursery Street
Sheffield S3 8GG
UK
www.greenleaf-publishing.com

Cover by LaliAbril.com
Printed in the UK on environmentally friendly, acid-free paper
from managed forests by CPI Group (UK) Ltd, Croydon

British Library Cataloguing in Publication Data:
  A catalogue record for this book is available from the British Library.

  ISBN-13: 978-1-906093-52-5 [paperback]
  ISBN-13: 978-1-909493-20-9 [electronic]

Contents

Introduction 1

1 Toward a focused, multinational, rare disease awareness initiative 7
Peter Saltonstall and E. Michael D. Scott

2 The challenges of scaling up an orphan drug enterprise 22
Hans Schikan

3 Building an entrepreneurial patient movement:
A global case study from the AKU Society 43
Oliver Timmis

4 The practicalities of clinical development of drugs for rare diseases 62
Anthony K. Hall

5 Navigating orphan drugs through the regulatory maze:
Successes, failures and lessons learned 87
Remco de Vrueh, Harald Heemstra and Michelle Putzeist

6 Drug repositioning strategies for rare and orphan diseases:
A cost-effective approach for new uses for existing drugs 114
Maria P. del Castillo-Frias, Andrew J. Doig and Farid Khan

7 Why patient registries are crucial for finding cures for rare diseases .. 150
Pat Furlong and Kyle Brown

8 Challenges, strategies and lessons learned for the setting up
and running of a European Reference Network for rare disease 159
Samantha Parker and Stephen Lynn

9 Managing research advances into a rare disease:
Case study of the Myrovlytis Trust 176
John Solly and Galina Shyndriayeva

10 The BLACKSWAN Foundation for rare diseases 193
Olivier Menzel and Silvia Panigone

11 The rise and fall of Sanfilippo syndrome 201
Karen Aiach

12 Lobbying for a national rare disease plan in the UK:
Lessons for rare disease patient alliances 207
Stephen Nutt

13 The global drug development process: What are the implications
for rare diseases and where must we go? 231
Sharon F. Terry with Jayson Swanson

Conclusion 263

Index 265

Introduction

Nicolas Sireau
AKU Society

I was introduced to the world of rare diseases 12 years ago, with the birth of my first child, Julien. We'd just taken him home from the hospital where he was born, when we noticed late one evening that his nappy was red-black. We were worried. Was it blood?

We immediately rang up the after-hours doctor, who turned up within the hour. He was a youngish doctor, with a cheerful face and cheeks red from the cold outside. He studied the nappy curiously, then tested for blood, but didn't find any. He scratched his chin and looked around our apartment as though expecting to find an answer.

Then he asked my wife, Sonya, what we'd been eating that day. It turned out that we'd had a delivery of organic fruit and vegetables, including red cabbage, which we'd eaten.

'Aha', said the doctor. 'That's the reason why. The red from the cabbage is going into the breastmilk, into the baby and into his urine'.

We weren't overly impressed by this diagnosis. Next day, we went to see our family doctor, who dismissed the other doctor's diagnosis of red cabbage as 'ridiculous' and had a range of tests carried out.

A few weeks later, the correct diagnosis arrived: alkaptonuria, an ultra-rare disease for which there is no cure. Our family doctor told us not to go and research it on the internet because we'd end up scaring ourselves. That's exactly what we did. We found out that alkaptonuria or (AKU for short), was the first inherited disease identified, in 1901, that it's called black bone disease because bones go black and brittle, that there was no support group in existence, and that some early-stage, tentative research into a treatment was being carried out at the National Institutes of Health (NIH) in the USA, but nowhere else.

After extensive online searching, I made contact with an AKU patient called Robert Gregory, who lived in Liverpool and was setting up the AKU Society as a charity in collaboration with a metabolic consultant called Dr L. Ranganath. The early years were tough: we had no money, no research projects and knew very few patients. Ten years later, we have an international consortium of pharmaceutical companies, biotechs, universities, hospitals, clinical trial centres, contract research organisations and AKU patient groups spanning Europe, North America, the Middle East and Asia. We've raised more than US$25 million, have set up the world's first AKU Centre, in Liverpool, and launched a five-year international clinical trial to obtain market authorisation for the promising drug originally studied by the NIH.

It's been quite an adventure, and lots of hard work, with many setbacks along the way. But our story is in no way unique, as this book will show. From the creation of the National Organization for Rare Disorders (NORD) in the USA, to the launch of the biopharma company Prosensa in the Netherlands, the BLACKSWAN Foundation in Switzerland, PatientCrossroads in the USA, Protein Technologies and the Myrovlytis Trust in the UK, and the Genetic Alliances in the USA and the UK, social entrepreneurs have been leading the drive to find treatments for the myriad rare diseases affecting hundreds of millions of people worldwide.

There is no unique model of social enterprise in the rare disease space. Some of us, such as the AKU Society, have gone for the single rare disease, patient group, charitable model. Others, such as NORD or the Genetic Alliances, have gone for the umbrella model, representing a broader segment of society and focusing on changing the overarching government policies that affect rare disease patients. Yet others, such as Prosensa and Protein Technologies, have adopted a more commercial approach as businesses focusing on drug development. This diversity is what makes up the strength of the rare disease sector, because all share the same vision: a better life for rare disease patients.

My background is in social entrepreneurship: the belief that individuals can make a big difference to society by harnessing the entrepreneurial methods and skillsets generally attributed to the commercial sector. Spearheaded originally by the Ashoka global fellowship of social entrepreneurs, social entrepreneurship is now mainstream and taught in top business schools around the world. Jargon such as social impact assessment, social return on investment and social value is used widely.

But social entrepreneurship is primarily a state of mind. It is born out of necessity. A social entrepreneur, whether they're setting up a solar enterprise in Africa, a microfinance scheme in India, or an anti-gang project in inner-city London, is driven by the need to solve a glaring social problem that nobody has yet resolved. Ultimately, social entrepreneurship thrives in areas of large unmet need.

Which is exactly the case for rare diseases. As you'll read many times in this book, there are 6,000 to 8,000 rare diseases, affecting 6–8% of the world's population: 3.5 million people in the UK; hundreds of millions worldwide. Yet only a small minority of these rare diseases have treatments. The rest are left to languish, with patients dying or living severely disabled lives. The unmet need is so huge and still so unrecognised that many people call these rare diseases by the name of 'orphan diseases': orphaned from society, orphaned from the medical profession, orphaned from research.

Yet it's a sector where social entrepreneurship is thriving, as this book will show. These social entrepreneurs generally fall into two categories: patients, parents and relatives frustrated by the lack of interest in rare diseases and wanting to make a difference; and researchers, scientists and clinicians wanting to help patients that nobody else is caring for, yet also fascinated scientifically by what these rare diseases teach us about the human body.[1] When this frustration or fascination is turned into effective action, a social entrepreneur is born.

But this book is more than just a few case studies of social entrepreneurship. It provides crucial information for social entrepreneurs who want to develop within the rare disease space. It tackles key issues such as the regulatory rules and regulations governing orphan drug development, the repurposing of drugs for rare disease indications, the policy framework and the need for patient registries. All of these are key for developing projects successfully.

Chapter 1 is by Peter Saltonstall and Mike Scott, respectively the CEO and Chairman of the National Organization for Rare Disorders (NORD). They make the case for a more focused and global public awareness campaign on rare diseases. They show how, despite the significant recent advances of the rare disease patient movement, awareness of rare diseases is still low among scientists, policy-makers, industry and the public. They suggest key messages that should be at the heart of such an awareness campaign and break down the target audiences that need to be reached. Indeed, strong communications is fundamental to achieving our goals of curing as many rare diseases as possible.

Chapter 2 is by Hans Schikan, the CEO of biopharma company Prosensa. In its early stages, Prosensa was financed mainly by funding from the muscular dystrophy patient groups to help it develop its first drug development initiatives. Now, Prosensa is in partnership with GlaxoSmithKline, to the tune of hundreds of millions of Euros, yet retains its strong links with the patient community. Hans explains Prosensa's journey and why patients have played such an important role in it from the start. He also looks at the challenges facing a company trying to scale up in the orphan drug space.

We then move on to a chapter that continues the theme of patient-driven action with the story of the AKU Society. Written by Oliver Timmis, Communications Manager at the AKU Society, it describes the growth of the AKU Society from its early days to now being at the centre of a worldwide movement seeking to develop a promising new treatment called Nitisinone. Oliver explains the steps taken to reach

---

1 Many rare diseases are extreme forms of common diseases or provide insight into common disease mechanisms. For instance, AKU is a chemical model of osteoarthritis, a very common disease, for which there is no treatment. Statins, used widely to treat high cholesterol, were developed initially for the rare disease familial hypercholesterolemia. Bisphosphonates, a class of drugs developed initially for a rare disease called hypophosphatasia, are now used extensively to treat bone disorders such as osteoporosis.

this stage, from the global campaign to identify AKU patients, to the need to raise funds and carry out strong fundamental and early clinical research, to the challenge of designing a clinical trial for such a rare disease.

Drug development is highly regulated, which is why Chapter 4, by orphan drug development expert Tony Hall, goes through the detail of the regulations and incentives facing any entrepreneur wanting to enter the orphan drug space. Tony is a successful entrepreneur himself, with years of experience in this field, and his advice on this is definitely worth reading. He explains the differences between the US and European legislations and what this means for drug developers. He finishes with a case study of Nitisinone's clinical development that builds directly on the material provided by Oliver in the previous chapter.

In Chapter 5, Dutch researchers Remco de Vrueh, Harald Heemstra and Michelle Putzeist put forward the results of their research into the successes and failures of navigating the orphan drug regulatory maze. They look at what factors predict whether an orphan drug will gain regulatory approval, such as whether the company has initiated early dialogue with the regulatory authority before launching the trial. It has often been said that the pharmaceutical industry is the most regulated industry after the airline industry, and hence all entrepreneurs in the orphan drug space should read this chapter to increase their chances of success.

Chapter 6 is the most scientifically complex, yet hugely exciting. Written by Manchester group Maria P. del Castillo-Frias, Andrew J. Doig and Farid Khan, it argues in favour of increased repurposing of existing drugs for rare diseases. Drug repurposing—or the re-use of drugs initially developed for other conditions and applying them to new conditions—is a cost-effective and efficient way of developing new treatments for rare diseases. Repurposed drugs often already have regulatory approval and are therefore considered safe. So the cost of redevelopment is much lower than starting from scratch, and the chances of success much higher. The authors discuss the use of compound libraries, systems biology and intellectual property rights, among other issues, and provide pointers for entrepreneurs.

We then move to a range of other important issues for social entrepreneurs in the rare disease space. Chapter 7, by Pat Furlong and Kyle Brown, tackles the complex problem of patient registries, the term used to describe the databases of patient information that are crucial for tracking and understanding the evolution of the disease. A key problem is that there is no uniformly accepted format for rare disease patient registries, which leads to a plethora of different types and packages that often don't communicate with each other and lead to suboptimal data. Pat and Kyle propose the model developed by PatientCrossroads, where patients and clinicians can both enter data, and which would provide a template for a global registry system for rare diseases.

Chapter 8, by Samantha Parker and Stephen Lynn, discusses the issue of European reference networks for rare diseases, which are specialised networks of expert centres. A major problem facing most rare diseases is that they don't have a specialist centre that patients can attend where clinicians, working as a multi-disciplinary team, are experts in the particular disease. Rare disease patients often go from doctor to doctor and hospital to hospital, trying to find the best treatment, but rarely receiving it. This chapter provides practical guidance for the development and management of European reference networks for rare diseases, building on experience gained through the pilot reference networks funded through the European Commission DG Sanco call for proposals 2006–2008.

In the next two chapters, we focus on case studies of two medical foundations researching rare diseases. Chapter 9, by John Solly and Galina Shyndriayeva, describes the case of the Myrovlytis Trust, which was set up to help cure genetic diseases, deciding to focus on Birt-Hogg-Dubé (BHD) Syndrome for its initial research programme. The authors explain how developing networks, trying to lower the barriers to research, and directly funding research projects have been factors behind the foundation's success so far.

Chapter 10 is another excellent example of social entrepreneurship. Written by Olivier Menzel and Silvia Panigone—both from the BLACKSWAN Foundation for rare diseases—it presents two exciting initiatives: the (RE)ACT Congresses on rare diseases, an international conference devoted exclusively to rare disease academic research, and the move to set up a social investment fund for rare disease start-up companies. Both of these initiatives have the potential to revolutionise the rare disease space.

Chapter 11 is an inspiring example of the creation of a biotech company by the parents of a rare disease patient. Karen Aiach tells of her anguish when her child was born with Sanfilippo syndrome, a particularly lethal rare disease with a central nervous system component. But rather than give in to despair, she and her husband set up Lysogene, a clinical stage biotechnology company that is already carrying out a phase I/II clinical study of a promising gene therapy that could ultimately treat a range of rare diseases.

Chapter 12 moves us into the realm of policy. Written by Stephen Nutt of Rare Disease UK (RDUK), it examines the background to the campaign for a plan for rare diseases in the UK, and the establishment and role of RDUK to lobby for a plan. It develops recommendations to inform other national alliances seeking to lobby their national governments to develop a rare disease plan. As policy plays such an important role in structuring the framework for research, clinical care and drug development for rare diseases, this chapter is important reading.

Chapter 13, by Sharon Terry with Jayson Swanson, closes the book with an overview of the key issues facing the rare disease sector: from the problem of funding, to the implications of the human genome project, whole genome sequencing, stratified medicine, biobanks, social media and the recent involvement of big pharma in the orphan drug space. The authors conclude with a plea for more openness, transparency and networking to accelerate the drug development process. I hope this book will help others to respond to this plea.

I hope you enjoy reading the book as much as I enjoyed editing it. It brings together leading thinkers in this field and will, I hope, spark some good debates.

Dr **Nicolas Sireau** is Chairman of the AKU Society, a medical charity that works to find a cure for and support patients with AKU, which affects his two sons. The AKU Society is a fast-growing patient movement, with formal patient groups in the UK, France, Italy, Germany, the Netherlands and North America. It is spearheading an international consortium of biotechs, pharma companies, universities, hospitals and clinical trial centres across Europe, the Middle East, Asia and North America. He is the Co-founder and Chairman of Findacure, a new charity that raises awareness and funds research into fundamental diseases: extreme and exceptional diseases that advance our understanding of medicine and help us discover potential new treatments. Dr Sireau is also a former non-executive Director of GenSeq, a bioinformatics company. He is a fellow of the Ashoka fellowship of social entrepreneurs and of the Royal Society of Arts. Dr Sireau's previous career was in international development, where he set up SolarAid, an award-winning social enterprise bringing solar power to Africa, and wrote several books on international aid. Dr Sireau has a PhD in Social Psychology, an MSC in Business Management, an MA in Journalism Studies, and an MA (Oxon) in History and Economics.

1

Toward a focused, multinational, rare disease awareness initiative

Peter Saltonstall and E. Michael D. Scott[*]

National Organization for Rare Disorders, USA

1.1 In the beginning

The tale of how rare diseases started to come to public consciousness began more than 30 years ago when Abbey Meyers, who was to become the founder of the National Organization for Rare Disorders (NORD), was concerned about a drug being taken by her oldest son.

Abbey, who described herself as 'a simple housewife from Connecticut with children who have a rare genetic disorder', first contacted the US Food and Drug Administration (FDA) in the late 1970s, when her oldest son was severely impacted by a rare disease.

As Abbey relates it:

> Finally he was put on an investigational drug, and it worked. But a few months later the manufacturer decided to stop development of the compound. I did not know at the time that the decision was based solely on

* Peter Saltonstall is the President and Chief Executive Officer of the National Organization for Rare Disorders (NORD) in Danbury, Connecticut; E. Michael D. Scott is an executive with Independence HealthCom Strategies Group, Inc. in Philadelphia, Pennsylvania, and is the current Chairman of the Board of Directors of NORD.

economic—not medical—reasoning. The drug was being developed for a prevalent disease and it was not effective for that condition. The manufacturer didn't care that it worked for my son's disease because the market was too small to be sufficiently profitable. In other words, it was an 'orphan drug'.

Abbey went on:

Since I had no answers as to why we couldn't get the drug, I phoned the FDA. Eventually I spoke to a woman in the Neuropharmacology Division and asked why development of the drug was being stopped. In particular, I wanted to know if my son was in danger; for example, did FDA find out that it caused a serious side effect such as cancer and therefore ordered the sponsor to discontinue the clinical trials?

The woman on the phone said, 'I can't talk to you until I speak to a Freedom of Information Officer', and she promised to call me back. A few hours later she did call me back. She said, 'I spoke to the Freedom of Information Officer, and he said I cannot talk to you'.

Needless to say, I hung up the phone in disbelief. That phone conversation, however, was the very beginning of a battle that culminated in passage of the *Orphan Drug Act of 1983*. I spoke with numerous rare disease support groups who felt the orphan drug dilemma needed to be solved, and that coalition evolved into NORD, dedicated to the identification, treatment, and cure of rare diseases through programs of education, advocacy, research, and services for patients and families. Ultimately the American orphan drug program became the model for an international effort to alleviate rare disease (Meyers 2005).

Until the US Congress passed the Orphan Drug Act, the terms 'rare disease' and 'rare disorder' had no special meaning, and the term 'orphan drug' had no meaning at all. The term 'orphan disease' was used but there was no standard definition for it. If you'd asked the typical healthcare professional what an 'orphan drug' or an 'orphan disease' was in 1983, the response would undoubtedly have been a puzzled look.

1.2 Where are we now?

Fast forward to the present time…and the world of rare diseases and orphan drugs (and devices) has changed—big time.

- NORD, which Abbey Meyers founded in 1983, remains the strong and principal US voice for the entire rare disease community, providing a spectrum of national advocacy and patient services

- EURORDIS (the European Organisation for Rare Diseases) is the European counterpart for NORD and represents the European rare disease community

- In virtually every part of the economically advanced world, there are national organisations that represent patients with rare diseases, but much more importantly there are disease-specific organisations, usually headed by a person with the disease or by a caregiver-relative, often a parent of a child, with the disease

- Government-supported entities worldwide, their regulatory officials, and government and private reimbursement personnel know exactly what is meant by a rare disease and by an orphan drug or orphan device

- Programmes, though not necessarily well-funded, exist throughout the world to support patients with rare diseases and to advance research into new therapies for them

- Members of the investment community—some, not all—have recognised that investing in the development of drugs and devices for rare diseases can be financially viable, and a number of companies have been formed solely for the purpose of developing and marketing orphan drugs and devices

- Major pharmaceutical companies have understood the potential of developing products for the treatment of rare diseases, and have acquired or established specific units to focus on these opportunities

As never before, and perhaps in a manner never envisioned by Abbey Meyers in 1983, the world rare disease community has started to develop cohesion and collaboration and even a sense of shared purpose.

But there is another side to this coin:

- The stark reality is that the vast majority of people on our planet, including many in positions of great power, still have no idea what a rare disease is, or how to define an orphan drug or device

- The stark reality is that government-approved therapies exist for only about 250 of the estimated 7,000 rare diseases

- The stark reality is that most patients with rare diseases still do not have the kind of support that they need to feel comfortable with their conditions or to get the levels of services that enable them to live comfortably with their disorders

- The stark reality is that many investors still shy away from investing in the development of orphan drugs and devices, presuming that the small number of patients who might benefit from the products cannot support a favourable return on investment, especially with constraining healthcare costs continuing to be the priority of every government

- And the stark reality is that even as medical progress provides glimmers of hope for many with rare diseases, the financial constraints on national healthcare delivery systems threaten to undermine the availability of possible new treatments

In short, the rare disease community has taken giant steps toward bringing together the interests of people with rare diseases and those capable of developing appropriate treatments; toward starting to take advantage of modern communications methods to bring patients together globally; and toward coordinating the various organisations that represent patients with rare diseases. These efforts are noteworthy and signal great interest and progress.

But the time has come to take the next logical steps: to massively broaden public awareness and understanding of rare diseases and their impact—not only on the individual patients and their families and caregivers, and the healthcare community that serves them, but also on society and medicine in a larger context.

We need a truly global initiative to foster extended awareness about the incidence, prevalence and scientific importance of rare diseases. We need to fully appreciate the extent to which what we learn about rare disorders can have profound consequences for our understanding of more common conditions. Wider global awareness of rare diseases will accelerate research and bring the patient community closer together. A global awareness initiative on rare diseases is especially critical because rare diseases are, by definition, rare, and only by understanding them and approaching them on a global basis can we can achieve successful treatments and enhanced quality of life for the affected people.

1.3 Efforts to date to increase awareness of rare diseases

For the past few years, the leaders of organisations representing the rare disease patient community have taken aggressive steps to increase awareness and international communications about rare diseases.

In the US, for example, NORD was very instrumental in creating a special caucus in the Congress consisting of Members of both the House of Representatives and the Senate to focus their attention on rare and neglected diseases. When the Food and Drug Administration Safety and Innovation Act was passed by Congress in 2012, in a rare demonstration of bipartisanship, rare diseases were singled out for special attention. In an agreement reached with the leadership of the FDA, the office in the FDA's Center for Drug Evaluation and Research (CDER) was designated to receive increased staffing and support. This agreement was actively advocated for and aggressively supported by NORD.

The leaders of both NORD and EURORDIS have established a number of joint programmes that have started to bring together people with rare diseases and the healthcare professionals who treat them, regardless of geographic location, and that serve to increase awareness on an international basis about the needs of patients.

These programmes merit mention because, as we move forward, we need to build on these programmes and create new ones, including broad outreach to enhance public awareness of rare diseases.

For example, EURORDIS and NORD have launched online disease-specific communities so that patients with rare diseases can communicate with each other no matter where they live. For people with rare diseases, this is especially important because, in the areas where they live, there might not be a single other person with the same disease. Communications can aid in understanding medical care, as patients share information with each other about symptoms and treatments, but perhaps equally importantly communications among people with rare diseases can provide an immeasurable psychological support. The online disease-specific communities often are an integral part of a patient's personal support network, so essential in treating any chronic disease.

EURORDIS and NORD have created numerous online disease-specific communities. In the future, EURORDIS and NORD will grow their joint efforts to create international online communities of patients and families, involving patient organisations from around the world when they exist, in order to raise their disease awareness internationally, to ease exchange and mutual support across countries and continents, and to promote new patient-generated knowledge.

Another example of the globalisation of rare diseases is International Rare Disease Day, an annual, awareness-raising event coordinated by EURORDIS and NORD. Rare Disease Day started in 2008. It always takes place on the last day in February, which, when February has 29 days, is the rarest day on the calendar.

During recent Rare Disease Days, national alliances across the globe, on every continent, organised activities that were designed to increase awareness of rare diseases generally. More than 60 countries participated in Rare Disease Day in 2012 and included local events, social media and viral communications. Rare Disease Day has served to raise public awareness and to attract attention of policymakers.

In the USA, in 2012, both the National Institutes of Health and the Food and Drug Administration held special events on their campuses to recognise Rare Disease Day. In the UK, the lobbying group Rare Disease UK, led by Genetic Alliance UK, published an excellent report called, *A Vision for a UK Rare Disease Strategy*.

The importance of an international Rare Disease Day cannot be overemphasised. The events that take place on Rare Disease Day help focus attention not just on the patient community with rare diseases, but also on the need for new and better treatments. The day's very existence and the enthusiasm generated by and among the patient community cause a bright light to shine on rare diseases and the special challenges they pose.

A third initiative with international implications are meetings that EURORDIS and NORD sponsor annually along with the Drug Information Association, to bring global focus to rare diseases. In the autumn in Washington, DC, and in the spring in Brussels, hundreds of leaders within the rare disease community gather to discuss the latest policy, regulatory and reimbursement issues, among others. (However, there will be no meeting in Brussels in 2013 because the International Rare Disease Research Consortium [IRDiRC] is scheduled to hold its meeting in Dublin, Ireland in March 2013.)

The singular theme that always emerges from these meetings is that advances can be made only through close collaborations among government, industry, the financial community and patients and their organisations. Whether the topic is medical, such as the critical need to develop natural histories for most diseases; or regulatory, such as the need to assure flexibility in the testing and approval process; or reimbursement, such as the need to assure that patients with lifelong chronic diseases have access to the medications they need, the solutions are all tied into collaboration among the various stakeholders.

There have been and are a large number of other initiatives designed to increase awareness of and bring coordination to rare diseases.

The International Conference on Rare Diseases & Orphan Drugs (ICORD), initially organised in Stockholm in 2005, and subsequently held in seven major cities around the world (Madrid [2006], Brussels [2007], Washington, DC [2008], Rome [2009], Buenos Aires [2010], Tokyo [2012] and Shanghai [2013]), has brought together leaders from patient advocacy organisations, public policy, academia and industry. ICORD has sought to create a core international community of rare disease leaders sharing the same vision and common objectives.

The IRDiRC, initiated in 2010 by the European Union with the United States, Canada, Japan and other countries as well as industry, promotes globally coordinated policy for the development of the knowledge base for rare diseases.

EURORDIS has a large number of projects that are designed to broaden awareness of rare diseases. For instance, the EU Rare Disease Patient Solidarity initiative has the objective of exchanging information—on a pan-European level—on ways of offering essential services to rare disease patients, their organisations and families. Other objectives are to compare the quality of services available in different EU Member States for such patients, organisations and families; to identify the main obstacles to the provision of high-quality services; to disseminate best practices in the services offered; and to provide services urgently needed to support patients, patient organisations and families, such as a European database for very isolated patients, new EU networks with dedicated web pages, and databases with information on relevant help-lines, respite care centres and summer camps.

EURORDIS was also involved in the Pan-European Patient Network for Information on Rare Diseases and Orphan Drugs. Its primary objective was to gather the information required to help develop public policies on rare diseases and improve access to quality information. The methodology was based on a survey, workshops both at European and country levels, an awareness-raising event in the form of the first European Rare Disease Awareness Week, and the publication of guidelines and pedagogical documents. This project involved more than 500 organisations from 19 European countries and greatly mobilised the rare disease community.

A noteworthy earlier EURORDIS project was designed to: strengthen existing national alliances (Denmark, France, Germany, Italy, Spain, Sweden, UK) and develop new national alliances in Europe around the theme of orphan medical products (Belgium, Netherlands, Portugal); develop partnerships among all alliances; identify needs and problems regarding orphan medicinal products in each country; share best practice and knowledge; and produce recommendations at both the national and European levels.

Another important network, NEPHIRD, coordinated by the Centro Nazionale Malattie Rare (Istituto Superiore di Sanità in Italy), includes public health institutions on rare diseases and has received EU support for several projects, including a European Network for Epidemiological and Public Health Data Collection on Rare Diseases (Phase 2). The specific objectives of the project have been to estimate the epidemiological indices (i.e. prevalence, incidence) of a group of rare diseases selected as models in collaboration with existing clinical/diagnostic networks, to assess the quality of life and quality of healthcare in rare disease management within the participating countries, and develop public health indicators for rare diseases.

At the country level, an effort being coordinated by the rare disease community in France is called the Patients' Consensus on Preferred Policy Scenarios for Rare Diseases, or POLKA. This project links the EU efforts to the Member States' initiatives and to the interests of patients. The project aims at developing 'strategies and mechanisms for exchange of information among people affected by rare diseases'. It also aims to 'support European Networks of Reference for rare diseases in an effort to establish guidelines for best practice on treatment, and to share knowledge on rare diseases, together with evaluation of performance'. This objective is pursued through collecting, analysing and presenting in EU conferences rare disease patients' experiences and views on health policy, with the support of healthcare professionals, at both national and EU levels.

There are many more projects under way that are designed to increase awareness of rare diseases and generate more coordination. The point is that the rare disease community has come a long way in recent years in awareness and coordination efforts.

It's now time for the multiple interest groups concerned about rare diseases to take the awareness effort to the next level.

1.4 The need for enhanced public awareness of rare diseases

Despite the very significant and effective efforts to date to increase international collaboration among organisations interested in rare diseases and to raise awareness of rare diseases, there is still a great deal more to do.

While awareness about factors affecting the management of rare diseases have been dramatically enhanced since Abbey Meyers first started talking with the US FDA in the late 1970s, many people who have the power (and potentially the will) to influence the future of rare diseases still are not aware of the scope of the problem or of the degree to which what we learn about and apply to rare diseases expands our knowledge about the more widespread ones.

The lack of awareness about rare diseases affects everything from fundraising and government support for research and services, to the ability of the medical community to accurately and promptly diagnose rare diseases, to the confidence needed in the scientific research and investment communities in investing time and money in seeking new treatments.

Research into rare diseases is still highly 'siloed'. A young researcher today—however much he or she may want to commit to research in the rare disease space—has to be concerned that such specialisation may present difficulties for career development over time. The scientific research community still has no major professional organisation that brings all basic researchers in the rare disease community together (in the way, for example, that the American Association for Cancer Research brings scientific researchers on cancer together).

Only through enhanced public awareness will the rare disease community be successful in encouraging governments to have a rare disease strategy and to allocate sufficient funding to rare disease research and to services for affected patients and families.

In brief, the benefits of increased public awareness about rare diseases are:

- Increased government support for research and services

- Positive public health policies to advance the needs of patients with rare diseases

- Better communication among patients with rare diseases, enhancing not only their own lives but also the ability to develop needed natural histories or to recruit for clinical trials

- Better and more focused incentives for healthcare professionals to dedicate their careers to serving rare disease patients

- More precise and more prompt diagnoses of rare diseases

- Enhanced regulatory reviews of innovative new therapies

- Better reimbursement for services and therapies needed by patients, families and caregivers

- More investment in research and service providers

1.5 The audiences

To say that knowledge about rare diseases should be universally understood is too simplistic. There can never be universal knowledge and understanding about anything.

Therefore, any systematic effort to increase 'public' awareness of rare diseases must, as must any communications and education effort, have targeted populations. Among the populations that need to have a better understanding of rare diseases and orphan products are:

- The **research community**, which holds the key to new therapies but which needs to understand why research into rare diseases is important and how their research potentially can be used to treat not only patients with rare diseases but also those with more prevalent diseases

- **Policy-makers**, who set public policies and government spending that affect the delivery of healthcare and who, in this universally cost-conscious environment, must understand the importance of assuring that the policies and expenditures affecting patients with rare diseases are well informed

- **Policy influencers** such as the media, bloggers and think-tank experts, whose views are important to the policy-makers and who often set the agenda for healthcare issues

- The **academic community**, which provides intellectual leadership and which also provides early direction for medical and scientific research

- **Government health researchers** on a global basis, who cumulatively control the largest research budgets and who can set future directions for both basic as well as translational research

- **Healthcare providers**, who historically have been slow to diagnose patients with rare diseases but who need to understand the high cumulative prevalence of rare diseases and the need to be alert to any patient whose symptoms are not readily recognised

- **Drug and device companies**—from their boards and other leaders—who set priorities for their research and marketing requirements based on likely return on investment and support from the medical and patient communities, and who make fundamental decisions about which drugs and devices get to market and how they are priced

- The **investment community**, which decides which companies and products to invest in and by doing so makes decisions about which drugs and devices are to be further developed for possible approval and commercialisation

- **Government regulators**, who serve as the gatekeepers for the availability of new drugs, devices and diagnostic tests and who set the standards for how to test their safety and effectiveness

- **Government reimbursement officials**, who decide which products and services are to be reimbursed and at what price, thereby providing the commercial world with incentives, or lack of incentives, to pursue certain avenues of research

This is not meant to be a comprehensive list of audiences. It does not include, for example, patients, families and organisations, who presumably by their very nature know about rare disease since they are affected by one every single day.

One audience that has not been mentioned thus far is the 'general public'. This audience is defined as people who have no special reason to be interested in rare diseases for either personal or professional reasons, but who influence public policy, reimbursement and other issues simply by being voters and voices in the political process. Reaching this audience may be the most difficult, but there is no reason why the 'man or woman in the street', so to speak, should not understand what is meant by a 'rare disease' or 'orphan drug', and there is no reason why they should not become advocates for more research and better funding. Every family faces the risk that the next child born in that family will have some form of rare disorder…but most of them are simply not aware of the degree to which they are at risk.

Two examples of how this works are:

- The success of the muscular dystrophy telethon in the US, which for four decades has raised millions of dollars for a disease with which most donors have no personal connection

- The annual rare disease telethon in France, sponsored by the patient community for nearly three decades, which raises almost €100 million a year in donations through a 30-hour TV programme. The telethon has changed the rare disease landscape in France. Everyone there has heard of the term 'orphan disease'

What is important to understand is that many different audiences in many different countries need to be more aware about rare diseases, the impact they have on affected people and what they need to do to make the world better for the rare disease community.

1.6 The messages

There are a number of obvious messages that everyone should know about rare diseases, such as:

- How many rare diseases there are

- How many people cumulatively are affected

- The fact that most rare diseases are genetic and affect children

- The fact that most of these disorders are chronic

- The fact that so few rare diseases have government-approved treatments

- The special services that people with rare diseases sometimes need

- The need to understand many diseases so much better than we do today, including such basic factors as how they progress (natural histories) and what interventions, beyond medicines, are needed

These messages, and others, are foundational and must be integrated into any and all mass communications programmes designed to reach out to any of the audiences identified above.

But there are some less obvious messages that are also important because they can serve as motivators for those who seldom think about rare diseases at all. For example, as already mentioned, research into rare diseases often has a value beyond its benefit to affected patients.

There should be widespread interest by all within the healthcare community or among people concerned with disease in advancing rare disease research on a global basis. Not only does research help the people with the specific rare disease, it also often helps in gaining a better understanding of the biology of more common diseases and in new treatments for them. Rare disease research has great value as a learning tool for the better diagnosis and management of more common diseases.

The reason is that many rare diseases are regarded as special forms of common disease. For instance, alkaptonuria (AKU), a genetic disease first characterized in the early 1900s, is a chemical model of osteoarthritis. Research into AKU has provided better insights into osteoarthritis, discoveries that could lead to new treatments.

Some rare diseases are specifically described as 'gateway' diseases because they are gateways to understanding common diseases. Dr Francis Collins, Director of the National Institutes of Health, discussed this point at a conference sponsored by NORD, EURORDIS and other organisations in October 2011. He pointed out that such rare disorders 'often have profound consequences for our understanding of more common conditions'. Sometimes investors who decide to invest in research on a rare disease do so because they hope that the findings will help unlock new understandings and treatments for common diseases.

A second counterintuitive message has to do with finances. Orphan drugs and devices, despite smaller patient populations, can be a good financial investment, beyond the satisfaction that comes from investing in therapies that truly help people. A number of companies have invested in rare disease research and orphan products not just because they want to help people with rare diseases but also because it can be good business.

A third message relates to where medicine and scientific knowledge is generally headed. The more that we learn about the molecular basis of disease and about genomics, the greater the possibility of providing more precise diagnoses and more individualised treatments. Some medical experts say, only partially tongue-in-cheek, that someday all diseases will be 'rare diseases' because we will be able to narrow the diagnosis to the individual level. Indeed, many cancers today receive very precise and narrow diagnoses, enabling them to be treated on a much more targeted basis than ever before. So one of the messages that must be communicated is that everyone knows someone with a rare disease, and the more we understand the nature of disease and treatment, the more we will understand how personal the rare disease community is.

Finally, the messages must focus on the special challenges faced by the research community in developing new therapies for rare diseases. These challenges can more readily be met and addressed with access to larger patient populations, something that is seldom available for patients with rare diseases.

The specific research challenges that all the target audiences need to understand, and that are best addressed on a global scale, include the following:

- The rarity of the disease means that usually less is known about it, and there are fewer resources for obtaining medical and patient perspectives. A global perspective adds to both the knowledge base as well as to the resource base

- The lack of natural histories for rare diseases creates a challenge for researchers seeking to establish focused clinical endpoints and inclusion and exclusion criteria for study design. The more patients whose medical records can be accessed, the more likely it is that accurate natural histories can be developed for rare diseases

- The number of healthcare professionals with knowledge of certain rare diseases is usually quite limited. The more global the effort to train new healthcare professionals and to develop new treatments and needed services for patients, the more likely it is that such knowledge can be transferred. The development of a more integrated rare disease research community is essential to assure advances in both treatments and services

- The relatively small number of patients with rare diseases makes recruitment into clinical trials challenging and potentially expensive, and can also influence the design and statistical analysis of the clinical trial. Clinical trials for new treatments for patients with rare diseases often must be global in nature to enable recruitment of sufficient numbers of patients. Plus, data from multi-centre and multi-country trials often have greater credibility than data from narrower sources

- Limited funding options for new treatments for rare diseases often make it difficult to raise the money needed to support research. The more widespread the geographic areas involved in seeking new treatments for rare diseases, the more likely it is that more resources could be available

1.7 How to increase awareness

In our information-saturated world, how can the rare disease community increase, on a global basis, the awareness of rare diseases?

Communicating today poses novel challenges. Yes, there are an infinite number of ways to communicate. Messages and interests are segmented—that is, people have TV shows, websites, magazines and other sources of information that target narrow interests. So reaching people outside their normal interest zones is challenging.

Some of the potential programme elements for increasing awareness are:

- Highly targeted communications aimed at specific audiences such as the research community that, on a periodic basis, keep them informed and interested in rare diseases

- Published studies that address many of the myths about rare diseases and orphan drugs, such as that orphan products do not merit financial investment because of the limited patient populations

- More published studies and better public understanding of how research on rare diseases can affect the understanding of more prevalent diseases and lead to better treatments

- Education for diagnosing physicians who need to be reminded that a patient who presents with unusual or persistent symptoms may have a rare disease, and there are Internet databases that can help in the diagnosis

- Use of some of the public techniques that have worked well in the past, such as telethons

- More political involvement by the rare disease patient community, to advocate on behalf of policies and funding

- Use of social and viral media, the new way of engaging people on a broad scale

- Use of public/celebrity spokespeople who can bring attention to rare diseases through their own personal involvement and appearances

- Further enhancement of existing efforts such as International Rare Disease Day whose purpose is to increase awareness of rare diseases

This is far from a comprehensive list of communications approaches that might be used, on a global basis, to increase awareness of rare diseases. But it is a start. In late 2011, NORD rewrote its vision statement to include the development of:

> A social, political, and financial **culture of innovation** that supports both the basic and translational research necessary to create diagnostic tests and therapies for all rare disorders.

We would respectfully suggest that this vision—of a society that understands and is determined to address the fundamental sociocultural problem of living with a rare disease—is the core issue that needs to be addressed if we are to solve many of the specific problems inherent in diagnosis and management of rare disorders.

Addressing that core issue needs a global determination among the rare disease community to speak up, in a well-coordinated way, and to teach our society's leaders, and our peers, about the problems and the opportunities that lie in front of us all.

1.8 Conclusion

Rare diseases affect millions of people on a worldwide basis. Since disease has no geographic bounds, rare diseases affect people in every corner of the world.

For the rare disease community to advance its interests in having more and better financed research and services for the patients, their families and their organisations, there needs to be more awareness of rare diseases. There are a number of audiences who will affect the future of the rare disease patient—researchers, policy-makers, investors, government officials, for example—and they all need to have a better understanding of rare diseases. Beyond that, the general public, which influences the environment, must also be involved in advocating for patients and their legitimate interests.

The leaders within the increasingly global rare disease community need to work closely together to provide the true leadership that is essential if public awareness is to increase. No priority is more important for them as they pursue programmes that serve the best interests of the patient with a rare disease.

Reference

Meyers, A. (2005) '2005 Wiley Lecture', Annual Meeting of the FDA Alumni Association, Washington, DC, www.rarediseases.org/docs/policy/2005Wiley.pdf, accessed 29 November 2012.

Peter L. Saltonstall has been the President and CEO of the National Organization for Rare Disorders (NORD) since 2008. In the past four years, he has forged new relationships between the patient community and Congress, FDA, National Institutes of Health (NIH) and Social Security Administration, as well as with drug/device companies and the medical/academic and investment communities. His efforts to build collaborations with all stakeholders stems from his view that advances for the patient community can be achieved best through joint efforts. Under Peter's leadership, NORD also has updated and expanded its Patient Assistance Programs, which include assistance to patients in need of medications that they cannot afford. In addition, he has initiated steps to globalise the rare disease patient community and to facilitate research into new therapies and assure access by patients. Before joining NORD, Peter had more than 30 years of healthcare experience in both for-profit and not-for-profit environments. He held senior positions with a number of major academic medical centres and organisations, including Harvard's Brigham and Women's Hospital, Tufts-New England Medical Center and St Elizabeth's Medical Center of Boston. He also helped launch Harvard Risk Management Foundation's start-up venture, Risk Management Strategies, and the

University of Pittsburgh Medical Center's private equity arm, Strategic Business Initiatives. In addition, Peter was the co-founder and CEO of SafeCare Systems, LLC, which developed one of the country's first patient safety management systems. He played an active role on Capitol Hill in the development of the Patient Safety Act of 2005, which dramatically improved the reporting of events that adversely affect patients. Peter serves on the Humana Cares Advisory Board, the FDA Cellular, Tissue & Gene Therapies Advisory Committee (CTGTAC), the Child Neurology Foundation Board of Directors, the CTSA Consortium Coordinating Center External Advisory Board, and is a member of the IRDiRC Executive Committee.

E. Michael D. ('Mike') Scott is the current Board Chairman of the National Organization for Rare Disorders (NORD) and an executive vice president of Independence HealthCom Strategies Group, Inc., a privately held healthcare communications group of companies based in Philadelphia, Pennsylvania, where he has worked in a variety of positions since moving from the UK to the USA in 1985. He had previously been the sole proprietor of a scientific and medical health care communications consulting company in the UK. He has spent his entire 40-year career in areas related to scientific and healthcare-related communications. His primary personal interests today are in professional and patient communications related to the development and clinical use of products for the diagnosis and treatment of various forms of cancer and rare disorders, and in issues affecting access to these therapies for appropriate patients. Mike is also a member of the Board of Directors of the International Myeloma Foundation (IMF) and the president and co-founder of Prostate Cancer International. Among other professional affiliations, he is a member of the American Society of Hematology, the Drug Information Association, and the Alliance for a Stronger FDA. He is an affiliate member of the American Society of Clinical Oncology and the American Urological Association.

2
The challenges of scaling up an orphan drug enterprise

Hans Schikan

Prosensa Therapeutics, The Netherlands

2.1 'This company is patient focused'

In early 2004, after spending the first 17 years of my pharmaceutical career working for Organon, I joined Genzyme as director Genzyme Netherlands.

'You need to realise that this company is patient focused', the head of human resources told me as I was signing my employment agreement. My reaction was predictable. 'Well sure, every company active in the healthcare space needs to be patient focused, otherwise it shouldn't be in healthcare'.

My new colleague looked at me, smiled gently, and said I would soon find out what he meant; that my experience of working with patients would be very different at Genzyme. Just *how* different was something I would discover a mere two weeks later.

In almost two decades at Organon the number of my direct interactions with patients had been limited. Our primary focus was on healthcare professionals—the doctors who prescribed our products and the pharmacists who delivered the products to the end-users. In fact, at that time, direct interactions between patients and the pharmaceutical industry were uncommon, and were perceived by many to be inappropriate. After all, the thinking went, it is physicians who are most knowledgeable about diseases and their potential treatments; they are the audience that pharmaceutical companies should 'target'. Circumventing the doctor by talking directly to patients and potentially creating the impression of influencing those patients could be interpreted as an unwanted promotional practice.

After a couple of weeks in my new position, I participated in an informal orphan drug 'café' workshop, coordinated by the Dutch Steering Group for Rare Diseases. The café was organised to foster networking between all stakeholders in the Dutch rare disease community. During the Q&A session following a presentation by a regulator I asked a question and, in doing so, introduced myself as the new country director of Genzyme in the Netherlands.

A little later, in a break between the presentations, a young woman in a wheelchair came up to me and began:

> So…You are the new guy at Genzyme. My name is Maryze, and I would like to invite you to come and have soup and sandwiches for lunch at my house so that I can tell you everything you need to know about my disease.

Remember, I had just come from 'big pharma'. My initial thought was: 'Am I allowed to do this? Is it OK for me to have direct contact with a patient, not having talked to her physician first?' But I bit the bullet and accepted the invitation. Just a few weeks later I was on my way to a small village in the eastern part of the Netherlands to meet with Maryze Schoneveld van der Linde and talk about Pompe disease, about patient advocacy and about the need for a treatment. It turned out to be one of the most inspiring meetings I have had in my nearly 30 years working in the biopharmaceutical industry.

2.1.1 Patients as a source of inspiration

When I got to Maryze's home, she was busy dealing with email. I rapidly realised that she was in contact with Pompe patients all over the world—to inform them about scientific progress, to advise them about new and ongoing clinical trials, and to help them look for ways in which they might be eligible for one of Genzyme's expanded access programmes. Via the virtual highway, she was in regular contact with her friends and peers, providing both information and hope. While we enjoyed the delicious soup and sandwiches, which her mother had prepared, Maryze talked about Pompe disease and about herself. She told me how her parents had first received the diagnosis and how the verdict that no treatment was available, as yet, came right thereafter. She described how her disease had progressed and how, year by year, she experienced more functional loss due to the glycogen storage in her body and the absence of the enzyme which should break down this glycogen. She told me how her parents wanted and encouraged her to experience everything that healthy kids can experience, like skiing, while her condition still allowed for it. Then she mentioned how she woke up one morning and heard on the radio that a Dutch company called Pharming had had a breakthrough in its research efforts towards development of a potential medicine for Pompe disease—and how her day was turned upside down. That very evening she was on prime time news; the TV channel wanted to feature a patient with this rare disease for which a Dutch company now had a possible treatment.

From that moment onward Maryze's future looked—and became—totally different. The disease by which she was affected, and which had resulted in her being wheelchair bound, suddenly seemed to be treatable. One of her remarks about the change this brought about in her perception of the future was that she now had to start worrying about having a pension. She had always assumed that her life would be shorter, and that a pension wasn't something she needed to worry about, but now there was at least a chance that she might need (and enjoy) a pension one day. Maryze showed me newspaper clippings of how the rights to the Pharming candidate medicine for Pompe were acquired by Genzyme a couple of years later and how eventually Genzyme had performed a study which formed the basis for the final choice of the most promising development candidate.

At the end of a most enjoyable, but also very inspiring afternoon, Maryze reminded me that it was Genzyme's task to make a difference and to ensure that in the not too distant future a drug would become available for her and all other patients affected by this terrible disease. These tasks were therefore my personal tasks, too.

2.1.2 One person can make a difference

Just a few years later—after Maryze had already been on expanded access with the enzyme provided by Genzyme for some time—the regulatory files were submitted to the European Medicines Agency for all the data to be reviewed (and hopefully approved) so that Genzyme's new drug could be made available to patients.

This regulatory review process is carried out for all new therapeutic agents, and new, innovative products are approved every single year. In that respect the regulatory review process for Genzyme's novel medicine for Pompe disease was no different from that for any other new drug. However, apart from the fact that it concerned an application for use of a product in a very rare muscular disease unmet by any other product, it was the very first time that any patient was allowed to participate in the meeting with the European regulators and give a patient opinion.

At the time of the submission of the data supporting approval of this product, Genzyme had studied its candidate medicine predominantly in infants. Experience with use of the product in juveniles and adults was limited, and there was a fair chance that initial approval for use of the product would be limited to infants. There were concerns that more studies would need to be done before use of this product could be approved in other age categories.

It was Maryze who made a strong and well-presented plea to the regulators for the medicine to be approved for all patients affected by Pompe disease—regardless of their age. I am convinced to this day that Maryze's personal appeal made a significant difference in the final decision by the regulators that the product could be prescribed for all patients, even though (at that time) it had been studied mainly in infants. One person can absolutely make a difference.

Obtaining approval is only one hurdle in the long road between the earliest idea for a new drug and its final use by patients. Reimbursement is an equally significant hurdle, especially in the world of orphan drugs. Due to the long development trajectory and the specific challenges that affect very rare diseases, the development costs for innovative drugs for such diseases are substantial. When the number of patients eligible for treatment with the resulting drug is small, the consequence is almost automatically that the price per patient becomes high, especially if the company providing this drug wants to continue investing in possible solutions for other unmet medical needs and build a sustainable presence in the orphan drugs space. Annual treatment costs between €200,000 and €300,000 per year are not uncommon, provided the medicine has a real impact on these patients and their families, and provided the rarity and severity of the disease justify this.

In the Netherlands, the minister of health at that time thought that these high-priced orphan drugs could be reimbursed from individual hospital budgets. He did not realise that this could result in a hospital in Amsterdam allowing treatment with a specific product for a specific rare disease, whereas a hospital in Rotterdam could decide not to cover this cost—for the very same type of patient with the same rare disease at exactly the same time.

This system of 'postcode reimbursement' was widely considered to be unfair to patients, and would undoubtedly have led to a lot of patient referrals. It would also have extended many patients' earlier 'diagnostic' odysseys by adding a reimbursement odyssey, thereby effectively delaying or even withholding much needed access to the fruits of innovation for patients in greatest need. Not only was this the view of the biopharmaceutical industry, it was also the view of many patient organisations focused on rare diseases. This alignment of views is not at all uncommon.

On 1 July 2004, the Netherlands took over the role of Chair of the European Union. The Dutch ministry of health subsequently organised a conference in The Hague about 'priority medicines', attended by several hundred participants, among whom were Maryze and her mother, Tanneke. During a break in the meeting, Tanneke walked up to the minister of health, who was surrounded by some 20 people, all of whom wanted to get his attention. She tapped him on his shoulder and said that her daughter, who was wheelchair bound, would also like to speak with him, but could not get through the crowd. The minister followed Tanneke and, after the initial introductions, Maryze made it very clear to the minster that his plans for postcode pharmacy and making hospitals decide whether they would or would not reimburse were not good for patients with a rare disease. Obviously, he was rather surprised by this direct approach and promised to visit the patient organisation to discuss the topic in more detail, which he did a few weeks later.

The bottom line was that, just a few months later, he decided to abandon his previous plan to let hospitals decide on reimbursement and a novel system was set up whereby specialised hospitals could get financial resources from a centralised fund to cover costs for orphan drugs. Again, one person can make a difference.

The coincidence is that, many years later, flying back from a rare disease conference in the USA, I ended up in the aeroplane sitting next to this same ex-minister of health. When I mentioned to him that, under his ministry, an excellent system was set up to allow access to orphan drugs for patients with a rare disease, he directly remembered Maryze, who made a real impression on him. One person can make a difference.

2.1.3 Parents with initiatives

The patients who are themselves affected by rare diseases tend to be the greatest advocates when it comes to 'getting something done'. They are a source of inspiration for all stakeholders, especially the researchers in the companies that are trying to find a solution.

However, there are also many highly inspiring examples of parents who have become key advocates in rare disease areas which have a major impact on one or more of their children and their family as a whole. There are numerous patient organisations founded by parents who would not accept no for an answer and who started to raise money that could be directed toward research and development efforts into their specific disease. The dilemma of spending as much time as you can with your child with a rare disease while going the extra mile to raise money and to steer innovation towards that specific disease cannot be easy. Still, there are many parents, such as John Crowley, who left a well-paid job in order to set up a biotech company to help his children affected by Pompe disease, and they are all role models for other parents who encounter a similar situation.

The field of Duchenne muscular dystrophy is especially well populated with examples of parents who wanted to make a difference: Pat Furlong, whose two sons died of Duchenne's and who founded Parent Project Muscular Dystrophy; Paul and Debra Miller who set up Cure Duchenne to raise money for research; Elizabeth Vroom, the founder of Duchenne Parent Project NL; Nick Catlin of Action Duchenne; Benjamin and Tracey Seckler of Charley's Fund; and many others. Their organisations may be in different geographies and may have different strategies, but the overriding goal is the same for all—to fight the progression of Duchenne and to help find a treatment for a disease which so far cannot be treated. Their drive, their determination and their energy are a constant motivation for us to do what we do at Prosensa, each and every day: to fight Duchenne.

2.2 The making of Prosensa

Prosensa is a young, dynamic biopharmaceutical company dedicated to finding effective and safe forms of treatment for Duchenne muscular dystrophy and other rare diseases with a high unmet medical need. Our primary focus is on Duchenne's, but we are also applying our proprietary platform technology (RNA modulation) to opportunities to affect other rare genetic disorders, such as myotonic dystrophy and Huntington's disease. Our mission is to help patients and their families affected by rare diseases and it is our ambition to make a difference in their lives. This may seem a rather generic statement, but when we received an email from India around Thanksgiving Day last year, saying '… you are making a difference in our lives…' it suddenly became much less generic and very personal.

2.2.1 The foundation

Back in 2002, two scientists and an entrepreneur came together to found a classic biotech start-up company, Prosensa. Very early on, the company obtained access to intellectual property from Leiden University Medical Center in the field of so-called 'exon skipping'.

'Exon skipping' is one type of ribonucleic acid (RNA) modulation technology. Basically, Prosensa's technology platform uses single-stranded RNA-based anti-sense oligonucleotides (AONs) to correct mutated forms of single-stranded messenger RNA (mRNA) that cause life-threatening disorders. Our AON compounds are designed to: interfere with splicing so as to induce exon skipping, enhance exon inclusion, or correct splicing mutations; remove mutant RNA or protein domains; or simply block RNA expression.

Prosensa directed its earliest efforts to the field of Duchenne muscular dystrophy, where researchers at Leiden University had obtained some intriguing preclinical results. Gert-Jan van Ommen, a professor in human genetics, had been working in this field for quite some time and had applied for a number of key patents.

Of course an essential nutrient for any start-up company (in addition to highly motivated people, a great idea and time) is money. It is thanks to support from organisations such as Cure Duchenne, Duchenne Parent Project NL, Charley's Fund, AFM and many others that Prosensa was able to start to grow and attract scientists to work on a possible medicine for this debilitating disease.

Remarkably, for the first 5 years of its existence, Prosensa was mainly funded by patient and parent organisations, until we were able to attract more substantial venture capital in 2007. In many therapeutic areas, patient organisations are funded by the pharmaceutical industry; in the case of Prosensa it was the other way around.

2.2.2 Prosensa's growth

Thanks to financial support from patient organisations, an initial venture capitalist and the Dutch government, Prosensa was able to expand from a start-up with three people in 2002 to an organisation with around 20 people some 6 years later. Since that time, two financing rounds have attracted more than €31 million. The company has become more professional. Laboratory space and office space increased by the year; the science has progressed; and key publications have appeared in top ranking scientific journals, such as the *New England Journal of Medicine*.

After extensive preclinical studies at Leiden University Medical Center, the first four patients were treated in a Prosensa-initiated clinical study to assess the safety of a very small dose of the candidate medicine—and its effects on muscle cells. All four patients showed clear and consequent expression of dystrophin, an essential structural muscle protein which is missing in boys with Duchenne's. The preliminary proof of principle had been achieved, but a long road of development with numerous challenges was still ahead of us.

2.2.3 Partnerships as a key ingredient

Patient organisations not only played a key role in the essential, early financing of the company. In both the first few years of its existence, and throughout its development from a start-up to a more professional and structured biopharmaceutical company, discussions between Prosensa and many patient organisations about relevant end-points in clinical studies, disease awareness, clinical trial awareness, natural history data and registries have occurred on a frequent basis. The collection of natural history data and the registry initiatives used to assemble such data on patients with rare disorders are of key importance, even in the absence of a possible treatment, to a complete understanding of the progression of rare diseases. Similarly, the ability to correlate the natural history of a disease to outcome data from clinical studies is of paramount importance for the accurate assessment of the impact of a specific treatment.

Close partnerships between companies developing orphan drugs and patient organisations acting in the interests of people with particular diseases are mandatory, but due care and attention must be paid to the degree of independence of the partners. Even though the goals and interests of both parties are often well aligned, mutual respect for each other's position is a key ingredient for success. The perception that any patient organisation has become an extension of the commercial arm of a biopharmaceutical company should be prevented by all means. Not only would this be ethically inappropriate, it would also be counterproductive. The separate and independent role of the patient organisation should in no way be jeopardised. At Prosensa, we believe it is an excellent development that guidelines are now available to define appropriate interactions between pharmaceutical companies and patient organisations, so that these partnerships can be as fruitful and transparent as possible.

2.2.4 Rare diseases and 'big pharma'

One of the pioneers in the development of orphan drugs for rare diseases was undoubtedly Genzyme, with its early success in gaining approval of a treatment for Gaucher disease.

The Orphan Drug Act in the USA (back in 1983) and similar legislation in Europe (starting in 2001) were key drivers in the discovery and development of drugs for rare diseases. Companies such as Genzyme, BioMarin and Shire (after its acquisition of the small biotech company TKT) became early and important role models for other companies in the orphan space. We should not be surprised that small biotech companies were quick to embrace the rare disease drug development model. They were able to make rapid and significant advances in the relevant biotechnological science; 'big pharma' was still focused on developing blockbuster drugs with a revenue base of over US$1 billion and huge potential patient bases.

Until very recently only a few of the larger biopharmaceutical companies had seriously recognised and committed themselves to the strategic opportunities presented by rare diseases. However, with the decreasing output from the research and development pipelines of many large pharmaceutical companies and a looming patent expiration cliff for older, blockbuster products, conversations in many big pharma board rooms turned to the success of Genzyme as a possible opportunity to refocus on rarer diseases and orphan drugs—uncharted waters for most 'big pharma' companies as little as 5 years ago.

The patent cliff, which is the popular name for the fact that many high-use, high-revenue medicines have lost their patent protection in the last few years (and many others will do so in the near future) is a considerable challenge for many big pharma companies. After a patent expires, a medicine can be copied by generic manufacturers and the revenue of the original developer can be dramatically reduced within just a matter of months. This is a particular challenge if a company's total revenue drops significantly. This will usually imply that fewer resources can be made available for research and development into new therapeutic areas. One answer to the patent cliff is to move into emerging markets, such as China, Russia, India and Brazil, and to set up operations in these growth markets. Another strategy is to work on so-called life-cycle extensions by means of more patient convenient formulations, new administration forms and novel indications. Last, but in the context of this book certainly not least, an anti-patent cliff strategy is to enter the field of rare diseases.

However, a word of caution is essential. Any company that thinks that an entry into the rare disease field will be simple and comes with few significant hurdles needs to know that the often uncharted waters can lead to devastating shipwrecks. The idea that the world of rare diseases necessarily is associated with shorter drug development paths, premium prices, little to no competition, self-selling products and a simple business model is a myth. Those who believe in this myth are clearly misguided.

In 2009 Prosensa signed a collaboration agreement with GlaxoSmithKline (GSK) for part of Prosensa's portfolio of candidate drugs for Duchenne muscular dystrophy. The objective for Prosensa was to broaden and accelerate the development pipeline for products to treat Duchenne's. Early in 2010, GSK announced that it would set up a dedicated rare disease unit, and the collaboration with Prosensa was highlighted as an example of this new direction. Soon after GSK's announcement, Pfizer followed the same path and also set up a rare disease unit. A new era of partnerships between small biotech innovators and big pharma in the rare disease space had become a fact.

2.3 Seven hurdles in developing orphan drugs

The world of orphan drugs and rare diseases is one with numerous hurdles. At the most basic level, the assumption that patients with a rare, unmet medical need are waiting in line for a solution to their problem, and that enrolment of such patients in clinical trials is easy and uncomplicated, is wrong. In fact, the usual hurdles which are common in the development of any new drug are equally present in the case of rare diseases. The development of a new medicine, from its first inception until the point where patients have real access, takes 12 to 15 years. The number of drug development failures is huge. And even though the processes by which research and development take place have become far more efficient than 20 years ago, the hunger for more data and better defined study results has increased over time as well.

2.3.1 The rarity of the disease

An orphan drug designation can be obtained if the disease for which the drug is intended has fewer than 200,000 patients in the USA or fewer than 5 patients per 10,000 inhabitants in Europe.

On a regular basis, Orphanet publishes an overview of rare diseases listed by their prevalence. The most recent such report was issued in May 2012 (Orphanet 2012). The first 11 pages of this report cover diseases with their prevalence expressed in cases per 100,000, with 'infantile Refsum disease' closing the list at 0.005 patients per 100,000 people. This would mean for a country such as the Netherlands, one patient. On the next 16 pages of the report, diseases are ranked based on the number of case reports or affected families known, with 'X-linked spastic paraplegia type 16' listed as the last disease, with one family knowingly affected. To identify and correctly diagnose patients with an ultra-rare disease is not easy since most physicians have barely been made aware of (let alone been exposed to) these very rare diseases during their education. This often leads to diagnostic odysseys by patients and their parents or caregivers, desperately looking for any specialist who can correctly diagnose their disease. It is not unusual for there to be a delay of many years before the right diagnosis is made, and all too often patients end up with the wrong diagnosis, which is even more problematic if a treatment really is available for their actual disorder. In Pompe disease, for example, because of the similarity of symptoms, many patients used to be incorrectly diagnosed as having limb girdle muscular dystrophy. When a treatment became available, physicians who had patients in their databases with limb girdle did not automatically think that these patients might be eligible for the approved enzyme replacement therapy for Pompe disease.

Correctly diagnosing patients is one thing; getting these patients enrolled in clinical trials is quite another. Due to the extreme rarity of many diseases, it is impossible to apply the same development standards as for more common diseases. Studies with 5,000 or 10,000 patients are unimaginable in any orphan space, where it is not unusual for fewer than 1,000 patients to have been identified globally. Novel and innovative development pathways need to be identified in order to make progress in this field.

2.3.2 Preclinical models

When a biopharmaceutical company has decided to embark on the long journey of drug development for a promising drug candidate, the key question is how to select the most appropriate candidate compounds. Before clinical work with patients can even start, preclinical models are applied to test a clinical hypothesis. For many common diseases there are now well-validated animal models that can be applied. However, for rare diseases the use of animal models is often restricted because either such models are not available or the available animal models have no validated correlation with the effects in humans. This means that more efforts have to be spent on preclinical work, which in turn leads to a slower overall development process.

2.3.3 Functional outcome parameters

How can we measure whether an orphan drug candidate has the right effects on patients from the points of view of both efficacy and safety? For most common disorders, again, there are now well-defined functional outcome parameters that are utilised as end-points in clinical studies. For many rare diseases, unfortunately, relevant functional outcome parameters are less well defined.

Before a test is validated and can be used in a clinical study as an appropriate reflection of the efficacy of a novel medicine, many discussions have been held with healthcare providers, with regulators and with patient organisations. The last-mentioned stakeholder is of key importance. It is the patient who defines which parameters are relevant. The established '6-minute walk test' may be useful to authorities who review a regulatory dossier, but may be of zero relevance to a young man with Duchenne muscular dystrophy who is wheelchair bound. In his case, being able to work on a computer and handle a mouse to stay in touch with the outside world via emails, Twitter and Facebook is far more important. In rare diseases, many such outcome parameters, which are deemed highly important by patients, have not been identified and validated yet. Registries and natural history studies can help to identify novel useful end-points that can then be applied to clinical studies.

2.3.4 Development issues

In the development of drugs for more common disorders, many different clinical pathways may have been explored, discussed and established as appropriate by regulators. In rare diseases and some other unmet medical needs, such pathways are usually not established or even that well defined. The use of a placebo arm in clinical trials is an example.

In clinical trials that use placebos, one group of patients receives the actual drug being tested and another group receives a placebo that looks like the drug being tested but is actually just an inactive substitute. This 'randomisation' of the patients to active drug or placebo can be carried out in such a way that none of the parties involved (i.e. the patient, the physician or the company developing the drug) actually knows whether a particular patient is being given the active drug or not.

These so-called randomised, double-blind, placebo-controlled studies aim to provide the highest level of confidence that a drug effect can be accurately measured with regard to efficacy as well as safety. However, it also means that, over the course of the clinical trial, which can often span 1 or more years, one group of patients is not receiving a potentially effective new medicine. In that time frame, the disease will continue to progress. For the patients getting the placebo, more and more functions will be lost, whereas the other patients are receiving a potentially effective new treatment. One can debate whether the use of placebos in progressively debilitating rare diseases is ethical. If natural history studies and registries are available, providing valuable insight into the progress of a rare disease, the use of a placebo arm in a direct comparison may be less essential. In fact, many of the orphan drugs already available today have never been tested against a placebo in the clinical studies leading to their approval by the regulatory authorities.

2.3.5 Manufacturing challenges

Thanks to the advancement of molecular biology and the significant steps taken in the science of human genetics, many rare diseases are better understood now than ever before. Such insights into the causes of rare diseases and their pathophysiologies, made possible through highly innovative science, have led to new opportunities and innovative approaches to tackle these diseases. Often opportunities are found in the clinical use of complex molecules that can pose a variety of manufacturing challenges. In the case of biologicals (i.e. medicines made from living organisms, such as proteins), manufacturing can be particularly challenging. The same is true for so-called gene therapy, where the manufacturing hurdles to bringing new medicines to patients can be enormous. These manufacturing challenges are not exclusive to orphan drugs, but in view of the fact that many approaches in rare diseases are based on biologicals, they are quite certainly not less in the field of rare diseases.

Such challenges have been well illustrated by Genzyme's history in the manufacture of enzyme replacement therapies for lysosomal storage disorders, which unfortunately led to a situation in which patients were temporarily deprived of access to their essential medicines. At Prosensa, we work on antisense oligonucleotides. These are complex molecules that require more than 60 manufacturing steps from the first chemical reaction to the last purification.

2.3.6 Regulatory pathways

Drug development is very highly regulated—and for good reason. It has been said that with the exception of the airline industry it is the most regulated industry in the world. The Food and Drug Administration (FDA) in the USA and the European Medicines Agency (EMA) are key regulators when it comes to reviewing registration files and approving medicines, and the safety, the efficacy and the quality of the envisaged medicine are the most important elements in their assessment processes. Thanks to orphan drug regulations, frequent interactions between companies and the regulators have become possible. Companies are now encouraged to seek and obtain scientific guidance from the regulators early in the development process for specific drug candidates, which is extremely useful, especially for smaller companies with less experience of working with the FDA or EMA.

One of the challenges in this field is the lack of sufficient harmonisation between regulators. A company may receive contradictory guidance from the two sides of the Atlantic Ocean. Moreover, since the establishment of yet another European regulatory body, the Pediatric Committee, a company may be faced with different, sometimes non-compatible recommendations from different regulators even within Europe. Efforts are being made to resolve such problems, but when it comes to rare diseases, every year lost due to inefficiencies in assessment processes is one year too many.

In this context, it can certainly be argued that for patients with severe unmet medical needs, the review process perhaps should be less stringent, with possibilities for conditional approval, allowing for swift access to new drugs for patients for whom there is no alternative.

2.3.7 Pricing and reimbursement

If, after many years of successful research and development, a medicine is finally approved by the regulators, access to patients is by no means guaranteed, since the final hurdle of pricing and reimbursement still needs to be overcome.

The development costs for a novel orphan drug are not necessarily lower than those for drugs for more common disorders, and the routine manufacturing cost of these often highly specialised medicines can be substantial. Since the number of patients for whom an orphan drug may be applicable is small, the actual cost per patient for a course of treatment (which may be lifelong) can be very high. This is certainly not always the case and there are many examples of orphan drugs that have prices in the same range as those of drugs for more common disorders. But there are also examples of orphan drugs for very small patient populations, but with a massive impact on patients' lives, where the treatment costs go beyond US$400,000 per patient per year.

According to an article by Schey *et al.* in the *Orphanet Journal of Rare Diseases* in 2011, the annual per patient cost of existing orphan medicines (in Europe) was shown to vary between €1,251 and €407,631, with a median cost of €32,242 per year. This evidently worries payers, and many reimbursement authorities are concerned about the financial impact of new orphan therapies. In the same article, it was predicted that the share of the total pharmaceutical market represented by orphan drugs will increase from 3.3% in 2010 to a peak of 4.6% in 2016, after which it is expected to level off through 2020.

Since the traditional health technology assessment tools used to calculate acceptable reimbursement levels are arguably less applicable to diseases with few patients, a new approach is warranted. Apart from the impact a new orphan medicine has on a disease, the severity and the rarity of individual diseases need to be taken into account. This is clearly still uncharted territory and various initiatives are being introduced and undertaken to tackle this.

In order to improve early access to orphan drugs, pre-approval access systems have already been put in place in a number of countries, allowing patients with high medical need to receive selected medications prior to all regulatory approvals being in place, but at the same time allowing companies to start generating limited revenues from these medicines.

2.4 Building blocks in rare disease drug development and treatment

What would be the key ingredients or building blocks for an integrated and sustainable healthcare system in which patients with a rare disease would have access to the medicines they need?

It is evident that an unmet medical need is best served by prompt diagnosis and an effective and safe medicine or other form of treatment. But that is certainly not enough. For many rare diseases, patients do not have access to the right medicines because of flaws in the system. The building blocks in the following sections are by no means meant to be comprehensive. Yet, they are essential components which will help to get the right drug to the right patient at the right moment in time.

2.4.1 A good diagnostic infrastructure

Unfortunately, as already mentioned, many patients with a rare disease must undergo a diagnostic odyssey in which they go from doctor to doctor without obtaining a clear diagnosis. Diagnostic delays of many years are not uncommon and can lead to premature death, despite the availability of a medicine. This is also the case if the evident symptoms can be caused by a variety of diseases. A patient can be incorrectly diagnosed, diagnosed with a very similar but incorrect disorder, and not be identified as being eligible for a clinical trial or a treatment once such options become available years after the initial, wrong diagnosis.

For this reason and many others, a good diagnostic infrastructure is the first and most important key building block. Thanks to prenatal and newborn screening programmes, many diseases can now be identified prior to birth or in the first few days of life. Such screening programmes will further develop and expand in the near future, thanks to improved access to DNA sequencing and the increased understanding of the human genome. One unresolved question, however, is whether diseases for which there are no treatments as yet should be part of any newborn screening programme. Opinions on this topic diverge. Many parents feel that they would like to know as soon as possible whether their child has a serious disorder so that they can try to help as much as they can, even if a treatment is not yet available. Others have argued strongly that the years during which they were not aware of their child's disease were the happiest in their lives, even though they suspected that something was not quite right. The same dilemma comes up with what to do about diseases where debilitating symptoms are only expressed much later in life. Should one burden a patient from the moment of birth with the knowledge that by the age of 40 the first serious problems due to the disease are likely to occur?

From a purely technological and scientific point of view, we are at the threshold of far better diagnostic tools with greater utility than ever before. From an ethical and philosophical perspective, quite a few questions remain unresolved.

2.4.2 A solid patient network

When a patient is first confronted with the diagnosis of a rare disease and comes home, often in considerable distress, the Internet is, in almost every case, the first next step in the search for hope. Information about the disease, about the most experienced treatment centres, about research and development efforts towards effective treatments or a cure are the primary focus in these situations. However, for most of the approximately 6,000 to 8,000 rare diseases we know of, little really good and reliable information is available as yet.

Peer contact between patients or parents/caregivers of patients can be a valuable tool to collect and exchange information. The initiation and organisation of a well-structured patient network can also be a key step. There are numerous, inspiring examples where parents took the initiative to try to make a difference by contributing to a possible solution for their kid's disease. The key question of whether one wants to spend time setting up a patient network or spend that same time with one's child never makes things easier, and certainly not when the child has a shorter life expectation. However, the examples from fields as diverse as Duchenne muscular dystrophy, Pompe disease, familial hemophilia, Fabry disease, Gaucher disease, alkaptonuria and the mucopolysaccharide storage (MPS) disorders are inspiring—as are many others.

We have already discussed, in some detail, examples of the ways in which patients and parents have made huge contributions to the collective knowledge, the development and the final access for patients to innovative medicines for rare disorders in discussing the experiences of both Genzyme and Prosensa. It is almost impossible to overestimate the importance of the insights that patients can bring to researchers working on potential treatments for specific rare disorders.

2.4.3 Centres of excellence

The majority of rare diseases have a prevalence which is far below even the European orphan drug designation threshold of fewer than 5 patients per 10,000 inhabitants. As a consequence, the chance that the average general or family practitioner will ever see a patient with an ultra-rare disease is very small. Logically, the chance that they will recognise the disease is even smaller, since the textbook of internal medicine which they studied as part of their training curriculum may only have contained part of one minor chapter, if anything at all, on that particular disease. Finally, the chance that they are fully up to date on the latest insights with regard to such a rare disease and that they are aware of the best treatment guidelines is equally small.

For all these reasons, many patients with rare disorders are referred to specialists who are likely to see more patients affected by the specific disease or rare diseases that fall into a group of similar rare disorders. In an ideal world, a patient can and will get treated at a centre where all the healthcare providers—including the physicians, the nurses, the pharmacists, the physiotherapists, the genetic counsellor, the psychologist and many others—are familiar with the latest insights into the disease and the best way forward. These centres of excellence are critical to optimal patient care. It may mean that patients have to travel further to visit such focused treatment centres, but the advantages of being treated by teams that are fully aware of the latest developments around a rare disease are substantial.

2.4.4 Registries

The collection of many types of data about a rare disease is of great importance to better understand that disease and consequently to provide optimal care. A well-defined database including relevant patient information can also facilitate the recruitment of patients for clinical trials, especially in the case of a very rare disease where trial enrolment might otherwise take years.

For many years now, registries have been a key component of the regulatory framework whereby biopharmaceutical companies are required to collect and monitor data on use and the impacts of the medicines that they develop and market. Such registries allow for better insight into the value of individual medicines from a longer-term perspective. They can be disease-specific, product-specific or some combination of the two. They provide a resource for physicians who want to mine data and publish their findings on a particular disease in the peer-reviewed scientific literature. While most registry data are entered and compiled by healthcare providers, patient-based registries are becoming more common and the combined collection of data potentially allows for improvements in knowledge and consequent improvements in patient care.

For all of these reasons, registries of various types are now a key building block in the development of knowledge about the optimal management of rare disorders. On top of that, registries can also become a tool for building a community around a rare disease. By contributing to a better understanding of a rare disease, patients and healthcare providers develop a sense of belonging to a small but important community where information about the rare disease they all deal with is exchanged and shared.

2.4.5 Expanded access

Once an investigational compound has reached its final development phase and the efficacy, safety and quality of manufacture of the product have met criteria that enable a manufacturer to approach regulators with a dossier containing all data that will allow the compound to be assessed for marketing authorisation, physicians and patients will often want to have early access to the product for the most urgent cases. In many countries, regulators have developed systems to allow for such early access in cases of unmet medical need.

Applications for such 'expanded access' are usually physician initiated, either for individual patients or for groups of patients. It is then up to the manufacturer whether or not to provide the still investigational medicine for these purposes. Evidently, there are risks involved for all parties. From the manufacturer's point of view, early access can potentially jeopardise the review and approval process for the product. For example, under less strictly controlled circumstances than those used in a formal clinical trial, in a rare individual case, there might be findings that had not previously been observed in the clinical development of the new drug. Such findings could substantially slow down or delay the review process, even if the findings were not, in fact, drug related at all.

Nevertheless, early access programmes are common in the rare disease space. Where there are significant, unmet medical needs, expanded access may be a key ingredient to optimal healthcare for patients with rare disorders, and if companies can provide their candidate medicines early enough, but not too early, increased patient benefit is a valued outcome. If such early or expanded access programmes are set up with the right degree of rigour and oversight, and the data submitted by the manufacturer in the regulatory dossier are strongly supportive of potential approval of the product in question, they are among the most tangible examples of how to allow patients to benefit quickly from the many years of research and development which went into that regulatory dossier. Conversely, for products that might get a negative review from regulatory authorities, leading to failure to obtain marketing authorisation for those products, the situation is more difficult. In such cases it would make perfect sense either not to start an expanded access programme or even to stop an expanded access programme that had already been initiated. Experience has shown that in situations such as these, full support of appropriate decisions from relevant patient organisations is essential.

2.4.6 Standards of care

Even in the absence of an approved medicine that can actually impact disease progression, optimal care for patients with rare disorders can be achieved by means of appropriate support services and interventions that can optimise quality of life or even postpone some of the debilitating effects of a rare disease. A multidisciplinary approach describing the highest standards of care by patient type and by stage of the disease is commonly valuable. Such definition of standards of care and practice guidelines is still equally important once a medicine is available, since age, disease severity and other specific circumstances may lead to the need for different approaches to optimise care. If the best minds in a particular rare disease can meet and define the applicable standards of care, the outcome could (and ideally should) be a published, scientific, peer-reviewed article which sets the standards to be applied by all healthcare providers involved in the management of that disease with their own patients. There are numerous examples of excellent management guidelines and standards of care, based on the collective experience of the most knowledgeable specialists in management of specific diseases. Creation of such a consensus document is a vital pillar of an optimal healthcare system in the orphan space.

2.4.7 Centralised funding

In order to prevent a situation in which patients have access to reimbursed medicines in one hospital, but not in another, within the same country, a system of centralised funding for coverage of relevant costs seems to be the most widely preferred approach. As we saw earlier, 'postcode pharmacy' is the term used when patients in a particular town or city are deprived of optimal care just because they happen to live in an area where, due to local budget constraints, an approved therapy is not reimbursed. This is an unacceptable situation and may lead to unnecessary patient travel or even migration. From a social equality perspective, such a system is not desirable. The United Kingdom had a regionalised funding system like this until centralised funding for management of ultra-rare diseases replaced it relatively recently.

2.4.8 A tight community

Patients affected by rare diseases (and their caregivers) often become part of small and tight communities of individuals who find each other via the Internet or through meetings organised by patient organisations. The initial reaction once the diagnosis of a rare and unmet medical need is confirmed is all too often one of frustration and despair. Shortly thereafter comes the initial search—commonly via the Internet—for information, for a potential treatment in development, and for other people in the same situation. Small virtual communities can quickly be built, often followed by a first 'get-together' at which patients with the same disease can meet each other. The virtual community is often expanded into a very closely knit group of patients and parents/caregivers. Other potential members of such small communities can include healthcare professionals who regularly see and treat patients with the specific rare disease and researchers with particular interests in the causes and effective treatment of the disease.

This sense of belonging to a community built around a particular rare disorder is an important ingredient in any sustainable healthcare infrastructure through which patients and others can work together towards optimal care. The combined power of patients, healthcare providers, pharmaceutical companies, policy-makers, regulators and payers can have a huge impact on access to optimal care for patients affected by a rare disease. Partnerships are a key ingredient for success in the rare disease space. When all the potential stakeholders involved in the management of a rare disease are represented and engaged, communities such as these can make an enormous difference.

2.5 The future for rare diseases

Every day new articles are published about rare diseases. Every day our insight into the pathophysiology of rare diseases is increasing. Every day science is advancing and every day we come a bit closer to solving the puzzles around rare diseases for which there are currently no treatments. The future for rare diseases is one of hope: hope that the combined efforts of patient organisations, healthcare providers, academia and companies will lead to treatment solutions that will improve the quality of life of patients and their families affected by such diseases. Will this all be realised in the next decade? The answer is, no. But will we get closer, step by step, to helping more patients than ever before? The answer is, yes.

2.5.1 Personalised medicine

With our ever-increasing understanding about the human genome, insight into pathways that cause many diseases and into the potential to find effective treatments for those diseases is growing. This is inevitably leading towards a situation in which 'old' diseases that we currently think of as affecting many patients will become more fragmented and selectively definable in the future. A striking example is breast cancer, where, thanks to the increased understanding of the causes and biology of the disease, specific treatment modalities for smaller groups of patients have become reality. Another example is in cystic fibrosis, where marketing authorisation was recently granted for a therapeutic product which is intended for clinical use in just about 5% of the entire cystic fibrosis patient population. These are just two examples; more will follow.

Prosensa and GSK are currently working on the development of several possible treatment options for Duchenne muscular dystrophy, each for a distinct subset of patients with a different genetic profile. Personalised medicine (or 'individualised' medicine if you prefer that term) is just around the corner. In other words, subsets of many of the more common diseases of today will meet criteria for rare diseases tomorrow. Rare diseases are pioneers in personalised medicine.

2.5.2 Accelerated development

The pharmaceutical development of a novel medicine can take up to 15 years. Recent increases in regulatory rigour, and in the data requirements before a drug can be approved, have extended drug development times to such a degree that there is very public discussion about whether all of these new requirements are fully justified.

In the case of patients with unmet medical needs, rare or common, for whom good treatments are not readily available, the need to bring such therapies to market quickly and efficiently is especially important. We know for sure that every day that a new treatment option is delayed, patients with some rare, progressive disease will move further down their slope of functional decline. Every year that an effective and safe medicine for a rare disorder or an unmet medical need is delayed in its development will lead to patients with lower quality of life and potentially loss of life entirely. At the same time, investigational compounds which have not been reviewed by regulators in terms of the right risk–benefit relationship may come with significant and unknown health risks. More and more regulators are taking this into account when assessing registration files presented by pharmaceutical companies. One should not expose rare disease patients to unacceptable risks, but the natural history and clinical background of a disease where the outcome is known and certain can provide an important and sometimes critical perspective. Fortunately, the possibility for accelerated review of innovative new agents now exists in many jurisdictions.

However, quite apart from what can be done to shorten time to market through expeditious regulatory review, a paradigm shift is required in the way we develop new medicines, certainly for very rare diseases. The standard process of conducting large, randomised, placebo-controlled trials is impossible in situations where there are very few patients. Concerted efforts are required to come to a new, sustainable process for efficient drug development. Without changes in this respect, innovation in medicine becomes an impossible enterprise.

2.5.3 Health and wealth

Health technology assessment tools are widely used today to assess the balance between the value of a new medicine and the costs of such a product. A direct consequence of the application of such technology assessment is that a medicine which is clearly valuable for some patients may not be reimbursed because the costs are perceived to be too high.

For many very rare diseases, the treatment costs per patient are substantial, because the high development costs must be spread over a very small patient population. This may lead to situations in which a payer is not willing to reimburse for a specific medicine and patients do not have access as a consequence. This is undesirable—from a healthcare perspective and also from an economic point of view. If a biopharmaceutical company has spent hundreds of millions of euros on the discovery and development of a new medicine, but the results of that innovation cannot lead to economically tangible results, it can certainly be seen as a waste of resources.

A well-integrated approach involving healthcare, economic and innovation departments in governments would make a lot of sense. Even when regulators are convinced that a novel medicine has passed the assessment hurdles of efficacy, safety and quality, we all know of situations—certainly with orphan drugs—in which the hurdle of value versus cost is still insurmountable. Under those circumstances, real access to patients is denied. We need to find a way to approach this dilemma of whether or not to pay for innovation from a holistic point of view, in which we better assess the value that a new treatment may bring to patients, their families and society at large on the one hand and the cost of providing such a new treatment on the other. While this is what the science of health technology assessment currently tries to do, in the case of many orphan medicinal products, the current, widely applied methodology is less than fully appropriate when one considers the rarity of some of the diseases.

2.5.4 Patients in charge

Thanks to the exponential growth in access to information, patients today can be and often are far more knowledgeable about their disorders and the possible treatment options than ever before.

Especially when it comes to rare diseases, we frequently find that patients or their parents/caregivers are more knowledgeable than many healthcare providers. Patients experience their disease every single day. They talk about it; they read about it; and they often become experts. This is even more evident with rare diseases, when patients often establish small, highly focused communities and exchange their experiences via various electronic communication channels. In the field of Duchenne muscular dystrophy, as one example of many, parent initiatives have led to the development of professionally managed organisations that play a key role in directing funds towards academia and biotech companies to advance the science of possible solutions to the challenges presented by this devastating rare disease. But it is not only in the field of fundraising that patient organisations are influential and can make a difference. Patient organisations can and do also play pivotal roles in the dissemination of information and knowledge about a disease; the setting up of communication groups, support teams and registries; and in helping to establish sustainable systems through which researchers, clinicians, patients and families with shared interests in a specific disease can work together to optimise care and opportunity. Patients with unmet needs are starting to take more and more control over how those needs can be addressed, and the orphan space is clearly a front-runner in this respect.

The fact that patient organisations, and especially those in the rare disease space, are now increasingly well represented on the advisory bodies to many regulatory authorities (such as the FDA and EMA) is a clear indication of how patients are taking the lead in finding solutions and building healthcare systems in which patients with a rare disease have access to appropriate treatment that is equal to that of patients with the more common diseases that we all know well.

References

Orphanet (2012) 'Prevalence of rare diseases: Listed in order of decreasing prevalence or number of published cases', Orphanet Report Series, Rare Diseases collection, no. 2, May 2012, www.orpha.net/orphacom/cahiers/docs/GB/Prevalence_of_rare_diseases_by_decreasing_prevalence_or_cases.pdf, accessed 17 October 2012.

Schey, C., T. Milanova and A. Hutchings (2011) 'Estimating the budget impact of orphan medicines in Europe: 2010–2020', *Orphanet Journal of Rare Diseases* 6: 62.

Hans G.C.P. Schikan, PharmD, is CEO of Prosensa, an innovative Dutch biopharmaceutical company focusing on the discovery, development and commercialisation of novel treatments for rare diseases such as Duchenne muscular dystrophy, myotonic dystrophy and Huntington's disease, using its RNA modulation platform. In 2009 Prosensa announced a key agreement with GlaxoSmithKline for part of its Duchenne compounds at a value of nearly US$700 million. Before joining Prosensa, Hans worked at Genzyme for five years in various executive roles, including as Vice President for Global Marketing and Strategic Development of Genzyme's portfolio of products for rare genetic diseases. Prior to Genzyme, he spent 17 years at Organon, both at corporate level and in country operations which included assignments in Asia and Europe. In addition to his role at Prosensa, Hans is currently Executive Board Member of the Dutch Top Institute Pharma, Non-executive Director of Sobi (Swedish Orphan Biovitrum) and member of the Regiegroep Top Sector Life Sciences & Health. He is also past Chairman of Nefarma, the Dutch Association of Research Based Pharmaceutical Industry. He has a PharmD from Utrecht University. Hans has given numerous presentations on orphan drugs, rare diseases and innovation.

3

Building an entrepreneurial patient movement

A global case study from the AKU Society

Oliver Timmis
AKU Society, UK

Each rare disease only affects a few people. The AKU Society has identified 81 UK patients with alkaptonuria, and nearly 700 patients worldwide. It is not that many people, and leaves some questioning whether it is worth investing significant time and money into a large-scale campaign to help these patients. 'Wouldn't our work be better focused on common diseases, like cancer or cardiovascular disease?' Well, collectively, rare diseases do affect a significant number of people.

There are 3.5 million people with a rare disease in the UK.[1] If for each of those, you include family members (an average of four people per family), that is 14 million people directly affected by a rare disease. With a UK population of 60 million, that is about 25% of the UK population with direct experience of rare diseases. That is a significant health problem.

Grouping all rare diseases as one health problem can be called short-sighted, as it covers a vast range of conditions, many dramatically different from the others.

1 Estimate from Rare Disease UK (www.raredisease.org.uk).

However, as work at the AKU Society and many other rare disease charities has shown, all patients diagnosed with a rare disease face very similar problems. Nearly all patients, regardless of the rare disease they have, explain the hopelessness they feel because of a lack of support from the medical profession and the feeling that their disease is misunderstood. And nearly every family member explains the feelings of uselessness; forced to watch as their loved one struggles with a health problem for which, usually, there is no help.

So, when we are asked if it is worth studying a rare disease, patient organisations can explain that rare diseases are one of the most overlooked and underestimated health problems in the world today. This chapter will focus on just one of the 7,000 rare diseases, the first inherited disease ever described: alkaptonuria (AKU).

AKU is an unusual rare disease to use as a case study—it is one of the few that has potential for a treatment, a drug called nitisinone. By understanding the early studies into the drug, this chapter will show how the AKU's strategy as a patient group has been directed at building the knowledge, resources and most importantly the people needed to finally launch an international phase III clinical study of nitisinone use in AKU patients.

3.1 What is AKU?

In 1902, Sir Archibald Garrod, a doctor practising in London, described four strange medical conditions (albinism, alkaptonuria, cystinuria and pentosuria) that he called 'inborn errors of metabolism' (Garrod 1908), providing one of the first explanations of the link between genetics and diseases. One of the four was characterised by its ability to turn urine black, and was named alkaptonuria or AKU for short.

We now know that AKU is a genetic disease and so inherited from your parents. A mutation in the third chromosome leaves patients with a non-functional homogentisate 1,2 dioxygenase (HGD) enzyme (Fernandez-Canon *et al.* 1996). The HGD enzyme plays a key role in the breakdown of an amino acid, tyrosine. Its malfunctioning in AKU means that tyrosine is only partially metabolised, stuck at the point it is converted to homogentisic acid (HGA). HGA increases to a level 2,000 times the normal, and accumulates in all tissues in an AKU patient (Phomphutkul *et al.* 2002).

HGA is a black pigment. The majority is excreted in the urine, meaning that the urine of AKU patients will turn black when exposed to air. About half of the patients known to us were diagnosed when their parents noticed the black urine staining their nappies. Worried their newborn children are passing blood, parents take their child to the GP to find out they in fact have AKU.

The HGA that remains in the body of an AKU patient, however, causes many problems. It accumulates in the eyes and ears, causing black spots; in the kidney and prostate, causing stones to form; in the blood vessels, causing heart disease; and in tendons and ligaments, causing painful ruptures. The most severe effect of HGA accumulation is seen in the cartilage and bone of AKU patients.

HGA binds to cartilage, turning it black and brittle. In their late 20s, patients feel this as severe joint and back pain—every movement that should be softened by smooth cartilage is instead jarred against abnormal cartilage four times harder than plastic. Soon, the damaged cartilage breaks away, injuring the underlying bone and, without the protection of a cartilage layer, allows bones to rub together. This is where the other half of patients are diagnosed with AKU, often having reported to the doctor with severe joint pain or later with early-onset, severe osteoarthritis.

A diagnosis of AKU in adult patients is often suspected because of the presence of the classic tetrad of features shown in Figure 3.1.

For an AKU patient, the pain of this severe form of osteoarthritis is extreme and debilitating to the point where patients can no longer walk or move comfortably. Currently, the only options for treatment are to offer a lifetime of painkillers, while waiting for multiple joint replacements. Regardless of the severe pain caused to an AKU patient, the lengthy treatment periods (up to 6 months for treatment and recovery of a joint operation) and restrictions to comfortable movement affect their quality of life. Many patients take early retirement, miss out on playing with their children and are forced to choose a less active life. For a patient group like the AKU Society, it is important to remember that the disease not only affects patients, but also their families and loved ones that care for them and also have to carry the burden of disease.

Figure 3.1 **Tetrad of diagnostic features of AKU. Note the dark urine, eye and ear pigment and joint ochronosis. The diagnosis of AKU relies on recognising the black urine present from birth, blue/ black ear pigment, black pigment in the whites of the eye and clinical arthritis. These features usually alert a physician to consider AKU as the diagnosis**

Note: For greater clarity, you may view the figure in colour at www.akusociety.org/symptoms.html

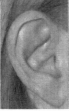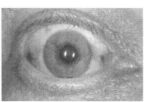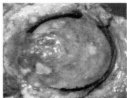

3.2 A potential treatment?

Our ultimate aim is to find a cure for AKU. Research into AKU began at the National Institutes of Health, in the USA in the 1990s. They completed their first study of AKU patients in 2002, publishing a 'Natural History of Alkaptonuria' (Phomphutkul *et al.* 2002). The paper was unique as it contained a very small sub-study where two patients were given a drug, nitisinone, for just over a week. The patients reported feeling less pain and analysis of their urine showed a reduction in HGA. The researchers were interested by this and so were keen to investigate the use of nitisinone a little further.

Nitisinone has a rather strange history. It started off life developed by ICI's Plant Protection Division, as a weedkiller. However, it turned out to be too effective and rather than focusing on the weeds to which it was applied, it would destroy any plant nearby. Analysis of its mode of action showed that nitisinone inhibited the tyrosine breakdown pathway (Fig. 3.2). In plants, this breakdown pathway leads to chlorophyll production. Nitisinone, therefore, killed plants by preventing them from producing chlorophyll and stopping them from using sunlight as energy. Chlorophyll also gives plants their green colour, a lack of which explains the bleaching effect when using nitisinone.

The tyrosine breakdown pathway is also present in humans, where it describes several diseases, as explained in Figure 3.2. AKU is caused by a mutation in

Figure 3.2 **Metabolic pathway of tyrosine metabolism. Enzymes in italics, disease names and drug in bold, with a cross denoting their interaction with the pathway**

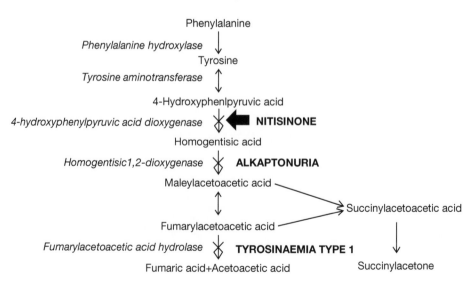

homogentisate 1,2-dioxygenase while hereditary tyrosinaemia type 1 is caused by a mutation in fumarylacetoacetic acid hydrolase.

The team at ICI realised that if nitisinone blocked tyrosine breakdown in plants, it should also work in humans. If so, then it could act as a treatment for hereditary tyrosinaemia type I (HT-1). HT-1 is a terrible disease, causing newborn infants to suffer kidney and liver disease; characterised by an extremely swollen liver. Patients were unlikely to live beyond their fourth birthday. However, treatment with nitisinone almost immediately causes a return to normal liver function and patients can expect to live a normal lifespan (McKiernan 2006). Heralded a 'wonder drug', nitisinone was officially licensed as a treatment for HT-1 in 1991. Last year, one of the first patients to receive nitisinone successfully gave birth—to a baby that never could have existed without treatment.

The use of nitisinone in HT-1 is a wonderful story demonstrating how good science can lead to unlikely chemicals, such as weedkillers, becoming life-saving drugs. Looking again at Figure 3.2, AKU is also present as a disease due to the malfunction of homogentisate dioxygenase. If nitisinone can treat HT-1, there is good reason to think that it could also treat AKU.

Emboldened by the knowledge that nitisinone could play a role in AKU treatment, and hints of success in the first study of AKU patients, the NIH researchers began a second study, this time looking at a larger sample of patients and several dosages in order to find the most suitable one for patients to take. 'Use of Nitisinone in Patients with Alkaptonuria' was published in 2005 and described the results of a study in nine patients taking nitisinone for 3 to 4 months (Suwannarat *et al.* 2005). The analysis looked promising: HGA dropped to near unidentifiable levels in blood samples; patients reported feeling less pain; and clinical tests such as hip rotation showed improvement. Encouraged by their finding, the researchers decided to move ahead to a phase III clinical trial—the stage where the effectiveness of a new drug is fully tested and required to gain a licence for its general use.

The first AKU phase III trial was done by the NIH, following on from their early studies. They recruited 40 patients who had already shown symptoms of AKU but had not yet had joint replacement surgery (Introne *et al.* 2011). Over 36 months, they would receive nitisinone and success would be based on hip rotation, a clinical test that had shown improvement in the previous study. Unfortunately this trial failed. It was underpowered and so did not have a statistically relevant result, and therefore could not be used to prove nitisinone's effectiveness in treating AKU. These results were disappointing for AKU patients, especially those who had taken part in the study and had reported feeling less pain while taking nitisinone and improvements to their health.

The AKU Society realised that we needed to ensure that the next phase III trial of nitisinone would be sufficiently powered. By learning from the NIH results, it was clear that there were several areas that needed to be improved:

- Not enough patients, so need to increase patient identification and collaboration with other countries

- Insensitive end-point, so need to learn more about the development of AKU in an individual by:

  - Increasing the basic science research into AKU and better understand how it affects the body

  - Increasing the clinical studies of AKU to see how it presents in a patient over time

  - Using the augmented knowledge to design a more thorough evaluation-based end-point

- Additional support from clinicians, researchers, statisticians, regulatory bodies and industry, so a need to increase networking and build a supportive framework to ensure the best team to work on an AKU treatment

These main points became targets for our work. By addressing these three major problems, we could put ourselves in a position where we could run another phase III trial; a trial with the best and fairest assessment of nitisinone.

3.3 The AKU Society

In 2003, an AKU patient at the Royal Liverpool University Hospital, Robert Gregory, decided that he needed to do something about the lack of knowledge of AKU and the lack of support for patients. He, along with his doctor, Dr Ranganath, started to build a group that would support patients. Together they began the AKU Society, with several aims:

- Support AKU patients and their families

- Provide the latest high-quality scientific information about AKU

- Recruit scientists and clinicians and promote their research into the causes, effects and treatments of AKU

- Help medical professionals find the best way to support new AKU patients

- Ultimately, to bring together all the resources needed to find a cure for AKU

We like to use these two founding members: one patient and one doctor, as a metaphor for the way the AKU Society works, uniting patients with the medical profession as well as researchers in order to mutually learn more about the disease. Only by thoroughly knowing the disease can we best examine treatments.

We are in a fortunate position that there is a potential treatment for AKU. Most rare diseases do not have a treatment and the majority have so little scientific knowledge about them that a treatment is a very long way off. However, knowing that the first phase III trial of nitisinone was not successful, the AKU Society had a duty to prepare and build to a second trial. For that and based on the findings during the first trials, we decided on three areas to improve. These formed the strategy for the AKU Society for the next few years, and will be the focus of the rest of this chapter:

- Increase identification of AKU patients

- Increase scientific knowledge of AKU

- Build an international network of patients, scientists, clinicians and industry, working together with the aim to cure AKU

3.3.1 The patient identification campaign

In 2007 the AKU Society built on its relationship with the Royal Liverpool University Hospital and, using funding from the Big Lottery Fund, we created the world's first AKU Information Centre. Based at an office in the Liverpool hospital, and run by a staff of two, it aimed to identify new AKU patients in the UK and worldwide.

Over two years, 11,151 UK GPs were sent letters including information packs about AKU, posters and a questionnaire (Ranganath *et al.* 2011). Around 20% responded, but this helped us to better understand the UK spread of AKU patients. When the society began, we knew of four patients; this campaign extended that to 75. Since then, more have been identified, and the number now stands at 81, but the bulk of the work was achieved through this basic campaign.

Of the GPs that responded, only 30% knew about AKU, and most of those admitted their knowledge was inadequate, little more than a vague memory from medical school. It was obvious that a general lack of knowledge and awareness was another problem to be met.

As a UK-based charity, much of our work has been focused in the UK. However, through our website and meetings with doctors at medical conferences, we have identified more than 700 patients worldwide (see Fig. 3.3).

To better approach and support these patients, we supported the development of several international AKU Societies. The first was l'Assocation pour la lutte contre l'Alcaptonurie (ALCAP), a French AKU Society, which has since identified a further 30 patients in France and built a strong relationship with a National Centre for Metabolic Disease at l'Hôpital Necker in Paris.

Then came l'Associazione italiana dei malati di alkaptonuria (AIMAKU), an Italian AKU Society; the AKU Society of North America, which supports patients in the USA and Canada; the Deutsch Selbsthilfegruppe für Alkaptonurie (DSAKU) in Germany, as well as upcoming groups in Slovakia and the Netherlands.

Each of these groups has one thing in common. All are led by a dedicated team of patients, family members and their doctors. We find it crucial that a patient group has the correct support in team leadership and so value the work achieved by

Figure 3.3 **World map of AKU patients by country (accurate as of the close of the patient identification campaign in 2010)**

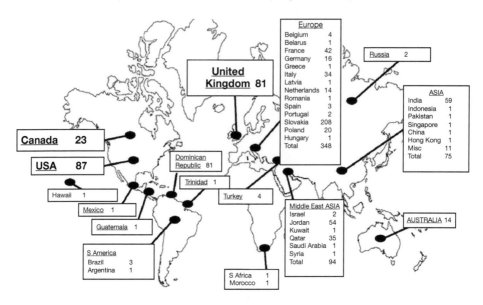

uniting patients and doctors, an ethos that has always run at the core of our work at the AKU Society.

3.3.2 Increase scientific knowledge of AKU

In 2006, we funded a PhD programme at the University of Liverpool. Building on connections at the Royal Liverpool University Hospital (where we were founded) and following the work on the autopsy of an AKU patient (Helliwell *et al.* 2008), awareness of AKU had grown to a point at the university where we felt confident that an investment would pay off. We were lucky, and the PhD candidate was an excellent student, dedicated to his work and keen to further AKU knowledge.

With an interested team at Liverpool, we could launch a major research initiative, the findAKUre project. With funding from the Childwick Trust and the Big Lottery Fund, we could create a multi-disciplinary approach to AKU research. This work has led to many developments, including an *in vitro* model, a cell model and an animal model. Just as useful, it led to an important collaboration with another academic centre at the University of Siena.

Together, the Universities of Liverpool and Siena developed an *in vitro* model of AKU ochronosis (Tinti *et al.* 2011). Ochronosis is the process whereby cartilage is turned black and brittle, and so can be studied by growing cartilage cells in a solution containing HGA (the pigment present in AKU). Schmorl's stain was used to highlight the pigment deposits for analysis under a microscope.

The researchers noticed a dose-related deposition of pigment in cells and that *in vitro* deposition was much more rapid than *in vivo*, indicating that protective mechanisms exist in living tissues. The results confirm that the concentration of HGA is the primary cause of ochronosis and, therefore, reducing the concentration of HGA should prevent AKU. We know nitisinone reduces HGA and so this work is good evidence that it may help treat AKU.

Our funded work at the University of Liverpool also led to the development of the world's first AKU mouse model (a HGD knockout (HGD$^{-/-}$), meaning the mice lack the enzyme that malfunctions in human form AKU). These mice were derived through a two year programme based on two mouse strains from the original mutant at the Institut Pasteur, and from a related mutant from Oregon Health and Science University. The AKU mouse (HGD$^{-/-}$) has proven to be a model of AKU biochemistry and of AKU joint pathology, and is therefore an appropriate model in which to test potential treatments, including nitisinone. By using the drug in the model, our researchers have shown that nitisinone administration in mice completely prevents ochronosis in joint cartilage (Preston *et al.* in press; Taylor *et al.* 2012).

In a group of nine mice maintained on nitisinone for 18 months, a comprehensive study of the knee joints revealed no pigmented chondrocytes, providing convincing evidence that ochronosis was prevented. In the control untreated group, all knee joints developed ochronosis, as shown by the positive staining of individual and small groups of cells in the cartilage. Electron microscopy has revealed the molecular interactions that represent the very earliest stage of ochronosis. Individual collagen fibres become decorated with pigment that binds to specific sites within the fibrillar structure, creating a regular striped pattern.

The basic science research has cemented the link between AKU and osteoarthritis. We often use this connection to gain attention, especially to funders who would prefer to be funding more common diseases. The connection has been very useful to us; apart from funding, it has helped us to recruit researchers and it is also a quick and easy way of explaining to people why they should care about a disease that otherwise would mean nothing to them. There are about 80 people with AKU in the UK, but over 8 million with osteoarthritis, so the public see it as more important and therefore more worthy of attention. We can use that to show the significance of researching AKU.

The basic science work has also led to biochemical evidence for the use of nitisinone in AKU. The work demonstrates that increased HGA leads to AKU ochronosis, and that using nitisinone in a mouse model reduces HGA and tissue pigmentation. If nitisinone reduces the chemical responsible for damage in AKU, it should act as an effective treatment. However, that argument alone is not enough to get a licence for nitisinone for use in AKU. For that, we need clinical evidence.

In 2008–2010, we funded and carried out a natural history study with the Royal Liverpool University Hospital on 17 patients (Ranganath and Cox 2011), which showed: 40% had aortic valve disease; cardiac dysrhythmias were seen in 40%; kidney and prostate stones occurred in 40% and 33%, respectively; 20% had renal or liver cysts; marked laryngeal ochronosis is well known and 25% noticed loss/weakness/alteration in voice; muscle (46%), tendon (20%) and ligament (7%) ruptures; osteopenia (47%), all fractures (53%) and fragility fractures (13%). Severe spinal disease commonly leads to kyphoscoliosis, nerve entrapment syndromes and spinal fusion.

The research has allowed us to understand the wide-ranging effects AKU can have on the body, yet there are still questions to be answered. We are unable to detect the earliest signs of ochronosis and so cannot correctly describe the evolution of disease over a lifespan. Our current understanding is explained in Figure 3.4. It is vital to know when disease starts, as only then can we make a decision on when to start treatment. Ideally, a patient would start treatment just before the disease begins to affect their body, and therefore avoid the complications of AKU. In practice, AKU starts to affect patients in the late 20s with back and joint pain, but we are

Figure 3.4 **Natural history of AKU: current understanding. One interpretation of overt ochronosis in the third decade is that it only starts to develop from this point onwards, as is indicated by the line 1. An alternative possibility is that ochronosis is continuously evolving from birth reaching a threshold for detection by the third decade of life (line 2). Slower and more rapid phases are recognisable in the ochronotic period (curved line 3)**

Source: L.R. Ranganath, A.M. Taylor, A. Shenkin, W.D. Fraser, J. Jarvis, J.A. Gallagher and N. Sireau (2011) 'Identification of Alkaptonuria in the General Population: A United Kingdom Experience Describing the Challenges, Possible Solutions and Persistent Barrier', *Journal of Inherited Metabolic Disease* 34: 1,153-62; with kind permission from Springer Science+Business Media B.V.

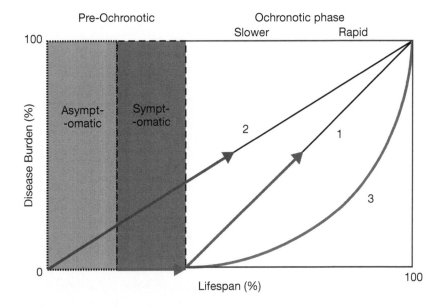

unable to know yet, whether the HGA is causing ochronosis in their joints 1 year or 20 years before that pain begins.

However, we have built a sufficient description of the natural history of AKU in order to develop better end-points for a new phase III clinical study of nitisinone. Learning from the NIH study, which used a single end-point of hip rotation, we realised the need to develop an all-encompassing score index that takes into account all aspects of AKU—kidney and prostate stones, aortic stenosis, bone fractures, tendon/ligament/muscle ruptures, kyphosis, scoliosis and many more clinical features. Drs Cox and Ranganath at the Royal Liverpool University Hospital united all these features, into a single AKU Severity Score Index (AKUSSI) (Cox and Ranganath 2011).

The research into AKU is now at a point where we have developed *in vitro* and animal models of the disease, accurate enough to test the effectiveness of any new treatments and the clinical evaluations have developed into a validated scoring index, robust enough to test those new treatments. The scientific programme into AKU has reached a stage where we feel confident enough to stage and accurately assess a second phase III study.

3.3.3 Build an international network

One of our first acts in 2012 was to submit a 140-page application to the European government for funding for a phase III clinical trial. For us, this was the conclusion of many years work, of building up an international database of patients, and advancing AKU research to a point where could confidently assess nitisinone—all we now need is to secure the funding to run the trials.

Our application includes 12 partners, each of them providing a unique and valuable contribution to a future study. This was the last piece of the puzzle to prepare for a trial, recruiting a network capable of running the next phase III clinical trial of nitisinone.

Our partners include several groups:

- **Academia**. University of Liverpool (UK), University of Siena (Italy) and Institute of Molecular Physiology and Genetics (Slovakia)

- **Clinical centres**. Royal Liverpool University Hospital (UK), Hôpital Necker Enfants Maladies (France) and National Institute of Rheumatic Disease (Slovakia)

- **Patient support**. AKU Society (UK) and ALCAP (France)

- **Industry**. Swedish Orphan Biovitrum International (Sweden), PSR Group (Netherlands), Cudos (Netherlands) and Nordic Bioscience (Denmark)

This is by no means a complete list of our partners. It does not include, for example, our colleagues at the NIH who ran the first studies; as this is European funding, they couldn't be a partner. Also not included are several centres running other basic research programmes, such as a gene therapy project at Imperial College London and a protein replacement project at Protein Technologies in Manchester. There are also several other AKU Societies (AIMAKU in Italy, the AKU Society of North America and DSAKU in Germany) who will be involved in patient recruitment for trials, but are not in the application as we limited it to groups based in countries with clinical trial centres (UK, France and Slovakia).

However, the list of 12 partners in the EU application is a good representation of the kinds of groups we partnered with in order to push towards a clinical trial.

3.3.3.1 Academia

I have explained how vital basic science research is to understanding AKU, and therefore allowing us to properly assess a drug. Research at the University of Liverpool was an obvious choice. The AKU Society was founded in Liverpool and so many trustees had a good connection with researchers interested in a similar disease, osteoarthritis. By funding a PhD student to begin looking at AKU, we could raise more attention to AKU, until we were able to fund the major programmes described in the previous section.

The University of Siena came on board through a student exchange scheme at the University of Liverpool. Our funded researchers already had pre-existing good links with Siena, and so were able to get Italian students to begin AKU work, leading to developments such as the joint work on the *in vitro* model of AKU.

The partner in Slovakia is due to a strange quirk of genetics. AKU is a rare disease in the UK, affecting up to 1 in 500,000 people. However, in Slovakia, the disease is much more common, with as many as 1 in 19,000 people suffering with AKU. The reasons for this are unclear—possibly due to a founder effect, as many cases are restricted to a historically tribal region in the north of the country—but are being studied by the group at the Institute of Molecular Physiology and Genetics. This is a good example of using natural events to our advantage. AKU happens to be more common in one country, and so researchers are better encouraged to study the disease.

3.3.3.2 Clinical centres

The AKU Society was founded at the Royal Liverpool University Hospital, and so has always been a home of AKU study. As mentioned above, Slovakia has a vested interest in AKU, because of its uncommonly high numbers of AKU patients, and the National Institute of Rheumatic Disease has studied ochronosis since the 1950s. With a 60-year history of studying AKU, and access to a few hundred AKU patients, the National Institute of Rheumatic Disease became a key partner.

The Hôpital Necker Enfants Maladies runs a Reference Centre of Inherited Metabolic Diseases. Therefore they have experience of treating AKU patients, as well as using nitisinone in treating hereditary tyrosinaemia patients. France has a long history of awareness of rare disease (for example, the public funding through the

French Telethon, a Comic Relief-style fundraising campaign for rare diseases) and so centres such as the one at Hôpital Necker are motivated places, with a good understanding of the issues surrounding the treatment of rare diseases. Enthusiastic clinical centres are vital resources for any rare disease group to seek out. This can be hard, but listen to your patient members and often they will find the clinicians and centres that have an innate curiosity to investigate and treat certain diseases.

3.3.3.3 Industry

Nordic Bioscience is a research company based in Denmark that has experience of working with the University of Liverpool researchers in order to develop tests to determine the presence of ochronosis in cartilage samples. This is yet another example of using your pre-existing networks in order to find new partners.

PSR Group is a CRO (contract research organisations) and Cudos is a consultancy, which together can plan and monitor the AKU clinical trials. These two specialise in rare diseases and so have years of experience with small group trials, perfect for helping the group plan an AKU clinical trial. We initially made contact through a chance meeting at a rare disease conference and after explaining AKU and the need to study nitisinone, they agreed to join the network.

Swedish Orphan Biovitrum International (Sobi) is the licence holder for nitisinone, and therefore an essential partner to study the drug. Sobi was one of the first supporters of the AKU Society, funding the creation of our first website back in 2003. Since then, we have worked hard to maintain a good relationship and learnt that good communication is key, ensuring that the company is informed of the latest news in AKU research and discussing how that could lead to studying nitisinone as a treatment. Ultimately, our partnership has resulted in Sobi pledging to supply nitisinone in the next trial, working with us to analyse its results and if successful, applying for its licence as a new treatment for AKU.

Many of our partners for the clinical trial bid were connections grown from previous partnerships. Our beginnings at the Royal Liverpool University Hospital led to work at the University of Liverpool, which in turn led to work at the University of Siena and at Nordic Bioscience. It is important to constantly be looking for new colleagues, which could be as simple as talking at conferences (PSR Group and Cudos), discovering areas with an unusual link to your disease (the two Slovakian centres) or working with pre-existing rare disease centres (Hôpital Necker). Our relationship with the pharmaceutical company, Sobi, is a good example of strengthening these collaborations, through constant communication, discussion and awareness of the reasons for both parties to get involved.

We have made progress with our original aims. Having identified hundreds of AKU patients worldwide, providing good evidence for HGA working to treat AKU in scientific models, producing effective clinical measurements of AKU and cementing partnerships with a bid to the EU government for clinical trial funding, the consortium is well on the way towards a second phase III clinical trial for nitisinone in AKU.

We aim for other patient groups to learn from our experience. AKU is one of 7,000 rare diseases, yet conclusions can still be drawn for them all. To that end, the next sections will look at three case studies, focusing on areas where change has been most needed:

- Fund research into rare diseases

- Minimise delays in diagnosis

- Centres for excellence

3.4 Research into rare diseases

The recent advancements that have helped us learn about AKU, the *in vitro* models, the animal models and the clinical evaluations among others, have allowed us to better understand AKU. Without this foundation of knowledge to understand the disease, it is impossible to be able to get to a position where a potential treatment can be found or effective clinical studies performed.

Yet many rare disease charities and patient organisations neglect research, either not seeing its importance or thinking that it is not their problem. Many other patient organisations have the attitude that doctors or scientists know better and they will handle the research, and so patient organisations step aside. Obviously, you need experts to do the actual work, but there is no reason why patient organisations cannot be intimately involved with that work. Rare disease patients should be passionate about research as they have the most to gain. The AKU Society has a good track record of research work, and that is due in no small part to constant updates with the patient group, jointly working on funding applications and keeping up to date with the work being done in the AKU labs. Patient groups have the most contact with patients, so they have as much invested into the research that could lead to a treatment as the researchers, so should be involved from the start and throughout.

Another reason for a lack of research into rare diseases is finding the funding. We have sometimes struggled to get money to start new projects, or even keep existing projects running; however, we have managed by constantly checking for new funding opportunities, applying to any that are relevant, and by knowing what funders are looking for.

Many medical research funders typically want to fund common diseases. They have a limited amount of money available for grants and so want to make the most of it; £100,000 for a rare disease could help 100 patients; whereas £100,000 for a common disease could help 1 million patients. It is frustrating to a rare disease charity who knows that its patients are just as deserving as others, but are stuck because their disease happens to be rare; but it is how many funders see the application.

However, there are two useful approaches to present a rare disease funding application in order to get around the problem:

- Make the link to a common disease. There are many similarities between AKU and osteoarthritis. Our basic science researchers at the University of Liverpool became interested in AKU work because they had a history of work on osteoarthritis; and so their research often overlaps both diseases. This is a useful point to highlight, and a funder is much more willing to fund a project that could have effects on a common disease. If there is the potential for a greater number of beneficiaries from the original research, then make it clear in the application

- Many common diseases are seeing diminishing returns. The most common diseases that people can name (cancer, heart disease, diabetes...) have had millions invested into their research. A further grant has little overall effect. A £100,000 donation to cancer research is nothing (0.08%) compared with the £123.4 million from Cancer Research UK (figure from their Annual Review 2010/11), but could easily start an entirely new research project for a rare disease

3.5 Minimise delays in diagnosis

One of the problems we often hear from AKU patients is that they had to fight for a diagnosis. AKU is unusual as there is an easy-to-spot symptom, black urine, but a few patients' urine is light enough to not cause that much of a darkening, and some patients ignore it. If your urine has always been black, there is no reason to worry when you notice it later on in life, and certainly no reason to link it to your bad back. Therefore, there is a good number of patients (about half the ones we know of) who are diagnosed late in life. However, many of those are not diagnosed immediately. Often, patients are sent away with a diagnosis of osteoarthritis; sometimes they are told they must be imagining the pain. We even know of one UK patient who was not diagnosed with AKU until she underwent a knee replacement operation, only for the surgeon to cancel the operation once he saw the opened knee was black with ochronosis.

The high rate of misdiagnosis is not unique to AKU. A report by Rare Disease UK (RDUK) (Limb *et al.* 2010) claims that 46% of patients were given incorrect diagnoses and 30% received three or more misdiagnoses. Even worse, RDUK found that rare disease patients face a long delay in finding that correct diagnosis. Almost half of patients with a rare disease had to wait over a year for a correct diagnosis, 20% had to wait over 5 years, and 12% waited over 10 years.

Many rare diseases are similar to common diseases; AKU presents in a similar way to osteoarthritis, and so misdiagnoses are understandable. However, to a rare disease patient, they can cause much distress, prevent them from finding the right information and getting the right support and cause a significant emotional toll to themselves and their families. Therefore, medical professionals should attempt to avoid or at least reduce misdiagnosis.

As a part of our Patient Identification Campaign, we send round information about AKU, including the classic symptoms—the tetrad of features seen in Figure 3.1: black spots in eyes/ears, black urine and black cartilage. This is a useful start but more could be done.

One idea would be to look at medical training. Some would call for more emphasis on rare diseases in medical schools, but this would be impracticable. Rare diseases are, by definition, rare, and so training should focus on diseases that doctors are more likely to need to diagnose. However, there should be an emphasis on looking out for the uncommon. It is easy to mistake AKU for osteoarthritis, but there are clues that should make you rethink. AKU affects patients at an earlier age than osteoarthritis and the pain is more generally felt over all joints rather than focused in one or two joints. Therefore, a better solution seems to be to include training to flag these inconsistencies—training should emphasise more research when a disease varies from the normal presentation. It could even be included in the computer prompts used by GPs to make diagnoses.

3.6 Centres for excellence

The Royal Liverpool University Hospital was made a Centre for Excellence for the treatment of AKU in early 2012. This means the hospital is a national centre that treats all patients with AKU in the UK with yearly check-ups and produces the reliable guidance for treating patients at their local hospitals and GP surgeries.

A Centre for Excellence is funded by the NHS, which has to justify the cost by moving funding from elsewhere. Therefore, the most persuasive argument is to show that a new centre for a rare disease is needed as costs are currently too high, and the intervention of early, directed treatment could reduce costs overall.

Currently, AKU is an expensive disease to treat. As it destroys joints, patients can expect to have several joint replacements throughout their lifetime. One UK patient has had 11 joint replacements, including both hips, both knees, both shoulders and elbows and several revisions. Joint replacement surgery is one of the most expensive operations offered by the NHS and, for us, it sparked an idea that AKU patients may be disproportionately expensive for the NHS.

In 2011, we recruited a volunteer, Michael Craig, to look at the cost of an AKU patient. Michael is a charted accountant and senior analyst in a large consulting company and was intrigued by our idea. He agreed to research the idea for us, and following a lengthy period of interviews with AKU experts, AKU patients and NHS staff, produced a report in 2011. He matched typical AKU symptoms with the testing techniques used by UK doctors and likely treatments (Fig. 3.5).

Figure 3.5 **Typical symptoms, tests and treatments for AKU patients in the UK**

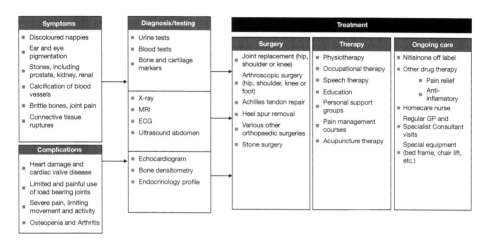

By estimating the costs of each procedure (as well as taking into account hospital staff time and possible overnight stays), he could then give a good idea of the cost of a single, typical AKU patient. His key findings were:

- Individual patient costs vary greatly depending on the stage of the disease they are in and the resulting number of surgeries and amount of patient care required. Direct costs from one patient for one year can be in excess of £90,000 without taking into account drug therapy and physical aids required to live as normal a life as possible. These additional costs bring the single possible direct patient total to over £100,000, and possibly even larger given the limit to which direct costs were captured for each patient

- Data from this research could be extrapolated to the current known AKU UK population. When extrapolated, calculations show that yearly direct health-care cost attributed to AKU range from £0.2 million to £3.0 million depending on the number of surgeries patients incur in any one year

- A weighted average of all possible scenarios shows that total direct healthcare costs of approximately £1.0 million may be a more reasonable conservative estimate

- A conservative approximation of the total costs of AKU in the UK including indirect costs (i.e. lost wage and production) is approximately £1.4 million to £2.0 million per year with the upper limit possibly being as high as £7.0 million

With this information, we were able to submit a persuasive application to the NHS Specialised Services and successfully get funding to make the UK's first Centre for Excellence for the treatment of AKU.

This study is a perfect example of the hidden burden of rare diseases. It often seems that rare diseases such as AKU are ignored because most people do not think they will affect them. It is true that most people will never meet an AKU patient, or even hear of the disease. However, they will be affected by another rare disease. Even if they are not in the 25% of the population who is closely related to someone with a rare disease, they will be affected by the financial strain to the NHS, and to the country.

An ignored health problem could be a significant drain to society, and is one of many reasons why the problem of rare diseases should be properly understood and addressed. To conclude, there are four key messages that have been learnt through work with the AKU Society. These messages should help anyone that wants to set up a rare disease group, or expand an existing one.

The first is obvious: **always act for the benefit of our patient members**. Our overarching aim has always been to cure the disease and that has guided most of our development.

The second is to **work alongside medical staff**. The AKU Society was founded by a patient talking to his doctor and their mutual agreement that more had to be done to treat and support AKU patients.

The third is similar, to **work alongside researchers**—you must fully understand a disease before you can treat and cure it, and we could not have got to the stage of launching a clinical trial without a lot of basic research. However an important thing to remember is not to be overruled by medical staff or researchers. While they may understand the science better, you understand the patients best, so always use the first message, and make sure you work for the benefit of patients foremost.

The final message is to **raise awareness, among patients, professionals and the general public**. One of the AKU Society's first tasks was to raise awareness among GPs and led to us identifying around 70 UK patients. Rare diseases are rare and instead of thinking that means no one should care, it just means we have to work harder to help people to understand them.

References

Cox, T.F., and L.R. Ranganath (2011) 'A Quantitative Assessment of AKU: Testing the Reliability of Two Disease Severity Scoring Systems', *Journal of Inherited Metabolic Disease* 34: 1153-62.

Fernandez-Canon, J.M., B. Granadino, D. Beltran-Valero de Bernabe, M. Renedo, E. Fernandez-Ruiz, M.A. Penalva and S. Rodriquez de Cordoba (1996) 'The Molecular Basis of Alkaptonuria', *Nature Genetics* 14.1: 19-24.

Garrod, E. (1908) 'The Croonian Lectures on Inborn Errors of Metabolism. Lecture II. Alkaptonuria', *Lancet* 2: 73-9.

Helliwell, T.R., J.A. Gallagher and L. Ranaganth (2008) 'Alkaptonuria: A Review of Surgical and Autopsy Pathology', *Histopathology* 53.5: 503-12.

Introne, W.J., M.B. Perry, J. Troendle, E. Tsilou, M.A. Kayser, P. Suwannarat, K.E. O-Brien, J. Bryant, V. Sachdev, J.C. Reynolds, E. Moylan, I. Bernardini and W.A. Gahl (2011) 'A 3-year Randomized Therapeutic Trial of Nitisinone in Alkaptonuria', *Molecular Genetics and Metabolism* 103.4: 307-14.

Limb, L., S. Nutt and A. Sen (2010) *Experiences of Rare Diseases: An Insight from Patients and Families* (London: Rare Disease UK).

McKiernan, P.J. (2006) 'Nitisinone in the Treatment of Hereditary Tyrosinaemia Type I', *Drugs* 66.6: 793-50.

Phomphutkul, C., W.J. Introne, M.B. Perry, I. Bernardini, M.D. Murphey, D.L. Fitzpatrick, P.D. Anderson, M. Huizing, Y. Anikster, L.H. Gerber and W.A. Gahl (2002) 'Natural History of Alkaptonuria', *New England Journal of Medicine* 347.26: 2111-21.

Preston, K., H. Sutherland, A.M. Taylor, L.R. Ranganath, J.A. Gallagher and J.C. Jarvis (in press) 'Osteoarthropathy in a Mouse Model of Alkaptonuria, and its Inhibition by Nitisinone', submitted to *Annals of Rheumatic Diseases*.

Ranganath, L.R., and T.F. Cox (2011) 'Natural History of Alkaptonuria Revisited: Analyses Based on Scoring Systems', *Journal of Inherited Metabolic Disease* 34.6: 1141-51.

Ranganath, L.R., A.M. Taylor, A. Shenkin, W.D. Fraser, J. Jarvis, J.A. Gallagher and N. Sireau (2011) 'Identification of Alkaptonuria in the General Population: A United Kingdom Experience Describing the Challenges, Possible Solutions and Persistent Barrier', *Journal of Inherited Metabolic Disease* 34: 1153-62.

Suwannarat, P., K. O'Brien, M.B. Perry, N. Sebring, I. Bernardini, M.I. Kaiser-Kupfer, B.I. Rubin, E. Tsilou, L.H. Gerber and W.A. Gahl (2005) 'Use of Nitisinone in Patients with Alkaptonuria', *Metabolism: Clinical and Experimental* 54: 719-28.

Taylor, A.M., A. Preston, N.K. Paulk, H. Sutherland, C. Keenan, P. Wilson, B. Wlodarski, M. Grompe, L.R. Ranganath, J.A. Gallagher and J.C. Jarvis (2012) 'Ochronosis in a Murine Model of Alkaptonuria is Synonymous to that in the Human Condition', *Osteoarthritis and Cartilage* 20.8: 880-86.

Tinti, L., A.M. Taylor, A. Santucci, B. Wlodarski, P.J. Wilson, J.C. Jarvis, W.D. Fraser, J.S. Davidson, L.R. Ranganath and J.A. Gallagher (2011) 'Development of an in vitro Model to Investigate Joint Ochronosis in Alkaptonuria', *Rheumatology* (Oxford) 50.2: 271-7.

Oliver Timmis is the Communications Manager for the AKU Society, an entrepreneurial patient organisation supporting those diagnosed with alkaptonuria (AKU), a rare genetic disease. He graduated with a BA (Hon) in Natural Science (Physiology, Development and Neuroscience) from Cambridge University in 2010 and has begun a MSc in Health Policy with the Centre for Health Policy at Imperial College London in 2012. While at the AKU Society, Oliver developed the scientific communications strategy, by strengthening relationships with AKU research teams, developing several online AKU rare disease platforms, and is a key point of contact with specialist healthcare PR agency Tudor Reilly, which offers pro bono PR support to the charity. Oliver also works on the fundraising strategies, including the applications to the UK Department of Health to create a National Centre for alkaptonuria and to the European Commission FP7 call to fund an international phase III clinical trial in AKU. He is a volunteer writer for BioNews, a news website focusing on medical issues.

4

The practicalities of clinical development of drugs for rare diseases

Anthony K. Hall

Cudos, The Netherlands

4.1 The regulations and incentives for orphan drug development

The development of medicines to treat diseases is a commercial business, driven by market forces as it has been for more than a century, spurred on by the high gains to be made from medicines for common diseases such as high cholesterol, asthma, cardiovascular disease, hypertension, diabetes and gastrointestinal disorders. With so many common diseases needing attention, it is perhaps not surprising that rare diseases received very little attention from the pharmaceutical industry. However, support groups and families of patients with rare diseases got together and, by 1982, had formed a coalition which was able to bring enough pressure to bear on the United States Congress to bring about the passing of the Orphan Drug Act (ODA) in early 1983 (US Congress 1983). This legislation was designed to advocate and support the development of drugs for treating rare diseases. The coalition has since evolved into the National Organization for Rare Disorders (NORD)[1] and is a powerful voice for rare diseases in the USA.

---

1 www.rarediseases.org, accessed 17 January 2013.

It took a long time before other countries followed this lead, but by 2000 legislation had been passed in Japan (1993), Singapore (1997), Australia (1998) and the European Union (2000) (European Parliament and Council of the European Union 1999). Again, it was largely due to the efforts of a patient advocacy group, the European Organization for Rare Diseases (EURORDIS),[2] formed in 1997, that this legislation came about in Europe. In this chapter, we will focus on the US and Europe (with the emphasis on Europe), since these are the main markets currently where orphan drug legislation is relevant because of the size of the markets and the development of the healthcare systems.

At the heart of the philosophy of the orphan legislation is the idea espoused in the European Regulation that 'Patients suffering from rare conditions should be entitled to the same quality of treatment as other patients' (European Parliament and Council of the European Union 1999). History has shown that traditional market forces are not enough to stimulate interest from the pharmaceutical industry in order to achieve this goal. The legislation introduced a range of incentives to make the development process more attractive. Being a European regulation, the legislation was binding in its entirety and directly applicable in law in each of the European Member States, although most of the consequences of the legislation are implemented at the EU level. The Regulation deals with commercial incentives to stimulate the *development* of orphan drugs; it does not deal with issues of pricing and reimbursement which are relevant after marketing authorisation, since EU Member States retain the responsibility for their own local budgets. This issue will be touched on later in the chapter.

The incentives of the orphan drug legislation are broadly similar in the US and Europe, as shown in Table 4.1.

Table 4.1 **Main incentives of the orphan drug legislation in the US and Europe**

	EU	US
Market exclusivity	10 years*#	7 years
Protocol assistance and follow-up	Yes	Yes
Reduced/waived regulatory fees	Yes	Yes
Tax credit on clinical trials	No	Yes
Dedicated subsidies for clinical trials	No^	Yes

* includes similar products for the same indication (unless significantly superior)
\# plus an extra 2 years if paediatric development included
^ the European Framework Programme has a Health call, which may include orphan drugs

2 www.eurordis.org, accessed 17 January 2013.

Of these incentives, most companies consider the market exclusivity to be the most important, although free advice and fee reductions from the regulatory agencies during the development programme can be extremely important for small companies with very tight budgets and a focus on the short-term. The EU is particularly interested in stimulating small and medium-sized enterprises (SMEs) to engage in the development of orphan drugs and the fee reductions have been revised twice recently (in Europe) in order to put more emphasis on assisting SMEs, as summarised in Table 4.2.

The market exclusivity, as defined for Europe, means that

> The EMA [European Medicines Agency] & Member States shall not, for a period of 10 years, accept another application for a marketing authorisation, or grant a marketing authorisation or accept an application to extend an existing marketing authorisation, for the same therapeutic indication, in respect of a similar medicinal product.' (European Parliament and Council of the European Union 1999: Article 8; Para 1)

This period may be reduced to six years if, at the end of the fifth year, it is shown on the basis of available evidence that the product is sufficiently profitable not to justify maintenance of market exclusivity. Exceptions to these rules exist if the original market authorisation holder gives consent, or the original market authorisation holder cannot supply sufficient product or the second applicant can show that their product is safer, more effective or otherwise clinically superior. The

Table 4.2 **Fee reductions in Europe for companies developing orphan medicinal products (OMPs)**

European Union	2007 (EMEA-H-4042-01-Rev.7)	2011 (EMA/60514/2011)	2013 (EMA/663496/2012)
Protocol assistance, initial and follow-up requests	100%	100% for SMEs 75% for non-SMEs	100% for SMEs 40% for non-SMEs (non-paediatric-related assistance) 100% for non-SMEs (paediatric-related assistance)
Pre-authorisation inspections	100%	100%	100% for SMEs
Initial marketing authorisation application	50%	100% for SMEs 10% for non-SMEs	100% for SMEs
Post-authorisation activities, including annual fee in the 1st year after MA	50% for SMEs	100% for SMEs	100% for SMEs

definitions of a 'similar medicinal product' and 'clinical superiority' can be found in Regulation (EC) 847/2000 (Commission of the European Communities 2000). In brief:

a 'similar medicinal product' means a medicinal product containing a similar active substance of [sic] substances as contained in a currently authorised orphan medicinal product, and which is intended for the same therapeutic indication;

'clinically superior' means that a medicinal product is shown to provide a significant therapeutic or diagnostic advantage over and above that provided by an authorised orphan medicinal product in one or more of the following ways:

(1) greater efficacy than an authorised orphan medicinal product (as assessed by effect on a clinically meaningful endpoint in adequate and well controlled clinical trials). Generally, this would represent the same kind of evidence needed to support a comparative efficacy claim for two different medicinal products. Direct comparative clinical trials are generally necessary. However, comparisons based on other endpoints, including surrogate endpoints may be used. In any case, the methodological approach should be justified;

or

(2) greater safety in a substantial portion of the target population(s). In some cases direct comparative clinical trials will be necessary;

or

(3) in exceptional cases, where neither greater safety nor greater efficacy has been shown, a demonstration that the medicinal product otherwise makes a major contribution to diagnosis or to patient care.

4.2 Some misconceptions about orphan drug development

There is a common belief, both within and outside the pharmaceutical industry, that it is quicker, easier and cheaper to develop an orphan drug compared with other drugs and yet it is still possible to achieve blockbuster revenues. This belief seems to be based on four main misconceptions:

- Owing to limited patient availability the regulators will automatically accept one small pivotal trial in place of the standard two pivotal phase III efficacy studies

- Orphan drugs are automatically eligible for expedited approval procedures

- Orphan drugs are automatically eligible for conditional approval

- Owing to the limited potential sales volume, companies can automatically demand a high price for orphan drugs

Although there are examples to support each of these assertions, they are the exceptions rather than the norm. Let us look at each in turn:

4.2.1 One small pivotal trial for market authorisation

Even though it might be extremely difficult to recruit enough patients to a clinical programme for an orphan drug, officially, the regulators demand the same level of proof of safety and efficacy for orphan drugs as for other drugs. In fact there is no *formal* requirement to include two or more pivotal studies from a phase III programme (neither in Europe nor the US), but in most cases this is needed in order to adequately demonstrate the usefulness of the product in the intended population. Both the FDA (US Food and Drug Administration) and the EMA (European Medicines Agency) have published guidance documents dealing with this issue and both agencies accept that there is no fixed rule for demonstrating substantial evidence of effectiveness. It is a matter of judgement.

The EMA has produced a guidance document that outlines the circumstances under which a single pivotal clinical trial may be acceptable for marketing authorisation. It is a stand-alone guidance document, in principle applicable to any drug, and is not part of the orphan drug legislation (CPMP 2001). The document endorses the fact that,

> [although] there is no formal requirement to include two or more pivotal studies in the phase III program…in most cases a program with several studies is the most, or perhaps only feasible way to provide the variety of data needed to confirm the usefulness of a product in the intended population.

In cases where the sponsor provides evidence from only one pivotal study, the study must be exceptionally compelling with respect to internal and external validity, clinical relevance, the degree of statistical significance, data quality and internal consistency. The FDA makes similar caveats in its guidance documents.

While it is clear, therefore, that it might be possible to obtain a marketing authorisation on the basis of a single pivotal trial, this should not be regarded as an easy option and, even in a rare disease, multiple confirmatory studies might be necessary.

Notwithstanding the above, it is clear that it is not always possible to meet conventional requirements with rare diseases. The small populations available for study, the often unknown natural history of the disease and lack of accepted clinical efficacy measures or surrogate markers can make it extremely difficult. Consequently, the regulators do exercise some degree of flexibility in the assessment of orphan drugs, as evidenced by the results of a recent study by NORD (Sasinowski 2011), which looked at 135 non-cancer orphan therapies approved as new chemical entities in the US between the enactment of the Orphan Drug Act in 1983 and June 2010. Of these 45 (33%) were classified as 'Conventional' approval, 32 (24%) as

'Administrative Flexibility', and 58 (43%) as 'Case-by-Case Flexibility'. An informal review of the EPARs (European Public Assessment Reports) for authorised OMPs in Europe indicates that the EMA has also adopted a somewhat flexible approach to the granting of marketing authorisation in many cases, always providing that the risk/benefit assessment is positive (A.K. Hall, unpublished).

The EMA has produced a specific guidance document for clinical trials in small populations (CHMP 2005a), which also explains how special trial designs or statistical approaches may be acceptable. However, again, this should not be over-interpreted and the document clearly states that:

> [the] approaches outlined in this document for situations where large studies are not feasible should not be interpreted as a general paradigm change in drug development. The methods described here to increase the efficiency of the design and analyses are also applicable for studies in large populations, but are often not used because of increased complexity.

4.2.2 Eligibility for expedited approval procedures

The FDA has special procedures designed to speed up the availability of new drugs for patients with serious conditions (FDA 2012).

- The Fast Track process is 'designed to facilitate the development, and expedite the review of drugs to treat serious diseases and fill an unmet medical need. The purpose is to get important new drugs to the patient earlier'

- The Accelerated Approval regulation was instituted in order to facilitate the earlier approval of drugs to treat serious diseases, and that fill an unmet medical need based on a surrogate end-point, 'mindful of the fact that obtaining data on clinical outcomes can take a long time'

- A Priority Review designation is given to drugs that offer major advances in treatment, or provide a treatment where no adequate therapy exists. A Priority Review means that the time it takes FDA to review a new drug application is reduced. The goal for completing a Priority Review is six months.

It will be noted from the above that the emphasis is on serious diseases and unmet medical need and the procedures are neither specific nor automatic for orphan drugs. However, it is clear that orphan drugs are likely to qualify more often than drugs for common indications where many treatments are already available.

In Europe, there is also an accelerated assessment procedure (similar to Priority Review) for medicinal products of major therapeutic interest. Under this procedure, the normal time limit for review of a Marketing Authorisation Application of 210 days is reduced to 150 days. The legal basis for the procedure is laid down in the Regulation on Community procedures for the authorisation and supervision of medicinal products for human and veterinary use (European Parliament and Council of the European Union 2004) and explained in detail in the guideline on the procedure for accelerated assessment (CHMP 2006a). The procedure is intended for where there is a high unmet medical need and is not specific for orphan drugs; the request for accelerated assessment must be justified and each case is assessed on its merits.

4.2.3 Eligibility for conditional approval

Conditional Approval in Europe can be considered as somewhat similar in its objectives to Accelerated Approval in the US, in the sense that approval may be granted on the basis of incomplete data, with the requirement that the sponsor provides additional data in the future. Note that the terminology is a little confusing, since Accelerated Approval in the US is not the parallel of Accelerated Assessment in the EU. Table 4.3 is included for additional clarity.

Once again, the procedure is neither specific nor automatic for orphan drugs, but is often particularly applicable to these products, because of the difficulty in collecting sufficient robust clinical data in these populations.

The legal basis for the granting of a conditional marketing authorisation in Europe is laid down in a Commission Regulation (Commission of the European Communities 2006) and the procedure is explained in detail in an EMA guideline (CHMP 2006b). The following points are particularly noteworthy:

Table 4.3 **Comparison of regulatory procedures in the US and EU designed to accelerate the approval of drugs which fulfil an unmet medical need**

FDA	EMA
Fast-track	No *direct* equivalent
To help expedite the process	
More meetings with FDA	
Eligibility for Accelerated Approval	
Eligibility for Priority Review	
Accelerated Approval	**Conditional Approval**
Specific for approval with a surrogate end-point	Incomplete data; not specific for surrogate end-point
Approval is conditional on post-approval trials showing a clinical benefit	Approval is conditional on supplying additional post-approval data
After confirmation, FDA grants a traditional approval	After confirmation, authorisation is converted to a normal approval
	(Approval under Exceptional Circumstances *can* also include a surrogate end-point)
Priority Review	**Accelerated Assessment**
Reduced time for review of NDA	Reduced time for review of MAA
Target review time is 6 months	Reduced from 210 to 150 days

- The data on which a conditional marketing authorisation may be granted may be less complete, but the risk–benefit balance should still be positive

- In a conditional marketing authorisation, only the clinical part of the application dossier should be less complete than normal

4.2.4 The price of orphan drugs

A detailed review of the pricing of orphan drugs is outside the scope of this chapter; however a brief look at this aspect is relevant here, since it is one of the drivers for companies to undertake the development of orphan drugs.

There is a common belief that the orphan drug legislation leads to high pricing, as evidenced by the series of articles in the November 2010 issue of the *British Medical Journal* (Ferner and Hughes 2010; Roos *et al.* 2010; Hawkes and Cohen 2010; Godlee 2010; Nicholl *et al.* 2010). In reality there is nothing in the orphan drug legislation about the final prices of orphan drugs once they reach the market; this is determined by the MAA (marketing authorisation application) holder at the time, while reimbursement is decided at a local level, since EU Member States retain the responsibility for their own national budgets.

Because there are very few patients with a particular rare disease, companies need to charge a relatively high price in order to recover the costs of development. However, where to set this price is a matter of much debate and a problem for health technology assessment (HTA) bodies, which are tasked with determining whether a nation's healthcare budget should be used to pay for such individually expensive treatments. The 'normal' criteria which HTAs use to assess the cost-effectiveness of a drug and to decide if they will pay for it are not very helpful for orphan drugs. As a result, there is a large variation in the availability of orphan drugs across Europe, even though each product has a marketing authorisation which is valid in all 27 Member States. It is therefore important that companies considering the development of an orphan drug think carefully about the price they expect to charge at the time of launch onto the market, taking into account the anticipated reimbursement environment at the time, as well as new initiatives being developed to improve the process.

Pricing issues will not be discussed further here; the interested reader is referred to a recent article in the *Orphanet Journal of Rare Diseases*, which looks in detail at the issues surrounding the pricing of orphan drugs and presents some innovative proposals for changes in the value assessment of orphan drugs (Hughes-Wilson *et al.* 2012).

4.3 The process of obtaining orphan designation

In order to qualify for the incentives, a sponsor must first obtain designation of its product as an orphan drug (more properly referred to as an orphan medicinal product in the EU). Orphan medicinal product designation (OMPD) can be requested at any stage *before* marketing authorisation application (MAA) and is applicable to new chemical entities (NCEs), new biological entities (NBEs), existing drugs with new formulations and existing drugs for new indications. Depending on the exact nature of the product, it can also be applicable for medical devices and medical foods.

In the US, the application for orphan designation is assessed by the Office of Orphan Products Development (OOPD), a branch of the FDA. In Europe it is assessed by the Committee for Orphan Medicinal Products (COMP), one of the committees established under the auspices of the EMA, as shown in Figure 4.1.

As laid down in the important Regulation 141/2000, the tasks of the COMP are:

- To assess applications for orphan medicinal product designation

- To advise the European Commission on policy issues relating to OMPs in the EU

- To assist in international liaison on OMP matters and with patient support groups

- To assist the EC in drawing up detailed guidelines

Although attempts have been made to harmonise the procedure for designation, such as the introduction of a common application form, there remain some differences between the procedure for the EU and the US. Table 4.4 highlights some of the main differences.

Of particular note is that, in the US, the emphasis is on demonstrating the scientific rationale and disease prevalence. It is necessary to demonstrate that the

Figure 4.1 **Committees of the European Medicines Agency**

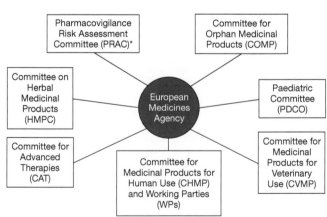

* since July 2012
(CHMP Pharmacovigilance Working Party retired as PRAC came into operation)

Table 4.4 **Main differences in the procedures for orphan designation in the US and Europe**

	EU	**US**
Terminology	Orphan medicinal product designation	Orphan drug designation
Application to	Committee for Orphan Medicinal Products	Office of Orphan Products Development
Timing	Timetable for submission and assessment published by EMA	Any time; no defined timelines
Prevalence criteria	Disease or condition affects <5 in 10,000 persons in the EU	Disease or condition affects <200,000 persons in the US
Core dossier	Sections A–E according to ENTR/6283/00	Nine parts according to 21 CFR 316.20(b)
Most important aspects of the application	Medical plausibility Prevalence Justification of significant benefit or why other methods are not satisfactory	Scientific rationale Prevalence
Place of establishment	Proof of establishment in EU	Not required
Translations	Translations of product name and proposed orphan indication into all official EU languages, plus Icelandic and Norwegian	Not required

disease or condition affects fewer than 200,000 persons in the United States, or, if it affects more than 200,000, then there should be no reasonable expectation that the cost of developing and making the drug available will be recovered from sales in the United States. Note that if the drug is a vaccine, diagnostic drug or preventive drug, then the criterion is that less than 200,000 persons per year will be administered the drug in the United States.

It is important to note that the prevalence criteria relate to the region where the agency operates, so for Europe the prevalence within Europe must be no more than 5 per 10,000 of the EU population. This means that diseases which are common in some other countries (e.g. malaria, which is very common in some countries) may still qualify for OMPD in Europe or the US because the prevalence is low in these regions.

It is worthwhile spending some time here to run through the processes of orphan designation in the US and Europe, since these underpin the development of medicines for rare diseases. The information provided here is top-line, to give a flavour of the procedures; more detail can be found in the relevant regulations and guidance documents (which are referenced in the text).

The US application is outlined in a Guidance for Industry document, although this is not very helpful and it is better to refer to the original Code of Federal Regulations (2006).[3] It comprises nine sections and it is strongly advised not to change this numbering. These are as follows:

1. Statement requesting orphan drug designation for a specific rare disease or condition

2. Name and address of the sponsor and primary contact person, generic and trade name of the drug or biologic, name and address of manufacturer if not the sponsor

3. A description of the rare disease or condition and why the proposed therapy is needed

4. A description of the drug and a discussion of the scientific rationale for using the drug to treat the rare disease or condition, including all data from nonclinical laboratory studies, clinical investigations, and other relevant data that are available to the sponsor, whether positive, negative or inconclusive. Copies of relevant papers are also required, whether published or unpublished

5. If a drug is the same as an already approved orphan drug for the same rare disease or condition, an explanation must be provided of why clinical superiority is expected

6. Where a drug is under development for only a subset of persons with a particular disease or condition, a demonstration that the subset is medically plausible

7. A summary of the regulatory status and marketing history of the drug around the world

8. Referenced documentation on disease prevalence or insufficient return on investment

9. A statement as to whether the sponsor submitting the request is the real party in interest of the development

In the EU, the requirements are slightly different. In order to receive orphan medicinal product designation, the product must meet the following criteria:

- A medicinal product intended for the diagnosis, prevention or treatment of a condition meeting the prevalence criteria, *and*

- Is life-threatening or chronically debilitating, *or*

3 Since this is almost impossible to find, a link is provided (www.gpo.gov/fdsys/pkg/CFR-2006-title21-vol5/pdf/CFR-2006-title21-vol5-sec316-20.pdf, accessed 17 January 2013).

- Is life-threatening, seriously debilitating or a serious and chronic condition that without incentives would not generate sufficient return to justify the necessary investment

and

- that there exists no satisfactory method of diagnosis, prevention or treatment of the condition in question that has been authorised in the Community, *or*

- if such method exists, that the medicinal product will be of significant benefit to those affected by that condition

These criteria may be better visualised in Figure 4.2.

If there is any product registered in the Community to treat the condition for which OMPD is sought, the EMA considers that a 'satisfactory method' exists. In this case, it is necessary in the application to give a convincing argument that the new product will have significant benefit over the existing method. Significant benefit means 'a clinically relevant advantage or a major contribution to patient care'. Assumptions of potential benefit(s) should be plausible and where possible based on sound pharmacological principles.

As detailed in the European guideline on the format and content of applications for designation as orphan medicinal products, 'In general a demonstration of potentially greater efficacy, an improved safety profile, and/or more favourable pharmacokinetic properties than existing methods may be considered to support the notion of significant benefit'(European Commission Enterprise Directorate-General 2007). This may be a new mechanism of action, an easier route of administration, a reduction in the number of pills to be taken or a reduced number of intravenous cycles, for example.

Figure 4.2 **Criteria for orphan medicinal product designation in the EU**
Source: Adapted from EURORDIS

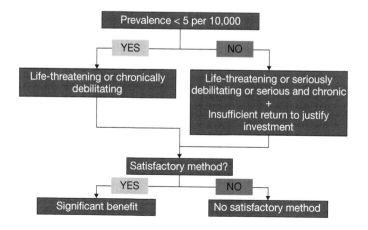

Figure 4.3 **The procedure and timelines for orphan designation in Europe**
Source: Adapted from EURORDIS

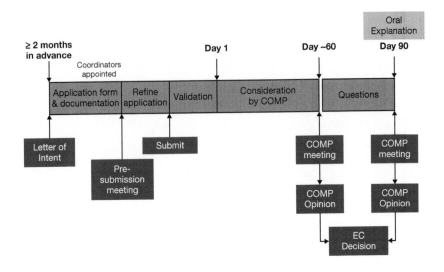

The complete procedure and timelines for OMPD decision are summarised in Figure 4.3. The dates of the deadline for submission of applications, the start of the procedure for validated applications and the COMP meetings are published on the EMA website.

The European application comprises five sections (A–E). Here we will briefly run through these sections, highlighting points of particular note.

4.3.1 Part A: Description of the condition

4.3.1.1 Details of the condition

This should include a description of the condition that the medicinal product is intended to diagnose, prevent or treat, based on published references where possible, or textbooks. Details of the causes and symptoms should be provided.

4.3.1.2 Proposed orphan indication

The choice of indication in the OMPD application is very important. Defining the actual orphan indication may be simple, but in many cases it can cause problems for the sponsor. It should be remembered that the orphan indication is a regulatory definition, which might differ from the clinical definition that the sponsor has in mind for development and which is decided at the time of marketing authorisation on the basis of the development programme which has been performed. The population included by the orphan indication might be broader than the population defined for the proposed therapeutic indication and the prevalence estimates should be based on the population for the orphan indication. This can lead the sponsor into difficulties if the prevalence of the former does not meet the criteria for designation, as described below.

Another aspect to watch out for is defining a condition which is in fact a consequence of the condition rather than a condition itself. For example, a wording such as '…for the treatment of pain secondary to giant cell arteritis' would probably not be accepted by the COMP. It might well be that the sponsor intends to develop its product for this specific indication, in which case the development plan will reflect this, but this would not be accepted for the purposes of OMPD.

If the product's effect is to reduce pain then (unless a very good argument exists to the contrary, based on the mechanism of action of the product) it will most likely also be effective in other types of pain and the above would be an invalid subset of patients. In this case, the true set of patients would exceed the prevalence threshold for OMPD, but the point is applicable even if this were not the case. But if the product's effect is on the arteritis, then this is the real condition being treated and the wording of the orphan indication should reflect this.

4.3.1.3 Medical plausibility

This section is one of the most important in the application and can cause difficulties if there is little or no preclinical or clinical data available on which to base the argument. In general, a rationale based only on theoretical grounds for the effectiveness of the product in the proposed orphan indication will not be sufficient to obtain designation.

The condition for which orphan designation of the product is requested should be well-defined and widely accepted. If the proposed orphan indication refers to a subset of a particular condition, a justification of the medical plausibility for restricting the use of the product to this subset would need to be argued, based on the characteristics of the condition and the mechanism of action of the product. A valid condition might be based on the pathophysiological, histopathological or clinical characteristics of the condition. Different degrees of severity or stages of a disease would generally not be considered as distinct conditions but would be considered to be invalid subsets within a condition. Details of the exact requirements for medical plausibility and valid subsets are described in an EMA Discussion Paper (COMP 2010).

4.3.1.4 Justification of the life-threatening or debilitating nature of the condition

As mentioned above, OMPD may be granted for a product which does not fulfil the prevalence requirements of no more than 5 per 10,000 persons in the Community, provided that 'it is unlikely that the marketing of the medicinal product in the Community would generate sufficient return to justify the necessary investment'. Regardless of whether the sponsor is applying for OMPD on the basis of rarity or insufficient return on investment, in both cases a statement justifying the seriousness of the condition needs to be provided, supported by references.

4.3.2 Part B: Prevalence of the condition

4.3.2.1 Prevalence of the orphan disease or condition in the Community

First of all, it is important to note that prevalence is not the same as incidence. Prevalence is the number of persons with a disease or condition at a specified instant in time in a given population, while incidence is the number of new cases arising in a given period of time (usually a year). The COMP wants to see the prevalence for the condition in the European Community at the time of the orphan designation application.

This can be quite challenging, as the epidemiology of many rare diseases is not well documented and what little information is available often refers to incidence rather than prevalence. However, it is important to be thorough in this section of the application and to provide a clear explanation of prevalence calculations and assumptions. It is also important to provide information from across Europe, not just one country, since the orphan designation (and any future marketing authorisation) is centralised and applies to the whole of the EU. Prevalence might vary significantly from one country to another and it is important to demonstrate that the figures provided in the application are relevant across Europe. The documentation should include a comprehensive review of authoritative references and should cover as many Member States as possible. There is a guidance document to help sponsors with this aspect of the application (COMP 2002).

The sponsor should not assume, just because someone else has been granted orphan designation for another product in the same indication, that this means they do not need to demonstrate prevalence or that the designation will be automatic. Each application is assessed individually on its own merits so it is important to be thorough.

If the prevalence figures are close to the cut-off of 5 per 10,000, the sponsor should be particularly careful with the calculations and provide strong supportive data. It is not unknown for sponsors to attempt to define a subset, as described above, in order to meet the prevalence criteria. Needless to say, such attempts to artificially create an orphan indication would be quickly spotted by the COMP.

4.3.2.2 Prevalence and incidence of the condition in the Community

If the orphan designation is based on the 'insufficient return on investment' argument, prevalence and incidence information should be provided in this section, for information purposes only. Otherwise this section is not applicable.

4.3.2.3 Information on participation in other Community projects

This section of the application should include any information on whether a disease or condition has been financially supported by European funding, such as the framework programmes. The COMP expects the sponsor to search the relevant public information services for this information.

4.3.3 Part C: Potential for return on investment

This section of the application only needs to be completed if the orphan designation application is based on the 'insufficient return on investment' argument. In this case, it is necessary to provide documentation to support all costs incurred or expected to be incurred during the course of development and marketing according to the following subheadings:

1. Grants and tax incentives

2. Past and future development costs

3. Production and marketing costs—past and first 10 years of marketing

4. Expected revenues—expected in first 10 years

5. Certification by registered accountant

This is not a commonly used route for orphan designation and will not be explored further here.

4.3.4 Part D: Existence of other methods of diagnosis, prevention or treatment

4.3.4.1 Details of any existing diagnosis, prevention or treatment methods

This section must be completed for all applications and if no methods currently exist, this should be stated. For many rare diseases, this may be the case. Where there are currently available treatments which do not have a marketing authorisation, these need to be discussed and it is the responsibility of the applicant to justify why such methods are not considered satisfactory. In general such methods could be considered satisfactory if there is consensus among clinicians or good scientific evidence as to their value. For products with a marketing authorisation in Europe, these are always considered to be satisfactory, the argument being that they would not have a marketing authorisation if they were not satisfactory. This includes products authorised nationally in at least one Member State, which might be old nationally approved products from before the country in question joined the EU. The sponsor must demonstrate that it has performed a comprehensive search for any products authorised in any Member States, a process which can be difficult. Where a satisfactory method exists, the applicant must justify why the new product seeking designation will be of significant benefit to those affected by the condition, as explained above.

4.3.4.2 Justification as to why methods are not satisfactory

If this section is completed, it is not necessary to complete section D3 regarding justification of significant benefit and vice versa.

4.3.4.3 Justification of significant benefit

This section and the one above are mutually exclusive and only one of them should be filled in. The criteria for demonstrating significant benefit are described above and are defined in detail in the EMA discussion paper (COMP 2010).

4.3.5 Part E: Description of the stage of development

4.3.5.1 Summary of the development of the product

Here, the sponsor needs to provide brief details of preliminary research, pharmaceutical development, pre-clinical and clinical investigation, details of planned Protocol Assistance, if known.

4.3.5.2 Details of current regulatory status and marketing history

A summary of the worldwide regulatory status and marketing history of the medicinal product should be provided, including clinical trials and marketing application status, and any adverse regulatory actions. This section should also include details of whether orphan status has been applied for or granted in other countries.

4.3.6 Part F: Bibliography

This section should contain all published references referred to in sections A to D, provided as a separate volume.

It is important to remember that an orphan designation is not a marketing authorisation. In many ways, it is just the start of the process (Fig. 4.4).

Figure 4.4 **Orphan designation may be the start of a long process**
Source: Adapted from EURORDIS

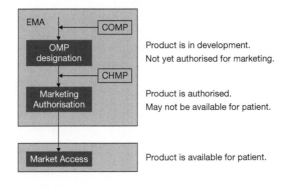

An orphan designation, once obtained by a sponsor, may be transferred to another sponsor by submitting an application to the EMA accompanied by the following documentation:

- A copy of the commission decision on the designation

- Identification of the sponsor of the designation to be transferred and the identification of the sponsor to whom the transfer is to be granted

- A document certifying that a complete and up-to-date designation application has been made available to or has been transferred to the person to whom the transfer is to be granted

- Proof that the sponsor to whom the designation is to be transferred is established in the EU

- A document stating the date on which the person to whom the transfer is to be granted can actually take over responsibility for the designation

Within 30 days of the submission of the required documentation as listed above, the EMA will give its opinion (European Commission Enterprise Directorate-General 2007).

4.4 The challenges of designing clinical trials for orphan indications

The clinical development of products for orphan indications can present many challenges, such as those listed below:

- Logistical issues (small populations available for study)

- Ethical issues (use of placebo; children)

- Lack of specialist centres

- Lack of knowledge of disease natural history

- Lack of accepted clinical efficacy measures

- Lack of accepted surrogate markers

- Lack of animal models for disease

- Lack of appropriate statistical tools

- Lack of established regulatory paradigm

All these issues are inter-linked, making the design of the clinical development programme a specialist area, somewhat removed from the traditional drug development programmes of products for common conditions.

To begin with is the question of exactly what to study. It may be that very little is known about the natural history of the disease and the presentation may be a complex syndrome of clinical features.

The difficulties of orphan drug development are very well illustrated by the rare disease alkaptonuria, which will be used as a case study here. As described in detail in Chapter 3, alkaptonuria (AKU) is a rare autosomal recessive disorder of tyrosine metabolism characterised by high plasma homogentisic acid (HGA) due to a deficiency of the enzyme homogentisate 1,2-dioxygenase (HGD). Despite efficient and marked urinary excretion, HGA undergoes conversion to a melanin-like polymeric pigment via benzoquinone acetic acid (BQA) in connective tissues, a process called ochronosis. Cartilage is selectively targeted for ochronosis leading to early-onset and severe arthritis affecting mainly the spinal and large weight-bearing joints such as hips and knees. Other important damage in AKU includes aortic valve stenosis/regurgitation (sometimes requiring valve replacement), stone formation in various sites (renal, prostate, gall bladder and salivary), osteopenia (sometimes leading to fractures), weakening of connective tissues (resulting in rupture of tendons, muscle and ligaments), and on occasion hearing loss (due to joint disease affecting the small bones of the auricular chain).

Nitisinone is a potent inhibitor of the enzyme 4-hydroxyphenylpyruvate dioxygenase (pHPPD), which catalyses the conversion of 4 hydroxyphenylpyruvate [pHPP] to HGA. It has a marketing authorisation for the treatment of hereditary tyrosinaemia type 1 (HT1). Therefore, nitisinone is expected to prevent the production of HGA by removing its substrate and, since HGA is thought to be the substance responsible for the development of ochronosis, nitisinone would be expected to prevent ochronosis.

Although there is good reason to believe, on theoretical grounds, that nitisinone would be effective in the treatment of alkaptonuria, together with a few anecdotal reports from patients that they 'feel better' when taking nitisinone (off-label), from a scientific and regulatory point of view the efficacy and safety of the product is unproven. In addition, for the team tasked with designing the clinical development programme for a product where the clinical features manifest themselves very gradually over several decades, this was a voyage into uncharted territory.

There was no information on which dose to select (although it was thought, on theoretical grounds, that this would be much lower than the 1–2 mg/kg required in HT1). And there were no animal models in which to study the disease and investigate the effects of nitisinone. Fortunately, because of the tenacity of the AKU Society and the interest of a group of researchers in Liverpool, money was raised to fund some basic research at the University of Liverpool. In mice genetically deficient in homogentisate 1,2-dioxygenase, the researchers were able to demonstrate that plasma HGA was elevated throughout their lifetime. Furthermore, administration of nitisinone to these mice reduced the levels of HGA. Together with data from human subjects in a few small clinical trials, this information could be used to demonstrate that nitisinone (as postulated, at a dose considerably lower than that required for the treatment of HT1) reduced HGA in the blood and urine. Unfortunately, in the initial model, the knock-out mice did not develop ochronosis and so it was not possible to show that reducing HGA levels with nitisinone had an effect on the course of the disease. Later, after refining the model, ochronosis could be demonstrated in these mice and, of great importance to the programme, it was shown that nitisinone completely prevented the development of ochronosis in these mice (Preston *et al.*, submitted).

Even with a useful animal model available and some limited dose information in a clinical setting, the way ahead was not straightforward. The lack of accepted clinical efficacy measures was an obvious problem in selecting an appropriate primary end-point for clinical trials. Furthermore, even though this is an inherited disorder which leads to raised HGA from birth, the clinical syndrome does not usually develop until around the third decade, after which the course, although relentless, is very slow and unpredictable.

In order to address the problem of efficacy measures, the University of Liverpool developed a clinical scale on which the severity of the disease could be assessed, based on a large number of features, some subjective and some objective. The resulting AKU Severity Score Index (AKUSSI) was published in the *Journal of Inherited Metabolic Disorders* (Cox and Ranganath 2011) and, although this is not automatically accepted by the regulators as an appropriate end-point, for the first time a tool was available which allowed clinicians to chart the course of the disease with both objective and subjective measures.

However, the AKUSSI was not the entire answer to the question of lack of accepted clinical efficacy measures. The clinical features of AKU develop slowly over several decades and, although there was now good experimental grounds (from the mouse model) to suppose that nitisinone could prevent ochronosis, its ability to reverse already established disease is much more questionable. In order to demonstrate that nitisinone could prevent ochronosis, in theory it would be necessary to perform a placebo-controlled clinical trial over several decades, something which is obviously impractical and unethical. Therefore, it was necessary to consider whether a different approach could be acceptable, but there was no regulatory precedent or guidance document for such an approach. The obvious target for study would be a reduction in HGA, which had been linked to the prevention of ochronosis in mice. But HGA has not been accepted as a surrogate marker for clinical outcome in AKU.

A surrogate end-point can be defined as a biomarker intended to substitute for a clinical end-point. 'Surrogate endpoints may be used as primary endpoints when appropriate (when the surrogate is reasonably likely or well known to predict clinical outcome)' (ICH Expert Working Group 1997).

Surrogate end-points can be very useful during a development programme for the following reasons:

- **Speed**. Clinical end-points may take years to measure

- **Smaller numbers**. reduced variability

- **To make possible what would otherwise be impossible**. 'When direct assessment of the clinical benefit to the subject through observing actual clinical efficacy is not practical, indirect criteria (surrogate variables) may be considered' (ICH Expert Working Group 1998)

There are, however, some disadvantages:

- **Clinical relevance**. Surrogate end-points may not be a true predictor of clinical outcome

- **Risk/benefit**. It may be difficult to measure clinical benefit against adverse effects

- **Reliability**. Relationship with clinical outcome may vary between drugs/classes

- 'There is no surrogate for safety' (Temple 1999)

In order to be considered acceptable by the regulatory authorities, a surrogate end-point needs to be validated. The validation of a surrogate end-point is described in ICH E8 (ICH Expert Working Group 1997), but in brief the requirements are:

- There must be a sound biological rationale for the surrogate

- The surrogate should be a prognostic marker for clinical outcome

- Treatment-induced changes in the marker should be prognostic for clinical outcome

- Effects of treatment on the marker should explain effects of treatment on clinical outcome

The EMA guideline on clinical trials in small populations (CHMP 2005a) mentions some of the limits of surrogate end-points:

> Also it has to be pointed out that surrogate markers cannot serve as final proof of clinical efficacy or long-term benefit. If they are intended to be the basis for regulatory review and approval then, unless they are properly validated, there should be a predetermined plan to supplement such studies with further evidence to support clinical benefit, safety and risk/benefit assessment.

Returning to our case study of AKU, it is important to note at this point that, even if HGA was accepted as a suitable surrogate end-point, it is still unknown:

- At what age treatment would need to begin in order to prevent ochronosis

- Whether treatment would need to begin before the onset of ochronosis or whether existing ochronosis could be halted or reversed

These questions could only be properly answered with extremely long and impractical studies. Therefore, the following development programme was conceived:

1. A phase II study in a small number of patients to study the effects of nitisinone at different doses on HGA levels, which is expected to form the cornerstone of the marketing authorisation. This study was relatively easy to design, since there was already some information available on the effect of different doses of nitisinone on plasma and urinary HGA. However, whether plasma or

urinary HGA is the best parameter to use and the level to which HGA needs to be reduced in order to prevent ochronosis are still open questions.

2. A phase III study over 4 years in patients with established ochronosis. This trial will not only confirm the long-term effect of nitisinone on HGA levels, but also show if nitisinone can halt or reverse established ochronosis and therefore whether there is any benefit to treating patients once they have reached this stage of their disease. Such a study is difficult to design, as there are many unknowns; in particular the anticipated effect size on the various clinical parameters is not known and this makes it difficult to develop a proper statistical rationale and calculate the number of patients required. This study will hopefully show a clinical benefit, but it is important to remember that the study says nothing about the preventive role of nitisinone. Hence a failure to show clinical benefit in this group of patients with established ochronosis cannot be interpreted as lack of efficacy of nitisinone in AKU per se and should not preclude authorisation.

3. A cross-sectional study to evaluate whether AKU progresses sub-clinically before overt ochronosis develops. This study will allow the group to make a reasonable judgement as to what age treatment should begin.

4. Even if a marketing authorisation is granted on the basis of the above clinical programme, perhaps based on the surrogate end-point, long-term data will also be needed to look at the use of nitisinone in real life, including the prevention of ochronosis in patients who are currently free of overt disease.

As seen above, it can be difficult to define an appropriate development programme, even in cases where the course of the disease lends itself more readily to study. It is therefore extremely important to seek the advice of the regulatory agencies (free advice for orphan drugs can be obtained from the regulatory agencies; see Table 4.2) when deciding on the clinical development programme and, in particular, the primary end-point for the clinical studies.

In addition to illustrating some of the clinical and regulatory challenges of developing a product for a rare disease, logistical and ethical issues will also have to be addressed. AKU affects somewhere between 1 per 500,000 and 1 per million of the population. Before the advent of the AKU Society (which now covers several countries) there was no mechanism for tracking and keeping in touch with patients and no specialist centres for looking after them. This situation is not unusual for rare disorders and presents huge challenges for recruitment into clinical trials. Fortunately, the recent developments in social media, coupled with the growing strength of patient groups, are making it easier for patients to obtain diagnoses, contact each other and find a specialist centre to treat them. For AKU, there now exists a number of local registries and a few specialist centres in Europe and the US, which should make recruitment to the clinical programme feasible.

However, this does not overcome the ethical issues to be faced. Where no treatment is available, it can be argued that a placebo-controlled trial is acceptable, at least until a treatment is proven to be safe and effective. But many rare diseases are genetic and affect children, so that the clinical trials need to be performed in this group, which raises special ethical concerns for the conduct of clinical trials and for the use of placebo in particular.

The AKU example is also useful for illustrating the need for new regulatory paradigms for the approval of products for rare diseases. As already explained, a pivotal regulatory study to demonstrate that nitisinone prevents ochronosis is neither practical nor ethical and an alternative approach must be found. At the time of writing, this has not been accepted by the regulatory authorities, but is presented here as an illustration of the fact that standard development approaches are often not feasible with rare diseases.

The phase II study described above is expected to generate data to show that nitisinone reduces HGA in a dose-dependent manner. There is already an extensive safety database available for nitisinone, which has been on the market for several years for the treatment of HT1. Using this safety database, the information from the animal model and a sound theoretical basis, it is hoped that the regulators will agree to a conditional marketing authorisation for nitisinone based on the results of this phase II study. The larger study in patients with established ochronosis should provide supportive clinical data.

Conditional approval is a path available in Europe in order to meet unmet medical needs of patients and in the interests of public health, as detailed in Section 4.2.3. In certain cases, the authorities recognise that 'it may be necessary to grant marketing authorisations on the basis of less complete data than is normally the case and subject to specific obligations'. In the case of a conditional marketing authorisation, authorisation is granted before all data are available if the sponsor can show that the benefits outweigh the risks. It is not intended to remain conditional indefinitely and, once the missing data are provided, it should be possible to replace it with a marketing authorisation which is not conditional. The sponsor must agree to certain post-authorisation commitments to further study the product and obtain more data.

Another non-standard route to marketing authorisation which is available in Europe and has been used for several drugs for rare diseases is the approval under exceptional circumstances. This may be necessary 'when a population is so small that comprehensive data may never become available, or the present state of scientific knowledge is insufficient, or it would be against generally accepted principles of medical ethics' (CHMP 2005b). In contrast to the conditional marketing authorisation, it will normally never be possible to assemble a full dossier in respect of a marketing authorisation granted in exceptional circumstances.

4.5 Conclusion

This chapter has outlined the history of the incentives for the development of products for rare diseases, the process of obtaining designation as an orphan drug and some of the key factors to consider when developing a drug to treat a rare disease. It will be clear to the reader that the development of an orphan drug requires a different approach, both in the thinking of the company doing the development and in the way the regulators make their assessment. Changes are slow in the highly regulated environment of drug development, in the interests of patients' safety. However, change is necessary if we are to realise the objective of providing treatments for people with rare diseases, particularly as we move towards an era of more personalised medicine and new technologies that no longer fit into the traditional models.

References

CHMP (Committee for Medicinal Products for Human Use) (2005a) *Guideline on Clinical Trials in Small Populations* (CHMP/EWP/83561/2005; London: CHMP, 27 July 2006).

CHMP (2005b) *Guideline on Procedures for the Granting of a Marketing Authorisation Under Exceptional Circumstances, Pursuant to Article 14 (8) of Regulation (EC) No 726/2004* (EMEA/357981/2005; London: European Medicines Agency, 15 December 2005).

CHMP (2006a) *Guideline on the Procedure for Accelerated Assessment Pursuant to Article 14 (9) of Regulation (EC) No 726/2004* (EMEA/419127/05; London: CHMP, 17 July 2006).

CHMP (2006b) *Guideline on the Scientific Application and the Practical Arrangements Necessary to Implement Commission Regulation (EC) No 507/2006 on the Conditional Marketing Authorisation for Medicinal Products for Human Use Falling Within the Scope of Regulation (EC) No 726/2004* (EMEA/509951/2006; London: CHMP, 5 December 2006).

Code of Federal Regulations (2006) *21 CFR Part 316 - Orphan Drugs - Subpart C—Designation of an orphan drug: Section 316.20 Content and format of a request for orphan-drug designation* (Washington, DC: US Government Printing Office).

Commission of the European Communities (2000) 'Commission Regulation (EC) No 847/2000 of 27 April 2000 laying down the provisions for implementation of the criteria for designation of a medicinal product as an orphan medicinal product and definitions of the concepts "similar medicinal product" and "clinical superiority"', *Official Journal of the European Communities* 28.4.2000.

Commission of the European Communities (2006) 'Commission Regulation (EC) No 507/2006 of 29 March 2006 on the conditional marketing authorisation for medicinal products for human use falling within the scope of Regulation (EC) No 726/2004 of the European Parliament and of the Council', *Official Journal of the European Union* 30.3.2006.

COMP (Committee for Orphan Medicinal Products) (2002) *Points to Consider on the Calculation and Reporting of the Prevalence of a Condition for Orphan Designation* (COMP/436/01; London: European Agency for the Evaluation of Medicinal Products, 26 March 2002).

COMP (2010) *Recommendation on Elements Required to Support the Medical Plausibility and the Assumption of Significant Benefit for an Orphan Designation* (EMA/COMP/15893/2009 Final; London: European Medicines Agency, 2 March 2010).

Cox, T.F., and L. Ranganath (2011) 'A Quantitative Assessment of Alkaptonuria: Testing the Reliability of Two Disease Severity Scoring Systems', *Journal of Inherited Metabolic Disorders* 34.6 (December 2011): 1,153-62.

CPMP (Committee for Proprietary Medicinal Products) (2001) *Points to Consider on Application With 1. Meta-Analyses; 2. One Pivotal Study* (CPMP/EWP/2330/99; London: CPMP).

European Commission Enterprise Directorate-General (2007) *Guideline on the Format and Content of Applications for Designation as Orphan Medicinal Products and on the Transfer of Designations from One Sponsor to Another* (ENTR/6283/00 Rev 3; Brussels: European Commission, 9 July 2007).

European Parliament and Council of the European Union (1999) 'Regulation (EC) No 141/2000 of the European Parliament and of the Council of 16 December 1999 on orphan medicinal products', *Official Journal of the European Communities* 22.1.2000.

European Parliament and Council of the European Union (2004) 'Regulation (EC) No 726/2004 of the European Parliament and of the Council of 31 March 2004 laying down Community procedures for the authorisation and supervision of medicinal products for human and veterinary use and establishing a European Medicines Agency', *Official Journal of the European Union* 30.4.2004.

FDA (US Food and Drug Administration) (2012) 'Fast Track, Accelerated Approval and Priority Review: Accelerating Availability of New Drugs for Patients with Serious Diseases', www.fda.gov/forconsumers/byaudience/forpatientadvocates/speedingaccesstoimportant newtherapies/ucm128291.htm, accessed 3 December 2012.

Ferner, R.E., and D.A. Hughes (2010) 'The problem of orphan drugs', *BMJ* 341: c6456.

Godlee, F. (2010) 'Stop Exploiting Orphan Drugs', *BMJ* 341: c6587.

Hawkes, N., and D. Cohen (2010) 'What Makes an Orphan Drug?' *BMJ* 341: c6459.

Hughes-Wilson, W., A. Palma, A. Schuurman and S. Simoens (2012) 'Paying for the Orphan Drug System: Break or Bend? Is it time for a new evaluation system for payers in Europe to take account of new rare disease treatments?' *Orphanet Journal of Rare Diseases* 7: 74.

ICH Expert Working Group (1997) *ICH Harmonised Tripartite Guideline: General Considerations for Clinical Trials* (E8; Geneva: ICH, 17 July 1997).

ICH Expert Working Group (1998) *ICH Harmonised Tripartite Guideline: Statistical Principles for Clinical Trials* (E9; Geneva: ICH, 5 February 1998).

Nicholl, D.J., D. Hilton Jones, J. Palace and 18 others (2010) 'Open letter to Prime Minister David Cameron and Health Secretary Andrew Lansley', *BMJ* 341: c6466.

Preston, A.J., C.M. Keenan, H. Sutherland, P.J. Wilson, B. Wlodarski, A. Taylor, D.P. Williams, L.R. Ranganath, J.A. Gallagher and J.C. Jarvis (submitted) 'Development of Ochronosis in a Mouse Model of Alkaptonuria and its Inhibition by Nitisinone', *Annals of the Rheumatic Diseases*, submitted.

Roos, C.P., H.R. Hyry and T.M. Cox (2010) 'Orphan Drug Pricing may Warrant a Competition Law Investigation', *BMJ* 341: c6471.

Sasinowski, F.J. (2011) *Quantum of Effectiveness Evidence in FDA's Approval of Orphan Drugs Cataloguing FDA's Flexibility in Regulating Therapies for Persons with Rare Disorders* (Danbury, CT: National Organization for Rare Disorders).

Temple, R. (1999) 'Are Surrogate Markers Adequate to Assess Cardiovascular Disease Drugs?' *Journal of the American Medical Association* 282.8 (August 1999): 790-95.

US Congress (1983) 'Orphan Drug Act: To amend the Federal Food, Drug, and Cosmetic Act to facilitate the development of drugs for rare diseases and conditions, and for other purposes', *Public Law* 97-414-Jan 4, 1983.

Dr **Anthony Hall (Tony)** graduated from King's College London with first class honours in physiology and pharmacology before going on to study medicine at the Royal Free Hospital. He joined the pharmaceutical industry in 1994 before starting his own company in 2001, providing drug development consultancy and other services to the biopharmaceutical industry. Since 2010, Tony has focused exclusively on the orphan drugs and rare diseases sector. He has built an in-depth knowledge of the orphan drug market, regulatory and clinical pathways. Tony has built trusted relationships with patient groups, providing pro bono advice on the development of medicines to treat their diseases. Tony is Co-Founder of Findacure Foundation, to which he devotes part of his time. The rest of his time, he works as a consultant, providing advice and guidance on the development of orphan drugs to the biopharmaceutical industry.

5

Navigating orphan drugs through the regulatory maze
Successes, failures and lessons learned

Remco de Vrueh
Rare Disease Matters, the Netherlands

Harald Heemstra
The Netherlands

Michelle Putzeist
Utrecht Institute for Pharmaceutical Sciences, the Netherlands

It is generally acknowledged that the introduction of specific orphan drug legislation in various jurisdictions across the globe has made, and is still making, an enormous difference in the lives of millions of rare disease patients (EMA 2005a; Haffner 2006). Over 400 orphan drugs in the US and 70 in the EU have been approved since the introduction of the US Orphan Drug Act in 1983 and the EU Regulation on Orphan Medicinal Products (OMPs) in 2000, respectively. One important contributor to this success has been the group of small and medium-sized bio-pharmaceutical companies, so-called SMEs. A large proportion (approximately 85%) of the orphan designation applications originate from SMEs (Torrent-Farnell 2005). For this group, the legislation provides an important opportunity to demonstrate the potential of their new technology platforms and drug products.

At the same time there is a growing interest from big pharma in orphan drugs and rare disorders, best exemplified by the introduction of specific rare disease units, for example at Pfizer and GSK, or by giving them a more prominent position in their business model, such as at Novartis (Shaffer 2010; Melnikova 2012). This growing interest should not be interpreted as a lack of activity by big pharma in the field of orphan drugs thus far. As depicted in Figure 5.1, big pharma companies have been involved from the start, in particular at the stage of market authorisation. Their role has just been slightly less prominent than SMEs (Haffner 2006).

In essence, nowadays, promising products may subsequently be licensed or sold to other (big) companies for further development or may be developed by SMEs under their own steam (Drews 2003; Wilgenbus 2007; Czerepak and Ryser 2008). The crucial question that senior management or an investor in a new SME or an academic start-up/spin-off will have to address is which of the aforementioned strategies is most likely to be successful. We realise that each situation is unique, and that, besides the technical development of the drug, other more economic and business-related issues have to be considered, which makes it impossible to define a set of ground rules. Nevertheless we feel it is important that those think-ing of entering or those that have just entered the orphan drug arena should be aware that approval of an orphan drug is certainly feasible, but is accompanied by difficulties, in particular during the clinical development stage. What we are interested in is to enhance understanding of what distinguishes successful from non-approved orphan drug development. What are the important lessons to be learnt? At the end of the day it is of utmost importance that products with real ther-apeutic value reach the patient.

In the remainder of this chapter we share some of our research findings and views on this matter. We start off with a concise overview of orphan drug development

Figure 5.1 **Descriptive statistics of EU and US orphan designations and market authorisations: total and top-50 pharma share (period 2000–2006)**

Source: Top 50 pharma from Wikipedia 2004

	 EU	 US
#designations (Total)	429	699
#designations (Top-50 Pharma)	65	115
#Market Authorisations (Total)	31 (a)	44
#Market Authorisations (Top-50 Pharma)	13	26

(a) Prevalence rare disorder: 0,01–50 per 100,000

in the US and the EU to emphasise the importance of understanding what distinguishes successful from non-approved orphan drug development. We highlight some differences between the US and the EU with regard to orphan drug development and share some remarkable findings. We address various sponsor, product, disease, clinical and regulatory aspects that we and others have investigated to shed some light on the question of what differentiates successfully approved orphan drugs from non-successful ones. Although patient access to orphan drugs also involves reimbursement of an orphan drug in each market, here we define successful development as drugs having obtained a positive CHMP opinion (the EMA's Committee on Human Medical Products). To allow early access to drugs that treat serious diseases in the EU and the US, regulators have specific regulatory instruments at their disposal. Although these instruments are not specific for orphan drugs, as rare diseases are by definition a chronically debilitating or life-threatening disease, orphan drugs in principle qualify. We provide a concise overview of these important regulatory instruments, and discuss their role in orphan drug approval thus far. Moreover, the ever-growing and important role of the rare disease patient in orphan drug development will be discussed. Finally, we describe what lies beyond orphan drug approval and that has raised and will increasingly continue to raise considerable discussion in the area of rare diseases: orphan drug reimbursement and patient access.

We have written this chapter with a small start-up company with an interest in orphan drug development in mind as the main target readership, providing a sound mix of the necessary theoretical and helpful practical information. This chapter is also of interest to representatives of venture capital firms, patient organisations and even more mature SMEs stepping into the orphan drug arena.

5.1 Overview of orphan drug development in the US and EU

Before discussing the subject of what distinguishes successful from failed orphan drug development, we believe it is important to start off with a concise overview of the orphan drug legislation in the US and the EU. Equally important is a quantitative and qualitative description of orphan drug development in the US and the EU, because this will help us to better understand the difference between successful and non-approved orphan drug development.

5.1.1 Orphan drug legislation in the US and EU: comparable but not identical

In essence, the orphan drug legislations introduced in the US and the EU in 1983 and 2000, respectively, are comparable, but not identical (see Table 5.1). Both legislations aim to stimulate drug development for rare disorders through a number of

Table 5.1 **Overview of orphan drug legislation in the EU and US**

	US	EU
Legislation	Orphan Drug Act	Regulation (EC) nr. 141/2000
Administrative authorities involved	FDA (OOPD)	EMEA (COMP)
Prevalence-criterion (within jurisdiction)	<200,000 (7.5:10,000) or insufficient ROI	<5: 10,000 or Insufficient ROI
Seriousness criterion	N.A.	Life-threatening or chronically debilitating Life-threatening, seriously debilitating or serious and chronic
Significance criterion	N.A.	No Satisfactory method or Medicinal product will be of signifcant benefit
Market exclusivity	7 years	10 years
Other incentives	Grant programme; tax credit clinical studies; technical assistance, fee reduction/waivers	FP, technical assistance, fee reduction/waivers, national measures
Accelerated approval	yes	yes

regulatory and economic incentives, of which a market exclusivity period of seven and ten years in the US and the EU, respectively, is regarded as the foremost. Other incentives included in both legislations are a number of regulatory fee reductions and/or waivers and technical assistance (= free scientific advice). The importance of the latter is not always recognised, but as we will show below, it can have a real added value to the success of an orphan drug development programme, especially for less experienced SMEs. The US has a tax credit incentive, which allows a sponsor a 50% tax reduction for its clinical trial expenses. It is important to understand that this tax credit can only be used when a company makes a profit: most SMEs do not in the first years of their existence. Although the EU does not have a tax incentive at communitarian level, EU Member States have implemented a variety of additional national economic, regulatory and other incentives. A description of these incentives goes beyond the scope of this chapter, but an extensive overview of national incentives in the EU is provided and updated at regular intervals (EUCERD 2009).

To benefit from the aforementioned incentives, a sponsor has to apply and obtain an orphan designation for its product from the Food and Drug Administration

(FDA) or European Medicines Agency (EMA)/European Commission in the US and the EU, respectively. Products intended for treatment, diagnosis or prevention of rare diseases that fulfil a set of predefined criteria are eligible for an orphan designation. Both EU and US orphan legislation include a definition of the rarity of the indicated disease (= **prevalence criterion**). In the EU, drugs indicated for a disease with a prevalence of fewer than 5 patients per 10,000 residents are eligible for an orphan designation. In the US, a rare disease is defined as a disease with a maximum of 200,000 patients (equivalent to 7 patients per 10,000 residents). The EU has two additional important criteria that have to be fulfilled. In the EU, an orphan designation will only be provided if the product is intended for the diagnosis, prevention or treatment of a life-threatening or chronically debilitating condition (= **seriousness criterion**). Moreover, the sponsor should establish that there exists no satisfactory method for the diagnosis, treatment or prevention of this condition, or if such a method exists, that the new product will be of significant benefit for those affected by that condition (= **significance criterion**). What this means is that if an approved product for the indicated disease already exists, the sponsor of a new product, a so-called follow-on, has to establish that its product has a clinically relevant advantage or a major contribution to patient care. The latter is generally justified by 'demonstration of potentially greater efficacy, an improved safety profile and/or more favorable pharmacokinetic properties than existing methods' (EMA 2009). Recently, Roos *et al.* (2010) claimed that the highly praised market exclusivity incentive basically creates a market monopoly that in their view has allowed manufacturers to charge 'exorbitant' prices for orphan drugs.

Tambuyzer, in contrast, argued that

> if an approved OMP is currently the only product on the market, it is either because a company was the first to develop a treatment for this disease and competitors have yet to enter the market or because the market is too small to attract competition, rather than because the incentives have created a monopoly (Tambuyzer 2010).

Brabers *et al.* (2011) provided evidence that absence of follow-on OMP development is more a matter of time or market size as argued by Tambuyzer, rather than the creation of a market monopoly as claimed by Roos *et al.* (2010). They revealed that approval of the first OMP for a rare disorder, and consequently a market exclusivity period of ten years, does not serve as a disincentive for the development and marketing of a follow-on OMP for the same indication in the EU. In both the EU and US, certain disease classes and rare indications—in particular oncology—are associated with a high number of orphan designations and approvals (EMA 2005a; Haffner 2006; Heemstra *et al.* 2009). US and EU orphan legislation allow multiple orphan drugs to be designated, but also approved for one rare disease as long as each consecutive product fulfils the aforementioned criteria (e.g. pulmonary arterial hypertension, see Box 5.1) (Braun *et al.* 2010; Brabers *et al.* 2011). Moreover, one

Box 5.1 **Pulmonary arterial hypertension (PAH)**

Source: Agarwal and Gomberg-Maitland 2011

PAH is caused by a narrowing of the pulmonary vascular bed, which results in a progressive increase in pulmonary vascular resistance. The condition is defined as a resting mean pulmonary arterial pressure higher than 25 mmHg, in addition to a pulmonary arterial wedge pressure lower than or equal to 15 mmHg. The prevalence of this condition is estimated at 1.5 per 100,000 inhabitants, with an estimated median survival of 2.8 years. The condition may be idiopathic, but also frequently occurs in different clinical conditions, such as connective tissue disease or human immunodeficiency virus (HIV). Since 1995, a number of new treatments have been approved for marketing that offer impressive progress in the survival of patients with PAH. However, a cure for PAH has not yet been developed.

---

product can have a designation as well as be approved for multiple rare diseases (e.g. Glivec [imatinib]).

Finally, it is important to be aware that several orphan products have been approved in the EU, but not in the US and vice versa. This may be due to the fact that a sponsor has made a strategic decision to restrict marketing of the product to the EU or US. A company may, for example, only have limited regulatory market access and/or marketing capacities, or a company may not have found a partner for development and marketing in one of these regions. However, even if a marketing authorisation application has been submitted in both jurisdictions, the final outcome of the marketing authorisation process can be different. For example, Firazyr (icatibant) and Replagal (alpha-agalsidase) have been approved in the EU, but (initially) rejected in the US. In contrast, Mylotarg (gemtuzumab ozogamicin) and Dacogen (decitabine) are authorised in the US, but rejected in the EU. Both US and EU regulatory systems share many similarities, and there is growing interaction and sharing of knowledge between the regulatory agencies. However, cultural and historical differences remain that can have an impact on the outcome.

5.1.2 Orphan drug development in the US

The FDA Office of Orphan Medicinal Products (OOMP) has written a number of papers on the subject of orphan drugs. Many of these papers contain very relevant descriptive statistics, and combined provide an excellent comprehensive overview of orphan drug development in the US (Braun *et al.* 2010; Burke *et al.* 2010; Cote *et al.* 2010; Freeman *et al.* 2010; Talele *et al.* 2010; Lev *et al.* 2011).

In the first 25 years of the orphan drug act, 1,892 products were designated as orphan, and 326 products were approved (Braun *et al.* 2010). These 326 products target more than 200 rare diseases and make a difference in the lives of millions of rare disease patients (Burke *et al.* 2010; Freeman *et al.* 2010; Talele *et al.* 2010). Interestingly, these products do not only target the more prevalent rare diseases, but also quite a number of very rare diseases (Braun *et al.* 2010). Apart from the orphan drug act, the other contribution to this success is that around the time of the introduction of the orphan drug act, the biotechnology revolution was picking up speed with important inventions such as cDNA cloning and various molecular biology techniques (e.g. PCR). First, the revolution resulted in improved understanding of many rare disorders and the knowledge that many of these have a genetic component. Second, it allowed the start of a number of US-based biotechnology companies, such as Genentech, Amgen and Genzyme, and the translation of rare disease knowledge into numerous highly innovative rare disorder therapies (Haffner *et al.* 2002; Haffner 2006).

Although in the last decade the annual number of orphan designations continues to grow, as depicted in Figure 5.2, the annual number of orphan drugs that has been approved remains more or less constant (Braun *et al.* 2010). Nevertheless, the number of non-orphan drugs approved has declined in the last decade, and consequently the proportion of all drug approvals that are orphan drugs has almost doubled in the last 20 years (Cote *et al.* 2010). There is no apparent reason to assume that this trend will change in the near future. Nevertheless, development

Figure 5.2 **Orphan drug approvals in the US (2001–2010)**

Source: FDA database; www.accessdata.fda.gov/scripts/opdlisting/oopd/index.cfm

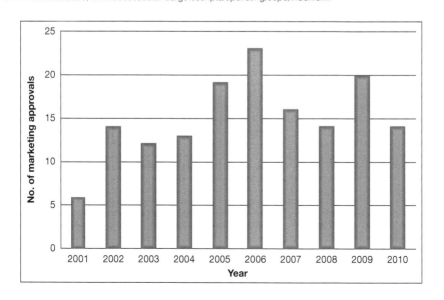

of an orphan drug, in particular the confirmatory (or pivotal) clinical trial stage, remains difficult for various reasons: limited number of patients, no clinical end-points or acceptance of surrogate end-points, lack of expertise, etc. Some of these issues will be addressed in more detail below. The FDA and Keck Graduate Institute provided a quantitative description of the scientific rationale on the basis of which promising compounds were designated as orphan drugs in 2009 (Lev *et al.* 2011). Only for 21 out of a total of 160 designations were phase III, or confirmatory trial stage, clinical data available.

5.1.3 Orphan drug development in the EU

Since the European Union (EU) Regulation on Orphan Medicinal Products (OMP) came into force in 2000, more than 70 OMPs have been approved for marketing and more than 900 medicinal products have received an orphan designation (OD) in the EU within the first decade of this regulation (COMP 2011). Both the Committee for Orphan Medicinal Products (COMP) at the EMA as well as several authors, including ourselves, have written a number of papers on the subject of European orphan drug development (Joppi *et al.* 2006, 2009; Heemstra *et al.* 2008a, b, 2009; Regnstrom *et al.* 2010; COMP 2011; Putzeist *et al.* 2012). Many of these papers contain very relevant descriptive statistics, and combined provide a comprehensive overview of orphan drug development in the EU.

We analysed orphan drug development between the introduction of the Regulation on Orphan Medicinal Products in 2000 and 2007 in Europe at a national level and unveiled a strong relationship between orphan drug development and pharmaceutical innovation performance in Europe (Heemstra *et al.* 2008b). Gaps in transition from science into orphan drug development were identified as important bottlenecks that exist in several European countries. Our findings underlined the importance of innovation-based policies to enhance the development of orphan drugs in Europe. Subsequently, we have extended the original dataset of 521 medicinal products with an orphan designation (OD) in the EU (August 2000 (= date first OD assigned) to December 2007) up to July 2010 and included a total of 759 orphan designations. Moreover, to allow a comparison between the first five and last five years at a national level the dataset was divided into two consecutive five-year periods.

In general, there has been a greater degree of development of orphan drugs at a national level in the last five years compared with the first period (see Fig. 5.3). Oddly, for France, a decrease in the number of orphan designations was observed. However, a logical explanation for this is that France already had a national plan for rare diseases when the EU orphan drug legislation came into force. Therefore, this should not be regarded as a decrease, but more as a consolidation of excellent work. Most orphan designations originate from the large countries, although a number of small countries appear to have entered the orphan drug discovery and development arena. In particular the Netherlands, Belgium and Switzerland have

Figure 5.3 **Absolute number of orphan designations (n = 414) originating from European countries divided in two equal five-year periods. Country of origin was defined as the country in which the company/institution was located that was leading the step from preclinical work to initial clinical development of the particular product for the designated indication (typically Phase I or Phase I/IIa clinical trials or proof-of-concept)**

Source: Adapted from Heemstra *et al.* 2008b and extended with new data (Jan 2008–July 2010) using the same methodology as described by Heemstra *et al.* 2008b

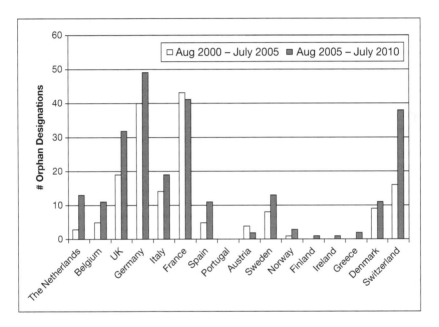

been active from the start of the legislation and show a more than average increase in number of orphan drugs.

A comparison of orphan drug output between European and Non-European countries also reveals that a considerable amount of European orphan drugs originate from outside Europe (see Fig. 5.4). Moreover, like European orphan drug development, there has also been considerable growth in non-European orphan drug development between 2000 and 2010. A total of 345 EU orphan designations originate from non-European countries, in particular the US (period 1: 105; period 2: 171). The latter provides encouraging evidence that US sponsors of orphan drugs also consider Europe as a potential market for their product.

Just like the US Orphan Drug Act (Haffner *et al.* 2002; Haffner 2006), the EU Orphan Drug Regulation is highly appreciated for its role in creating a favourable orphan drug development environment (EMA 2005a; COMP 2011). Unlike the

Figure 5.4 **Absolute number of EU orphan designations (n = 759) originating from European and non-European countries divided in two equal five-year periods**

Source: Adapted from Heemstra *et al.* 2008b and extended with new data (Jan 2008–July 2010) using the same methodology as described by Heemstra *et al.* 2008b

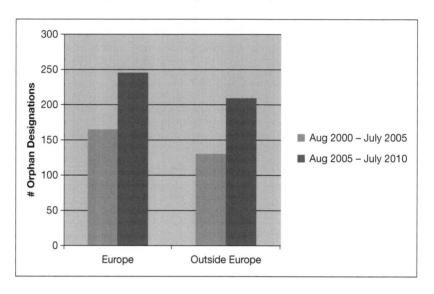

US, annual approval of orphan drugs in the EU in the last decade has been vari-able (see Fig. 5.5). This is probably best explained by the fact that the US Orphan Drug Act, active since 1983, has been fully adapted by US industry and regulators, whereas the EU orphan drug legislation is relatively new and still maturing.

Although the number of EU orphan drug approvals has been impressive, the number of EU orphan drugs for which a marketing authorisation was submitted, but eventually withdrawn or refused (= non-approval) has been equally impres-sive (see Fig. 5.5). A similar trend was observed in the US: between 1998 and 2007 there were 15 non-approved orphan new drug applications (NDAs) (Heemstra *et al.* 2011). Regnstrom *et al.* (2010) compared marketing authorisation applica-tions (MAAs) involving orphan drugs with MAAs with non-orphan drugs (108/138, 78%) during 2004–2007 and found a lower approval rate for orphan drugs (58% ver-sus 78%). These findings further emphasise the need to understand what differ-entiates successfully approved orphan drugs from non-successful ones. However, better understanding of the orphan drug development process is warranted for two additional reasons. First, enhanced understanding will hopefully increase the efficiency of the application process, thereby stimulating innovation and promot-ing the regulatory goal of assuring drug safety and efficacy (Heemstra *et al.* 2008b; Eichler *et al.* 2008). Second, and perhaps more importantly, it will help to speed the availability of much-needed therapies for life-threatening and/or chronically debilitating rare disorders.

Figure 5.5 **Orphan drug applications in the EU and the outcome (2001–2010)**

Source: Adapted from Putzeist *et al.* 2012 and extended with data from EU orphan drug register & EMA website (European Public Assessment Reports [EPARs] + applications withdrawn)

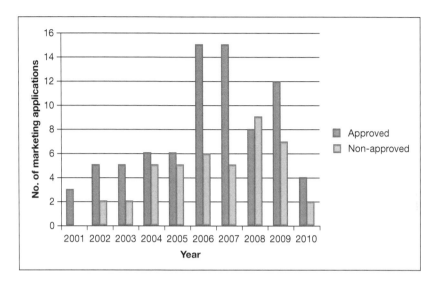

5.2 What differentiates successfully approved orphan drugs from non-successful ones?

In the last decade, successful approval of a regular drug has become increasingly more difficult, resulting in an unacceptably high attrition rate. Some have argued that this is due to the continuous expansion of the US and EU regulatory framework, both pre-and post-approval. In the EU alone, since 2000, specific orphan, paediatric, advanced therapies and pharmacovigilance legislations have come into force. As stated by Bouvy *et al.* (2012) the pharmaceutical industry is considered one of the world's most intensively regulated industries. Others argue that regulatory authorities have become risk-averse, and as such seriously delay pharmaceutical innovation (Scannell *et al.* 2012). An extensive elaboration of this subject is beyond the scope of this chapter, but for those interested we can recommend a number of interesting papers (Kola and Landis 2004; Elias *et al.* 2006; Pammolli *et al.* 2011; Morgan *et al.* 2012). What is important is that the aforementioned problem is partly responsible for the growing interest in orphan drug development by the pharmaceutical industry, in particular big pharma (Shaffer 2010; Melnikova 2012). We believe this trend provides one explanation for the fact that, in contrast to regular drug approval, successful orphan drug approval has remained more or less stable in the last decade (Meekings 2012). However, we have also shown above that successful orphan drug approval is accompanied by considerable non-successful orphan drug approval. Since both non-orphan and orphan medicinal products have to comply with the criteria of quality, safety and efficacy, one explanation is that orphan drugs that have not obtained marketing authorisation have unfavourable characteristics or the sponsor of the product has not been able to show the favourability of the product characteristics. In this section we will discuss some of the critical aspects that we and others have revealed to be related to achieving marketing approval in the EU and/or the US. A concise description of the various studies is depicted in Table 5.2. The focus will be primarily on the regulatory and clinical development aspects of orphan drug development, sponsor, product and disease characteristics, namely:

- Pivotal clinical trial stage
- Size/experience of sponsor
- Regulatory dialogue

Of course, many additional/other technical, economic and business-related aspects exist that differentiate successful from non-successful drug development. However, these aspects are not unique for orphan drugs, but a more generic challenge in pharmaceutical innovation. As such we consider them beyond the scope of this chapter.

Table 5.2 **Studies that investigated critical aspects of orphan drug development**

Study	Study period	Title
Heemstra et al. 2008a	April 2000–October 2006	Predictors of orphan drug approval in the European Union
Heemstra et al. 2011	1998–2007	Characteristics of orphan drug applications that fail to achieve marketing approval in the USA
Putzeist et al. 2012	2000–2009	Determinants for successful marketing authorisation of orphan medicinal products in the EU
Regnstrom et al. 2010	2004–2007	Factors associated with success of market authorisation applications for pharmaceutical drugs submitted to the European Medicines Agency
Joppi et al. 2006	2000–2004	Orphan drug development is progressing too slowly (EU)
Kesselheim et al. 2011	2004–2010	To define characteristics of orphan cancer drugs and their pivotal clinical trials and to compare these with non-orphan drugs (US)
Mitsumoto et al. 2009	1983–2007	Pivotal studies of orphan drugs approved for neurological diseases (US)

5.2.1 How important is the pivotal clinical trial stage?

The key issue with rare diseases is that they are fundamentally different from prevalent diseases. This becomes most painfully clear during the clinical development stage: too small a number of patients, logistics, ethics (e.g. use of placebo), lack of validated biomarkers and surrogate end-points, poor diagnostics, limited clinical expertise and expert centres. Being different has been the primary reason for the introduction of specific orphan drug legislation. Because rare diseases differ from common diseases, some have argued or suggested that regulatory agencies have been more lenient towards orphan drug MA (marketing authorisation) applications than regular drug MA applications (Joppi *et al.* 2006; Mitsumoto *et al.* 2009; Kesselheim *et al.* 2011). Joppi *et al.* commented in 2006 that the low approval rates for European orphan drugs may be due to the poor documentation underpinning the applications, and that many orphan drugs were approved under exceptional circumstances, without comprehensive data on the safety and efficacy of the product (Joppi *et al.* 2006). Deficiencies included the use of clinically irrelevant surrogate end-points, a low number of study subjects, inappropriate use of a comparator and the absence of adequately conducted randomised controlled trials (RCTs). As shown above, Regnstrom *et al.* (2010) compared MAAs involving orphan drugs with MAAs with non-orphan drugs (108/138, 78%) during 2004–2007 and found a lower approval rate for orphan drugs (58% versus 78%). We consequently believe that regulatory authorities have certainly not become more lenient. The approval of orphan drugs in the last decade has been accompanied by a considerable number of non-approved orphan drugs (see Fig. 5.5). In our view, regulatory authorities act within the regulatory framework. However, where deemed necessary in the interest of patients they make use of specific legislations, such as exceptional circumstances, accelerated and conditional approval, to allow earlier market access for drugs for serious diseases. Interestingly, some argue that regulatory authorities are not lenient enough, in particular to orphan drugs for ultra-rare disorders (Miyamoto and Kakkis 2011). We will elaborate on this subject below.

What is more relevant and important is to determine whether the pivotal clinical trial stage has specific characteristics that provide an explanation for why certain orphan drugs have been successfully approved and others not. We therefore performed two analyses with FDA and EMA data, respectively. The first study compared failed marketing applications for orphan drugs in the US between 1998 and 2007 with approved orphan drugs (Heemstra *et al.* 2011). The second study compared approved orphan drugs in the EU between 2000 and 2009 with non-approved orphan drugs (Putzeist *et al.* 2012). The first study revealed that two characteristics of the clinical trial design correlated with non-approval: failing to achieve the primary end-point of the pivotal trial and not identifying the most appropriate target population (Heemstra *et al.* 2011). Although the focus of the second study was on successful approval instead of failure, these findings were more or less confirmed by the outcome of the second analysis. In addition, the EMA study revealed the selection of a clinically relevant end-point and the submission of sound dose finding data as critical success factors (Putzeist *et al.* 2012). These factors were not included in the FDA study. The FDA study revealed no statistical significance for total exposed population, total number of patients, gender of study participants and choice of primary end-point (overall survival/cure versus progression-free survival or other) in the pivotal clinical trial. These factors were not included in the EMA study.

With regard to the rigour of the pivotal clinical design, the two analyses provided somewhat contradicting results. In the FDA study, no statistical significance could be established, whereas the EMA study showed 'providing RCT data as pivotal study' as a success factor. Perhaps the latter is the result of the aforementioned intrinsic difficulties with clinical development of orphan drugs, specific differences between the US and EU regulatory frameworks, or the existence of cultural differences between US and EU regulators.

5.2.2 Does the size and/or experience of a company matter?

One aspect that has been suggested as relevant in terms of influencing the likelihood of approval is the potential of the sponsor to carry out suitable clinical trials (Wästfelt *et al.* 2006). A case-control analysis between randomly selected authorised and a matched sample of not-yet authorised orphan drugs in the EU (2000–2006) revealed that orphan drug approval was strongly associated with previous experience of the sponsor in obtaining approval for another orphan drug (Heemstra *et al.* 2008a).

This finding was confirmed in two additional analyses with FDA and EMA data. The first study compared failed marketing application for orphan drugs in the US between 1998 and 2007 with approved orphan drugs (Heemstra *et al.* 2011). The second study compared approved orphan drugs in the EU between 2000 and 2009 with non-approved orphan drugs (Putzeist *et al.* 2012). Unfortunately, multivariate analysis was not possible for practical reasons (US study) or did not reach statistical significance (EU study). Apart from experience, the role of company size was also investigated in all three studies. The outcome in each study suggested that size of a company is an important factor, but again, multivariate analysis was not possible for practical reasons or did not reach statistical significance.

Although not conclusive, the data are in line with opinions expressed by many experts, that orphan drug development can be complicated for a variety of reasons and will require in-depth experience in developing and marketing an orphan drug to increase the likelihood of subsequent marketing approval. In particular the pivotal clinical trial stage is complex as shown in the previous section. Moreover, orphan drug development by inexperienced companies and/or SMEs can be hampered by a limited geographical outreach with poor access to patients and a lack of regulatory knowledge and experience in RCT design (Haffner *et al.* 2002). To overcome the gap of inexperience, several strategies are being employed, either separately or combined. The first strategy is, as many former SMEs with one or more approved orphan drugs have done, to bring on board management with the necessary experience at an early stage. A second valuable strategy, and in our opinion still underused, is to make full use of the scientific advice/protocol assistance instruments available at the FDA, the EMA and also various regulatory agencies of the individual EU members. We will discuss this aspect and its added-value in more detail in the next section.

Finally, in line with opinions expressed by many experts, and perhaps the most important strategy for SMEs with limited experience is to collaborate with an experienced partner in bringing a product to the market. Big pharma with its vast clinical development experience and financial resources may fulfil the missing link between early innovation by academic spin-offs and SMEs and orphan drug approval. Although big pharma has been active in the field of orphan drugs from the start, it appeared to keep a low profile. This is rapidly changing: some have introduced specific rare disease units (Pfizer and GSK), while others are giving it a more prominent position in their business model, such as Novartis (Shaffer 2010; Melnikova 2012). Whether the increased interest in orphan drug development by big pharma will have a positive impact on the number of approved orphan drugs remains to be determined. A good example of a combination of all aforementioned strategies is the Duchenne product, based on exon-skipping technology, which is in development at Prosensa in collaboration with GSK (for more information, see Chapter 2 and www.prosensa.eu)

5.2.3 The role of regulatory dialogue: Friend or foe?

Another strategy that we would like to bring forward is to engage with the various regulatory agencies and to make use of their scientific advice instruments. We have provided in Table 5.3 a list of regulatory agencies that provide scientific advice.

Most sponsors are aware of and appreciate that the FDA and the EMA provide free scientific advice or protocol assistance to sponsors of orphan drugs. However, a recent survey in the Netherlands that was presented at the MEB (Medicines Evaluation Board) annual meeting in 2011 indicated that more experienced SMEs are aware of the existence of scientific advice at member state level, but academic spin-offs and inexperienced SMEs in general are not (De Vrueh and Gispen-de Wied 2011). In general, a frequent strategy that was applied by more experienced SMEs to successfully navigate their product through the early clinical trial stage consisted of: 1) consulting relevant in-house expertise; 2) consulting their external network and/or hiring consultants with relevant expertise; 3) applying for scientific advice at national regulatory agency with relevant experience (e.g. in the past national agency acted as rapporteur for comparable product); and 4) applying for scientific advice at the EMA/FDA level.

The importance of regulatory dialogue during the (pivotal) clinical trial stage has been included in a number of studies (Regnstrom *et al.* 2010; Heemstra *et al.* 2011; Putzeist *et al.* 2011, 2012). Regnstrom *et al.* (2010) reviewed all market authorisation applications (non-orphan and orphan) in the EU in the period 2004–2007 with the aim to identify factors associated with successful drug approval. They showed that requesting scientific advice at the EMA was not associated with approval. However, complying with scientific advice was identified as a predictive factor for successful drug approval (Regnstrom *et al.* 2010). We would like to highlight three relevant clarifications the authors mention in their discussion. First, complying with scientific

Table 5.3 **Examples of EU Member State regulatory agencies that provide scientific advice**

Note: Websites accessed 4 December 2012

Regulatory agency	Jurisdiction	For further information
College ter Beoordeling van Geneesmiddelen (Medicines Evaluation Board)	Netherlands	www.cbg-meb.nl/CBG/en/human-medicines/scientific-advice/default.htm
Laegemiddelstyrelsen (Danish Medicines Agency)	Denmark	http://laegemiddelstyrelsen.dk/en/topics/authorisation-and-supervision/licensing-of-medicines/marketing-authorisation/request-for-scientific-advice
Läkemedelsverket (Medical Products Agency)	Sweden	www.lakemedelsverket.se/english/product/Medicinal-products/Scientific-advice/
Medicines and Healthcare Products Regulatory Agency	UK	www.mhra.gov.uk/Howweregulate/Medicines/Licensingofmedicines/Informationforlicenceapplicants/Otherusefulservicesandinformation/Scientificadviceforlicenceapplicants/index.htm
Bundesinstitut für Arzneimittel und Medizinprodukte (Federal Institute for Drugs and Medical Devices)	Germany	www.bfarm.de/EN/BfArM/BfArMService/AdviceProcedure/adviceProcedure-node.html
Agence française de sécurité sanitaire des produits de santé (French Agency for the Safety of Health Products)	France	http://ansm.sante.fr/var/ansm_site/storage/original/application/607bb3de8571b95963830b8b14b4f538.pdf
Agencia Espanola de Medicamentos y Productos Sanitarios (Spanish Agency for Medicines and Health Products)	Spain	www.aemps.gob.es/en/industria/asesoriasCientificas/home.htm
Bundesamt fur Sicherheit im Gesundheitswesen (Austrian Federal Office for Safety in Health Care)	Austria	www.basg.gv.at/en/medicines/before-authorisation/national-scientific-advice/
L'Agenzia Italiana del Farmaco (Italian Medicines Agency)	Italy	www.agenziafarmaco.gov.it/it/content/linee-guida-0
Federaal Agentschap voor Geneesmiddelen en Gezondheidsproducten (Federal Agency for Medicines and Health Products)	Belgium	www.fagg-afmps.be/en/human_use/medicines/herbal_medicinal_products/research_development/scientific_advices/

advice 'should not be viewed as a reward for following the regulators' views'. Scientific advice is clearly intended as a moment during which sponsors can enter into dialogue with regulators to argue their case. If needed, a follow-up scientific advice meeting can be requested. The final scientific advice is often the outcome of this dialogue and/or follow-up. Second, the authors speculate that scientific advice is requested for 'more challenging medicinal products and development programmes and in situations where regulatory guidance is missing'. Orphan drugs certainly fall within one or perhaps even both categories. Finally, in line with the size and/or experience being a predictive factor for success, it will not come as a surprise that the authors observed that 'large companies not only asked for SA (scientific advice) more frequently than medium-sized and small pharmaceutical companies but, importantly, they were significantly more compliant with the SA given than their smaller peers'. A limitation of the study is that it only includes the regulator's view. It would have been interesting if the sponsor's view somehow had been included as well. Putzeist *et al.* (2011), in a cross-sectional analysis of scientific advice by the Dutch Medicines Evaluation Board between 2006 and 2008, revealed that the number of clinical questions about pharmacokinetics asked by small companies was significantly larger than the number asked by medium-sized and large companies (Putzeist *et al.* 2011). A similar finding was found for the number of quality and non-clinical questions. A plausible explanation for this outcome may be that in general small companies are less experienced and are more active in the preclinical or early clinical stage rather than the late clinical stage of drug development.

The importance of compliance with scientific advice as a predictive factor for successful drug approval was also confirmed for orphan drugs by Heemstra *et al.* (2011) using US data. By providing scientific advice and allowing a dialogue, regulatory authorities can play a crucial role in successful orphan drug development that may not be fully appreciated by drug developers. In our view, what is evident is that this incentive is still underused.

Apart from scientific advice, regulatory authorities also play a pivotal role in the application and interpretation of specific legislations that allow early market access of drugs for serious diseases, such as orphan drugs, which we will discuss in the next section.

5.3 Early market access of orphan drugs: Theory and practice

As clearly depicted on the FDA website,[1] 'speeding the development and availability of drugs that treat serious diseases [is] in everyone's interest, especially when the

---

1 www.fda.gov/ForConsumers/ByAudience/ForPatientAdvocates/SpeedingAccesstoImportant NewTherapies/ucm128291.htm, accessed 2 March 2012.

drugs are the first available treatment or have advantages over existing treatments'. As depicted in Table 5.4a and b, both the US and EU have implemented similar approaches to allow earlier market access of such drugs.

An elaborate description of the approaches depicted in Tables 5.4a and b is beyond the scope of this chapter. If you are interested, we can highly recommend the FDA or EMA websites for relevant pages and/or guidance (FDA 2012; EMA 2005b, 2006a, b).

Although these approaches are not specific for orphan drugs, since a rare disease is by definition a chronically debilitating or life-threatening disease, orphan drugs in principle qualify. For obvious reasons, sponsors of orphan drugs will be attracted by the perspective of an accelerated approval process. Therefore, it is important to realise that orphan drugs do not automatically qualify for the aforementioned approaches. It is true that many orphan drugs in the EU have been granted

Table 5.4a **Approaches implemented in the US to allow early market access of drugs with a high medical need**

Source: FDA 2012

Approach	Aim	Description
Fast track	Get important new drugs to the patient earlier (e.g. more frequent meetings and written correspondence with FDA)	Drug that treats serious diseases and fills an unmet medical need by providing a therapy where none exists or providing a therapy which may be potentially superior to existing therapy (e.g. superior effectiveness, improved toxicity profile, improved diagnosis resulting in improved outcome)
Accelerated approval	Allow earlier approval of drugs to treat serious diseases and that fill an unmet medical need based on a surrogate end-point	Approval of a drug based on a surrogate end-point is given on the condition that post-marketing clinical trials verify the anticipated clinical benefit. The FDA bases its decision on whether to accept the proposed surrogate end-point on the scientific support for that end-point. The studies that demonstrate the effect of the drug on the surrogate end-point must be 'adequate and well controlled' studies, the only basis under law for a finding that a drug is effective
Priority review	Completing review in a six month time frame (standard review time frame is ten months)	Drugs that offer major advances in treatment, or provide a treatment where no adequate therapy exists (e.g. increased effectiveness, improved toxicity profile). Can apply to drugs that are used to treat serious diseases and to drugs for less serious illnesses

Table 5.4b **Approaches implemented by the EU to allow early market access of drugs with a high medical need**
Source: EMA 2005b, 2006a, b

Approach	Aim	Description
Exceptional circumstances	To allow authorisation of drugs for which it is unable to provide comprehensive data on efficacy and safety. Subject to a requirement to introduce specific procedures, in particular concerning the safety of the medicinal product	Indications for which the drug is intended are encountered so rarely that provision of comprehensive evidence cannot reasonably be expected
		In the present state of scientific knowledge, comprehensive information cannot be provided
		It would be contrary to generally accepted principles of medical ethics to collect such information
		A marketing authorisation may be granted subject to certain specific obligations (e.g. additional studies, supply-related)
Conditional approval	To meet unmet medical needs of patients and in the interests of public health, allow marketing authorisation of a drug with positive benefit–risk balance, but on the basis of less complete data than is normally the case and subject to specific obligations	Medicinal products which aim at the treatment, the prevention or the medical diagnosis of seriously debilitating diseases or life-threatening diseases
		Medicinal products to be used in emergency situations, in response to public health threats duly recognised either by the World Health Organisation or by the Community
		Medicinal products designated as orphan medicinal products
		Unmet medical needs means a condition for which there exists no satisfactory method of diagnosis, prevention or treatment or, even if such a method exists, in relation to which the medicinal product concerned will be of major therapeutic advantage to those affected
Accelerated assessment	Time frame period for CHMP to reach opinion reduced from 210 to 150 days	Medicinal products for human use which are of major interest from the point of view of public health and in particular from the viewpoint of therapeutic innovation

approval under exceptional circumstances (See Table 5.5 for overview). However, most approvals under exceptional circumstances have been granted in the first years of the EU orphan legislation. Nowadays, it appears that granting approval of orphan drugs under exceptional circumstances has become more exceptional. The increasing number of non-approved orphan drugs in recent years may suggest that the EMA has become less inclined to advise approval under exceptional circumstances (see Fig. 5.5). However, another explanation may be that sponsors no longer apply for approval under exceptional circumstances.

Table 5.5 **Orphan medicinal products with a marketing authorisation under exceptional circumstances in the EU (2000–2011)**

Source: EMA website, www.ema.europa.eu/ema/index.jsp?curl=pages/medicines/landing/
epar_search.jsp&mid=WC0b01ac058001d125, accessed 3 January 2013

Medicine name	Active substance	Authorisation date
Vyndaqel	tafamidis	16/11/2011
Firdapse	amifampridine	23/12/2009
Ilaris	canakinumab	23/10/2009
Rilonacept Regeneron (previously Arcalyst)	rilonacept	23/10/2009
Ceplene	histamine dihydrochloride	07/10/2008
Yondelis	trabectedin	17/09/2007
Atriance	nelarabine	22/08/2007
Increlex	mecasermin	03/08/2007
Elaprase	idursulfase	08/01/2007
Evoltra	clofarabine	29/05/2006
Naglazyme	galsulfase	24/01/2006
Revatio	sildenafil	28/10/2005
Orfadin	nitisinone	21/02/2005
Prialt	ziconotide	21/02/2005
Xagrid	anagrelide	16/11/2004
Onsenal	celecoxib	17/10/2003
Ventavis	iloprost	16/09/2003
Aldurazyme	laronidase	10/06/2003
Carbaglu	carglumic acid	24/01/2003
Zavesca	miglustat	20/11/2002
Tracleer	bosentan monohydrate	15/05/2002
Trisenox	arsenic trioxide	05/03/2002
Glivec	imatinib	07/11/2001
Fabrazyme	agalsidase beta	03/08/2001
Replagal	agalsidase alfa	03/08/2001

The majority of drugs with a conditional marketing authorisation in the EU involve innovative therapies for two life-threatening diseases: HIV and cancer (Boon *et al.* 2010). Boon *et al.* (2010) have studied whether exceptional circumstances and conditional approval lead to earlier access to innovative drugs. As the authors state, their study 'shows that neither of these regulatory pathways accelerates the approval process for innovative drugs'. Interestingly, their study reveals that innovative cancer and HIV drugs following the conditional approval route have a shorter clinical development time than those approved via the normal route. The opposite is true for innovative cancer and HIV drugs approved under exceptional circumstances. These products are associated with a longer clinical development period. Unfortunately, as depicted in Table 5.6, orphan medicinal products with conditional marketing authorisation are limited, but this may be, although not likely, due to the fact that the conditional approval legislation is fairly young (it came into force in 2005).

Similar to conditional approval in the EU, implementation of the accelerated approval regulation in the US in 1992 has been the driving force behind therapeutic innovation for cancer and HIV. During the first 16 years of the regulation 26 innovative cancer drugs and 29 HIV drugs were approved (Miyamoto and Kakkis 2011). In particular, the availability of current HIV therapies demonstrates that the accelerated approval route has had, and can have, a profound impact on delivering much needed treatments for patients with a life-threatening disease. Unfortunately, similar to the EU, in the US accelerated approval of therapies for rare and ultra-rare diseases has been limited. Only one drug (agalsidase beta or Fabrazyme) among 73 new chemical entities has successfully followed the accelerated approval route (Miyamoto and Kakkis 2011). In their study, Miyamoto and Kakkis (2011) build a convincing case that more appropriate use of the accelerated approval route could have a profound impact on driving therapeutic innovation for rare diseases, in particular ultra-rare ones. As the authors demonstrate 'better Accelerated Approval access could reduce development costs by approximately 60%, increase investment value, and foster development of three times as many rare disease drugs for the same investment'. Through extensive lobbying by numerous stakeholders, including patient organisations, new legislation to allow early access of orphan drugs in the US may soon become a reality in the US (FAST Act, TREAT Act, ULTRA Act). How well these new legislations will work is currently a subject for discussion (*Nature Biotechnology* 2012).

Table 5.6 **Orphan medicinal products with a conditional marketing authorisation in the EU (2000–2011)**

Source: EMA website, www.ema.europa.eu/ema/index.jsp?curl=pages/medicines/landing/ epar_search.jsp&mid=WC0b01ac058001d125, accessed 3 January 2013

Medicine name	Active substance	Authorisation date
Votubia	everolimus	02/09/2011
Arzerra	ofatumumab	19/04/2010
Cayston	aztreonam lysine	21/09/2009
Diacomit	stiripentol	04/01/2007
Sutent	sunitinib	19/07/2006

5.4 Growing role for the patient in orphan drug development

Nowadays, the role of rare disease patients in rare disease research and orphan drug development is enormous and at all stages of the drug innovation cycle: from lab bench to clinic and from clinic to lab bench. Rare disease patients or their parents initiate research, provide the necessary funding, provide input to research agendas, own patents, initiate product development programmes, maintain registries and biobanks, and even start their own companies. To give three examples:

- In France, Lysogene, a company founded by a parent of a child with Sanfilippo syndrome type IIIA (mucopolysaccharidosis IIIA), is working on a gene therapy product (www.lysogene.com)

- At the same time, in the US, another parent of twins with Niemann-Pick type C has discovered that a sugar molecule, cyclodextrin, might be beneficial. In the US as well as EU an orphan designation has been granted for the product (www.addiandcassi.com)

- Finally, the Alkaptonuria Society is collaborating with academia and industry to study the potential clinical effect that nitisinone, a product approved for tyrosinaemia type I (Orfadin), may have in alkaptonuria (www.alkapton uria.info)

With regard to orphan drug development, apart from well-established sources of funding such as governmental grants and venture capital, patient-initiated research foundations can also represent an important source of funding. Funding of translational research as well as (pre-) clinical proof of concept studies is not only directed to academic institutes, but also academic spin-offs/start-up companies and more mature SMEs. This does not mean that patient organisations that are not funding research are doing less. Far from it. Activities such as uniting patients, providing and allowing exchange of information, education, and advocacy are just as or even more important.

Several patient-initiated research foundations have been around for some time and have grown considerable funds; others have just been founded and are still small. If you are interested, we highly recommend visiting www.rarediseasematters.org, which contains a growing list of patient-initiated research foundations, and will provide a source of inspiration. For a broader interest in patient organisations we highly recommend the databases that NORD and Orphanet have created and continue to expand (www.rarediseases.org; www.orpha.net). An intriguing question that remains unanswered is what is their combined impact on rare disease research and orphan drug development?

5.5 Beyond orphan drug approval: market access of orphan drugs

A growing hurdle for the successful delivery of new orphan drugs to patients is the uncertain access and reimbursement of orphan drugs after marketing approval. For various reasons, including pressure on national healthcare budgets, access and reimbursement of orphan drugs vary between the individual member countries within the EU. A 2007 survey by Eurordis, the European organisation for patients with a rare disease, showed that access to orphan drugs in Europe was highly variable between countries (Eurordis 2007). Only in 4 out of 28 countries did patients have access to at least 20 out of 22 orphan drugs one year after approval. The variability in access to orphan drugs may also be the result of other factors: in its 2007 survey report, Eurordis revealed a longer delay for countries with a smaller population. A number of orphan drugs are in development by (small) companies that do not have a sales force in all European countries and may consequently need more time to be able to reach smaller markets. In the end, without access to the approved orphan drugs for the patient, the product has no benefit. Moreover, a delay in market access of orphan drugs to the European market will be a disincentive for sponsors of potential orphan drugs and may reduce the number of new orphan drugs that will be developed in the long term. Consequently, obtaining access and reimbursement for an authorised orphan medicinal product is of great importance for the sponsor and for the patient. Although an in-depth discussion on the challenges of obtaining reimbursement for orphan drugs is beyond the scope of this chapter, this phase of orphan drug development has many similarities with the above-described regulatory phase. The reader should therefore keep in mind that much of the advice given above is also valid for obtaining reimbursement. For those interested to learn more about this subject, we can recommend a number of interesting papers (McCabe *et al.* 2010; Simoens 2011; Schey *et al.* 2011).

References

Agarwal, R., and M. Gomberg-Maitland (2011) 'Current Therapeutics and Practical Management Strategies for Pulmonary Arterial Hypertension', *American Heart Journal* 162.2: 201-13.

Boon, W.P., E.H. Moors, A. Meijer and H. Schellekens (2010) 'Conditional Approval and Approval under Exceptional Circumstances as Regulatory Instruments for Stimulating Responsible Drug Innovation in Europe', *Clinical Pharmacology & Therapeutics* 88.6: 848-53.

Bouvy, J.C., M.A. Koopmanschap, R.R. Shah and H. Schellekens (2012) 'The Cost-Effectiveness of Drug Regulation: The Example of Thorough QT/QTc Studies', *Clinical Pharmacology & Therapeutics* 91.2: 281-88.

Brabers, A.E., E.H. Moors, S. van Weely and R.L. de Vrueh (2011) 'Does Market Exclusivity Hinder the Development of Follow-on Orphan Medicinal Products in Europe?' *Orphanet Journal of Rare Diseases* 6: 59.

Braun, M.M., S. Farag-El-Massah, K. Xu and T.R. Coté (2010) 'Emergence of Orphan Drugs in the United States: A Quantitative Assessment of the First 25 Years', *Nature Reviews Drug Discovery* 9.7: 519-22.

Burke, K.A., S.N. Freeman, M.A. Imoisili and T.R. Coté (2010) 'The Impact of the Orphan Drug Act on the Development and Advancement of Neurological Products for Rare Diseases: A Descriptive Review', *Clinical Pharmacology & Therapeutics* 88.4: 449-53.

Committee for Orphan Medicinal Products and the European Medicines (COMP), K. Westermark, B.B. Holm, M. Söderholm, J. Llinares-Garcia, F. Rivière, S. Aarum, F. Butlen-Ducuing, S. Tsigkos, A. Wilk-Kachlicka, C. N'Diamoi, J. Borvendég, D. Lyons, B. Sepodes, B. Bloechl-Daum, A. Lhoir, M. Todorova, I. Kkolos, K. Kubáčková, H. Bosch-Traberg, V. Tillmann, V. Saano, E. Héron, R. Elbers, M. Siouti, J. Eggenhofer, P. Salmon, M. Clementi, D. Krieviņš, A. Matulevičiene, H. Metz, A.C. Vincenti, A. Voordouw, B. Dembowska-Bagińska, A.C. Nunes, F.M. Saleh, T. Foltánová, M. Možina, J. Torrent-Farnell, B. Beerman, S. Mariz, M.P. Evers, L. Greene, S. Thorsteinsson, L. Gramstad, M. Mavris, F. Bignami, A. Lorence and C. Belorgey (2011) 'European Regulation on Orphan Medicinal Products: 10 Years of Experience and Future Perspectives', *Nature Reviews Drug Discovery* 10.5: 341-49.

Coté, T.R., K. Xu and A.R. Pariser (2010) 'Accelerating Orphan Drug Development', *Nature Reviews Drug Discovery* 9.12: 901-902.

Czerepak, E.A., and S. Ryser (2008) 'Drug Approvals and Failures: Implications for Alliances', *Nature Reviews Drug Discovery* 7: 197-98.

De Vrueh, R., and C. Gispen-de Wied (2011) *Collegedag 2011 (annual MEB meeting): Wetenschappelijk advies: voor groot, maar zeker ook voor klein.*

Drews, J. (2003) 'Strategic Trends in the Drug Industry', *Drug Discovery Today* 8.9: 411-20.

Eichler, H.G., F. Pignatti, B. Flamion, H. Leufkens and A. Breckenridge (2008) 'Balancing Early Market Access to New Drugs with the Need for Benefit/Risk Data: A Mounting Dilemma', *Nature Reviews Drug Discovery* 7.10: 818-26.

Elias, T., M. Gordian, N. Singh and R. Zemmel (2006) 'Why Products Fail in Phase III', *In vivo* 24: 49-56.

EMA (European Medicines Agency) (2005a) 'COMP report to the Commission in Relation to Article 10 of Regulation 141/2000 on Orphan Medicinal Products', EMEA/35218/2005 Final, www.ema.europa.eu/docs/en_GB/document_library/Report/2010/04/WC500089638.pdf, accessed 3 January 2013.

EMA (2005b) 'EMEA/357981/2005, Guideline on procedures for the granting of a marketing authorisation under exceptional circumstance, pursuant to article 14 (8) of regulation (EC) No 726/2004', www.ema.europa.eu/docs/en_GB/document_library/Regulatory_and_procedural_guideline/2009/10/WC500004883.pdf, accessed 2 March 2012.

EMA (2006a) 'EMEA/509951/2006, Guideline on the scientific application and the practical arrangements necessary to implement Commission Regulation (EC) No 507/2006 on the conditional marketing authorisation for medicinal products for human use falling within the scope of Regulation (EC) No 726/2004', www.ema.europa.eu/docs/en_GB/document_library/Scientific_guideline/2009/10/WC500004908.pdf, accessed 2 March 2012.

EMA (2006b) 'EMEA/419127/05, Guideline on the procedure for accelerated assessment pursuant to Article 14 (9) of Regulation (EC) No 726/2004', www.ema.europa.eu/docs/en_GB/document_library/Regulatory_and_procedural_guideline/2009/10/WC500004136.pdf, accessed 2 March 2012.

EMA (2009) 'Recommendation on Elements Required to Support the Medical Plausibility and the Assumption of Significant Benefit for an Orphan Designation', EMA/COMP/15893/2009 Final, www.ema.europa.eu/docs/en_GB/document_library/Regulatory_and_procedural_guideline/2009/09/WC500003778.pdf, accessed 3 January 2013.

EUCERD (2009) '2009 Report on Initiatives and Incentives in the Field of Rare Diseases of the European Union Committee of Experts on Rare Diseases', nestor.orpha.net/EUCERD/upload/file/Reports/2009ReportInitiativesIncentives.pdf, accessed 13 March 2012.

Eurordis (2007) 'Eurordis Survey on Orphan Drugs Availability in Europe', www.eurordis.org/IMG/pdf/2007ODsurvey-eurordis.pdf, accessed 7 May 2012.

FDA (2012) 'Fast Track, Accelerated Approval and Priority Review: Accelerating Availability of New Drugs for Patients with Serious Diseases', www.fda.gov/ForConsumers/ByAudience/ForPatientAdvocates/SpeedingAccesstoImportantNewTherapies/ucm128291.htm, accessed 2 March 2012.

Freeman, S.N., K.A. Burke, M.A. Imoisili and T.R. Coté (2010) 'The Orphan Drug Act and the Development of Stem Cell-Based Products for Rare Diseases *Cell Stem Cell* 7.3: 283-87.

Haffner, M.E. (2006) 'Adopting Orphan Drugs: Two Dozen Years of Treating Rare Diseases', *New England Journal of Medicine* 354.5: 445-47.

Haffner, M.E., J. Whitley and M. Moses (2002) 'Two Decades of Orphan Product Development', *Nature Reviews Drug Discovery* 1.10: 821-25.

Heemstra, H.E., R.L. de Vrueh, S. van Weely, H.A. Büller and H.G. Leufkens (2008a) 'Predictors of Orphan Drug Approval in the European Union', *European Journal of Clinical Pharmacology* 64.5: 545-52.

Heemstra, H.E., R.L. de Vrueh, S. van Weely, H.A. Büller and H.G. Leufkens (2008b) 'Orphan Drug Development across Europe: Bottlenecks and Opportunities', *Drug Discovery Today* 13.15-16: 670-76.

Heemstra, H.E., S. van Weely, H.A. Büller, H.G. Leufkens and R.L. de Vrueh (2009) 'Translation of Rare Disease Research into Orphan Drug Development: Disease Matters', *Drug Discovery Today* 14.23-24: 1166-73.

Heemstra, H.E., H.G. Leufkens, R.P. Rodgers, K. Xu, B.C. Voordouw and M.M. Braun (2011) 'Characteristics of Orphan Drug Applications that Fail to Achieve Marketing Approval in the USA', *Drug Discovery Today* 16.1-2: 73-80.

Joppi, R., V. Bertele and S. Garattini (2006) 'Orphan Drug Development is Progressing too Slowly', *British Journal of Clinical Pharmacology* 61.3: 355-60.

Joppi, R., V. Bertele and S. Garattini (2009) 'Orphan Drug Development is Not Taking Off', *British Journal of Clinical Pharmacology* 67.5: 494-502.

Kesselheim, A.S., J.A. Myers and J. Avorn (2011) 'Characteristics of Clinical Trials to Support Approval of Orphan vs Nonorphan Drugs for cancer', *Journal of the American Medical Association* 305.22: 2320-26.

Kola, I., and J. Landis (2004) 'Can the Pharmaceutical Industry Reduce Attrition Rates?' *Nature Reviews Drug Discovery* 3.8: 711-15.

Lev, D., C. Thorat, I. Phillips, M. Thomas and M.A. Imoisili (2011) 'The Routes to Orphan Drug Designation: Our Recent Experience at the FDA', *Drug Discovery Today* 17.3-4: 97-99.

McCabe, C., R. Edlin and J. Round (2010) 'Economic Considerations in the Provision of Treatments for Rare Diseases', *Advances in Experimental Medicine and Biology* 686: 211-22.

Meekings, K.N., C.S. Williams and J.E. Arrowsmith (2012) 'Orphan Drug Development: An Economically Viable Strategy for Biopharma R&D', *Drug Discovery Today* 17.13-14 (February 2012): 660-64.

Melnikova, I. (2012) 'Rare Diseases and Orphan Drugs', *Nature Reviews Drug Discovery* 11.4: 267-68.

Mitsumoto, J., E.R. Dorsey, C.A. Beck, K. Kieburtz and R.C. Griggs (2009) 'Pivotal Studies of Orphan Drugs Approved for Neurological Diseases', *Annals of Neurology* 66.2: 184-90.

Miyamoto, B.E., and E.D. Kakkis (2011) 'The Potential Investment Impact of Improved Access to Accelerated Approval on the Development of Treatments for Low Prevalence Rare Diseases', *Orphanet Journal of Rare Disease* 6: 49.

Morgan, P., P.H. Van Der Graaf, J. Arrowsmith, D.E. Feltner, K.S. Drummond, C.D. Wegner and S.D. Street (2012) 'Can the Flow of Medicines be Improved? Fundamental Pharmacokinetic and Pharmacological Principles toward Improving Phase II Survival', *Drug Discovery Today* 17.9-10 (May 2012): 419-24.

Nature Biotechnology (2012) 'Editorial: Reforming Accelerated Approval', *Nature Biotechnology* 30.4: 293.

Pammolli, F., L. Magazzini and M. Riccaboni (2011) 'The Productivity Crisis in Pharmaceutical R&D', *Nature Reviews Drug Discovery* 10.6: 428-38.

Putzeist, M., A.K. Mantel-Teeuwisse, C.C. Gispen-De Wied, A.W. Hoes and H.G. Leufkens (2011) 'Regulatory Scientific Advice in Drug Development: Does Company Size Make a Difference?' *European Journal of Clinical Pharmacology* 67.2: 157-64.

Putzeist M., H.E. Heemstra, J.L. Garcia, A.K. Mantel-Teeuwisse, C.C. Gispen-De Wied, A.W. Hoes and H.G. Leufkens (2012) 'Determinants for Successful Marketing Authorisation of Orphan Medicinal Products in the EU', *Drug Discovery Today* 17.7-8: 352-58.

Regnstrom, J., F. Koenig, B. Aronsson, T. Reimer, K. Svendsen, S. Tsigkos, B. Flamion, H.G. Eichler and S. Vamvakas (2010) 'Factors Associated with Success of Market Authorisation Applications for Pharmaceutical Drugs Submitted to the European Medicines Agency', *European Journal of Clinical Pharmacology* 66.1: 39-48.

Roos, J.C., H.I. Hyry and T.M. Cox (2010) 'Orphan Drug Pricing May Warrant a Competition Law Investigation', *BMJ* 341: c6471.

Scannell, J.W., A. Blanckley, H. Boldon and B. Warrington (2012) 'Diagnosing the Decline in Pharmaceutical R&D Efficiency', *Nature Reviews Drug Discovery* 11.3: 191-200.

Schey, C., T. Milanova and A. Hutchings (2011) 'Estimating the Budget Impact of Orphan Medicines in Europe: 2010–2020', *Orphanet Journal of Rare Disease* 6: 62.

Shaffer, C. (2010) 'Pfizer Explores Rare Disease Path', *Nature Biotechnology* 28: 881-82.

Simoens, S. (2011) 'Pricing and Reimbursement of Orphan Drugs: The Need for More Transparency', *Orphanet Journal of Rare Disease* 6: 42.

Talele, S.S., K. Xu, A.R. Pariser, M.M. Braun, S. Farag-El-Massah, M.I. Phillips, B.H. Thompson and T.R. Coté (2010) 'Therapies for Inborn Errors of Metabolism: What Has the Orphan Drug Act Delivered?' *Pediatrics* 126.1: 101-106.

Tambuyzer, E. (2010) 'Rare Diseases, Orphan Drugs and their Regulation: Questions and Misconceptions', *Nature Reviews Drug Discovery* 9.12: 921.

Torrent-Farnell, J. (2005) 'International Conference on Rare Diseases and Orphan Drugs in Stockholm, ICORD 2005', www.icord.cc/stockholm_2005.php?p=speaker_presentations, accessed 15 March 2012.

Wästfelt, M., B. Fadeel and J.I. Henter (2006) 'A Journey of Hope: Lessons Learned from Studies on Rare Diseases and Orphan Drugs', *Journal of Internal Medicine* 260.1: 1-10.

Wilgenbus, K., R. Hill, A. Warrander, S. Kakkar, E. Steiness and R. Wessel (2007) 'What Pharma Wants', *Nature Biotechnology* 25.9: 967-69.

Remco de Vrueh works as senior adviser at Schuttelaar & Partners, a Dutch communications consultancy firm that strives to promote greater health and sustainability. As a personal initiative, he founded Rare Disease Matters at the beginning of 2012 to continue his research and teaching in the area of orphan drug development. Prior to this he worked for the Netherlands Organisation for Health Research and Development (ZonMw) as adviser to various (orphan) drug innovation programmes. Between 2006 and 2011 he was active as Orphan Product Developer for the Dutch Steering Committee on Orphan Drugs. He was responsible for stimulating development of orphan drugs by the Dutch pharmaceutical industry. Apart from industry, he also actively interacted with academia and patient organisations. Remco de Vrueh (co-)organised meetings, has given presentations, provided training and teaching, and is the (co-)author of several scientific publications. In the same period he also fulfilled interim project management positions for the European and Developing Countries Clinical Trials Partnership and the Dutch Medicines Evaluation Board. Before joining ZonMw he worked for seven years at OctoPlus, a Dutch pharmaceutical company. Remco de Vrueh holds a PhD degree in Biopharmaceutical Sciences from the Leiden-Amsterdam Center for Drug Research in the Netherlands.

Harald Heemstra undertook a PhD research programme at the Utrecht Institute for Pharmaceutical Sciences, Division of Pharmacoepidemiology & Clinical Pharmacology, Utrecht University, the Netherlands, aimed at identifying strategies for enhancing the development and marketing of orphan drugs. The research involved close collaboration with all stakeholders in the field of rare diseases and orphan drugs, including the Dutch Ministry of Health and the Dutch Steering Committee on Orphan Drugs. Moreover, several studies were performed during internships at both the Food and Drug Administration (FDA) and the European Medicines Agency (EMA). Harald (co-)authored several scientific publications on orphan drug development and has provided presentations at meetings and conferences in the Netherlands and abroad. Thereafter, he worked as a senior research consultant in the field of market access for innovative new medicines at Pharmerit, Rotterdam. Harald is currently employed in a market access function for the pharmaceutical industry.

Michelle Putzeist, PharmD, is a PhD-candidate at Utrecht University, the Netherlands. Her PhD thesis aims to identify factors for successful marketing authorisation of new medicinal products, in particular orphan drugs approved at the European Medicines Agency. The association between the orphan drug development plan, its clinical outcomes, clinical relevance and marketing authorisation were studied. The role of the scientific dialogue between pharmaceutical companies and regulatory authorities is another main theme. These studies are conducted via agreements with the Medicines Evaluation Board in the Netherlands and the European Medicines Agency. Michelle holds a Master's degree in Pharmacy and Epidemiology at Utrecht University.

6

Drug repositioning strategies for rare and orphan diseases

A cost-effective approach for new uses for existing drugs

Maria P. del Castillo-Frias and Andrew J. Doig
Manchester Institute of Biotechnology, University of Manchester, UK

Farid Khan
PharmaKure Ltd, Manchester Science Park, Manchester, UK

Over the last decade, large pharmaceutical companies have held the belief that many new drugs will be discovered using combinatorial synthesis and advanced screening technologies. This has largely failed, however. Coupled to the fact that many of the currently used drugs have already or will soon be patent-expired, the need for new drugs has become more urgent. In addition, there is a lack of interest in the industry in developing therapeutic options for orphan and neglected diseases because they do not generate attractive revenues compared with those generated by Western diseases. Western diseases are those characteristic of many Western societies that are not commonly found in developing countries. They include heart disease, diabetes, inflammatory bowel diseases, obesity, autoimmune diseases, Alzheimer's disease (AD) and many forms of cancer. An orphan disease may be a rare disease (according to US criteria, a disease that affects fewer than 200,000 people). Common (neglected) diseases are those that have been ignored (such as tuberculosis, cholera, typhoid and malaria) because they are far more prevalent in developing countries than in the developed world. As a result, there is an urgency in finding new cost-effective strategies to yield drugs that will be approved by regulatory bodies. Drug repositioning, whereby drugs are 'recycled' and used in the treatment of diseases other than those for which it was developed, has emerged as a promising model able to address both these problems: namely, to increase drug productivity and at the same time generate new treatments for orphan and neglected diseases. This chapter describes the current drug discovery processes and then focuses on drug repositioning strategies and finally highlights collaborative efforts between industry, academia and charities towards a cure for alkaptonuria, a rare metabolic disease.

6.1 Drug discovery technologies

It typically takes 10–15 years to develop one drug from the time it is discovered to when it is available for treating patients. One recent estimate for the average cost of research and development (R&D) of a successful drug is US\$800 million to US\$1 billion (DiMasi *et al.* 2003). This number includes the cost of the thousands of failures. Notably, for 5,000–10,000 compounds that enter R&D, ultimately only one typically receives approval.

In the early 1990s, the introduction of combinatorial chemistry opened the possibility of generating a large number of compounds in a short period of time. High throughput screening (HTS) techniques emerged and gained popularity rapidly as the solution to test the compounds generated by combinatorial chemistry. During this period, the pharmaceutical industry had great expectations that this approach would not only reduce the drug discovery timelines, but also would increase the productivity of successful drugs for clinical studies. Unfortunately, after hundreds of millions of dollars of investment in high throughput screening platforms the expected results were not obtained (Macarron 2006; Keserü and Makara 2009).

The failure of traditional HTS can be attributed to several factors. First of all, the compound libraries consisted of approximately 10^4 to 10^7 compounds. This number of compounds, however, represented only a small proportion of the vast chemical space, as the total chemical space is estimated to be between 10^{40} to 10^{70} compounds (Macarron 2006). In other words, the compound 'universe' is likely to contain a minute number of compounds which could possibly have therapeutic activity and would miss the best compounds. Second, a compound which shows positive bioactivity in an assay against a selected target (known as a 'hit') would be further chemically modified, resulting in significant differences in the physical, chemical and biological properties from the original hit molecule, rendering the lead candidate inactive. Furthermore, the generation of compounds from combinatorial chemistry can be random such that those molecules with drug-like (e.g. which follow Lipinski's rules; Lipinski *et al.* 2001) properties, such as molecular weight, bipartition coefficient or no solubility in water are created (Fox *et al.* 2006). In addition, there has been a high rate of false positive hits associated with HTS which has resulted in wastage of resources and time in chasing up those compounds. Finally, the majority of HTS was undertaken using *in vitro* assays (as opposed to more biologically relevant cell-based assays), which generated a considerable quantity of hits that are not suitable as therapeutic agents, which also explains the high rates of failures associated with this technique (Parker and Bajorath 2006; Martis *et al.* 2011). In the decade that followed HTS, high content screening (HCS) technology emerged with advances in development of CCD cameras (charge coupled device cameras) and fluorescence-based image analysis. HCS allowed the simultaneous measurement of multiple biochemical and morpho-logical parameters and many targets in cell-based models of disease as opposed to single target *in vitro* based HTS campaigns. The large datasets produced by HCS would typically contain spatially resolved, quantitative data which can be used for building systems-level models and simulations of how cells and organisms function. In the near future, systems biology models of cell function would permit prediction of why, where and how the cell responds to external changes, growth and disease.

6.2 Stages of development of new drugs

Drug leads that are discovered by HTS and HCS are followed by pre-clinical (animal) and clinical trials (human). Figure 6.1 shows the various stages of drug development. If drugs have a new structure and are therefore novel, they are known as new chemical entities (NCEs) or new molecular entities (NMEs). These compounds will require detailed safety tests to determine toxicity, pharmacokinetics and metabolism in

Figure 6.1 **The drug discovery process. Typically, after HTS, for every 5,000–10,000 promising compounds that are taken into the R&D programmes only 250 compounds enter into preclinical trials. Only one drug reaches manufacture after successful clinical trials**

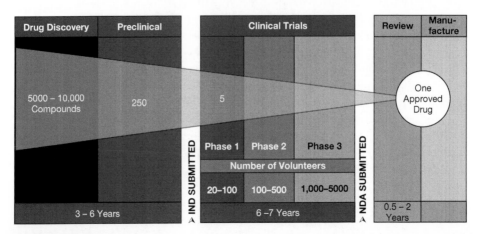

humans. The physical and chemical (e.g. stability and solubility) properties of the NCE are also important factors as they determine the final formulation and route of administration in patients. The synthesis and manufacturing scale up (from lab scale to production scale) from kilogram to ton scale will also be established. Further clinical data is obtained for the dosage, route (e.g. oral tablet, capsules, intravenous/subcutaneous injection) and formulation of the drug. These processes are commonly termed as chemistry, manufacturing and control or CMC.

The process of clinical drug development is tightly regulated by licensing authorities such as the Food and Drug Administration (FDA) in the United States and the Medicines Healthcare Products Regulatory Agency (MHRA) in the United Kingdom. Clinical drug development involves a series of trials of new drugs which are designed to elucidate any major side effects and toxic effects. If the drugs are NCEs, animal trials would be required prior to first use in humans. *In vivo* testing of toxicity is required whereby toxicity effects are measured in the major organs (e.g. heart, lungs, brains, kidney, liver and intestinal tract) in addition to its targeted site (e.g. if the drug is delivered through the skin).

Once the toxicity data from animal studies and from CMC are obtained, this can be submitted as an investigational new drug application or IND to the regulatory authorities. If the IND is accepted, the next development phase would be human clinical trials.

6.2.1 Clinical phases

There are three phases to clinical trials: phase I trials are in healthy volunteers to determine safety and dosing; phase II trials are in a small number of sick patients to determine efficacy and to evaluate the toxicity; and phase III trials are in larger numbers of sick patients in which a critical and statistical evaluation of the safety and efficacy of the drug is evaluated.

In tandem to the clinical trials, there are other long-term effects which are monitored, particularly with NCEs. Examples include effects on the reproductive and immune systems. Drug candidates will also be tested for their ability to cause cancer.

If the drug candidate proves to have acceptability toxicity and a significant effect against the disease in question, it could then be submitted for marketing approval in countries where it will be sold. In the US, such a submission is called a new drug application or NDA. It must be noted, however, that the majority of NCEs fail during clinical trials because of toxicity effects of the compound or because they are not statistically efficacious against the disease.

6.3 The business of drug discovery

The true costs of bringing a new drug such as a NCE to market—from research and development, discovery though to clinical trials approval—has been difficult to elucidate. This has been due in part to large pharmaceutical companies including expenditure of 'capital costs' and/or R&D costs, typically over a ten year period. Often when figures are stated for the development costs of a new drug, it is often not stated whether a given figure includes the capitalised cost or comprises only out-of-pocket expenses. Another complication is that drug companies do not release the breakdown of their costs as the information is deemed confidential and if any such numbers are released this is on a voluntary basis. Thus, such figures cannot be independently verified. This leads to controversial figures and in some cases drug companies have been challenged to justify the high prices that they demand.

In a recent paper in *Nature Reviews* by Paul *et al.* (2010), the costs of many drug discovery programmes are compared. This analysis dissects capitalised costs and the out-of-pocket costs and applies assumptions in the discovery process. The authors conclude with an estimate of the capitalised cost as ~US$1.8 billion, with out-of-pocket costs of ~US$870 million.

In a previous publication by diMasi *et al.* in 2003, it was estimated that the actual value or 'capitalised costs' of a single drug development programme was US$800 million. This cost was further divided by half into 'opportunity costs' of US$400 million. The opportunity costs are the difference between the actual value resulting from such use and that of an alternative possible usage (i.e. as another use of the same resources or an investment of equal risk but greater return). A later study by Adams and Brantner in 2006 came to the figure of US$500 million to $2 billion to bring a single drug to market. The costs were dependent on the type of drug therapy being developed or the particular pharmaceutical company in question. Although a more recent publication in 2010 in the *Journal of Health Economics* criticised the methods used by diMasi *et al.*, the authors however, estimated even higher costs of US$1.2 billion (Adams and Brantner 2010). However, Marcia Angell, a former editor of the *New England Journal of Medicine*, has called that number grossly inflated, and estimates that the total is closer to US$100 million (Angell 2005). A more recent 2011 study, also critical of the diMasi methods, puts average costs at US$55 million (Light and Warburton 2011).

Drug lead compounds from HTS or HCS might theoretically include from 5,000 to 10,000 chemical compounds which may lead to one successful drug. There are high attrition rates and on average about 250 of these will show sufficient promise for further evaluation using laboratory tests, mice and other test animals. Approximately ten of these will qualify for clinical trials in humans (Kasapi and Mihiotis 2011) A study conducted in the 1980s and 1990s, by the Tufts Center for the Study of Drug Development, found that only 21.5% of drugs that start phase I trials are eventually approved for marketing (DiMasi *et al.* 2004).

6.4 Drug discovery downfall

At present, the drug development industry faces a challenge: despite the increasing cost of bringing new drugs into the market every year, the number of new chemical entities approved by regulatory entities such as the FDA remains the same or is even declining (Fig. 6.2) (Sleigh and Barton 2010; Lekka *et al.* 2011). Many of the most profitable drugs which have represented up to 40% of the overall sales have now expired their patents or are about to expire their patents, and this has had a dramatic effect on the economic stability of the industry (Alazraki 2011). A clear example is Zyprexa, the most profitable drug for Elli Lilly, the patent for which expired in 2011. To readdress this imminent financial loss, Elli Lilly reacted by substantial reduction of its staff and its R&D programmes to save US$5 billion in costs (Rasch William 2012). In fact, the majority of major pharma companies lack drug pipelines that would compensate for economic loss generated from patent expiration (Drews 2003). They have become more diligent in the choice of therapeutic targets to invest in, giving priority to the systemic diseases such as cancer, diabetes and nervous system diseases, such as Alzheimer's disease, which are deemed more profitable than rare diseases. Moreover, the industry has invested in technology platforms such as genomics, high-throughput screening, bioinformatics and molecular imaging that has resulted in the parallel analysis of many drug compounds. Despite these technologies, to date they have not provided many new

Figure 6.2 **Number of FDA drug approvals versus R&D expenses. This graphic depicts the current drug productivity gap. Despite that R&D expenditure has increased significantly, the number of drugs approved is not increasing**

Source: Sleigh and Barton 2010; FDA 2009, 2010, 2011

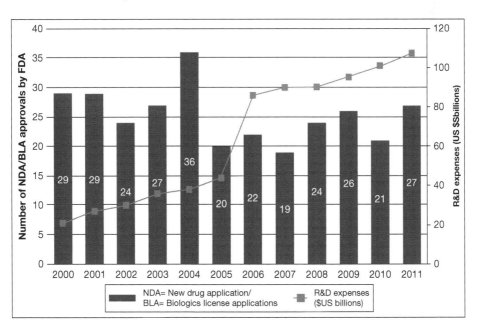

drug entities (Willmann *et al.* 2008). The lack of new drug pipelines together with the economic pressures is driving companies to adopt new models that have lower risks of failure and which are cost-effective.

The most common strategies to reduce the risks of drug development are: (a) developing new formulations of existing drugs; (b) in-licensing of clinical stage programmes, frequently the core strategy of so-called NRDO (no research, development only) companies; and (c) repurposing or repositioning of existing drugs or discontinued compounds to identify novel uses or therapeutic properties.

The 'drug repositioning' model, whereby existing drugs are utilised for other diseases, allows a paradigm shift in drug discovery. It is a powerful and alternative strategy to fill the vacuum for targets for other indications and also for rare and neglected diseases. For example, Seroxat was a drug originally licensed for the treatment of depression, but it has been repositioned to include treatment of social anxiety disorder, obsessive compulsive disorder, post-traumatic stress disorder and panic disorder. Of the 50 top selling brands in 2004, 84% have had additional indications approved since their initial launch in the US, and a further 6% are known to have subsequent indications in development (Paul 2007).

6.5 Drug repositioning as a strategy

Drug repositioning can be defined as the discovery of new therapeutic applications for existing or previously approved drugs (Fox *et al.* 2006). Traditional drug discovery relies on identification of a target, typically an enzyme or receptor-ligand, where it is hoped that binding to the target will elicit a desired biological response. Large libraries of compounds are tested for target binding using HTS methods and hits are then optimised for activity and other desirable properties. The times associated in bringing repositioned drugs to the market may vary between 3 and 12 years, which is still much faster than the conventional drug discovery of at least 15 years, and the investment costs are lower in comparison with new drug entities (Tartaglia 2006; Padhy and Gupta 2011). Progression of these initial hits through the stages of drug development remains very disappointing. Attrition rates through optimising hit structure, absorption, distribution, metabolism and excretion (ADME) properties, efficacy in a transgenic mouse or other animal, and phase I, II and III stages in humans are high for drug development in general and particularly poor for neurodegenerative diseases, such as Alzheimer's. The great majority of chemicals are entirely unsuitable as drug candidates, as shown, for example, by the utility of simple rules, such as Lipinski's rules, to summarise desirable properties in a drug. Hence, nearly all molecules found to be effective by high throughput screening, will fail if taken further in drug development.

The drug repositioning strategy has been growing in importance within the industry because of several advantages:

- Existing drugs are already known to exert a biological response in humans (Grau and Serbedzija 2005). This response may be beneficial for additional conditions. For example, studies of patients taking cholesterol lowering statin drugs revealed an unexpected link between cholesterol levels and AD, with patients on statins having a lower risk of AD (Fonseca *et al.* 2010)

- Such molecules are already usually known to be bioactive, safe, bioavailable and have FDA approval for use in humans. In addition, some can cross the blood–brain barrier, which is often problematic for a drug for neurodegeneration

- Many of the steps in drug development, such as determining ADMET properties and phase I clinical trials, have already been done, hence reducing drug development costs, accelerating drug development and improving chances of success (Chong and Sullivan 2007)

This drug repositioning or repurposing strategy has already led to several blockbuster drugs (e.g. Viagra and Rogaine) (Ashburn and Thor 2004). Up to 2011, 34 reports were published where groups screened libraries of FDA-approved drugs against various whole cell or target assays (Ekins and Williams 2011). None was for AD. Each screen identified at least one compound with a novel bioactivity.

Finally, a smaller compound library allows small biotech companies or research academic groups to pursue screening campaigns with the aim of finding repositioned drugs. These include the discovery of systemic diseases, infectious diseases associated with drug resistant microorganism or parasites, and rare diseases.

The rest of this chapter will elaborate on the principles of how academic and industry partnerships interact to perform drug repositioning programmes with the aim of finding new treatments for neglected diseases, rare diseases and some Western diseases. Illustrative examples of drugs in development that have been discovered by such strategies will be covered.

6.6 Drug repositioning principles

The literature considers that there are two main types of drug repositioning supported by two scientific principles:

- **Known compound–new target**. This is based on the 'promiscuous' nature of many drugs which interact with multiple targets or pathways. These interactions with 'off-targets' may be responsible for the side-effects of a drug. However, in some cases the interaction with a secondary target could produce a desirable effect to treat other disease (Grau and Serbedzija 2005; Sardana *et al.* 2011). As an example, we can mention the recent studies which suggest that the nonsteroidal anti-inflammatory drug (NSAID) Ibuprofen could provide a neuroprotective action against Parkinson's disease (Gao *et al.* 2011)

- **Known mechanism–new indication**. This principle indicates that a biological target may be relevant to more than one disease, pathway or process. In this case the repurposing of the drug is by finding a relationship between the known target and the new disease (Grau and Serbedzija 2005; Sardana *et al.* 2011). For instance: Duloxetine was approved by the FDA in 2004 to treat depression. During the development of this drug it was suggested that its mechanism of action which consists in blocking the re-uptake of serotonin and noradrenalin could be relevant to treat stress urinary incontinence (SIU). This is because it is known that both neurotransmitters have an effect on the urethral sphincter preventing the leakage of urine. While this drug was not approved to be marketed in the USA, it was approved by the regulatory agency in the European Union (EMEA) in 2004 (Ashburn and Thor 2004; Sweeney and Chancellor 2005)

Using different technology platforms, drug repositioning can find new uses for drugs which fall into the following categories (Grau and Serbedzija 2005; Sleigh and Barton 2010):

- Drugs that are still in clinical development. These drugs have been demonstrated to have mechanisms of action that may be relevant to more than one disease and have passed phase I clinical trials confirming that they have acceptable safety profiles. Phase II clinical trials to confirm proposed therapeutic applications are run in parallel

- Drugs that failed in late stages of drug development (phase II and phase III) through lack of evidence to demonstrate efficacy, but not for safety issues

- Drugs that were dropped during drug development for commercial reasons

- Marketed drugs whose patents are expired or about to expire

- Drugs that have launched in emerging markets (Latin America, Asia, etc.) to treat endemic diseases, but not in large markets such as the US or Europe

Initially, the new use of existing drugs for new purposes was found by serendipity. One of the most remarkable examples is the drug sildenafil, otherwise known by its trade name, Viagra. Originally, this drug was developed for the treatment of angina, a cardiovascular condition.

This drug failed to demonstrate cardiovascular activity during clinical trials; however, patients reported prolonged erections after the ingestion of the pill. Based on these findings, further clinical trials were performed to confirm the effectiveness of sildenafil to treat erectile dysfunction and by 1998 it was launched in United States as the first oral therapy to treat erectile dysfunction (Renaud and Xuereb 2002; Ashburn and Thor 2004). Undoubtedly, the discovery of this blockbuster drug along with the current economic situation has driven the use of systematic strategies to find new drugs by drug repositioning.

6.6.1 Drug repositioning compound libraries

In 2007, Chong and Sullivan estimated that there about 10,000 drugs used in clinical medicine. There is no current library which includes all these drugs. The largest available compound library is the Johns Hopkins Clinical Compound Library (JHCCL) which currently includes 3,500 drugs available for screening at a small charge (Chong and Sullivan 2007; JHSPH 2012). As an example, the Johns Hopkins research group screened this library to find antiangiogenic compounds based on the hypothesis that angiogenesis plays a key role in diseases such as prostate, lung and breast cancer. This study found that itraconzale has the potential to be used as an antiangiogenic compound. This drug is now in phase II clinical trials to evaluate its efficacy for the treatments of prostate and non-small-cell lung cancer. Studies to test its efficacy for breast cancer have also started (Chong *et al.* 2007; Aftab *et al.* 2011). There are other commercial libraries which include off-patent FDA-approved drugs which have also been used to screen drugs for new purposes (Table 6.1).

In addition to these collections, some contract research organisations (CROs) offer the use of their own compound collections for screening. One such service is the German-based company, European Screening Port (ESP), which works exclusively with academic and research institutes.[1] ESP provides a complete drug discovery service covering all stages from target validation via small molecule screening to candidate selection. An attractive feature of ESP services is that all derived hits and IP (intellectual property) are given back to the customer for full commercial exploitation.

Table 6.1 **Examples of available compound libraries**

Compound library	Number of compounds
Prestwick Chemical Library (Prestwick Chemical Library 2006)	1,200 small molecules approved by FDA
Microsource (MicroSource Discovery Systems 2012)	
Pharmakon	1,600 known drugs from US and international pharmacopoeia
US Drug Collection	1,040 drugs that have reached some phase of clinical trials in USA
International drug collection	320 drugs that are marketed in Europe and Asia
ENZO Life Sciences (Enzo Life Sciences 2012)	640 compounds approved by FDA
LOPAC 1280™ (Sigma-Aldrich 2012)	1,280 pharmacologically active compounds
NCGC Pharmaceutical collection (Huang *et al.* 2011)	2,400 drugs approved by FDA, EMEA NHI and Canadian authorities (HC)

1 screeningport.com, accessed 30 January 2012.

In a new initiative to create an open innovation platform in drug discovery, approximately 80 representatives from the pharmaceutical industry, government and academic institutions met in April 2011 (Mullard 2011). The key topic was to discuss repositioning and rescue efforts for old and new drugs. The US National Institutes of Health (NIH) officials asserted that the different sectors could better capitalise on advancing science and accumulating clinical data by working together on a systematic approach for screening clinical-stage, abandoned and approved compounds for new uses. Currently, all the major pharmaceutical companies are becoming more receptive to the idea of offering drug libraries to academic institutions and CROs for drug discovery. For example, a wide range of compounds from AstraZeneca and the UK Medical Research Council (MRC) will be made available to UK medical researchers in 2012 (AstraZeneca 2011). Though making individual compounds available to external academic investigators is not unusual, the breadth and open-innovation nature of this collaboration is unique because it provides unprecedented access to well-characterised clinical and pre-clinical candidate molecules to investigators across all UK academic institutions. The MRC will judge and select the best scientific proposals and award up to £10 million in total to fund research across a broad range of human diseases.

6.6.2 Database mining using systems biology

In addition to the public and private compound availability of compound libraries, there is much knowledge, literature and clinical data on the effects of many drugs. New disciplines, such as systems biology, which will allow the mapping of drug interactions within entire organisms (at the cellular, tissue organ level to pathology), and text mining, which will allow creation of databases storing the relationships between clinical, biochemical and compound data, are likely to prove invaluable. This ability to examine possible relationships between biological targets, metabolic pathways and available data on drugs and diseases (e.g. side-effects of drugs which may act as a possible second use of a drug) may be an effective and low-cost strategy in discovering new drugs for repositioning.

There has been a concerted collaboration of a number of groups to create powerful databases which can be utilised by the scientific community. For example, the PROMISCUOUS network database of about 25,000 drugs includes withdrawn drugs, 12,000 proteins, and 21,500 protein–protein interactions (von Eichborn *et al.* 2011). By association of structural similarity of drugs and side-effects, this network is able to establish possible networks between drugs and possible targets. This database represents an accessible first step for research groups interested in drug repositioning. The later confirmation and validation of the possible target–drug connections suggested by this database can be validated at an affordable cost. This resource was recently launched in 2011; however, the system has not been the subject of any subsequent publications, so it is difficult to evaluate the performance of this database.

In addition, although drug repositioning offers a large number of advantages, intellectual property issues must also be considered.

6.7 Intellectual property issues

It is an often misunderstood concept that exploiting old drugs for new uses is not novel drug discovery. However, the definition of novelty is the discovery of new therapeutic options to treat a disease and there are many ways in which to create novelty in drug development. The discovery that an existing drug is beneficial for a new condition can be novel IP and hence patentable. One important fact to consider about drugs that have being previously tested in humans is their associated patents. In some cases, the prior art (i.e. information derived from previous, publicly accessible knowledge or reports) around a drug subject to repositioning can be a difficult or even impossible hurdle to overcome.

Defending a repositioned drug can be more challenging than trying to defend a *de novo* drug. In general, the intellectual property issues can fall into two groups: the IP has broad claims for other disease indications and the compound of interest is owned (e.g. manufacturing and synthesis) by a third party; or, the compound has already lost its patent and there are already generics in the market. In the first case, the most common strategy is to reach a licence agreement with the company owner of the compound. In the second case, the drug can be patentable, claiming the new use of the proposed drug. In addition to the above-mentioned strategies, the development of new formulations, administration forms, combination of drugs and geographic strategies can be generated as ways to create some entry barriers for competitors (Ashburn and Thor 2004).

6.8 Repositioned drugs from screening small libraries

High-throughput screening in drug development can be defined as the techniques useful to screen and assess a huge number of chemical compounds derived from different origins against selected targets (Martis *et al.* 2011). Despite the drawbacks of traditional HTS, a lower-throughput approach has been widely used in drug repositioning. There are many advantages of using this approach.

As a starting point the number of drugs that have being tested in patients clinically are typically around 10,000 in contrast to the 10^{40} to 10^{70} of the chemical space. The availability of FDA-approved libraries from commercial vendors allows the real possibility of finding new indications for drugs (Macarron *et al.* 2011) and makes it feasible for small companies and academia to enter the business of drug

Table 6.2 **Examples of repositioned drugs**

Drug	Original indication	New indication
Celecoxib (Ashburn and Thor 2004)	Osteoarthritis	Familial adenomatous polyposis
Minidoxil (Ashburn and Thor 2004)	Hypertension	Hair loss
Paclitaxel (Ashburn and Thor 2004)	Cancer	Restenosis
Topiramate (Padhy and Gupta 2011)	Epilepsy	Obesity
Amantadine (Ekins *et al.* 2011)	Influenza	Parkinson's
Amphotericin (Oprea *et al.* 2011)	Fungal infection	Leishmaniasis
Aspirin (Padhy and Gupta 2011)	Inflammation, pain	Antiplatelet
Bromocriptine (Ekins and Williams 2011)	Parkinson's	Diabetes mellitus
Nitroxoline (Ashburn and Thor 2004)	Antibiotic	Antiangiogenic
Tiagabine (Ashburn and Thor 2004)	Antiepileptic	Neuroprotective agent
Ketorolac (Ekins and Williams 2011)	Nonsteroidal anti-inflammatory	Ovarian cancer
Tadalafil (Oprea *et al.* 2011)	Inflammation	Male erectile dysfunction
Zidovudine (Oprea *et al.* 2011)	Cancer	HIV/AIDS

repositioning. In addition, since these drugs have already been tested in humans, the failure risk associated with toxicity compared with *de novo* compounds at drug discovery stage is much lower. Another advantage is that, once a drug demonstrates efficacy against a selected target, it may not be necessary for lead optimisation steps (i.e. further modification of the chemical structure for efficacy).

6.8.1 NF-kB inhibitors

Miller *et al.* performed a screening of approved drugs from the NIH Chemical Genomics Center Pharmaceutical Collection (NPC) to search for inhibitors of nuclear factor-kappa (NF-kB) (Miller *et al.* 2010). This factor is associated with the cellular process implicated in inflammatory responses to infection. The activation of NF-kB signalling has been found to be relevant in some types of tumours, so the blockage of this signalling may be a target for anticancer drugs. A library of about

280 clinically approved compounds was tested using 15 different concentrations of each compound using a high-throughput screening format. Nineteen compounds were identified as inhibitors of NF-kB signalling. Some of the 19 are already used to treat cancer, but their activity as NF-kB inhibitors was unknown until the results of this study (Miller *et al.* 2010). The most effective inhibitor was ecteinascidin, which is already used for the treatment of ovarian cancer (Haupt and Schroeder 2011). This example provides clear evidence that in addition to finding new uses for existing drugs, the screening of compounds can result in a deeper knowledge regarding mechanisms of action of drugs and validating or finding new targets relevant for other diseases (Haupt and Schroeder 2011).

6.8.2 Antibiotics as neuroprotective agents

It is known that glutamate is one of the principal excitatory neurotransmitters. This neurotransmitter is regulated by the glutamate transporter protein (GLT1). Dysfunction of GLT1 plays a key role in chronic neurological disorders; such as amyotrophic lateral sclerosis (ALS), stroke and brain tumours (Rothstein *et al.* 2005). A blinded screening of 10^{40} approved drugs was performed in organotropic spinal cord slices to mimic the cellular metabolism and cell interactions presented *in vivo* for the transporter protein GLT1 (Rothstein *et al.* 2005; O'Connor and Roth 2005). This assay found that 20 compounds, including the β-lactam antibiotics and cephalosporins, showed a high activity, increasing GLT1 protein expression. Based on these results, additional assays provided molecular and *in vivo* evidence of the potential action of β-lactam and cephalosporins as neuroprotective agents. Further studies have been performed and the results have confirmed the action of Ceftriaxone as a neuroprotective agent in stroke (Neumann 2010). In addition, there are clinical phase III trials which demonstrate effectiveness of Ceftriaxone in ALS (Amy 2012). Considering that these studies were initiated in 2005, this is a clear demonstration of fast-tracking of drug repositioning, as a strategy in speeding up drug development timelines.

6.9 Drug repositioning for neglected diseases

The current drug discovery 'productivity gap' and the expiration of patents means that the pharmaceutical industry is pushing to find new ways to generate new chemical entities (NCE) and at the same time recover revenues. In the recent past, the industry was focused on developing blockbuster drugs for chronic diseases, as the possible revenues associated with such treatments were higher. However, in the current economic decline, drug repositioning has emerged as an interesting model to find treatments for neglected diseases. In addition, governmental and internationally recognised institutions such as WHO (World Health Organisation) and FDA are beginning initiatives to promote the development of treatments for neglected diseases.

Owing to the advantages of drug repositioning, a systematic approach has gained popularity in the drug development industry. New companies whose business model is based on licensing new uses for existing drugs to bigger pharmaceutical companies have been created in the past decade (Muthyala 2011). In addition, large pharmaceutical companies, such as Pfizer and GlaxoSmithKline (GSK), are using their own clinic tested libraries to find treatments for neglected diseases (Gilbert *et al.* 2010). In these cases, drug repositioning is very attractive as a possible method to extend the market life of a compound. Table 6.2 includes examples of some drugs that have been proposed for use in other therapeutic applications using systematic approaches (Aftab *et al.* 2011; AstraZeneca 2011).

6.10 Repositioned antimicrobials

Undoubtedly, the discovery of antimicrobials was one of the most significant medical advances of the 20th century (Powers 2004). With their introduction, the high mortality rates associated with infectious diseases were greatly reduced (Coates *et al.* 2002). Most antibiotics available in the market were developed between the 1940s and 1960s (Norrby *et al.* 2005). Their effectiveness and fast development led many to think that infectious diseases would soon be entirely eradicated. However, antibiotic resistance to antimicrobials swiftly appeared (Bax *et al.* 2000). Nowadays, antibacterial resistance has increased considerably, becoming an important global health issue (Smith and Coast 2002). It is estimated that about 70% of microbes causing intra-hospital infections are resistant to at least one antimicrobial (Parket and Bajorath 2006; Martis *et al.* 2011) Although the above facts highlight the necessity of developing new antimicrobials, since 2000, only five new antimicrobials were approved by the FDA (Coates *et al.* 2002; Theuretzbacher 2009; Moellering 2011). This alarming situation has raised global concern in the medical community and the Infectious Disease Society of America (IDSA). In addition, WHO has launched the initiative 10×20 with the goal of approving 10 new antimicrobials by 2020 (Powers 2004; Gilbert *et al.* 2010).

6.11 Repositioned parasiticides

6.11.1 Trypanocidals

Trypanosoma brucei is known as the causal organism of human African trypanosomiasis. In the current pharmacopoeia there are only four approved drugs to treat this disease. Moreover, it is estimated that drug resistance against the first line of treatment, melarsoprol, has increased, resulting in up to 10% mortality in infected patients (Paul *et al.* 2010). Mackey *et al.* developed an ATP-bioluminescence assay to screen a compound library of 2,160 FDA-approved drugs to search for those that exhibited a cytotoxic activity against *Trypanosoma brucei* (Mackey *et al.* 2006).

They found 33 compounds, of which 16 were already known to have a trypanocidal effect. One new compound is Orlistat, a lipid inhibitor commonly used to treat obesity which possesses a very good safety profile (Mackey *et al*. 2006). Complete results from this investigation are available in the public domain with the intention to incentivise further investigation of the hits.

6.11.2 Antimalarials

Plasmodium falciparum is the causal parasite of human malaria. This disease causes around 3 million deaths annually and resistance to current treatments is growing (Shahinas *et al*. 2010). Chong *et al*. (2006) screened a library of 1,937 FDA compounds to find inhibitors of *P. falciparum*. Preliminary screening revealed 189 compounds which showed >50% inhibition of growth. After eliminating drugs which exhibit topical action and known antimalarial and cytotoxic drugs, a second screening of 87 remaining molecules was performed. From this screening, astemizole, currently used as an antihistamine, demonstrated the strongest cytotoxic activity against the parasite. The antimalarial activity of astemizole was confirmed *in vivo* using two mouse models of malaria (Chong *et al*. 2006).

6.11.3 Leishmanicidals

Leishmaniasis is a group of diseases caused by parasites known as 'trypanosomatids' from the genus *Leishmania*. The disease is spread by the sandfly vector and persists in 88 tropical and subtropical countries; approximately 350 million people are at risk of contracting the disease (Piscopo and Mallia Azzopardi 2007). In fact, it is one of the most neglected tropical diseases, and affects the majority of the poorer populations. Worldwide, the number of infected persons is rising. This may be due to the lack of vaccines, failure to eradicate the sandfly and the increasing number of parasites resistant to chemotherapy. Amphotericin B is a newly repositioned drug for visceral leishmaniasis (VL) (Kafetzis *et al*. 2005), which was previously used intravenously for systemic fungal infections. Amphotericin B is a natural product which was originally extracted from the bacterium *Streptomyces nodosus* in 1955 at the Squibb Institute for Medical Research.

In addition to the previous case studies outlined, there are other research groups in discovery programmes to find antimicrobials in the existent pharmacopoeia using approaches other than HTS, such as bioinformatics or systems biology (Kinnings *et al*. 2009).

6.12 Drug development for rare and orphan diseases

This review will not differentiate between 'rare diseases' and orphan diseases, as both of these categories of disease affect a small percentage of the population. An orphan disease was usually referenced to the lack of treatment and resources, for which it was perceived that the development of therapeutics was not economically viable. There are approximately 6,000–7,000 rare diseases documented to date according to the European Organisation for Rare Diseases (EURODIS), the majority (over 80%) of which are of genetic origin and thus are present throughout the person's entire life, even if symptoms do not appear immediately. According to the European Society for Paediatric Oncology (SIOP Europe 2009), 75% of rare cancers affect children and 30% die before reaching the age of five. There is no internationally agreed cut-off number for which a disease is considered rare. The problem in definition is also related to the geographical occurrence of rare diseases. For example some rare diseases may be common in some countries and yet be rare in others. According to the US Rare Disease Act of 2002 a rare disease is defined in terms of population, i.e. 'those which affect small patient populations, typically smaller than 200,000 individuals in the United States' (Rare Diseases Act of 2002, 6 November 2002 Public Health Service Act to establish an Office of Rare Diseases at the NIH). In contrast, The European Commission on Public Health focuses on the severity of the disease, defining it as 'life-threatening or chronically debilitating diseases which are of such low prevalence that special combined efforts are needed to address them' (European Commission 2009). Furthermore, the term 'low prevalence' was defined as less than 1 in 2,000 suffers.

6.12.1 Biotherapeutics and enzyme replacement therapy

Although this review focuses on small molecule compounds as drugs for the treatment of diseases, the use of biologically derived drugs or biotherapeutics (mostly proteins) for the remediation of many diseases is becoming more and more important. These biotherapeutics are composed of various types of biological molecular entities and even whole cells such as stem cells, and have revolutionised the treatment of a variety of human diseases ranging from cancer and autoimmune diseases to rare genetic disorders over the past three decades. The first biotherapeutic was recombinant insulin for diabetes, developed by Eli Lilly in the early 1980s; subsequently over a thousand different biotherapeutic products have been marketed (Johnson 1983). Advances in recombinant expression technologies (especially in mammalian cells) has led to the production of many protein-based drugs such as erythropoietin in treating anaemia resulting from chronic kidney disease and antibodies such as Adalimumab (also known as Humira, by Abbott laboratories), approved for the treatment of rheumatoid arthritis, psoriatic arthritis, ankylosing spondylitis, Crohn's disease, moderate to severe chronic psoriasis, and juvenile idiopathic arthritis (Shim 2011). In 2003, there were 703 biotherapeutics in development globally (pre-clinical to registration); in 2008 this had grown to 845; 94 biological medicines have been licensed in the USA since 2003, and the top 20 accounted for US$82 billion of sales worldwide in 2008 (total pharmaceutical sales were about US$740 billion), compared with US$33 billion (total small molecule drugs US$499 billion) in 2003 (IMS 2011). Clearly, the future market growth for biotherapeutic products is on the increase.

In the case of rare diseases, biotherapeutics should become therapeutics of choice in the near future. For example, inherited rare diseases, which are due to mutational defects in the gene, produce malfunctioned proteins (e.g. enzymes, receptors or protein carriers), which in turn affect critical metabolic processes. In cases where a defective enzyme is inherited, the most obvious drug intervention is enzyme replacement therapy (ERT). With the advances in recombinant technologies in production and optimisation of proteins, the reduction in the cost of manufacture and taking in to consideration the high costs of healthcare, the business of drug development for rare diseases is fast becoming a viable business model.

The first ERT was developed for the treatment of the rare disease known as Gaucher disease, which was first described in 1882 by Philippe Gaucher. The disease results from the defective activity of glucocerebrosidase (GCase) and the subsequent storage of glucosylceramide in lysosomes of the macrophages. There are three classifications: type 1 (non-neuronopathic) with an incidence of 1 in 57,000, and types 2 and 3 (acute and sub-acute neuronopathic, respectively) with an incidence of 1 in 100,000. Type 1 disease has an increased incidence in the Ashkenazi Jewish population of 1 in 855 (Meikle *et al.* 1999). Gaucher disease type 1 results in enlargement of the liver, anaemia, reduction in platelets (thrombocytopenia), and severe bone complications. Patients with type 1 disease have no central nervous system (CNS) involvement. Individuals with type 3 disease may have varying degrees of visceral involvement and the presence of CNS manifestations, such as involuntary seizures. Infants with Gaucher disease type 2 have rapidly progressive CNS disease and pulmonary complications and die by 2 years of age (Grabowski 2008). Almost 20 years ago, Genzyme Corporation produced the first ERT product, imiglucerase (Cerezyme) (Weinreb 2008), which has proven to be effective at reducing the size of the liver and spleen to normal or near normal levels with simultaneous improvements in anaemia, thrombocytopenia and bone complication within 2 years. Regular ERT has been shown to restore health and reverse disease manifestations for most patients, allowing them to lead near-normal lives.

Another example of a rare genetic disease is the group of disorders known as the lysosomal storage diseases (LSDs). The LSDs are a group of over 40 different disorders characterised by the lack of sufficient enzymatic activity to prevent the accumulation of specific macromolecules, such as glycosphingolipids (a variety of different lipids), mucopolysaccharides, or glycogen, in various tissues. Each unique disorder is caused by deficiency or dysfunction of a different enzyme. LSDs include phenylketonuria (PKU), galactosaemia, and medium chain acyl carnitine deficiency (MCAD). Before the discovery that a controlled diet could change the outcome of LSDs, there was no hope for sufferers of these diseases and they were often lethal genetic disorders. However, administration of corrective enzymes in each of the LSDs by means of ERT moves the treatment of these disorders from symptomatic management and comfort care to therapeutic interventions that address the underlying metabolic defect. ERT is not a cure for these disorders, though it can greatly modify or attenuate the clinical manifestation (the signs and symptoms and severity of the condition) and disease progression. The success of ERT has proved that development of pharmacologic treatments for the LSDs is economically feasible and that development of better treatment options is worthwhile (Beutler 2006; Connock *et al.* 2006).

6.12.2 Small molecule drugs

A distinct strategy, in which repositioning of small molecule drugs may be used as therapies for rare diseases, is the remediation of biological activities of defective proteins through the direct molecular interaction of drug compounds. This approach has tremendous potential in the treatment of genetic diseases, where usually the cause of the disease is a protein malfunction due to a mutation on the wild-type sequence. In particular, this approach should be especially beneficially in those genetic-based diseases where the underlying metabolic functions and biological targets are known (e.g. protein sequences, mutations are characterised and animal models exist). The underlying mechanistic action which demonstrates the viability of this approach is through:

- Enzyme activation/inactivation by drug binding (e.g. through allosteric binding)

- Protein stabilisation/destabilisation by small molecule binding (pharmacological chaperones or cofactor binding)

The activity of enzymes can be altered by the binding actions of molecules to the enzyme in question. This is known as the 'allosteric effect' and such molecules are known as 'effector' molecules which include drugs or antibodies. Effector molecules modify allosteric enzymes by changing their structure, thereby affecting either a positive or negative effect on the activity of the enzyme in question. In fact the allosteric mechanism is commonly found in biochemical processes in living systems, allowing control of metabolic pathways. Allosteric enzymes can be either multimeric units composed of more than one enzyme (Monod *et al.* 1965) or single (monomer) enzymes (Gohara and Di Cera 2011).

In a similar manner to modulation of activity of allosteric enzymes, protein targets may be stabilised (or destabilised) by the binding action of effector molecules. If the effectors are small molecule drugs, these are known as 'pharmacological chaperones' or 'pharmacoperones' as their mode of action is through the stabilisation of unstable proteins. In many rare diseases, mutation of proteins often causes molecular misfolding, which results in protein misrouting within the cell. The mutated proteins may retain proper function but end up in parts of the cell where the function is inappropriate, or even deleterious, to cell function. Misfolded proteins are usually recognised by the quality-control system of the cell and retained (and often destroyed or recycled) in the endoplasmic reticulum. The absence of functional protein is the primary cause of rare diseases and pharmacological chaperones aid the recovery of such functionality, thus preventing further development of the diseases. Alternatively, pharmacological chaperones may also be used to prevent the aggregation of proteins observed in other diseases such as amyloidosis. Pharmacological chaperones have been reported to be successful in the treatment of Fabry's disease, Tay Sachs, Sandhoff disease, GM1-gangliosidosis and Pompe disease (Porto *et al.* 2009). The stabilisation effects of the pharmacoperones have not been explicitly measured in most systems and the efficacy is highly dependent on mutations.

The rare disease, N-acetylglutamate synthase (NAGS) deficiency, can be treated by allosteric action. NAGS deficiency results in an excess of ammonia in the blood (hyperammonaemia) resulting from disruption of the NAGS enzyme in the urea cycle (Bachmann *et al.* 1982). It is a very rare disease, and its frequency in the population has not been determined. Although the disease can manifest itself at any age, it is commonly diagnosed in newborns. The common symptoms include vomiting, diarrhoea, poor feeding, seizures, reduced motor and brain development and respiratory complications. Excess accumulation of ammonia can result in hyperammonaemic coma. NAGS is a genetic disease that can be passed down to children. The disease results from mutations in the NAGS gene leading to either a complete or partial loss in enzyme activity. The catalytic product of NAGS is N-acetylglutamate (NAG) which in turn is an allosteric activator of carbamylphosphate synthetase I (CPSI), the enzyme catalysing the first step in ureagenesis (Enns *et al.* 2010). The method of choice for treatment of NAGS activity is with daily administration of N-carbamyl-L-glutamate (NCLG), which mimics NAG, thereby activating CPSI. This successful regime has been approved as an orphan drug treatment for NAGS deficiency since 2003 in the European Union (Morizono *et al.* 2004). In the majority of cases, the effects of NCLG treatment are dramatic, allowing the restoration of normal life to patients.

A pharmacological chaperone has been successfully used in the treatment of phenylketonuria (PKU). PKU affects Caucasian populations in the US at a rate of 1 in 10,000 (Bickel *et al.* 1981). There is a wide variance of the disease between different countries. The largest incidence is in Turkey with 1 in 2,600 births, in comparison with Finland and Japan which have 1 in 100,000 births. PKU is a genetic disorder which affects the amino acid metabolism due to mutations in the gene for the hepatic enzyme phenylalanine hydroxylase (PAH). Mutation causes the enzyme to mis-fold, thereby rendering it non-functional. Normally, PAH converts the amino acid phenylalanine (Phe) to the amino acid tyrosine. If untreated, PKU can lead to mental retardation, seizures and other serious medical problems. The usual treatment for classic PKU sufferers is a diet which excludes Phe (Enns *et al.* 2010). The natural cofactor of PAH, tetrahydrobiopterin (BH4), has been demonstrated as a pharmacological chaperone for PAH which can remediate the enzyme function. Sapropterin dihydrochloride, the synthetic form of BH4, was recently approved as the first pharmacological chaperone to correct the loss-of-function phenotype (Burton *et al.* 2007). However, BH4 shows limited efficacy in some PKU genotypes and its chemical synthesis is very costly. To readdress these limitations, a number of promising new pharmacological chaperones with high *in vivo* efficacy have been discovered (Santos-Sierra *et al.* 2012).

6.13 A case study: New enzyme and drug therapy approaches for alkaptonuria

Alkaptonuria (black urine disease or alcaptonuria; AKU) is a rare inherited genetic disorder of phenylalanine and tyrosine catabolism, which is described in Chapter 3. The disease results from mutations in the enzyme homogentisic acid 1,2 dioxygenase (HGO), rendering the enzyme inactive, resulting in the accumulation of its substrate, homogentisic acid (HGA). Currently, there is no cure for AKU.

6.13.1 Enzyme therapy as a rational approach

The mechanistic action of HGO cleaves the aromatic ring of HGA during the metabolic degradation of Phe and Tyr to produce maleylacetoacetic acid (Fig. 6.3A).

Crystal structures of apo-HGO (without iron) and holo-HGO (containing an iron atom) have been determined at 1.9 and 2.3 Å resolution, respectively (Titus *et al.* 2000) (Fig. 6.3B). The HGO protein, which contains a 280-residue N-terminal

Figure 6.3 **Catabolic pathway of phenylalanine and tyrosine (A) and crystal structure showing as a dimer of two HGO trimers (B)**

Source: Reprinted by permission from Macmillan Publishers Ltd on behalf of Cancer Research UK: *Nature Structural & Molecular Biology*; G.P. Titus, H.A. Mueller, J. Burgner, S. Rodríguez de Córdoba, M.A. Peñalva and D.E. Timm, 'Crystal Structure of Human Homogentisate Dioxygenase', *Nature Structural & Molecular Biology* 7: 542-46. Copyright 2000.

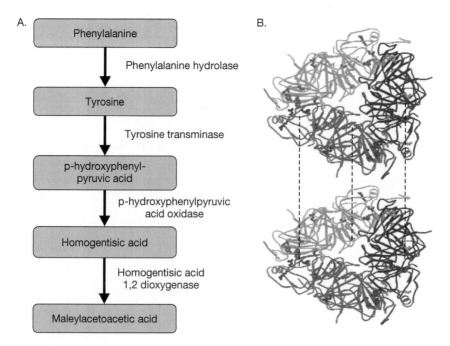

domain and a 140-residue C-terminal domain, associates as a hexamer and is arranged as a dimer of trimers. The active site binds an iron atom which is coordinated near the interface between subunits in the HGO trimer by a Glu and two His side chains. HGO represents a new structural class of dioxygenases. The largest group of AKU associated mutations affect residues located in regions of contact between subunits (Titus *et al.* 2000).

More than 84 mutations in the HGO gene have been identified in patients diagnosed with AKU (Rodriguez *et al.* 2000). Most of these mutations relate to single amino acid changes. For example, a substitution of valine for methionine at protein position 368 (i.e. Met368Val) is the most common HGO mutation in European populations. It is widely believed that these mutations result in disruption of the structure and function of the HGO enzyme thereby increasing the levels of HGA.

The crystal structure of HGO solved by Titus *et al.* (2000) allows molecular engineering of the enzyme and further understanding of the structural basis for the AKU mutations. Coupled with the fact that the human HGO can be recombinantly expressed and that the enzyme activity can be easily measured, enzyme replacement therapy (ERT) offers a promising therapeutic potential for AKU patients. A further advantage of ERT over drug-based therapies (such as the use of nitisinone; Introne *et al.* 2011) is that there would potentially be fewer adverse side-effects as the enzyme would restore the high HGA levels to normal levels in plasma of patients. However, HGO is a large and complex protein, consisting of a molecular mass of 300 kDa for the hexamer. The protein is unstable during freezing and thawing and aggregates in solution. In order for ERT to become a real and viable therapeutic option, the following key challenges remain:

- Demonstration of efficacy and longevity of action of the recombinant HGO in pre-clinical studies in AKU mouse models

- Production of HGO in high yields

- Increasing the stability, reduction of aggregation of HGO and retention of enzymatic activity

- Formulation of HGO for administration in patients (e.g. oral or intravenous injection)

In recognition of these challenges, the AKU Society (see Chapter 3) forged a successful academic–industry partnership in 2011 with the strategic aim of ERT for alkaptonuria. The partners included the University of Liverpool and Protein Technologies Ltd (PTL) in the United Kingdom.

Protein Technologies Ltd is a specialist contract research organisation (CRO) focused on engineering of proteins for stability and enhancing biological activities, protein expression (in bacteria, yeast and mammalian cells) and protein production. As a small to medium-sized enterprise (SME), PTL is able to rapidly turn over projects in contrast to the 'inertia' of larger companies, which have to overcome inter-departmental processes (e.g. protein expression and assay development) and management hurdles to undertake projects. PTL produced recombinant enzyme variants within a six-month intensive programme to express, purify and kinetically characterise the human recombinant protein in *Escherichia coli*. The rapid development of recombinant HGO was achieved at low cost (funded through the AKU society), utilising gene synthesis and only one full-time research assistant at PTL (recombinant expression and purification) and an adaptation to a 96-microwell *in vitro* spectrophotometric assay for HGO (Fig. 6.4). Although highly active HGO preparations were produced, the half-life of activity of the enzyme was limited to several days as the enzyme suffered from activity losses due to protein aggregation.

Following the successful production of an active recombinant HGO, the enzyme was intravenously injected into AKU mouse models developed by The Institute of Ageing & Chronic Disease at The University of Liverpool. The Liverpool group thus demonstrated significant reductions of plasma levels of HGA over several hours. Further pre-clinical studies using a larger number of mice and dosage are currently being undertaken.

In February 2012, an MSc six-month project student was appointed by the University of Manchester to PTL for studies to improve the expression yields, stability and formulation of HGO. After successive screening of the enzyme against a wide range of stabilisers and cryopreservatives, the enzyme was successfully formulated such that aggregation was prevented and concomitant retention of activity was achieved. Another major step forward was the tenfold increase in the yield of recombinant HGO (~50 mg/L in shaker flasks) by optimisation of *E. coli* growth media. This allows large-scale production of HGO by standard fermentation methods.

Figure 6.5A summarises the use of publicly financed human resources combined with academic expertise and facilities at universities and industry which has resulted in cost-effective discovery of promising ERT options for AKU patients. These initial but promising results could not have come at a better time, considering that AKU was the first genetic disease characterised over 100 years ago by Sir Archibald Edward Garrod in 1902. In general, this approach has tremendous potential in the treatment of many other genetic diseases, where usually the cause of the disease is an enzyme malfunction due to a mutation on the wild-type sequence.

Figure 6.4 **Schematic of homogentisic acid (HGA) to maleylacetoacetic acid by HGO (A) as measured by an absorbance assay in a 96-well microplate at 330 nm (B)**

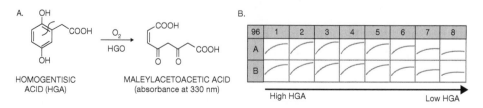

Figure 6.5 **Collaborative partners for enzyme replacement therapy (A) and drug repositioning (B). The partners include the AKU Society (a charity), private biotech companies (Protein Technologies Ltd and Lumophore Ltd) and Universities (Liverpool and Manchester)**

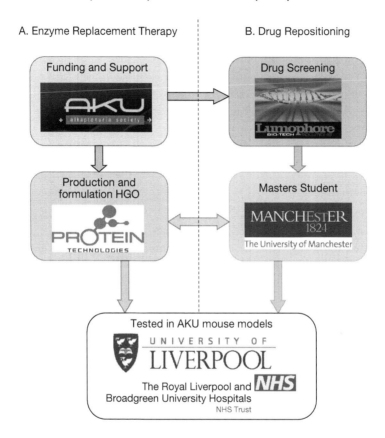

The next step in the development of ERT for alkaptonuria is to undertake phase 1 clinical trials and this is where traditionally there has been a funding gap. Phase I trials are usually sponsored by pharmaceutical companies if there is a clear commercial benefit; however with neglected diseases, this is often not the case, therefore charities and public funding, through government initiatives have been launched to address this issue. For example, the Innovative Medicines Initiative (IMI) is Europe's largest public–private initiative aiming to speed up the development of better and safer medicines for patients. The IMI has a €2 billion budget, which supports collaborative research and builds networks of pharmaceutical companies and academic experts in Europe. In the United Kingdom, the Technology Strategy Board, the government's premiere innovation agency, has launched the Biomedical Catalyst programme with £180 million invested in health-related projects, which is open to academics and SMEs. Projects include early stage exploration of commercial and technical potential through to proving utility in the field (which may involve human clinical trials) and development of new medicines prior to commercialisation. A number of European organisations such as ERA-Net for Research Programmes on Rare Diseases and the Wellcome Trust's Path Finders programme funds academic–industry partnerships to develop early-stage applied research and development projects in orphan and neglected disease areas. In the US, the National Organization for Rare Disorders (NORD) is a unique federation of voluntary health organisations dedicated to helping people with rare 'orphan' diseases and assisting the organisations that serve them. NORD is committed to the identification, treatment and cure of rare disorders through programmes of education, advocacy, research and service.

6.13.2 Drug therapies and repositioned drugs

6.13.2.1 Nitisinone

One potential drug intervention for AKU is the use of the herbicide nitisinone, for which a 3-year clinical phase II trial in 2009 was completed by the National Human Genome Research Institute (Introne *et al*. 2011). This trial was carried out on 40 AKU patients, 20 taking nitisinone, 20 taking a placebo, and the clinicians tested a series of movements on the patient's joints before, during and at the end of the trial. Although there was some improvement, it was not statistically significant. The report required further clinical evidence (tests of improvement) and trials to demonstrate the positive effects of the drug (see Chapter 4 for further details). The major side-effect is irritation of the cornea, and there is a concern that it will cause the symptoms of hereditary tyrosinaemia type III because of the possible accumulation of tyrosine or other intermediaries (Suwannarat *et al*. 2005). Severe tyrosinaemia can produce liver and kidney damage and mental retardation and if untreated it can be fatal.

6.13.3 Repositioned drugs strategy

Knowledge of the HGO protein structure allows one to understand mechanistic interactions in *in vitro* studies, such as structure–enzyme activity relationships of drugs–enzyme interactions (e.g. as allosteric activators of enzyme activity). The structure also permits *in silico* screening and design of novel drugs using computational approaches, such as virtual screening. An excellent review by Ekins *et al.* (2011) summarises *in silico* repositioning of approved drugs for rare and neglected diseases.

In March 2012, the AKU Society partnered with Lumophore Ltd, a specialised drug repositioning company in rare and neglected diseases, to investigate drug repositioning as a strategy for AKU (Fig. 6.5B, see also Table 6.3). The presence of highly active recombinant human HGO and a miniaturised assay, previously developed by PTL, were key prerequisites for screening for allosteric activators of HGO. The compounds used for the screening against HGO were previously FDA-approved and patent -expired drugs. The screening of 1,000 drugs resulted in the identification of three drug candidates which increased the enzymatic activity by 20% at 1μM concentration of the drug (Yu-Chen *et al.* 2012). These drugs will be tested further in AKU mouse models to demonstrate reduction of HGA levels in plasma and urine. The fact that these drugs have already been tested in humans, and thus have known toxicity profiles will enable them to be fast-tracked for use in human trials. If successful, such drugs could be used as off-label prescriptions. In the UK, the British General Medical Council stipulates that off-label prescriptions must better serve patient needs than alternatives and must be supported by evidence or experience to demonstrate safety and efficacy. Up to one-fifth of all drugs are prescribed off-label and, among psychiatric drugs, off-label use rises to 31% (Radley *et al.* 2006).

6.14 Drug repositioning businesses

To quote from Melior Discovery's president and CEO, Andrew Reaume (Netterwald 2008):

> Repositioning is not really a new idea. The concept was floated in the early 1990s, but rapidly gained momentum in the post-genomic era when drug developers realised that there are far fewer targets than the 100,000 to 150,000 initially stated. There was not a deep well of targets. So determining how we were going to find new drugs became a big dilemma for the industry and repositioning became one of the answers.

A number of big pharmaceutical companies are investing into therapies for rare diseases, not only because it improves public relations, but it allows much-needed revenue as well. Drug repositioning is an especially attractive commercial proposition because it extends the markets for a compound and finds new uses for near patent and patent-expired drugs at lower financial risk and in a shorter time. For example, FDA approval of Eli Lilly's Cymbalta (duloxetine), a serotonin-norepine-phrine reuptake inhibitor for fibromyalgia, offers another example of a successful drug repositioning programme. Initially developed as an antidepressant, the FDA approved its use for fibromyalgia, a chronic pain disorder, in 2008 (Lilly 2008; Russell *et al.* 2008). Sanofi Aventis has formed a dedicated Systems Biology team headed by Dr Edgardo Ferran based in Toulouse, France. The group has focused on drug repositioning for tuberculosis, malaria, trypanosomiasis and leishmaniasis, using *in-silico* methods, complemented with phenotypic experimental testing. Table 6.3 summarises the repositioned drugs that have come out of large pharmaceutical companies up to 2004.

Table 6.3 **Selected long-standing pharmaceuticals that had been repositioned during or prior to 2004**

Source: Reprinted by permission from Macmillan Publishers Ltd on behalf of Cancer Research UK: *Nature Reviews Drug Discovery*; T.T., Ashburn and K.B. Thor, 'Drug Repositioning: Identifying and Developing New Uses for Existing Drugs', *Nature Reviews Drug Discovery* 3.8: 673-83. Copyright 2004.

Generic name	Trade name, original indication (originator)	Trade name, repositioned indication (repositioner)
Celecoxib	Celebrex, osteoarthritis and rheumatoid arthritis (Pfizer)	Celebrex, familial adenomatous polyposis, colon and breast cancer
Minoxidil	Trade name N/A, hypertension (Pharmacia & Upjohn)	Rogaine, hair loss (Pfizer)
Topiramate	Topamax, epilepsy (Johnson & Johnson)	Trade name N/A, obesity (Johnson & Johnson)
Lidocaine	Xilocaine, local anaesthesia (AstraZeneca)	Trade name N/A, oral corticosteroid-dependent asthma (Corus Pharma)
Buproprion	Wellbutrin, depression (GlaxoSmithKline)	Zyban, smoking cessation (GlaxoSmithKline)
Fluoxetine	Prozac, depression (Eli Lilly)	Sarafem, premenstrual dysphoria (Eli Lilly)
Duloxetine	Cymbalta, depression (Eli Lilly)	Duloxetine SUI, stress urinary incontinence (Eli Lilly)

Such rich pickings are not restricted to the big pharma; a number of university-based spin-offs and small biotech businesses have been launched with a central focus on drug repositioning. This has been made possible by the relatively low costs of screening, as some compound libraries are commercially available and only a few thousand compounds are required for screening, negating the need for expensive liquid handling/robotic systems. Some new and upcoming drug repositioning companies are listed in Table 6.4, together with their disease target areas, and some examples are discussed further, below.

SOM Biotech is a Spanish drug repositioning company established at the Barcelona Science Park. The company has focused on pre-clinical validation, patenting and licensing of already known drugs for their commercial use in rare diseases. These include psoriasis, TTR amyloidosis, glioblastoma and T-cell lymphoma (Som Biotech 2011). The company utilises a proprietary virtual screening platform, based on an *in-silico* computer-modelling approach and the drug development is driven by a dedicated team of experts and strategy advisers.

In terms of Western diseases, a larger number of repositioning companies have emerged. For example, the US-based drug repositioning company, BioVista, has focused on eye disorders, diabetes (macular degeneration, glaucoma and diabetic retinopathy), obesity, CNS and oncology. They have discovered 12 drugs with significant potential in Parkinson's, Alzheimer's, epilepsy, depression and sleep

Table 6.4 **Examples of drug repositioning companies**

Drug repositioning company	Drug repositioning activity	Company location
Advinus Therapeutics	Diabetes, obesity, chronic obstructive pulmonary disease (COPD), irritable bowel syndrome (IBS), Parkinson's disease, leishmaniasis, dengue fever, tuberculosis, leprosy and malaria	Pune, India, www.advinus.com
BioVista	Eye disorders, diabetes, diabetes/obesity, CNS, oncology	Virginia, USA www.biovista.com
DesignMedix	Antimalarials and antimicrobials (e.g. MRSA)	Oregon, USA www.designmedix.com
Galapagos NV	Rheumatoid arthritis and orphan diseases (cystic fibrosis)	Mechelen, Belgium www.glpg.com
H.M. Pharma	Consultancy offering drug reposition services, specialist in CNS, eye disorders and cardiorespiratory medicine	Vienna, Austria www.hmpharmacon.com
Lumophore Ltd	Antimicrobials (e.g. MRSA, *C. albicans* and *E.coli*), antimalarials and rare diseases (alkaptonuria)	Manchester, UK www.lumophore.com
Medivir	Hepatitis C virus (HCV)	Stockholm, Sweden www.medivir.se/v4/en
Melior Discovery	Diabetes, IBS, atopic dermatitis	Pennsylvania, USA www.meliordiscovery.com
Napo Pharmaceuticals	HIV/AIDS, chronic diarrhoea, irritable bowel syndrome and cholera	California, USA www.napopharma.com
PharmaKure Ltd	Alzheimer's, diabetes and tuberculosis (TB)	Manchester, UK www.pharmakure.com
PolyMedix Inc	Antimicrobials, malaria, TB, cancer and cardiovascular	Pennsylvania, USA www.polymedix.com
Sequella, Inc.	TB, *H. pylori* infections, *C. difficile* and Crohn's disease	Maryland, USA www.sequella.com
Sosei	COPD, oropharyngeal candidiasis	Tokyo, Japan www.sosei.com
SOM Biotech	Psoriasis, TTR amyloidosis, glioblastoma, T-cell lymphoma	Barcelona, Spain www.sombiotech.com
Tau Therapeutics	Broad spectrum of anti-cancer	Virginia, USA www.tautherapeutics.com
Verva Pharmaceuticals	Diabetes and obesity	Melbourne, Australia www.vervapharma.com
Vichem Chemie Ltd	Oncological kinase targets (e.g. EGFR, Aurora, mTOR, Axl and FGFR), infectious disease targets (influenza, HIV, tuberculosis) and CNS/inflammatory targets (epilepsy, neurogenic, rheumatoid arthritis)	Budapest, Hungary www.vichem.hu

disorders. The company is in the process of filing for novel use patents for these drugs. BioVista's core strategy is on potential therapies for the new indications and to ensure that there is no prior art in the patent or scientific literature linking them to the new indications. In addition, they screen for at least equivalent efficacy with current standards of treatment, and with equal or lower risk profiles.

Melior Discovery has taken the drug MLR-1023 to a clinical stage ready to enter phase II studies for type 2 diabetes (Lilly 2008; Russell *et al.* 2008). The drug is a potential 'next generation' insulin sensitiser that works independently of a PPAR mechanism. MLR-1023 is a potent and selective allosteric activator of lyn kinase *in vitro* that improves glucose tolerance *in vivo*. MLR-1023 was formerly in development by Pfizer as an antiulcer compound in the 1970s, but clinical development was halted for lack of efficacy in phase II (Saporito *et al.* 2012). The drug, however, was shown to be safe and well tolerated in several clinical trials. Analysis of blood glucose in those trials provides an early, statistically significant, indication that the drug has therapeutic potential towards diabetes (Saporito *et al.* 2012).

Sosei is a Japanese drug company which has also identified new uses for established drugs and has exploited its unique position within Japanese, European and North American pharmaceutical markets by acquiring compounds from, and bringing compounds into, Japan. It has developed two drugs for chronic obstructive pulmonary disease. NorLevo® is its oral emergency contraceptive, containing only levonorgestrel as an active ingredient.[2]

Tau Therapeutics is developing oncology drugs for solid tumours that selectively inhibit the T-type calcium channel. The company's approach, called Interlaced Therapy™, capitalises on the central role of calcium influx through T-type calcium channels during cancer cell growth.[3] T-type calcium channel blockade with Tau's drugs is intended to arrest tumour cells at their most vulnerable metabolic point in the cell cycle, uniquely amplifying the effects of conventional therapies and overcoming drug resistance. Tau's first product candidate, mibefradil, was originally developed by Roche for the treatment of hypertension and chronic angina pectoris. It has been used extensively in humans and its safety profile is well known. Mibefradil is now entering clinical trials for brain cancer with support from the National Cancer Institute.

PharmaKure is newly launched repositioning company, based in the UK, which is a spin-off from the University of Manchester.[4] The company's primary focus is on Alzheimer's disease by discovering new uses for old drugs, which offers great promise for quickly bringing new therapeutic options to patient care. PharmaKure has patented its first drug, A-77636, for the treatment of Alzheimer's disease (Modak *et al.* 2012). A-77636 was first discovered in the 1980s, as a possible treatment for Parkinson's disease and cocaine addiction, by Abbott Laboratories, though it has never been previously tested for Alzheimer's (Kebabian *et al.* 1992). The drug was

---

2 www.sosei.com/en, accessed 6 December 2012.
3 www.tautherapeutics.com, accessed 6 December 2012.
4 www.pharmakure.com, accessed 6 December 2012.

tested in cell-based assays and has demonstrated inhibition of β-amyloid cell toxicity. Importantly, previous data from animal trials have shown that the drug is orally active, non-toxic and crosses the blood–brain barrier in primate brains, a crucial requirement for an Alzheimer's drug. In addition, PharmaKure's approach of drug screening using cell-based models for AD has led to the identification of a number of promising hits and analogues which will further increase the company's success and product portfolio.

In addition, specialist consultancy companies such as H.M. Pharma, based in Austria, are leaders in the business of drug repositioning.[5] Their services include surveying markets for unmet therapeutic needs, business risk assessment, comprehensive assistance with writing patent applications, freedom-to-operate searches and drafting replies to patent offices.

6.15 Conclusion

Existing drugs have been shown to be safe in patients, so if these drugs could be found to work for other diseases, especially for neglected and rare diseases, then this would dramatically reduce drug development costs, timelines and risks, creating a huge investment potential, too. The 'repositioning methodology' has now been adopted as a mainstream strategy in major drug companies with many successfully launched drugs. In particular, the strategy is well suited to smaller companies as the numbers of existing and ex-patent drugs are relatively small. Company partnerships with academic institutes coupled with government funding and charities have led to successful drug candidates for a number of diseases, and this trend is set to grow. As such, the future of cost-effective and accelerated discovery for neglected and rare diseases and indeed for many other diseases is assured and bright.

References

Adams, C.P., and V.V. Brantner (2006) 'Estimating the Cost of New Drug Development: Is it Really $802 million?' *Health Affairs* 25.2: 420-28.

Adams, C.P., and V.V. Brantner (2010) 'Spending on New Drug Development', *Health Economics* 19.2: 130-41.

Aftab, B.T., I. Dobromilskaya, J.O. Liu and C.M. Rudin (2011) 'Itraconazole Inhibits Angiogenesis and Tumor Growth in Non–Small Cell Lung Cancer', *Cancer Research* 71.21: 6764-72.

Alazraki, M. (2011) 'The 10 Biggest Selling Drugs That Are About To Lose Their Patent', Daily Finance, An AOL Money & Finance Site, www.dailyfinance.com/2011/02/27/top-selling-drugs-are-about-to-lose-patent-protection-ready, accessed 15 January 2013.

5 www.hmpharmacon.com, accessed 6 December 2012.

Amy, M. (2012) 'Phase 3 Trial of Ceftriaxone in ALS Stopped', *MDA/ALS News Magazine* 17.4 (Oct-Dec 2012).

Angell, M. (2005) *The Truth about the Drug Companies: How they deceive us and what to do about it* (New York: Random House Inc).

Ashburn, T.T., and K.B. Thor (2004) 'Drug Repositioning: Identifying and Developing New Uses for Existing Drugs', *Nature Reviews Drug Discovery* 3.8: 673-83.

Astra-Zeneca (2011) 'Ground Breaking Scientific Collaboration Gives UK Academia Access to Compounds to Advance Medical Research', www.astrazeneca.com/Media/Press-releases/ Article/20110512-groundbreaking-scientific-collaboration-and-uk-academia, accessed 6 December 2012.

Bachmann, C., J. Colombo and K. Jaggi (1982) 'N-acetylglutamate Synthetase (NAGS) Deficiency: Diagnosis, Clinical Observations and Treatment', *Advances in Experimental Medicine and Biology* 153: 39.

Bax, R., N. Mullan and J. Verhoef (2000) 'The Millennium Bugs: The Need for and Development of New Antibacterials', *International Journal of Antimicrobial Agents* 16.1: 51.

Beutler, E., (2006) 'Lysosomal Storage Diseases: Natural History and Ethical and Economic Aspects', *Molecular Genetics and Metabolism* 88.3: 208-15.

Bickel, H., C. Bachmann, R. Beckers, N.J. Brandt, B.E. Clayton, G. Corrado, H.J. Feingold, O. Giardini, G. Hammersen and D. Schönberg (1981) 'Neonatal Mass Screening for Metabolic Disorders', *European Journal of Pediatrics* 137.2: 133-39.

Burton, B.K., D.K. Grange, A. Milanowski, G. Vockley, F. Feillet, E.A. Crombez, V. Abadie, C.O. Harding, S. Cederbaum, D. Dobbelaere, A. Smith and A. Dorenbaum (2007) 'The Response of Patients with Phenylketonuria and Elevated Serum Phenylalanine to Treatment with Oral Sapropterin Dihydrochloride (6R-tetrahydrobiopterin): A Phase II, Multicentre, Open-Label, Screening Study', *Journal of Inherited Metabolic Disease* 30.5: 700-707.

Chong, C.R., and D.J. Sullivan (2007) 'New Uses for Old Drugs', *Nature* 448: 645-46.

Chong, C.R., X. Chen, L. Shi, J.O. Liu and D.J. Sullivan Jr (2006) 'A Clinical Drug Library Screen Identifies Astemizole as an Antimalarial Agent', *Nature Chemical Biology* 2.8: 415-16.

Chong, C.R., J. Xu, J. Lu, S. Bhat, D.J. Sullivan Jr and J.O. Liu (2007) 'Inhibition of Angiogenesis by the Antifungal Drug Itraconazole', *ACS Chemical Biology* 2.4: 263-70.

Coates, A., Y. Hu, R. Bax and C. Page (2002) 'The Future Challenges Facing the Development of New Antimicrobial Drugs', *Nature Reviews Drug Discovery* 1.11: 895-910.

Connock, M., A. Burls, E. Frew, A. Fry-Smith, A. Juarez-Garcia, C. McCabe, A. Wailoo, K. Abrams, N. Cooper, A. Sutton, A. O'Hagan and D. Moore (2006) 'The Clinical Effectiveness and Cost-effectiveness of Enzyme Replacement Therapy for Gaucher's Disease: A Systematic Review', *Health Technology Assessment* 10.24: 3-4, 9-136.

DiMasi, J.A., H.G. Grabowski and J. Vernon (2004) 'R&D Costs and Returns by Therapeutic Category', *Drug Information Journal* 38.3: 211-23.

DiMasi, J.A., R.W. Hansen and H.G. Grabowski (2003) 'The Price of Innovation: New Estimates of Drug Development Costs', *Journal of Health Economics* 22.2: 151-85.

Drews, J. (2003) 'Strategic Trends in the Drug Industry', *Drug Discovery Today* 8.9: 411-20.

Ekins, S., and A.J. Williams (2011) 'Finding Promiscuous Old Drugs for New Uses', *Pharmaceutical Research*: 1-7.

Ekins, S., A.J. Williams, M.D. Krasowski and J.S. Freundlich (2011) 'In Silico Repositioning of Approved Drugs for Rare and Neglected Diseases', *Drug Discovery Today* 16.7: 298-310.

Enns, G.M., R. Koch, V. Brumm, E. Blakely, R. Suter and E. Jurecki (2010) 'Suboptimal Outcomes in Patients with PKU Treated Early with Diet alone: Revisiting the Evidence', *Molecular Genetics and Metabolism* 101.2: 99-109.

Enzo Life Sciences (2012) 'FDA Approved Drug Library', www.enzolifesciences.com/BML-2841/fda-approved-drug-library, accessed 30 January 2012.

Eurordis (2005) 'Rare Diseases: Understanding this Public Health Priority, 2005', www.eurordis.org/ IMG/pdf/princeps_document-EN.pdf, accessed 15 January 2013.

European Commission (2009) 'Useful Information on Rare Diseases From an EU Perspective', ec.europa.eu/health/ph_information/documents/ev20040705_rd05_en.pdf, accessed 6 December 2012.

FDA (2009) 'New Molecular Entity Approvals for 2009', www.fda.gov/downloads/Drugs/DevelopmentApprovalProcess/HowDrugsareDevelopedandApproved/DrugandBiologic ApprovalReports/UCM091096, accessed 26 January 2012.

FDA (2010) 'New Molecular Entity approvals for 2010', www.fda.gov/Drugs/Development ApprovalProcess/HowDrugsareDevelopedandApproved/DrugandBiologicApprovalReports/ ucm242674.htm, accessed 26 January 2012.

FDA (2011) 'New Molecular Entity Approvals for 2011', www.fda.gov/Drugs/Development ApprovalProcess/DrugInnovation/ucm285554.htm, accessed 26 January 2012.

Fonseca, A.C., R. Resende, C.R. Oliveira and C.M. Pereira (2010) 'Cholesterol and Statins in Alzheimer's Disease: Current Controversies', *Experimental Neurology* 223.2: 282-93.

Fox, S., S. Farr-Jones, L. Sopchak, A. Boggs, H.W. Nicely, R. Khoury and M. Biros (2006) 'High-Throughput Screening: Update on Practices and Success', *Journal of Biomolecular Screening* 11.7: 864-69.

Gao, X., H. Chen, M.A. Schwarzschild and A. Ascherio (2011) 'Use of Ibuprofen and Risk of Parkinson Disease', *Neurology* 76.10: 863-69.

Gaucher, P.C.E. (1882) *De l'epithélioma primitif de la rate: hypertrophie idiopathique de la rate sans leucémie* (Paris: Octave Doin).

Gilbert, D.N., R.J. Guidos, H.W. Boucher, G.H. Talbot, B. Spellberg, J.E. Edwards Jr, W.M. Scheld, J.S. Bradley and J.G. Bartlett (Infectious Diseases Society of America) (2010) 'The 10 × '20 Initiative: Pursuing a Global Commitment to Develop 10 New Antibacterial Drugs by 2020', *Clinical Infectious Diseases* 50.8: 1081-83.

Gohara, D.W., and E. Di Cera (2011) 'Allostery in Trypsin-Like Proteases Suggests New Therapeutic Strategies', *Trends in Biotechnology* 29.11: 577-85.

Grabowski, G.A., (2008) 'Phenotype, Diagnosis, and Treatment of Gaucher's Disease', *The Lancet* 372.9645: 1263-71.

Grau, D., and G. Serbedzija (2005) 'Innovative Strategies for Drug Repurposing', *Drug Discovery & Development* 8.5: 56-61.

Haupt, V.J., and M. Schroeder (2011) 'Old Friends in New Guise: Repositioning of Known Drugs with Structural Bioinformatics', *Briefings in Bioinformatics* 12.4: 312-26.

Huang, R., N. Southall, Y. Wang, A. Yasgar, P. Shinn, A. Jadhav, D.T. Nguyen and C.P. Austin (2011) 'The NCGC Pharmaceutical Collection: A Comprehensive Resource of Clinically Approved Drugs Enabling Repurposing and Chemical Genomics', *Science Translation Medicine* 3.80: 80ps16.

IMS Institute for Healthcare Informatics (2011) 'The Use of Medicines in the United States: Review of 2010', www.imshealth.com/imshealth/Global/Content/IMS%20Institute/Documents/ IHII_UseOfMed_report%20.pdf, accessed 6 December 2012.

Introne, W.J., M.B. Perry, J. Troendle, E. Tsilou, M.A. Kayser, P. Suwannarat, K.E. O'Brien, J. Bryant, V. Sachdev, J.C. Reynolds, E. Moylan, I. Bernardini and W.A. Gahl (2011) 'A 3-year Randomized Therapeutic Trial of Nitisinone in Alkaptonuria', *Molecular Genetics and Metabolism* 103.4: 307-14.

JHSPH (Johns Hopkins Bloomberg School of Public Health) (2012) 'US Tox21 to Begin Screening 10,000 Chemicals', altweb.jhsph.edu/news/current/tox21screening.html, 30 January 2012.

Johnson, I.S. (1983) 'Human Insulin from Recombinant DNA Technology', *Science* 219.4585: 632-37.

Kafetzis, D.A., I.M. Velissariou, S. Stabouli, M. Mavrikou, D. Delis and G. Liapi (2005) 'Treatment of Paediatric Visceral Leishmaniasis: Amphotericin B or Pentavalent Antimony Compounds?' *International Journal of Antimicrobial Agents* 25.1: 26-30.

Kasapi, Z., and A. Mihiotis (2011) 'Management as Applied to New Products Penetration in the Competitive Environment of Pharmaceutical Industry', *Interdisciplinary Journal of Research in Business* 1.10: 73-85.

Kebabian, J.W., D.R. Britton, M.P. DeNinno, R. Perner, L. Smith, P. Jenner, R. Schoenleber and M. Williams (1992) 'A-77636: A Potent and Selective Dopamine D1 Receptor Agonist with Antiparkinsonian Activity in Marmosets', *European Journal of Pharmacology* 229.2: 203-209.

Keserü, G.M., and G.M. Makara (2009) 'The Influence of Lead Discovery Strategies on the Properties of Drug Candidates', *Nature Reviews Drug Discovery* 8.3: 203-12.

Kinnings, S.L., N. Liu, N. Buchmeier, P.J. Tonge, L. Xie and P.E. Bourne (2009) 'Drug Discovery Using Chemical Systems Biology: Repositioning the Safe Medicine Comtan to Treat Multi-Drug and Extensively Drug Resistant Tuberculosis', *PLoS Computational Biology* 5.7: e1000423.

Lekka, E., S.N. Deftereos, A. Persidis, A. Persidis and C. Andronis (2011) 'Literature Analysis for Systematic Drug Repurposing: A Case Study from Biovista', *Drug Discovery Today: Therapeutic Strategies* 8.3-4: 103-108.

Light, D.W., and R. Warburton (2011) 'Demythologizing the High Costs of Pharmaceutical Research', *BioSocieties* 6.1: 34-50.

Eli Lilly and Company (2008) 'FDA Approves Cymbalta for the Management of Fibromyalgia', press release, 16 June 2008, newsroom.lilly.com/releasedetail.cfm?releaseid=316740, accessed 15 January 2013.

Lipinski, C.A., F. Lombardo, B.W. Dominy and P.J. Feeney (2001) 'Experimental and Computational Approaches to Estimate Solubility and Permeability in Drug Discovery and Development Settings', *Advanced Drug Delivery Reviews* 46.1-3: 3-26.

Macarron, R. (2006) 'Critical Review of the Role of HTS in Drug Discovery', *Drug Discovery Today* 11.7-8: 277-79.

Macarron, R., M.N. Banks, D. Bojanic, D.J. Burns, D.A. Cirovic, T. Garyantes, D.V. Green, R.P. Hertzberg, W.P. Janzen, J.W. Paslay, U. Schopfer and G.S. Sittampalam (2011) 'Impact of High-Throughput Screening in Biomedical Research', *Nature Reviews Drug Discovery* 10.3: 188-95.

Mackey, Z.B., A.M. Baca, J.P. Mallari, B. Apsel, A. Shelat, E.J. Hansell, P.K. Chiang, B. Wolff, K.R. Guy, J. Williams and J.H. McKerrow (2006) 'Discovery of Trypanocidal Compounds by Whole Cell HTS of *Trypanosoma brucei*', *Chemical Biology & Drug Design* 67.5: 355-63.

Martis, E., R. Radhakrishnan and R. Badve (2011) 'High-Throughput Screening: The Hits and Leads of Drug Discovery-An Overview', *Journal of Applied Pharmaceutical Science* 1.1: 2-10.

Meikle, P.J., J.J. Hopwood, A.E. Clague and W.F. Carey (1999) 'Prevalence of Lysosomal Storage Disorders', *Journal of the American Medical Association* 281.3: 249-54.

MicroSource Discovery Systems (2012) 'Microsource Library', www.msdiscovery.com, accessed 30 January 2012.

Miller, S.C., R. Huang, S. Sakamuru, S.J. Shukla, M.S. Attene-Ramos, P. Shinn, D. Van Leer, W. Leister, C.P. Austin and M. Xia (2010) 'Identification of Known Drugs that Act as Inhibitors of NF-κB Signaling and their Mechanism of Action', *Biochemical Pharmacology* 79.9: 1272-80.

Moellering, R.C. (2011) 'Discovering New Antimicrobial Agents', *International Journal of Antimicrobial Agents* 37.1: 2-9.

Monod, J., J. Wyman and J.P. Changeux (1965) 'On the Nature of Allosteric Transitions: A Plausible Model', *Journal of Molecular Biology* 12: 88.

Morizono, H., L. Caldovic, D. Shi and M. Tuchman (2004) 'Mammalian N-acetylglutamate Synthase', *Molecular Genetics and Metabolism* 81: 4-11.

Mullard, A. (2011) 'Could Pharma Open its Drug Freezers?' *Nature Reviews Drug Discovery* 10.6: 399-400.

Muthyala, R., (2011) 'Orphan/Rare Drug Discovery through Drug Repositioning', *Drug Discovery Today: Therapeutic Strategies* 8.3-4: 71–76.

Netterwald, J., (2008) 'Recycling existing drugs', *Drug Discovery & Development*, January 2008: 1.

Neumann, C., (2010) *Variations Effect of β-lactam-antibiotic Ceftriaxone in Experimental Stroke and its Influence on Astrocytic Glutamate Transporter GLT-1* (dissertation; Berlin: Freie Universität Berlin).

Norrby, S.R., C.E. Nord and R. Finch (2005) 'Lack of Development of New Antimicrobial Drugs: A Potential Serious Threat to Public Health', *The Lancet Infectious Diseases* 5.2: 115.

O'Connor, K.A., and B.L. Roth (2005) 'Finding New Tricks for Old Drugs: An Efficient Route for Public-Sector Drug Discovery', *Nature Reviews Drug Discovery* 4.12: 1005-14.

Oprea, T.I., J.E. Bauman, C.G. Bologa, T. Buranda, A. Chigaev, B.S. Edwards, J.W. Jarvik, H.D. Gresham, M.K. Haynes, B. Hjelle, R. Hromas, L. Hudson, D.A. Mackenzie, C.Y. Muller, J.C. Reed, P.C. Simons, Y. Smagley, J. Strouse, Z. Surviladze, T. Thompson, O. Ursu, A. Waller, A. Wandinger-Ness, S.S. Winter, Y. Wu, S.M. Young, R.S. Larson, C. Willman and L.A. Sklar (2011) 'Drug Repurposing from an Academic Perspective', *Drug Discovery Today: Therapeutic Strategies* 8: 61-69.

Padhy, B., and Y. Gupta (2011) 'Drug Repositioning: Re-investigating Existing Drugs for New Therapeutic Indications', *Journal of Postgraduate Medicine* 57.2: 153.

Parker, C.N., and J. Bajorath (2006) 'Towards Unified Compound Screening Strategies: A Critical Evaluation of Error Sources in Experimental and Virtual High-Throughput Screening', *QSAR & Combinatorial Science* 25.12: 1153-61.

Paul, S.-K. (2007) 'Drug Repurposing', www.msi.co.uk/drug-repurposing, accessed 26 January 2012.

Paul, S.M., D.S. Mytelka, C.T. Dunwiddie, C.C. Persinger, B.H. Munos, S.R. Lindborg and A.L. Schacht (2010) 'How to Improve R&D Productivity: The Pharmaceutical Industry's Grand Challenge', *Nature Reviews Drug Discovery* 9.3: 2.

Piscopo, T.V., and C. Mallia Azzopardi (2007) 'Leishmaniasis', *Postgraduate Medical Journal* 83.976: 649-57.

Porto, C., M. Cardone, F. Fontana, B. Rossi, M.R. Tuzzi, A. Tarallo, M.V. Barone, G. Andria and G. Parenti (2009) 'The Pharmacological Chaperone N-butyldeoxynojirimycin Enhances Enzyme Replacement Therapy in Pompe Disease Fibroblasts', *Molecular Therapy* 17.6: 964-71.

Powers, J., (2004) 'Antimicrobial Drug Development: The Past, the Present, and the Future', *Clinical Microbiology and Infection* 10.s4: 23-31.

Prestwick Chemical Library (2006) 'Prestwick Chemical Library', www.prestwickchemical.com/index.php?pa=26, accessed 30 January 2012.

Radley, D.C., S.N. Finkelstein and R.S. Stafford (2006) 'Off-label Prescribing among Office-Based Physicians', *Archives of Internal Medicine* 166.9: 1021.

Rasch William, P.D. (2012) 'Antidepressant Drug Market', www.wikinvest.com/concept/Antidepressant_Drug_Market, accessed 26 January 2012.

Renaud, R.C., and H. Xuereb (2002) 'Erectile-Dysfunction Therapies', *Nature a-z index* 1.9: 663-64.

Rodriguez, J.M., D.E. Timm, G.P. Titus, D. Beltrán-Valero De Bernabé, O. Criado, H.A. Mueller, S. Rodríguez De Córdoba and M.A. Peñalva (2000) 'Structural and Functional Analysis of Mutations in Alkaptonuria', *Human Molecular Genetics* 9.15: 2341-50.

Rothstein, J.D., S. Patel, M.R. Regan, C. Haenggeli, Y.H. Huang, D.E. Bergles, L. Jin, M. Dykes Hoberg, S. Vidensky, D.S. Chung, S.V. Toan, L.I. Bruijn, Z.Z. Su, P. Gupta and P.B. Fisher (2005) 'β-Lactam Antibiotics Offer Neuroprotection by Increasing Glutamate Transporter Expression', *Nature* 433.7021: 73-77.

Russell, I.J., P.J. Mease, T.R. Smith, D.K. Kajdasz, M.M. Wohlreich, M.J. Detke, D.J. Walker, A.S. Chappell and L.M. Arnold (2008) 'Efficacy and Safety of Duloxetine for Treatment of Fibromyalgia in Patients with or without Major Depressive Disorder: Results from a 6-month, Randomized, Double-Blind, Placebo-Controlled, Fixed-Dose Trial', *Pain* 136.3: 432-44.

Modak, S., A.J. Doig and F. Khan (2012) 'New Therapeutic use: field of invention: A-77636 for the treatment of diseases or conditions that are associated with β-amyloid induced toxicity, such as Alzheimer's disease', UK Patent Application Office; application number 1206984.5.

Santos-Sierra, S., J. Kirchmair, A.M. Perna, D. Reiss, K. Kemter, W. Röschinger, H. Glossmann, S.W. Gersting, A.C. Muntau, G. Wolber and F.B. Lagler (2012) 'Novel Pharmacological Chaperones that Correct Phenylketonuria in Mice', *Human Molecular Genetics* 21.8: 1877-87.

Saporito, M.S., A.R. Ochman, C.A. Lipinski, J.A. Handler and A.G. Reaume (2012) 'MLR-1023 is a Potent and Selective Allosteric Activator of Lyn Kinase in vitro that Improves Glucose Tolerance *in vivo*', *Journal of Pharmacology and Experimental Therapeutics* 342.1: 15-22.

Sardana, D., C. Zhu, M. Zhang, R.C. Gudivada, L. Yang and A.G. Jegga (2011) 'Drug Repositioning for Orphan Diseases', *Briefings in Bioinformatics* 12.4: 346-56.

Shahinas, D., M. Liang, A. Datti and D.R. Pillai (2010) 'A Repurposing Strategy Identifies Novel Synergistic Inhibitors of Plasmodium falciparum Heat Shock Protein 90', *Journal of Medicinal Chemistry* 53.9: 3552-57.

Shim, H. (2011) 'One Target, Different Effects: A Comparison of Distinct Therapeutic Antibodies against the Same Targets', *Experimental & Molecular Medicine* 43.10: 539-49.

Sigma-Aldrich (2012) 'Validation Libraries', www.sigmaaldrich.com/chemistry/drug-discovery/validation-libraries.html, accessed 2 February 2012.

SIOP Europe (2009) 'Rare Diseases', www.siope.eu/SIOPE-EU/English/SIOPE-EU/Advocacy-Activities/Rare-Diseases/page.aspx/148, accessed 6 December 2012.

Sleigh, S.H., and C.L. Barton (2010) 'Repurposing Strategies for Therapeutics', *Pharmaceutical Medicine* 24.3: 151-59.

Smith, R.D. and J. Coast (2002) 'Antimicrobial Resistance: A Global Response', *Bulletin of the World Health Organization* 80.2: 126-33.

Som Biotech (2011) 'Pipeline', www.sombiotech.com/index.php?option=com_content&view=article&id=4&Itemid=22.

Suwannarat, P., K. O'Brien, M.B. Perry, N. Sebring, I. Bernardini, M.I. Kaiser-Kupfer, B.I. Rubin, E. Tsilou, L.H. Gerber, W.A. Gahl (2005) 'Use of Nitisinone in Patients with Alkaptonuria', *Metabolism* 54.6: 719-28.

Sweeney, D.D., and M.B. Chancellor (2005) 'Treatment of Stress Urinary Incontinence with Duloxetine Hydrochloride', *Reviews in Urology* 7.2: 81.

Tartaglia, L.A. (2006) 'Complementary New Approaches Enable Repositioning of Failed Drug Candidates', *Expert Opinion on Investigational Drugs* 15.11: 1295-98.

Theuretzbacher, U., (2009) 'Future Antibiotics Scenarios: Is the Tide Starting to Turn?' *International Journal of Antimicrobial Agents* 34.1: 15-20.

Titus, G.P., H.A. Mueller, J. Burgner, S. Rodríguez de Córdoba, M.A. Peñalva and D.E. Timm (2000) 'Crystal Structure of Human Homogentisate Dioxygenase', *Nature Structural & Molecular Biology* 7: 542-46.

von Eichborn, J., M.S. Murgueitio, M. Dunkel, S. Koerner, P.E. Bourne and R. Preissner (2011) 'PROMISCUOUS: A Database for Network-Based Drug-Repositioning', *Nucleic Acids Research* 39 (suppl 1): D1060-66.

Weinreb, N.J. (2008) 'Imiglucerase and its Use for the Treatment of Gaucher's Disease', *Expert Opinion on Pharmacotherapy* 9.11: 1987-2000.

Willmann, J.K., N. van Bruggen, L.M. Dinkelborg and S.S. Gambhir (2008) 'Molecular Imaging in Drug Development', *Nature Reviews Drug Discovery* 7.7: 591-607.

Wang, Y.C. (2012) *Small Drug Activation of Human Homogentisate Dioxygenase: Towards Drug Repositioning for Alkaptonuria* (MSc in Biotechnology and Enterprise, thesis; Manchester, UK: University of Manchester).

Zatková, A., D.B. de Bernabé, H. Poláková, M. Zvarík, E. Feráková, V. Bosák, V. Ferák, L. Kádasi and S.R. de Córdoba (2000) 'High Frequency of Alkaptonuria in Slovakia: Evidence for the Appearance of Multiple Mutations in HGO Involving Different Mutational Hot Spots', *American Journal of Human Genetics* 67.5: 1333.

Priscila del Castillo-Frias is a recent Master's graduate from the University of Manchester in Biotechnology and Enterprise. Her MSc project was on 'finding new antimicrobials through drug repositioning'. She has previously worked for three years as a clinical research associate in monitoring clinical phase 2 and 3 trials. She has a BSc in Pharmacy (at La Salle University, ULSA) and a postgraduate diploma in clinical pharmacology.

Professor **Andrew Doig** graduated in Chemistry from the University of Cambridge, where he stayed to complete his PhD on protein folding and peptide binding with Professor Dudley Williams, FRS, in 1991. He then carried out post-doctoral research in the Biochemistry Department at Stanford with Professor Robert Baldwin before joining UMIST in 1994. He is now a Professor of Biochemistry in the Faculty of Life Sciences at the University of Manchester. In addition to being an expert on Alzheimer's disease and protein structure, Professor Doig was one of the founders of Senexis, a Cambridge-based company focused on novel treatments for diseases resulting from the toxicity of amyloid-like proteins.

Dr **Farid Khan** has several years of running biotech companies and has brought over £5 million of grants and revenue into his business ventures. Recently, in 2009–10 he led his own research group at the University of Manchester in the development of novel molecular diagnostics and prior to this he worked at the Manchester Centre for Integrative Systems Biology. Dr Khan has worked for GlaxoSmithKline in drug discovery, assay development and screening (1997–2000) and obtained his PhD from Cambridge University in biophysics on the structural studies of GFP (2004). Currently, Dr Khan is Chief Scientific Officer of Protein Technologies Ltd (PTL), a biotherapeutic company based in Manchester. Dr Khan's team at PTL has taken the lead in developing a new enzyme replacement therapy for alkaptonuria. Dr Khan is also co-founder and CEO of PharmaKure Ltd, a drug repositioning company focused on finding a cure for Alzheimer's disease. He is named inventor on several patents which span from novel applications of fluorescent proteins, repositioned drugs to smartphone diagnostic devices. He has received multiple Technology Strategy Board awards and Bill & Melinda Gates Foundation grand challenges prizes for his technological innovations. Dr Khan is also a consultant and adviser of new biotechnologies to a number of large pharmaceutical companies and biotech investors and has honorary fellowship positions at the Universities of Manchester and Cambridge.

7

Why patient registries are crucial for finding cures for rare diseases

Pat Furlong
Parent Project Muscular Dystrophy, USA

Kyle Brown
Patient Crossroads, USA

By definition, rare disease populations are small and geographically dispersed. Drug manufacturers will not invest hundreds of millions of dollars in research if rare disease communities are not organised and quantified. Patient registries supported by both industry and patient advocacy organisations are critical to collect natural history information, diagnostic testing results and family history information. The patient community is ready and willing to help researchers understand their disorders and tapping into this valuable resource is critical to understand disease and recruit participants for clinical trials and studies that accelerate research.

Because these disorders are so uncommon, no single institution, and in many cases no single country, has sufficient numbers of patients to conduct generalisable clinical and translational research. Geographic dispersion of patients has been a major impediment to patient recruitment into clinical trials (Rubinstein *et al.* 2012).

A registry is a systematic collection of standardised data on a group of patients. The starting point of a registry is to develop a list of patients. Once a patient group is defined, a variety of different data can be collected. Data can be entered into a registry by patients, clinicians, researchers or directly imported from electronic health records. Scientists and pharmaceutical companies are more likely to conduct research on a given rare disease if they find a patient registry in place. By defining a population of patients, registries enable the formation of various types of research, educational and outcomes improvement infrastructure.

Best estimates are that fewer than 20% of rare diseases have registries, and patients' organisations or academic researchers operate most of these registries. Although many registries are country-specific, there are an increasing number of international efforts that are demonstrating the benefits of combining data across international boundaries by simply translating a single rare disease registry into multiple languages. Allowing international participation in a one-disease-one-registry model ensures the largest number of patients can be included in a single registry programme that can quantify global rare disease patient populations.

In a typical rare disease registry, patients and caregivers opt-in to disease-specific registries, answer a questionnaire regarding their medical history and provide electronic versions of confirmatory testing results. A registry may have a coordinator who verifies the patient submitted information. In this model, information is tracked longitudinally and email reminders can be sent to participants missing testing results or with out-of-date accounts.

Registries can support various types of research, education and outcomes improvement initiatives, including:

- Learn among the community
- Knowledge dissemination
- Encourage research and plan trials
- Recruit patients
- Understand the disease
- Evaluate effectiveness
- Safety monitoring
- Quality and outcomes improvement: treatment, practice, surveillance/monitoring
- Genotype/phenotype associations
- Hub to link other registries, repositories and data sources

The most effective registry programmes allow researchers and clinical investigators to register to gain access to de-identified data through a researcher portal. Interested researchers can register to gain access to data and query tools. De-identified data may be exported to Excel for further research.

No identifying information should be accessible in a researcher portal. If a researcher wishes to contact patients, he or she should contact the source patient registry that maintains the identifying information and the sponsor of those registries would send branded emails to the patients. Response rates and recruitment into trials are more effective when trusted sources such as patient advocacy foundations send the emails on behalf of researchers.

7.1 Involving patients and families

Rare disease research benefits from the active participation of patients and their families. Through tools such as patient-driven registries, individuals and their families are no longer bystanders, passively watching the research process unfold. Today, patients are engaged and empowered to make personal contributions that accelerate discovery and research, and are critical for clinical trials, government intervention, funding, awareness and advocacy. Patient and family involvement is the key determinant of the success of a registry and they are the key beneficiaries of new knowledge.

Patients can join registries and provide detailed medical history, family history and even confirmatory test results. A subset of the collected information can be shared with the international data repositories managed by government and institutional resources. Data shared with international repositories is first de-identified, removing any personal identifiers such as name, address or other information. The goal of these programmes is to share medical information with scientists and other researchers, while still protecting patients' privacy.

Approved scientists and researchers can use the registry data to:

- Study why individuals have different symptoms

- Learn whether treatments work

- Improve the medical care for patients

- Notify participants who may be interested in clinical research studies or clinical trials

Registries should allow patients to state their preference regarding whether they wish to be contacted with information about new research studies/clinical trials from the scientists who use the collected data. Any such messages are sent from the registry coordinators, so that the patient's privacy is protected. Patients can then request additional information from the researcher, if they so choose.

Participants spend valuable time answering the survey questions, so in return de-identified, summarised data should be provided in easy to understand graphs and charts. Patients and families can explore the data in their registry and learn about others with similar diagnosis, treatments or symptoms to better understand how they or their child fits within the disease community. The collected data can be also be used to develop standards of care or care considerations, thereby improving medical care available to patients.

7.2 Patient self-report vs. physician-entered registry strategies

Physician/clinician-entered registries capture patient data about patients directly from healthcare professionals. This method of collecting information can be costly and time consuming, but the data has a higher perceived value to researchers and pharmaceutical companies because a medical professional has validated it.

Patient self-report registries take the approach of allowing patients to opt-in to a registry and provide detailed medical histories and confirmatory testing results themselves. This model results in higher patient participation at a lower cost, but the value of the data is lessened because it was not input by a healthcare professional.

A hybrid approach to capturing patient medical history is quickly gaining acceptance. In the hybrid model, patients provide their medical history and medical professionals ensure accuracy, resulting in larger pools of potential clinical study candidates at a lower overall cost. In this hybrid approach, patients answer a survey regarding their medical history and attach electronic versions of testing results to their profile. Authorised medical professionals (curators) can view and enter patient-provided testing results, review patient data and tag the record for additional testing, follow-up or to confirm the information as clinically validated. This hybrid approach results in greater volumes of clinically validated patient data at a fraction of the cost of clinic data capture systems.

Regardless of the model a registry chooses to utilise, the de-identified patient data should be shared with a globally accessible and shared researcher portal, making this wealth of patient data available to researchers and drug manufacturers for recruiting patients into clinical trials or studies and to follow the natural history of disease.

Registry operators must be able to easily pinpoint clinical trial candidates that meet ever-narrower inclusion criteria. Email reminders can keep patients engaged by reminding participants to provide testing results and to update their profiles periodically. Email newsletters can enable an organisation to keep in contact with registered families informing them of new clinical trials and the latest research findings.

7.2.1 Consent, privacy and ethical considerations

Because patient registries are collecting very detailed, personal medical history and potentially test results, privacy and ethical considerations must be considered before committing to any patient registry programme. Patients are volunteering to join a registry, and if they do not understand the ramifications of participation and how their information is safeguarded, participation rates will be low and lessen the value of the registry programme.

It can be challenging to ensure that participants receive the information and background material necessary to understand and make a fully informed decision to participate in a registry. Materials, such as consent forms and supplemental reading, can help inform both participants and investigators about how participant data may be used.

Participating registries and databases must provide information to participants that explains the purpose and use of data contributed to the registry, the ability of external researchers to access repository data, ownership of the repository data and protection of patient's privacy, among other elements. Informed consent documents developed by the registry should include the agreement by the participant to share their de-identified medical information with other databases for biomedical research.

The consent and privacy considerations vary based on the registry model being implemented. If a registry is based at an academic research organisation, these institutions will often require IRB (institutional review board) approval before collecting any patient data. An IRB will review the consent process and documentation to ensure that patients fully understand their participation in the registry, who will have access to their data and what rights they are assigning to their personal medical information.

IRB approval can take several months to receive based on the use of the patient data and privacy issues with the data collection process. If an academic researcher is hosting and entering data into the patient registry, most certainly the academic institution will require IRB approval before the researcher will be allowed to proceed.

In a patient opt-in registry, managed and hosted by a non-academic institution, the IRB process can be greatly expedited by using an external IRB. These professional IRB organisations can quickly approve patient opt-in registry consent forms, often in a matter of days. If a registry is not managed at an academic institution and patients are opting in to contribute their data, an IRB is not technically required because of the voluntary nature of the registry. However, best practices would suggest an IRB approval should be pursued to ensure that patients fully understand their participation in the programme.

Data security and protection of patient data is critical in any patient registry programme. In clinician/physician-entered patient registries, these organisations often fall into the definition of a 'covered entity' which means they are subject to the Health Insurance Portability and Accountability Act of 1996 (HIPAA) and other government-mandated patient privacy regulations. For patient opt-in registries managed by foundations and other organisations that are not a 'covered entity', security is not mandated by government organisations.

Patient opt-in registries, though not necessarily subject to HIPAA restrictions, should operate using HIPAA and other data security best practices. By operating in a secure manner, these organisations can provide a comfort level to their patients that their information is protected, secure and managed by a trusted organisation that will govern access to their data.

Many countries have varying levels of patient protection requirements. Before implementing any patient registry, organisations should review the requirements in their governing country before accepting any patient data.

7.3 NIH Office of Rare Diseases Research Global Rare Disease Registry case study

Identifying patients and gathering genetic test results and clinical status parameters for many rare diseases is laborious and expensive. The Global Rare Diseases Patient Registry and Data Repository (GRDR) allows any rare disease population, regardless of size, to collect patient data that can identify clinical trial candidates and fuel research. By assembling many small patient registries into a common data repository, economies of scale can be realised and researchers will have the ability to look beyond a single gene/indication which may reveal non-obvious associations between genes and diseases.

The Office of Rare Diseases Research (ORDR) in collaboration with Patient Crossroads, the Children's Hospital of Philadelphia and WebMD, has launched a programme to establish a GRDR to collect de-identified patient clinical information for clinical research. Through the development of this registry database, ORDR can lead the community in establishing a shared, trusted resource of patient natural history information to accelerate research.

The GRDR serves rare disease patients and advocacy groups seeking help and information. It will also serve researchers developing new knowledge, clinicians treating patients, epidemiologists analysing disease data and investigators seeking patients for new clinical trials and initiating natural history studies. GRDR seeks to create private–public partnerships with different sectors of the community including advocacy, research and industry to ensure the long-term sustainability of the registry programme.

The goal of GRDR is to enable analyses of data across many rare diseases and to facilitate clinical trials and other studies. A web-based template allows any patient organisation to establish a rare disease patient registry. Guidance is available to patient groups to establish a registry and to contribute de-identified patient data to the GRDR repository.

A major deliverable of the GRDR programme is to develop a repository of commonly asked patient medical questionnaires that can be leveraged by any group interested in developing a rare disease patient registry. If many registries exist in a single disease, as long as they are collecting the same data, the information can be aggregated into a common repository. If all organisations collecting data in a single disease area collect varying information, there is little hope of sharing this wealth of knowledge. A CDE (common data elements) library will publish commonly used patient-oriented questionnaires so new registries can be deployed faster in a more standardised fashion enabling researchers to collect de-identified data from existing registries through mapping of their data to the CDE.

The GRDR has developed the capability to link patients' data and medical information to donated biospecimens by using a global unique patient identifier. The identifier enables the creation of an interface between the patient registries

that are linked to biorepositories and the Rare Disease Human Biospecimens/
Biorepositories: Rare Disease Hub (RD-HUB).[1]

Figure 7.1 illustrates an overview of the Global Rare Disease Registry and Data
Repository.

Figure 7.1 **GRDR process flow diagram**

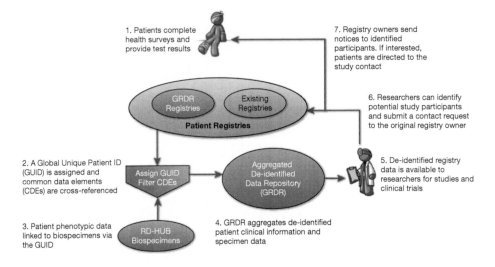

1. Patients complete health surveys and provide test results

7. Registry owners send notices to identified participants. If interested, patients are directed to the study contact

GRDR Registries   Existing Registries

Patient Registries

6. Researchers can identify potential study participants and submit a contact request to the original registry owner

2. A Global Unique Patient ID (GUID) is assigned and common data elements (CDEs) are cross-referenced

Assign GUID Filter CDEs

Aggregated De-identified Data Repository (GRDR)

5. De-identified registry data is available to researchers for studies and clinical trials

3. Patient phenotypic data linked to biospecimens via the GUID

RD-HUB Biospecimens

4. GRDR aggregates de-identified patient clinical information and specimen data

7.4 DuchenneConnect case study

Research activity in Duchenne and Becker muscular dystrophy (DBMD)
has surged in recent years, requiring robust information networks to support therapeutic development... In addition, the publication in 2010 of
care recommendations for Duchenne [Bushby *et al.* 2010a, b] marked a
watershed moment for families affected by and clinicians caring for individuals with DBMD.

This recent progress makes close communication between stakeholders in the DBMD community even more vital, e.g., to disseminate and educate about care recommendations, provide feasibility data to researchers
and industry, collect natural history data, and facilitate recruitment into
research studies. Established by Parent Project Muscular Dystrophy in
late 2007, DuchenneConnect was created to bridge the information gap
between care providers, researchers and the patient community, thereby
addressing medical care needs and accelerating the pace of therapeutic
advancements...

...DuchenneConnect is a patient-report registry and educational
resource for individuals with Duchenne and Becker muscular dystrophy

1 biospecimens.ordr.info.nih.gov, accessed 10 December 2012.

[and] carrier females. [Built using the proven PatientCrossroads self-report registry infrastructure[2]] the registry data is entered by parents/guardians of affected individuals, individuals with DBMD, and rarely by healthcare providers. Each participant's data is accessed through a unique ID and password, which maintains security and allows participants to update their data. Participant data is curated by the DuchenneConnect Coordinator and we request updates to participant profiles every 6–12 months. Data are maintained in a HIPAA-compliant database…

…DuchenneConnect is the largest US-based registry of Duchenne/Becker muscular dystrophy. As of June 2011, the registry represents 1,595 patients with muscular dystrophy, 98 carrier or at-risk females and more than 300 professionals with an interest in muscular dystrophy [see Fig. 7.2]. Of all patient participants, 69% (n = 1,213) have submitted a health history survey. Eighty-six per cent (n = 1,366) of patient participants report having genetic testing, of which 47% (n = 647) have submitted a copy of their genetic test results (Rangel *et al.* 2012).

As of June 2011, the registry data and established patient base have been used to feature 24 clinical trials, and to send targeted notifications regarding 11 studies to 1,416 pre-screened participants.

Figure 7.2 **Examples of patient registry data**

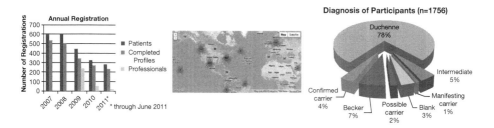

References

Bushby, K., F. Finkel, D.J. Birnkrant, L.E. Case, P.R Clemens, L. Cripe, A. Kaul, K. Kinnett, C. McDonald, S. Pandya, J. Poysky, F. Shapiro, J. Tomezsko and C. Constantin (2010a) 'Diagnosis and Management of Duchenne Muscular Dystrophy, Part 1: Diagnosis, and Pharmacological and Psychosocial Management', *Lancet Neurology* 9: 77-93.

Bushby, K., F. Finkel, D.J. Birnkrant, L.E. Case, P.R. Clemens, L. Cripe, A. Kaul, K. Kinnett, C. McDonald, S. Pandya, J. Poysky, F. Shapiro, J. Tomezsko and C. Constantin (2010b) 'Diagnosis and Management of Duchenne Muscular Dystrophy, Part 2: Implementation of Multidisciplinary Care', *Lancet Neurology* 9: 177-89.

2 www.patientcrossroads.com, accssed 10 December 2012.

Rangel, V., A.S. Martin and H.L. Peay (2012) 'DuchenneConnect Registry Report', *PLoS Currents: Muscular Dystrophy* 4 (http://currents.plos.org/md/article/duchenneconnect-registry-report/, doi: 10.1371/currents.RRN1309, accessed 7 January 2013).

Rubinstein, Y.R., S.C. Groft, S. Hull Chandros, J. Kaneshiro, B. Karp, N.C. Lockhart, P.A. Marshall, R.T. Moxley III, G.B. Pollen, V. Rangel Miller and J. Schwartz (2012) 'Informed Consent Process for Patient Participation in Rare Disease Registries Linked to Biorepositories', *Contemporary Clinical Trials* 33.1: 5-11 (doi: 10.1016/j.cct.2011.10.004).

Pat Furlong is the Founding President and CEO of Parent Project Muscular Dystrophy (PPMD), the largest non-profit organisation in the United States solely focused on Duchenne muscular dystrophy (Duchenne). Their mission is to end Duchenne. They accelerate research, raise their voices in Washington, demand optimal care for all young men, and educate the global community. Duchenne is the most common fatal, genetic childhood disorder, which affects approximately 1 out of every 3,500 boys each year worldwide. It currently has no cure. When doctors diagnosed her two sons, Christopher and Patrick, with Duchenne in 1984, Pat didn't accept 'there's no hope and little help' as an answer. Pat immersed herself in Duchenne, working to understand the pathology of the disorder, the extent of research investment and the mechanisms for optimal care. Her sons lost their battle with Duchenne in their teenage years, but she continues to fight—in their honour and for all families affected by Duchenne. In 1994, Pat, together with other parents of young men with Duchenne, founded PPMD to change the course of Duchenne and, ultimately, to find a cure. Today, Pat continues to lead the organisation and is considered one of the foremost authorities on Duchenne in the world.

Kyle Brown is the founder and CEO of PatientCrossroads, a provider of patient registry solutions to the rare and neglected disease community. PatientCrossroads collects patient-provided medical history and testing results in order to gain insight into disease progression and to recruit patients for inclusion in clinical studies and trials. Kyle is a respected authority on rare disease patient registries and is a frequent speaker at research conferences educating the non-profit and research community on the need for universally accessible, de-identified patient information. Kyle's passion is to change the economics of patient-provided information from closed, proprietary access, to universally available, self-funding programmes that accelerate disease research.

8

Challenges, strategies and lessons learned for the setting up and running of a European Reference Network for rare disease

Samantha Parker
Orphan Europe Recordati Group

Stephen Lynn
Newcastle University, UK

This chapter aims to provide practical guidance in the development and management of European reference networks for rare diseases. Recommendations build on experience gained through the pilot reference networks funded through the European Commission DG Sanco call for proposals 2006–2008. This chapter will give a brief overview of the current legal framework and sources of funding for networks; these topics are evolving rapidly as the European Commission is building European Reference Networks as part of healthcare systems, which will be implemented at a national level. The chapter focuses on addressing a number of challenges, difficulties and solutions in building and managing a multicultural, multi-stakeholder pilot network for one or a group of rare diseases. While recognising that different diseases in different populations will pose different problems, it is hoped that describing experience will assist other groups intending to embark on a similar project.

Figure 8.1 **Vision of what a European reference network could look like**

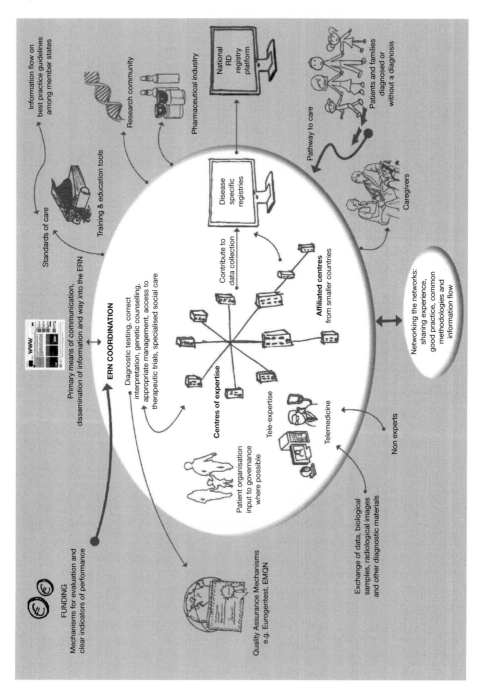

European pilot reference networks for rare diseases are specialised networks of expert centres. They exist because the care of rare disease patients is often based on a single centre's limited experience. Most often evidence-based guidelines do not exist and there is lack of uniformity in clinical practice; there is wide variation in the infrastructure, expertise, resources, access to diagnosis, time to diagnosis, treatment and outcome of patients between European countries. Therefore the philosophy of a network is that all individuals with a rare disease should have equal access to the most up-to-date care and advice wherever they live and it is a specific goal to reach out to underrepresented countries. It is nonetheless recognised that care is massively influenced by national healthcare systems. Shortcomings in the development of national services cannot be fully compensated by networks. Central is also the participation and empowerment of patients and families.

Networks demand a holistic approach and long-term vision with close collaboration between clinicians, diagnostic laboratories, scientists, patients and their families (see Fig. 8.1). Networks should consider the demands of governments, health authorities, healthcare professionals and national rare disease centres of expertise. A secondary target group includes the pharmaceutical industry, which can have a supporting role in: co-funding the network or specific activities, such as registries, through public–private partnerships; know-how in the development of potential new therapies; and management skills. The challenges in managing this complex multi-stakeholder network are commensurately large.

8.1 Background

8.1.1 Legal framework

The concept of a European Reference Network has been developed by the European Commission Communication on rare diseases of 11 November 2008, the Council Recommendation of 9 June 2009 and by Art. 12 of the Directive 2011/24/EU of the European Parliament and of the Council of 9 March 2011 on the application of patients' rights in cross-border healthcare. The cross-border directive gives incentives to Member States to reinforce the continued development of European Reference Networks (ERNs). The directive provides the legal framework in which:

> The Commission shall support Member States in the development of European reference networks between healthcare providers and centres of expertise in the Member States, in particular in the area of rare diseases. The networks shall be based on voluntary participation by its members, which shall participate and contribute to the networks' activities in accordance with the legislation of the Member State where the members are established and shall at all times be open to new healthcare providers which might wish to join them, provided that such healthcare providers fulfil all the required conditions and criteria (Directive 2011/24/EU of the European parliament).

The main goal of this directive is to facilitate improvements in the diagnosis and treatment across the EU by the delivery of high-quality, accessible and cost-effective healthcare for medical conditions requiring concentration of expertise or resources and in conditions where expertise is rare. The Directive is to be transposed by Member States into national law by October 2013. The deployment process on the establishment of the ERNs will take place from the end of 2013 through to 2015. In terms of designation, ERNs for rare diseases (RD) should be as inclusive as possible in terms of number of diseases and number of centres involved, and access to an ERN should be provided to those patients still seeking a diagnosis: diagnostic systemic networks may be prioritised with the long-term aim to cover all RD patient needs. Networks will be required to cross-link with other areas in RD, cancer and other cross-border healthcare-related provisions such as e-health and health technology assessment (HTA). Discussions of the Committee on Cross Border Healthcare are currently confidential.

A parallel group at the EUCERD (European Union Committee of Experts on Rare Diseases) has looked at the experience of EC-funded pilot ERNs. In January 2012, the EUCERD organised a workshop on concepts and criteria for ERN and a scoping paper has been developed to provide advice and recommendations on quality criteria for ERNs to the European Commission.[1] Recommendations of the EUCERD to the European Commission and the Member States on Rare Disease ERNs (RD ERNs) are expected to be adopted by the committee in early 2013. The recommendations propose a structure for the RD ERNs, and have identified a number of components of networking, such as databases, registries, biobanks, tele-expertise tools, guidelines, information packages and training tools covering the medical and social dimensions of diseases. These recommendations are designed to be complementary to the advice of the Cross-Border Healthcare Expert Group on ERNs and will help to develop the specific vision and strategy for RD ERNs.

From the patient perspective, a position paper from EURORDIS Rare Diseases Europe was published in May 2012.[2]

Core to the move from the pilot ERNs to the development of RD ERNs under the terms of the cross-border healthcare directive is the possibility to embed RD ERNs in the healthcare systems of the EU so that the sustainability of such networking is ensured and no longer driven by short-term projects.

8.1.2 Sources of finance

Approximately 15 pilot ERNs have been financed by the European Commission Directorate General for Health and Consumers (DG Sanco) through calls for proposals for pilot projects in 2006 and 2007 and through its operating grants which support the continuation of the pilots and other networks.[3] A number of projects financed through the European Commission Directorate General for Research Framework programmes, although focused on specific research questions, also

---

1 www.eucerd.eu, accessed 10 December 2012.
2 www.eurordis.org, accessed 10 December 2012.
3 A list of the pilot networks is available in EUCERD 2011.

include spin-off networking activities that are similar to the public health networks. Other networks exist, but have not been identified through these sources. Currently the networks funded focus on one or a few related diseases. The setting up and running costs are relatively small, ranging from €400,000 to €1 million for 3 years (Montserrat, personal communication, European Conference on Rare Diseases and Orphan Drugs (ECRD), May 2012).

Limited resources have meant that in 2013 some of these pilot networks are no longer funded by the European Commission. Either these networks will stop functioning or will continue to work with reduced activity. There is concern that less developed countries or structures will be most disadvantaged when having to find national or local funding.

There are an estimated 6,000–7,000 rare diseases. The patient federation EURORDIS states in its position paper that all rare disease patients should be covered by at least one ERN and no patient should be left outside. Therefore current policy is debating the advantages and disadvantages of an overarching network to cover a cluster of RD into diagnostic systemic areas. This would mean that a limited number of ERNs for RD will be financed in the 3rd Health Programme of the European Commission Directorate General for Health and Consumers (2014–2020) 'Health for Growth'. The networking activities of the ERN could be financed at a European level while the Member States finance their centres of expertise including active participation of the centre of expertise to attend meetings and workshops. At this stage, it is unclear how the ERNs will cluster the different rare diseases; however, it is foreseeable that they will look at the current structures and regrouping of centres of expertise in countries such as France or the UK's commissioning services.

These networks will primarily require European funding for staff to run the network, networking meetings and to maintain core activities such as a registry, biobank and laboratory external quality assessment schemes. Some of these activities may be sustained through external funding, for example laboratory external quality assessment schemes or registries and databases. Laboratory schemes can be funded through registration fees, while registries can be partly funded through the development of public–private partnerships with pharmaceutical companies. As companies outsource their registry activity to academically governed registries, their primary concern will be for the quality of any data held, and ensuring this is up to date and checked on a regular basis.

8.1.3 General objectives and main activities

Networks have historically been established between experts in national centres who have worked well together in the past, have common interests or objectives and are able to achieve funding to develop the network activities.

European networks for rare diseases should serve as research and knowledge centres, updating and contributing to the latest scientific findings, treating patients from other European countries, when no expert is available, and ensuring the availability of subsequent laboratory and treatment facilities where necessary. Therefore the main activities will include much of the following:

- Identifying expertise
- Coordination of the network
- Management of a website to ensure regular updating of information for patients and healthcare professionals
- Sharing expertise for patient management through telemedicine and sharing of difficult cases
- Offering training opportunities to healthcare professionals
- Developing, translating and disseminating evidence-based best practice guidelines for diagnosis and management, including the provision of recommendations for effective practice in clinical situations where variations in practice are known to occur and where effective care may not be delivered uniformly
- Setting up independent laboratory external quality assurance schemes or partnering with existing schemes such as the European Molecular Genetics Quality Network (EMQN) or ERNDIM Quality Assurance in Laboratory testing for inborn errors of metabolism
- Setting up and continuation of patient registries and biobanks
- Empowering patients and encouraging the establishment of patient groups
- Improving clinical research. The network provides the platform for sharing new ideas
- Many of these activities will require significant, ongoing funding to support the management and delivery of the network

The network members come to be regarded as experts both in the disease and in specific activities that can be generalisable to other rare diseases and healthcare in general. A formal system for sharing experience between ERNs in the field of rare diseases may be implemented (networking the networks) where good practice and common methodologies will be shared.

8.2 Challenges, strategies and lessons learned

8.2.1 Governance structure

8.2.1.1 Challenge

The governance structure specifies the distribution of rights and responsibilities in the network and spells out the rules and procedures for making decisions. The administrative responsibilities of the European Commission funded networks are commensurately large. The coordinator and network manager take the burden of these duties which include annual reports, chasing partners for financial information, budget control, ensuring active participation from patient organisations and staff recruitment. The networks are based on voluntary participation by their members. The incentives for members to participate are discussed in Section 8.2.6 on 'Clinician cooperation'. There is considerable variation in the infrastructure of national centres and the resources available for members to contribute to a network. Some partners, despite goodwill, cannot commit to the necessary time to respect the project timelines. The coordinator will spend enormous amounts of energy in addressing delays and related issues.

8.2.1.2 Strategy

The network should have different levels of management and strategic decision-making to alleviate responsibilities from the coordinator. A typical network will be composed of a large group with all members, sometimes called an advisory board or network. A small executive group or steering committee will be the strategic decision-making group, which writes the grant applications, reports and checks the project progress against objectives. At the beginning, the members of this core group will most likely have been the individuals who achieved the initial funding. Members of this group will often take on the responsibility of a specific activity or work-package. The network coordinator must be supported locally for logistical and financial reporting. A part-time project manager, ideally with some knowledge of the network and diseases, should be employed to manage the week-by-week activities. Depending on the scope of the network this could require further support, web/IT manager, public relations or communication support.

8.2.1.3 Lessons learned

The coordinator must be supported by a programme manager, a local team and a small steering committee of 5–6 members. Oversight and governance should be carefully defined, with participation clearly communicated with all stakeholders. A network charter defining the rules for publication, access to data/information and so on, should be agreed and signed by all partners. It should be possible to exchange network charters between ERNs. Collaborating partners who work on a voluntary basis usually cannot overcome the significant disadvantage of not receiving EU funding for their contribution. Therefore the activity of these partners is usually significantly lower than that of associate partners. This is a relevant shortcoming for the establishment of patient registries and other project-related activities.

8.2.2 Decision-making

8.2.2.1 Challenge

In order to meet its aims, the network needs to agree on standardised care and best practice. It needs to make decisions in which the network members take on the responsibility for the outcome. The governance and management of a network has all the decision-making complexity of any organisation. Coordinators will balance fast autocratic decision-making with slow consensus agreement.

8.2.2.2 Strategy

The steering group should be the first level of decision-making. Coordinators should not be required to take decisions alone. The advantage is the involvement of other perspectives. This is especially valuable when a network member may be affected negatively by the decision: for example, when addressing underperformance. When addressing standards of care and consensus guidelines, all members of the network are totally involved in the decision and responsible for the outcome. Everyone must agree and 'buy in' to the decision. If total commitment and agreement by everyone is not obtained, the decision becomes democratic (i.e. majority vote). The problem with majority vote is that no individual is responsible and members may say 'I didn't vote for that'. This is obviously particularly important in rare disease when members are expected to use the guidelines developed by the network in their daily practice.

8.2.2.3 Lessons learned

Most incremental decisions can be taken by the small steering committee while decisions which need members' buy in should be made at a group level.

8.2.3 Membership criteria

8.2.3.1 Challenge

Reference networks are established between centres of expertise designated at a national level or are centres that are recognised as having the necessary expertise. At the same time it is also important to ensure that less experienced centres that do not meet the criteria of a centre of expertise are allowed to join the network to train, learn and develop their competences and knowledge.

8.2.3.2 Strategy

The European Porphyria Network (EPNET) has defined clear qualitative and quantitative membership criteria.[4] It requires that centres follow the network quality assurance scheme, are able to distinguish using biochemical testing between all types of porphyria and are able to offer specialist detailed interpretation of results with clinical advice on management. Centres that do not achieve the criteria, on application, are accepted as conditional members for two years. They are expected to achieve the criteria within this period.

4 www.porphyria-europe.org, accessed 10 December 2012.

8.2.3.3 Lessons learned

Networks should establish membership criteria. This will ensure that members have the necessary resources to contribute and support the rare disease network. Less experienced centres should be given a conditional membership and time period to improve standards and services provided. This requires sufficient funding. Membership criteria for industry and patient groups should also be thought through.

8.2.4 Identifying expertise

8.2.4.1 Challenge

Identifying expertise is facilitated in countries with a culture of referring rare diseases to a central institution; however it is still complex, particularly in multi-system diseases such as Wilson's disease where patients are normally either under the care of a neurologist or a hepatologist with little dialogue between them. Furthermore, an increasing number of patients with rare disease are now being seen as adults, either because, with improved paediatric management, they have survived childhood and adolescence, or because it is increasingly recognised that some rare diseases present in adulthood. It is therefore an important part of a network to involve the adult clinicians. An additional problem in identifying expertise can be seen in ultra-orphan rare diseases for which not all countries will have a centre of expertise.

8.2.4.2 Strategy

It is of particular importance that the network will bring together the multidisciplinary specialists who might not meet in any other forum, thus promoting dialogue and continuity of care. Different mechanisms should be used to reach out to different specialities. In the UK, EuroWilson identified patients seen by neurologists by adding Wilson's disease to the British Neurology Surveillance Unit (BNSU). Laboratories performing genetic tests can be asked to send a letter to clinicians with all new diagnosis. Paediatricians should inform the adult doctors treating their older patients about the network. Patient organisations should encourage their treating clinicians (centres of expertise) to join the network. Identifying expertise will be facilitated by the Member States' implementation of centres of expertise and is thus a top-down approach to networking. Other strategies to identify expertise include: promotion through the international or national scientific societies, personal contact and presentations, submitting abstracts to relevant congresses, working with pharmaceutical companies who may assist in dissemination activities, producing a website included in the main search engines, information disseminated via Orphanet and so on. In countries where it is not possible to identify a centre of expertise, the ERN could, if sufficiently funded, provide travel grants for training at a specialist centre to facilitate the establishment of a centre in an underrepresented country. The setting up of a centre for a group of countries can also be addressed for feasibility.

8.2.4.3 Lessons learned

Networks demand close collaboration between clinicians, diagnostic laboratories, patient organisations and pharmaceutical companies to maximise communication efforts and identify expertise.

8.2.5 Patient organisation involvement

8.2.5.1 Challenge

Participation and empowerment of patients should be the ultimate goal and focus of an ERN. Patient groups should have a role in the translation and interpretation of patient information provided by the network. Patients should be represented on the network committees to ensure integrity and openness. Their comments on the science and medicine are also extremely perceptive and valuable. The patients' views on symptoms, side-effects of medication, quality of life and hence research priorities must be given equal if not greater weight than the doctors. This information can be collected through the registries and databases. EURORDIS recommends that the participation of relevant patient organisations as full partners should be one of the criteria of eligibility for funding. The challenge is that often there is no European federation for specific diseases or groups of diseases, which implies that one or two national patient organisations should become full members of the network. Their role with other national patient organisations needs clarification.

8.2.5.2 Strategy

The partner patient organisation(s) could be given the responsibility and funding to build a European patient group with the lead members of each national organisation. All members should be equal. Different national patient organisations (POs) can be given different responsibilities in the network. This group should be fully integrated into the network but also have the opportunity to meet alone, share experience and 'tricks'. This group should have a major role in the evaluation of the network activities and achievement of its long-term goals.

EURORDIS has developed rare disease patient online communities. This can be a complementary activity for a network which can support the patient community through short video interviews and explaining patient questions in patient-friendly language; by agreeing to answer questions via email for a Frequently Asked Questions section; by inviting patients and caregivers to scientific conferences and meetings.

8.2.5.3 Lessons learned

Patient organisations need to be equal and full partners in the network. They should have access to the necessary resources for collaboration and sharing of experience, particularly the tools they can offer to patients in countries with no patient organisation. A simple tool to develop for patient groups is a website repository for material that can be translated and used in any other country.

POs should also be involved in the governance and evaluation of ERNs when disease relevant POs exist and are structured to be able to do this. In rare diseases, the involvement of POs is of particular relevance because of their special role in patient support, knowledge about the conditions and involvement in registries and clinical trial design. Multiple examples exist of such cooperation, within the European Medicines Agency (EMA) for example and in the completed or ongoing pilot and other networks. EURORDIS can support the development of European Federations of Patient Organisations where these do not already exist.

8.2.6 Clinician cooperation and team working

8.2.6.1 Challenge

Clinicians, patients and other experts donate their time to the network as part of their normal organisational duties. There is no financial compensation for the additional work and services provided. Centres may receive a small amount of money for travel to meetings and part-time staff to enter initial data into a registry. Being part of a network which successfully achieves European funding may not provide individuals with satisfactory measures of esteem required in their organisations. Team working and keeping up enthusiasm in a network is one of the hardest and most time-consuming occupations for the coordinator and project manager. This is particularly the case for an ERN financed through the DG Sanco operating grant system in which only the coordinating centre is financially and contractually bound to the commission or for 'collaborating partners' in a project grant who do not receive financial compensation.

8.2.6.2 Strategy

The network activities can be broken down into smaller working groups in which all members can equally contribute, receive funding and which may generate publications. For example an ERN may have a registry working group, quality assurance working group and guideline working groups. The lead partners should be selected based on experience, personality, willingness, local resources and time available for the network. Other incentives to contribute to the network include centre and services offered listed on the ERN website.

8.2.6.3 Lessons learned

Not all network members will be committed or cooperate at the same level. The coordinator and steering committee should avoid spending too much time on trying to achieve universal commitment. Mistakes may include giving a key piece of work to an experienced but uncommitted member. Some groups, historically, will work better together than others and it could be that the rarer and more severe the disease, the greater the incentive to collaborate. Patient groups can also have a major role in improving clinical cooperation.

8.2.7 Dealing with conflicts

8.2.7.1 Challenge

Conflicts among members of a network may include disagreement in analysis of data from the registry and discrepancy in diagnosis procedures and best practice.

8.2.7.2 Strategy

All members of the network should be required to sign up to a network charter or standard operating procedure (SOP) which clarifies who owns knowledge held by the network, accesses to information held in the registry and publication, authorship and acknowledgment rules. The SOP sets out the expected rules by which members approach patients whose data will be entered into a registry. It describes the management rules and network functioning.

8.2.7.3 Lessons learned

The charter should be simple and understandable to non-law professionals. A system should be set up for sharing charters and SOPs between networks. Industry members of the network should also sign up to a confidentiality agreement and commitment to the network. Each partner can sign an agreement with the coordinating centre.

8.2.8 Telemedicine/tele-expertise

8.2.8.1 Challenge

Telemedicine and tele-expertise are two distinct concepts. Telemedicine is a relationship between a healthcare professional and a patient in a different location, whereas tele-expertise is the relationship between two or more healthcare professionals in different locations. Tele-expertise has been very successful within networks. Members will make personal contact with other network members to ask for advice or services. Some networks provide tools which allow sharing of images and data. All network meetings provide time for experts to share clinical conundrums. The professionals receiving the expertise use this knowledge to decide on a course of action in the management of their patient.

In the case of telemedicine, the network's public website will receive numerous hits and generate enquiries from patients, many of which demonstrate the continuing need for expertise and information. Network members are cautious in communication with patients as they are not in possession of all the laboratory and clinical information.

8.2.8.2 Strategy

Effort will be made to put the patient into contact with the most appropriate centre of expertise. The network will also propose laboratory services for testing. Google translate has been a useful resource for translating patient enquiries. In most cases a centre of expertise speaking the patient's language will be asked to take care of the enquiry. This is coordinated by the partner responsible for the website.

8.2.8.3 Lessons learned

It is important to set up a network of clinicians able to rapidly respond to enquiries. Some enquiries concern emergency management issues and a system for ensuring a prompt solution should be proposed. If questions concern a specific treatment, the pharmaceutical company should be informed. Many requests come from outside of Europe and dealing with these requests needs to be addressed. The coordinator should keep a table of enquiries and ensure that some form of follow-up is provided.

8.2.9 Sustainability

8.2.9.1 Challenge

A major concern in maintaining the dynamic of a network is its sustainability, as the infrastructure (website, meetings and registry) and coordination (personnel) have a cost. The cross-border directive provides the legal basis for sustainability; however there are a number of tactics and strategies that can be implemented over the long-term.

8.2.9.2 Strategies

- External quality schemes, after the initial pilots, these schemes should become self-sustaining through subscription fees from all members. Participating in an external quality scheme, when available, should be one of the mandatory membership criteria

- Current literature defines between 6,000 and 7,000 individual rare diseases. It will not be sustainable to set up so many European Reference Networks. Therefore networks need to cluster diseases into diagnostic systemic areas, such as rare metabolic diseases or rare renal disorders. EURORDIS proposes 20 to 30 ERNs covering a broad range of diseases. The major strategic and practical disadvantage of clustering is that the core data set might significantly decrease with the number of diseases that need to be integrated in one network. This is the consequence of increasing discrepancies of relevant clinical, biochemical, follow-up and therapy-related parameters with increasing number of diseases (even belonging to the same group of diseases)

- Many networks have a core registry activity. Funding is required for the initial data entry but follow-up can be entered during regular visits. Sustainability can be built into registries by several different mechanisms. First, by discussing public–private partnerships with the pharmaceutical industry which often need post-marketing surveillance data for their orphan drug or need to collect health technology assessment data. Second, through national rare disease plans which include the collection of core data elements for all rare diseases. This work is funded by the national health ministers, for example the BAMARA project in France. Registries should include the core data set and/or links with national databanks. Third, patients know their disease better than anybody and strategies need to be developed, in Europe, to support patients to access and enter their own data. The National Institutes for Health (NIH) in the USA has financed the Global Rare Disease Registry Network (GRDR) to set up 12 natural history registries and 12 external registries where patients opt-in and complete a medical questionnaire. However a hybrid between the patient entering his or her own data and clinicians entering the more technical data is required

- Coordination with other disease networks such as the EPIRARE project,[5] the International Rare Diseases Research Consortium (IRDiRC), RD-Connect and the sharing of experience, tools and standard operating procedures

8.2.10 Determining improvement in diagnostic, analysis and management quality in centres

8.2.10.1 Challenge

The characteristics of rare diseases imply that single centres or countries make choices based on their own, often very limited experience. As a result, care is not optimal; there are significant differences in the infrastructure, expertise, diagnostic procedures, time to diagnosis and outcome. This causes significant inequalities for patients. Standardising care and improving the outcome of patients and their families is a priority. However, it is complex to measure the direct impact an ERN has on improving outcome.

8.2.10.2 Strategy

The network should set up an evaluation committee composed of internal and external auditors. Central will be the participation of patients in this evaluation committee. Indicators can be determined, the most objective and easy to measure are process indicators; for example, how well is the network working: items to be

5 European Platform for Rare Disease Registries, www.epirare.eu, accessed 10 December 2012.

included in registry; quality and completeness of records; agreed contents of website; meetings held on schedule. Output indicators can also be objectively measured, for example, hits and enquiries on the website or access to consensus care protocols. Less tangible is the measurement of the outcome indicators: what are the real benefits of the network? It is possible to measure the improvement in diagnosis over time, look at changes in treatment strategies and outcome, and patient satisfaction surveys asking about services provided in their centre. These indicators can only be measured over long periods of time.

8.2.10.3 Lessons learned

Engage patient organisations in the design and measurement of outcome indicators. It would be a good idea to produce a core set of common indicators with expandable modules for the ERNs which should be flexible on a case-by-case basis.

8.2.11 Dissemination

8.2.11.1 Challenge

An ERN's overarching aim is to promote the care of patients with a rare disease and patients' access to information. To achieve this ERNs should be visible to the wider public. Public relations and communication managers are useful to ensure this visibility but they have a cost.

8.2.11.2 Strategy

One of the first tasks of a newly formed network is the development of a public website to diffuse expertise and facilitate patient access to updated information on their disease. This website should provide up-to-date information for healthcare professionals, patients and families in their own language. A list of centres of expertise and contact details can be provided. Patient organisations should be involved to help translate or back-translate documents. Up-to-date issues discussed in the network should be disseminated through the web (see Fig. 8.2).

Information is divided into different sections. The first is for patients and their relatives. It contains a general description of the disease(s) in the patient's own language. Information is provided for different age groups. YouTube can also be considered for communication with adolescents and young adults. The second section is for the non-expert healthcare professional. The third section provides information on the network, newsletter facility, details of centres offering clinical, diagnostic and research services, patient associations and related websites. Links should be provided to wider stakeholder groups including the pharmaceutical industry so that they can interact with the network. Access to the registry is password protected and governed by an oversight body. Other dissemination activities should include publishing in peer-reviewed journals.

Figure 8.2 **Typical website structure**

Source: adapted from the e.imd.org website and developed by CYIM

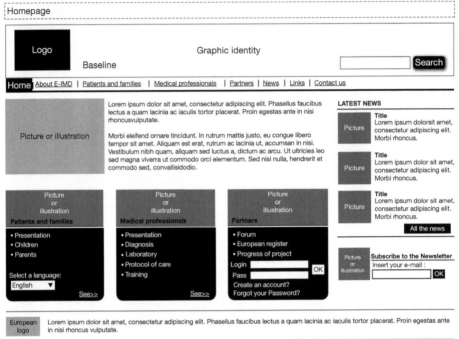

8.2.11.3 Lessons learned

The website should be developed with full collaboration from the patient organisations. Patients should be able to receive a small fee for providing the translation of relevant information or reading through translations prepared by the centre of expertise. A person must be designated responsible for regular updates of the website.

8.3 Conclusions

European Reference Networks are fundamental hubs for all stakeholder groups interested in specific disease areas. They should be a one-stop shop for: a patient looking for a specialist; a healthcare professional looking for best practice; industry developing new therapies; or scientists with a research idea. ERNs can succeed beyond expectations in the objective of improving healthcare for patients with a rare disease and their families. The network of participating centres is often larger than planned with a geographical coverage that extends beyond Europe. Partners enthusiastically embrace the principles of widening access to and improving quality of diagnostic and clinical services. Information for patients, families and non-expert clinicians in a variety of European languages is a priority for networks and there is often a commitment of partners to expand this library to include more international languages where possible. Audit and assessment of the quality of laboratory diagnosis allows for key diagnostic criteria to be defined and services to be measured against these standards which enhance quality. Collection of detailed biological, genetic and clinical data into a database or registry builds knowledge on the incidence and prevalence, provides a platform for research and defines the level of disease burden. Finally European Reference Networks engender a momentum and enthusiasm among professionals working in this field.

References

EUCERD (European Union Committee of Experts on Rare Diseases) (2011) 'Preliminary Analysis of the Outcomes and Experiences of Pilot European Reference Networks for Rare Diseases', ec.europa.eu/health/rare_diseases/docs/eucerd2011_report_european_ref_net.pdf, accessed 21 December 2012.

Official Journal of the EU (2011) 'Directive 2011/24/EU of the European Parliament and of the Council of 9 March 2011 on the Application of Patients' Rights in Cross-Border Healthcare', *Official Journal of the EU* L88/45.

Samantha Parker has been working for Orphan Europe Recordati Group for 12 years, a pharmaceutical company dedicated to the development of orphan drugs for rare diseases. Samantha runs the Orphan Europe Academy rare disease training programme (www.orphan-europe-academy.com) and has recently launched an e-learning platform for rare metabolic diseases. Her current role also includes collaboration with European Reference Networks (ERN): EPNET (www.porphyria-europe.org), EuroWilson (www.eurowilson.org) and E-IMD (www.e-imd.org). Specific activities in these networks include: expanding the expert disease community of healthcare professionals, patients, industry and regulators; building disease registries; developing consensus care guidelines; building measures to improve quality of diagnosis and patient care, in particular addressing differences between countries. She currently focuses on building the bridge between academically governed registries and those run by the industry for post-marketing surveillance and risk management plans and establishing public–private partnerships. Samantha is a member of the European Committee of Experts on Rare Diseases (EUCERD) and the International Rare Disease Research Consortium (IRDiRC).

Stephen Lynn is employed by Newcastle University and has worked as the manager of the TREAT-NMD Neuromuscular Network since early 2007. In addition, since early 2012, Stephen manages the EUCERD Joint Action project to support the mandate of the EC and EUCERD committee in formulating and implementing the Community's activities in the rare disease field, and foster exchange of experience, policies and practices. Stephen previously worked in the Science and Innovation Network in San Francisco as part of the UK Government's Foreign and Commonwealth Office. Stephen has a PhD in Physiology and Genetics from Newcastle University and has published on rare mitochondrial diseases.

9

Managing research advances into a rare disease

Case study of the Myrovlytis Trust[*]

John Solly and Galina Shyndriayeva
Myrovlytis Trust, UK

9.1 Creation of the Myrovlytis Trust

9.1.1 Rationale

There are about 7,000 rare diseases, of which 80% are genetic (EURORDIS 2005: 4). The definition of a rare disease varies between countries—defined as affecting <1 in 1,500 people in the USA, <1 in 2,500 people in Japan and <1 in 2,000 people in Europe[1]—but although each particular disease affects very few people, rare diseases as a group are not rare, with 3.5 million people in the UK alone estimated to be affected by a rare disease at some point in their life.[2]

Our vision is the cure of rare genetic diseases: it is unclear to us why anyone should be disadvantaged just for having inherited a rare genetic disorder. In late 2007 we created the Myrovlytis Trust to try to turn that vision into reality.

[*] The authors would like to thank Dr Vicki Colledge, Dr Sanjay Thakrar and Dr Arianne Matlin for critical reading of the text at various stages and for useful comments.
1 USA: Orphan Drug Act of 1983; Japan: Pharmaceutical Affairs Law (JPMA, 2008); EU: Regulation (EC) No. 141/2000.
2 www.raredisease.org.uk, accessed 12 December 2012.

9.1.2 How did we plan back in 2007?

Given the large number of rare diseases, we wanted to avoid spreading our effort thinly across several diseases and having no impact. Our aim was to focus on one condition to try to make a significant difference, and then to broaden our work by applying what we had learned, initially to related conditions. This was based on the assumption that information about one condition can provide insight into related conditions, both common and rare, and it raised two questions: how to focus on one condition and which condition to focus on?

We considered four options:

- Support patients, for example by developing a patient group

- Lobby for more money and support to raise awareness for the specific condition

- Screen for drugs based on current scientific knowledge

- Directly support scientific and medical research to increase scientific knowledge and generate insights for possible therapies

Dedicated patient support is invaluable, but we did not feel that we could improve on existing support, neither on organisations set up and run by driven, empathetic patients, nor on government-funded programmes such as the wonderful facilities provided by the US Government's National Institutes of Health. We considered lobbying to be outside our area of expertise, so unlikely to be successful. Drug screening and direct support for research seemed to be closely related: funding research would generate biological insights, which could inform further research and also provide leads for drug development and other therapies (Heemstra *et al.* 2009) (Fig. 9.1).

There were several additional reasons to support research, based on the unprecedented current rate of medical innovation which makes now a particularly fruitful time for rare diseases research:

Figure 9.1 **Assumed benefit of funding: research leads to insight which drives further research; from the insight comes therapy**

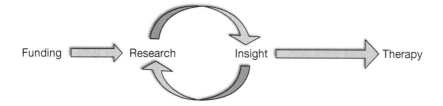

- Falling cost of technology (cost to sequence one human genome has fallen from US$100 million in 2001 to US$10,000 in 2012)[3] opens up the field of personalised therapies (see for example Human Genomics Strategy Group 2012)

- Improved technology, including computational modelling, which generates new scientific predictions (Orman *et al.* 2011; Navlakha and Bar-Joseph 2011), and the Internet which has obviously revolutionised access to information, collaborations and ideas

- Changing attitudes to public access to research (for example Public Library of Science[4] and *eLIFE*, the recently launched open access journal supported by Wellcome Trust, the Howard Hughes Medical Institute and the Max Planck Society)[5]

These are changing how research is done, are generating a step change in the value of research and make the present a uniquely promising time for medical research. If growing concerns over, for example, personal genomics data slow down future research, we may currently be living in even more of a research golden age than we realise (Greenbaum *et al.* 2011). We are passionate about maximising this opportunity to develop treatments for rare genetic disorders. Therefore, we decided to try to support drug screening and scientific and medical research.

Given our small size, how could we most effectively promote research in the shadow of such established and effective organisations as the Wellcome Trust and Cancer Research UK? We considered three approaches:

- Award a prize. This could highlight achievement, like the Nobel Prizes, or could stimulate research, like the X prizes,[6] or prizes for research into neglected diseases[7]

- Fund proposals. This would be similar to many government (e.g. the USA's NIH and Singapore's National Research Foundation) and non-government (e.g. Howard Hughes Medical Institute and the Wellcome Trust) funding agencies around the world. This funding could form seed grants, project grants or larger programme grants, and this approach would only be worthwhile if our narrow focus and manoeuvrability compensated for our lower level of funding

- Identify and fund people committed to researching a particular disease, like the McArthur Foundation but more narrowly focused, and give them free(ish) reign

---

3 www.genome.gov/sequencingcosts, accessed 12 December 2012.
4 www.PLoS.org, accessed 12 December 2012.
5 www.elifesciences.org, accessed 12 December 2012.
6 www.XPrize.org, accessed 12 December 2012.
7 For example: www.stoptb.org/global/awards/kochon and www.tbsurvivalproject.org/prize/winners.html (both accessed 12 December 2012).

How best to promote research would depend on which rare genetic disorder we focused on. We wanted to study a condition:

- Known to be genetic (with the relevant gene already identified), but with very little else known about it, therefore probably underdiagnosed

- With very few labs working on it

- With no dedicated funding body

- Known to be related to other conditions, so that any research we would support would be relevant for these other conditions

We chose Birt-Hogg-Dubé syndrome (BHD).[8] BHD is an autosomal dominant monogenic condition that leads to benign skin growths on the head and upper torso (fibrofolliculomas), pulmonary cysts, increased risk of pneumothorax and increased risk of kidney cancer (renal cell carcinoma). The BHD gene, which encodes the protein folliculin (FLCN),[9,10] was identified in 2002 (Nickerson *et al.* 2002) but very few laboratories anywhere in the world were working on the condition and there was no dedicated funding body.[11] BHD shares phenotypic and cell biological similarities with several other conditions, including von Hippel-Lindau disease (VHL),[12] tuberous sclerosis complex (TSC)[13] and lymphangioleiomyomatosis (LAM),[14] so insights into BHD might also provide insight into these related conditions. At least three organisations were already working in this disease space—the VHL Family Alliance,[15] the Tuberous Sclerosis (TS) Alliance[16] and The LAM Foundation[17]—which raised the valuable possibility of synergistic cooperation. Notably, all three organisations were founded, are based in and focus on (to a greater or lesser extent) the USA.

8   www.BHDSyndrome.org, accessed 12 December 2012.
9   www.uniprot.org/uniprot/Q8NFG4, accessed 12 December 2012.
10 omim.org/entry/607273, accessed 12 December 2012.
11 Before the creation of the Myrovlytis Trust in late 2007, 117 papers had been published on BHD since the condition was first described in 1977—an average of 3.8 per year. Since the Myrovlytis Trust was founded, 129 papers have been published on BHD (2008 to 30 April 2012)—an average of 29.8 papers per year.
12 omim.org/entry/193300, accessed 12 December 2012.
13 omim.org/clinicalSynopsis/191100, omim.org/clinicalSynopsis/613254, accessed 12 December 2012.
14 omim.org/entry/606690, accessed 12 December 2012.
15 The VHLFA has awarded more than US$1.3 million in research grants over 15 years, created a tissue bank and organises international research and family symposia (www.VHL.org, accessed 12 December 2012).
16 The TS Alliance has annual revenues of ~US$3.6 million (2011), spent ~US$2 million on research in 2011, supports a tissue bank, and facilitates natural history and mutation databases (www.TSAlliance.org, accessed 12 December 2012).
17 The LAM Foundation has raised US$15 million, most of which has been spent supporting research (www.TheLAMFoundation.org, accessed 12 December 2012).

9.1.3 Funding

The Myrovlytis Trust was set up initially with private funding and we strongly believe that philanthropy is a good thing per se. We anticipated that this would enable us to be more manoeuvrable compared with perhaps a government funding agency, and more willing to take risks than a funder that has responsibilities to donors from the general public. Clearly, this would release us from an initial need to spend time and effort raising money, but it would risk squandering resources. There has been surprisingly little study into the relative effectiveness of research funded from different types of sources. Diamond (2006) has suggested that privately funded research, at least in chemistry, leads to papers being more highly cited. However, it is unclear if this would apply to medicine, or whether citation is a good measure of usefulness, or whether increased citation and private funding are both just corollaries of something else, such as a proactive researcher (i.e. more proactive in applying for private funding and more proactive in getting his or her paper published in a more highly ranked journal). We considered alternative models, including the growing area of venture philanthropy, but felt that this would be a more useful model in the future once we had a candidate therapy.

9.1.4 Plan summary

From all these considerations our mission developed: to promote research into rare genetic disorders. To fulfil this mission, we developed a strategy based around medical research via direct grants, by increasing knowledge-sharing (e.g. by collating and disseminating public data and resources) and by facilitating collaboration (e.g. enabling scientific meetings and providing travel grants).

9.2 The first four years: BHD syndrome

9.2.1 The Myrovlytis Trust as a research hub

The Myrovlytis Trust aimed to be a research hub, acting as a central focus for the formation of a collaborative global BHD community. An international organisation that is seen to be disinterested and not competing directly with any other stakeholder can play the primary driving role in creating a community.

This applies to the field of rare diseases, but catalysing collaboration in this area faces specific challenges caused by the nature of a tightly focused research area. For example:

- The absence of research infrastructure, such as a centralised tissue bank or efficient system for sharing bench research materials, which delays research

- Geographical spread of research groups working on the same disease, which can lead to intellectual disconnection and unknowing duplication of experiments

- Small patient population, which makes it more difficult to recruit enough patients for a clinical trial

Sharing knowledge is fundamental to medical research and, as mentioned above, is more difficult for rare diseases. Successful research projects in all fields increasingly involve large teams with complementary expertise across different disciplines and countries, which makes collaboration ever more important. The current funding system in medical research strongly encourages scientists not to share their data until published, to minimise the chance of a competitor publishing first, which would decrease the scientist's chances of obtaining the next grant or the next promotion. This rational but defensive behaviour benefits the individual researcher in the short term, but hinders the research field, and in the long term may be counterproductive for the individual researcher because he or she may miss out on possible collaborations. Developing cooperation based on mutual trust is crucial to overcoming this systemic flaw, and would improve the efficiency of research, which is something that should be of interest to all funders, including taxpayers and philanthropists, as well as to the researchers themselves.

Since the 1990s—the start of the modern wave of goal-oriented philanthropic money being used to initiate and fund research—rare disease foundations have responded to these challenges (Kanellopoulou 2009: 194-95). They have addressed the rare disease funding gap that exists between the basic research often funded by governments and late stage clinical trials funded by private industry by recognising that a highly collaborative and synergistic network of stakeholders with different perspectives and areas of expertise—scientists, health professionals and patients—is one of the most valuable factors for successful research.[18] They have built on this insight to vigorously pursue avenues to potential therapies (Terry *et al.* 2007: 158). Creating such a network can decrease the barriers to research and development, for example by making the process of recruiting patients for clinical trials smoother and faster.

Several countries have national research hubs, such as the National Institutes of Health in the United States. However, an international organisation can act as a global hub, and an organisation that does not do research itself (such as the

---

18 As Kanellopoulou (2009: 195-96) remarked, 'By identifying and providing access to affected families, securing data and samples, sharing the costs of research, and developing research resources and clinical outcomes, advocacy groups greatly facilitate both research and its translation to healthcare… Numerous examples of advocacy groups now provide valuable resources for the realisation of studies that may not have otherwise been possible. Their role is increasingly valuable as they become essential in encouraging research on rare disease, fostering alliances and accelerating provision of therapies'. While Kanellopoulou was referring to advocacy groups, his description is also applicable to the Myrovlytis Trust.

Myrovlytis Trust) can be seen as an 'honest broker'. A number of successful medical research charities follow and exploit this research hub position. For example, The LAM Foundation in the United States is a focus for a clinical network of LAM experts.[19] The Multiple Myeloma Research Foundation (MMRF) has spearheaded advances in myeloma treatment; by emphasising a collaborative model to develop research insights into viable treatments, the MMRF has seen the approval of four innovative drugs since 2003.[20]

For the Myrovlytis Trust to successfully nudge and catalyse research, we needed to build on this history and become a global research hub for BHD syndrome.

9.2.2 Managing research so that the end goal is the focus

We aim to manage research so that the emphasis is continually on the end goal of treatment—our approach is to support research with high translational potential. To avoid the classic fate of uncontrolled, unconsidered growth leading to squandering of resources, our approach was to start small and grow organically. We aimed to misuse no resource and support no superfluous research effort—this included avoiding scientific overlap, either between projects funded by the Myrovlytis Trust, or with a project that is funded elsewhere. To enable this, and to support our role as a research hub, the Myrovlytis Trust has several members of staff trained to doctoral level in the biological sciences, who engage fully with research projects. All project applications are initially screened within the Trust and the successful ones, with the applicant's permission, are then externally peer reviewed.

We support research in the full spectrum of basic to clinical investigations. The study of basic biology can lead to possible targets for drug development: elucidation of a protein signalling pathway can lead to the identification of appropriate therapeutic targets (including repurposing of existing drugs), or determination of the structure of Folliculin protein can aid in drug design. More clinically orientated research describes the phenotype of FLCN variants, enables determination of best management guidelines and allows definition of diagnostics. We also support researchers developing experimental treatments, such as renal gene therapy. We are committed to acting on the results of these research projects to accelerate the pace of research and develop treatments for BHD as efficiently as possible. This extends into preparing a clear route for commercial development of possible therapies, so we seek to protect intellectual property wherever appropriate.

We decided to identify projects in two ways: proactively, by identifying current gaps in the understanding of BHD, finding researchers with expertise in those areas and approaching those researchers to see if they would consider a project; and reactively by waiting to receive ad hoc applications and by approaching researchers currently working on BHD for project ideas. This organic growth reflected not

19 www.thelamfoundation.org
20 www.themmrf.org, accessed 12 December 2012.

only our caution about squandering resources but also our approach to creating a BHD research community, described further below.

The Myrovlytis Trust's disinterest when evaluating competing research projects for funding combines with its global outlook and in-house expertise to make us an attractive funder for researchers. Our unbiased position and our internal firewalls ensure that we are perceived by researchers in the field as unbiased, so they are willing to share data with us. This extends beyond unpublished data from projects that we are funding to data from other projects, which is a clear mark of the trust and sense of community that we have engendered in the BHD research field. Being uniquely aware of unpublished BHD research from many different labs around the world—effectively a bird's eye view of BHD research—while maintaining the integrity of confidential information, means that we can identify valuable research paths to follow, decrease time spent by researchers on cul-de-sac or duplicate projects, and encourage useful bilateral collaborations between researchers.

9.2.3 Formation of collaborative research community

9.2.3.1 Creating the network of people

It is individuals who drive a project to completion or propose a consequential strategy. This applies in scientific research no less than any other field, where individual scientists influence the pace, increase the rigour and set the direction of research: Shapin (2008: 1, 4-5) has argued that individuals continue to be vital even in a research system that perceives itself to be as impersonal as possible.

For this reason we aimed to connect with an effective group of researchers and partners to create a strong network. These partners are committed to our mission, and the strength of the network (for example, we regularly visit the labs we support and we keep in very close contact with BHD researchers across the world) prevents us from defaulting to a general and distant prize-making organisation.

We decided to seed a network by identifying existing leaders in the field and then letting it grow, based on the assumption that such a network would be more stable than one imposed top-down. These leaders were people who were already active in the field and so had an interest in the intellectual problem and access to resources. However, they were also people with the expertise to take the field forward and the professional stature to attract new researchers, i.e. to act as a research node. We initially identified three laboratories with recognised expertise and a history of working in BHD or related conditions, and asked these leaders to form our Scientific Advisory Board (SAB). The network grew in two ways: the initial leaders developed their own collaborations, and we also identified gaps in the current scientific knowledge and tried to pique the interest of people who had the expertise to fill those gaps. Additionally, we always welcomed researchers with an interest in BHD syndrome—as in many other areas, intellectual curiosity and enthusiasm is important. One example of the success of our collaborative model was a recent paper by Preston *et al.* (2011). This paper reported research conducted by members of six laboratories from three countries, spanning clinical and functional biology; the researchers had been introduced to each other by the Myrovlytis Trust. By 2010 the principal investigators had fostered core groups of young researchers working on BHD; the results of the paper suggest a potential therapeutic approach to treating BHD.

In 2008 we initiated the formation of a researcher-led European BHD Consortium (EBC). This Consortium comprises researchers and clinicians and provides a highly trusted platform for collaboration, sharing ideas and resources. Functioning as a regional (European) network, it allows initiatives to be tested before they are expanded globally. It can be useful to create these intermediate regional bodies that comprise countries in similar situations, rather than directly launching a global collective that might face a number of difficulties, such as the logistics of meeting or struggling to encompass different healthcare systems and research environments. The EBC has developed national BHD patient registries such as a UK registry based at the University of Birmingham, published clinical guidelines for the management of BHD (Menko *et al.* 2009), created a pool of freely available laboratory resources and collections of biological samples, and created a *folliculin* mutation database.[21] The freely available database, hosted by the Leiden Open Variation Database, lists sequence variations in *FLCN*, and submissions are encouraged, whether from published or unpublished data, from researchers or clinicians, from any hospital or institution worldwide. The *FLCN* mutation database is one of the EBC's most wide-reaching resources; by April 2012, 623 submissions have been made by 57 submitters from 21 countries across the world. EBC members are also active in their home countries: for example, PREDIR, the French national centre of expertise in familial renal cancers, is led by an EBC member.[22]

Developing an international clinical network created a pool of patients large enough to study genotype-phenotype correlations (something that would be impossible with a small, country-specific group of patients) and enables clinicians to refer patients to each other. Additionally, it overlaps and complements the basic research network.

People with a FLCN mutation and their families are an essential focus, within the context of our twin aims of promoting research and educating the public (this latter aim is not discussed in this chapter). The Myrovlytis Trust provides information to families affected by BHD, including the 'For Families' section of BHDsyndrome.org offering information on diagnosis, symptoms and available treatment options,[23] an online Forum,[24] a BHD Worldwide map,[25] interviews with researchers

21 www.lovd.nl/flcn, accessed 12 December 2012. The clinician who established and curates this database was funded directly by the Myrovlytis Trust.
22 www.predir.org, accessed 12 December 2012.
23 www.bhdsyndrome.org/for-families, accessed 12 December 2012.
24 www.bhdsyndrome.org/forum, accessed 12 December 2012.
25 www.bhdsyndrome.org/features-and-events/bhd-worldwide, accessed 12 December 2012.

and patients,[26] and a series of pamphlets.[27] Hearing from individuals affected by BHD enables us not only to maintain contact with a group of patients who will hopefully be involved in clinical trials but also to remain focused on the goal of translational research. The Second BHD Symposium (discussed below) emerged as a successful model of an integrated gathering of medical professionals, laboratory researchers and people affected by BHD. The programme for families included a talk with a genetic counsellor, Q&A sessions with specialists in BHD syndrome and joint clinical research sessions. We now use this model every year.

9.2.3.2 Annual BHD Symposium

We have initiated an annual global BHD Symposium. Enabling researchers to meet regularly is crucial to advance any medical field but, we emphasise again, particularly so in a rare disease where researchers are geographically isolated. The inaugural BHD Symposium was held in Roskilde, Denmark in 2008, the second in Washington, DC, in 2010, the third in Maastricht, the Netherlands in 2011, and the fourth in Cincinnati, OH, in 2012. We believe that this annual symposium has several important benefits:

- Creates and develops relationships within the BHD research community, building mutual trust and creating space for collaborations to form and strengthen

- Bringing patients, researchers and clinicians together allows data to be shared and ideas to spark. It also enables people from different research (e.g. biochemists and geneticists) or clinical (e.g. renal surgeons and dermatologists) perspectives to learn from each other to inform their own and each other's work

- Collaborating with related organisations, or placing the symposium adjacent to another medical conference, raises the profile of BHD and increases possible interactions. We organise our annual Symposium so as to allow 'cousin' researchers to attend[28]

- Encouraging outside speakers—experts in an area tangentially related to BHD—provides a perspective that might be fresh to the core BHD field

- The physical location of the conference helps to raise awareness of BHD in the local research community and helps to engage patients from around the world

---

26 www.bhdsyndrome.org/features-and-events/video-interviews; www.bhdsyndrome.org/features-and-events/written-interviews, accessed 12 December 2012.
27 www.bhdsyndrome.org/for-families/additional-resources/telling-others-about-bhd, accessed 12 December 2012.
28 This includes holding the Symposium adjacent to another meeting (the Inaugural BHD Symposium was adjacent to an International VHL meeting, the 2nd and 4th BHD Symposia were held adjacent to the American Association of Cancer Research's annual meeting (AACR). It also includes hosting a session dedicated to a related area (the 3rd BHD Symposium included sessions on hereditary leiomyomatosis renal cell carcinoma (omim.org/entry/150800, accessed 12 December 2012), and the 4th BHD Symposium was held in Cincinnati, which is a world centre of expertise for TSC and LAM.

9.2.3.3 Networks for a small community

The limited size of the research community can cause complications. On the positive side, a small community can react more quickly to new data and insights and is more conducive to fostering closer personal relationships, leading to freer communication, more natural sharing of ideas and higher levels of trust.

However, conflicts of interest and professional competition can have a disproportionate impact on the field, over-reliance on the same perspectives can make the field stale, and there is a risk of insularity and perhaps decreased momentum. To counteract this, we try to encourage cross-disciplinary interaction, engage with researchers who have expertise in areas related to BHD, and encourage as global a community as possible.

Recent technical innovations, for example in genetic sequencing, have helped to reveal the steps required to analyse a genetic disorder. As a charity driving research into, initially, one monogenetic disorder, we have been able to take advantage of this by working with the relevant experts to optimise this process.

9.2.4 Online resources

Wherever possible, we have tried to make use of the Internet and email to compensate for the geographical scattering of BHD researchers, to provide information to families, and to provide information and access to resources for researchers. We have created several websites and work with social media, but our main effort in this area has been the primary online reference for BHD syndrome, www.BHD Syndrome.org.

9.2.4.1 www.BHDSyndrome.org

BHDSyndrome.org aims to provide information and resources to families and researchers, and to initiate public discussion around BHD. The site aims to be a central hub, focusing on both families and researchers; we hope that this dual focus creates a richer source of information about BHD syndrome, as well as encouraging families to find out more about current research, and reminding researchers of the goal of their work. The 'For Families' section[29] provides high-quality information that has been reviewed by clinical experts in BHD and awarded Information Standard certification in recognition of its quality, safety and reliability.[30] Aimed at families, it is also useful for researchers new to the BHD field.

---

29 www.bhdsyndrome.org/for-families
30 The Information Standard is an independent certification scheme for health and social care information, supported by the Department of Health in England: www.theinformation standard.org, accessed 12 December 2012.

9.2.4.2 BHDSyndrome.org resources for researchers

The 'For Researchers' section includes several types of resource.[31] These comprehensive resources are updated continually and aim to provide a 'one stop shop' for BHD researchers.[32] They include:

- Comprehensive list of antibodies that have been published or are commercially available, for FLCN and other relevant proteins

- Comprehensive list of all published FLCN-null cell lines and BHD animal models, including mouse, rat, dog, zebra fish and fruit fly

- Details of any current clinical trials

- Summary listing of all publications on BHD syndrome, highlighting the aims and results of these studies, along with a literature library offering full text where possible

- A 12,000 word, comprehensive review of BHD syndrome, incorporating the most recent research and written in the style of an academic publication. 'What is BHD?'[33] covers all aspects of current research and knowledge on BHD syndrome and considers future research avenues and possible therapies

- An original signalling diagram showing FLCN's known role and interactions within the cell[34]

- Quarterly newsletter

- Forum for researchers[35]

BHDSyndrome.org is exceptional in developing, collating and freely offering these resources to the research community. Ensuring that the scientific information on BHDSyndrome.org is freely available to anyone, from anywhere, helps to break down the barriers erected by publishing companies, etc. and encourages people to join the debate.

9.2.4.3 Blog and other social media

Since 2009 we have written a weekly BHD Research Blog.[36] Typically, the blog summarises and analyses a recent research article or scientific conference, putting it into context for the BHD field. As a voice and platform, it enables us also to profile active BHD researchers and discuss interesting studies with an impact of the

31　www.bhdsyndrome.org/for-researchers, accessed 12 December 2012.
32　www.bhdsyndrome.org/for-researchers/resources, accessed 12 December 2012.
33　www.bhdsyndrome.org/for-researchers/what-is-bhd, accessed 12 December 2012.
34　www.bhdsyndrome.org/for-researchers/what-is-bhd/4-folliculin-associated-signalling-pathways, accessed 12 December 2012.
35　www.bhdsyndrome.org/forum
36　www.bhdsyndrome.org/topics/bhd-research-blog, accessed 12 December 2012.

BHD field. We also use the blog as a more discursive form of news, reporting on the annual BHD Symposium, or to promote events such as Rare Disease Day.[37]

We have set up a Facebook page, which has become a very useful way of meeting individuals affected by BHD and creating a more informal space for sharing concerns and support.[38] We have a Twitter account, which raises the profile of BHD syndrome, and provides a rapid means for us to disseminate information.[39]

9.2.4.4 www.MyrovlytisTrust.org

MyrovlytisTrust.org describes our aims[40] and our work on BHD.[41] It includes description of some of the researchers we support[42] and their projects, which are showcased to share their diligent efforts in understanding BHD and developing therapies. We also implemented a crowd-funding scheme, enabling donors to choose a research project to support; their donations are used to offset the amount already awarded to that project.[43]

We hope these efforts to create a central space for BHD researchers online have led, and continue to lead, to the sense of a BHD community and a BHD research field. As a further consequence, we hope that individuals and families affected by BHD will also investigate the researchers' area, read the BHD Research Blog, join our Facebook group and follow us on Twitter.[44]

9.2.5 Summary of the first four and a half years

The Myrovlytis Trust has created a collaborative global BHD community that we continue to support and develop. We work with exceptional researchers from around the world and have, to date, awarded around £4.5 million in grants; this is the cornerstone of our work. BHD was first described in 1977. Between 1977 and 2007, when we set up the Myrovlytis Trust, 117 papers were published on BHD—an average of 3.8 per year. Since the Myrovlytis Trust was founded, 129 papers have been published on BHD (from 2008 to April 2012)—an average of 29.8 papers per year. This is an almost eightfold increase in publication rates. Interestingly, the BHD work we are supporting is starting to have implications for related genetic kidney diseases.

37 www.rarediseaseday.org, accessed 12 December 2012.
38 www.facebook.com/bhdsyndrome, accessed 12 December 2012.
39 https://twitter.com/BHDSyndrome, accessed 12 December 2012.
40 www.myrovlytistrust.org/about-us, accessed 12 December 2012.
41 www.myrovlytistrust.org/our-work/promoting-research/bhd-research, accessed 12 December 2012.
42 www.myrovlytistrust.org/our-work/advancing-education/researcher-profiles, accessed 12 December 2012.
43 www.myrovlytistrust.org/get-involved/donate/research-projects, accessed 12 December 2012.
44 We recently conducted a survey showing that these individuals do regularly read the blog.

9.3 The next four years: The kidney

Our work promoting research into BHD syndrome increasingly provides insight into other disorders: increased knowledge of cell signalling pathways, gene expression levels and protein–protein interactions involved in BHD are increasing our understanding of the genes and proteins known to cause related conditions. This is in addition to the renal gene therapy research which is potentially applicable to any genetic kidney disorder.

Given this overlap, it is a logical progression for us to try to create synergy by expanding our vision to encompass other genetic kidney disorders. To facilitate this progression, in 2011 we updated our organisational model by forming the BHD Foundation[45] to oversee all work pertaining to Birt-Hogg-Dubé syndrome. Having a constituent organisation responsible for all activities related to one specific disorder provides valuable flexibility and clarity: we aim to replicate for related genetic kidney disorders the support and structure that we have provided for BHD.

9.3.1 Lessons from the first four years

Several aspects of our model's design and implementation were unsuccessful or could have been improved.

Creating active networks of people involved in BHD syndrome has been effective and we strongly recommend it. The approach of identifying leaders in the field and working with them has, in general, worked well. However, the clinical and research networks have tended to reflect the current global scientific centre of gravity by being centred on North America and Europe. We have had less success in encouraging researchers and clinicians from other countries. This partly reflects the smaller volume of research being done there, but there are many countries with genuine clinical excellence around BHD with whom we are simply not working closely enough, such as Japan where the research and knowledge of BHD is outstanding but our relationships have not developed sufficiently. Improving and extending these networks would also raise the profile of BHD.

Our method of identifying projects has been relatively effective, both specifically and as a catalyst for the BHD field (more than sevenfold increase in publication rates of BHD papers since the Myrovlytis Trust was founded). There have been some unsuccessful projects, and we have learned to pay close attention to applicants' general approach to collaboration and how closely their professional values and aims reflect ours. There is a continual tension between grant recipients' needs to further their career and follow their scientific curiosity, and the Myrovlytis Trust's aim to better understand BHD. These motivations can never be fully aligned and acknowledging this is important for us and for the grant recipient.

---

45 www.BHDSyndrome.org/about-us/bhd-foundation, accessed 12 December 2012.

BHD is considered to be underdiagnosed. Raising the profile of BHD among families and patients would have an educative value, as well as creating a larger potential patient cohort for clinical trials. Current awareness and engagement is highest in the Anglosphere, perhaps because our websites, Facebook page, Twitter feed and pamphlets are in English. We have enabled translation of BHDSyndrome. org through Google, but we have not produced any professionally translated material—this is an area that we could look at.

One way to engage both professionals and families from under-represented countries could be through the BHD Symposium. This could include providing travel grants, or we could consider holding the BHD Symposium outside Europe or North America

Initially, we focused on promoting research into BHD syndrome by working exclusively with clinicians and researchers. This was based on the premise that anything else was a distraction; however, this was a mistake. Knowing that this is a common mistake committed by many, including some of the world's largest health foundations, was little practical use. Now, after four years, as the Myrovlytis Trust's profile has naturally increased and the global rare disease space has developed,[46] we work much more closely with other organisations. This is an area that we hope to expand significantly in the future: possibilities could include joint funding, with another single rare disease organisation, of research projects relevant to a range of conditions.

To become more effective, the Myrovlytis Trust will need to develop its fundraising capacity. Crossing the 'valley of death'—transforming a promising compound or technology into a marketable product—is a very costly process. We will start to develop a more robust fundraising programme, to enable us to efficiently propel a novel treatment to the bedside when appropriate.

We are excited about expanding our support to related genetic kidney diseases. We feel that the synergy and benefits will outweigh any potential loss of focus, and we would urge other research-focused, single-disorder organisations to consider a similar approach. This could involve directly funding research for related diseases or could be a collaboration with a similar organisation that focuses on a related condition. As the organisation, in addition to funding, has already established the centralised support, resources, research infrastructure and patient health information and communications for one disease, it might be relatively easy to duplicate them for a related condition. High impact activity in the rare disease research

---

46 Rare Disease Day was started in 2008, and its theme in 2012 was 'Solidarity' (www.rare diseaseday.org/article/rare-disease-day-2012-focus). This reinforces the point that although individual rare diseases are varied and distinct, each one faces many of the same challenges and that it is effective for the community to work together, for example when consulting on national policies or providing public health information. This is evident with the creation of organisations such as the International Rare Diseases Research Consortium (IRDiRC) (ec.europa.eu/research/health/medical-research/rare-diseases/irdirc_en.html), EURORDIS (www.eurordis.org), Orphanet (www.orpha.net) and NORD (www.rarediseases.org). All websites accessed 12 December 2012.

sphere should not be limited to the creation of more philanthropic organisations—the large pool of talent and resources in the private sector would make greater interest in rare diseases from this area very valuable. As well as direct research funding, contributions could include: incorporating rare disease research in their corporate social responsibility planning; donating resources, such as access to technical facilities or products; and allowing employees to donate time to advise charities and serve on charity boards.

9.4 Summary

There are 7,000 rare diseases and 80% them are genetic (EURORDIS 2005: 4). Over the last four and a half years, against a global backdrop of unprecedented medical innovation, the Myrovlytis Trust has tried to promote research into one rare disease, Birt-Hogg-Dubé syndrome, by developing networks, trying to lower the barriers to research, and directly funding research projects. This BHD research has generated insight into related conditions, which has encouraged us to progress to promote research into related genetic kidney disorders. We anticipate that our experience over the last four and a half years, and the resources that we have developed, will make the next four and a half years even more exciting and fruitful.

References

Diamond, A.M. (2006) 'The Relative Success of Private Funders and Government Funders in Funding Important Science', *European Journal of Law and Economics* 21: 149-61.

EURORDIS (2005) 'Rare Diseases: Understanding this Public Health Priority', www.eurordis. org/IMG/pdf/princeps_document-EN.pdf, accessed 24 April 2012.

Greenbaum, D., A. Sboner, X.J. Mu and M. Gerstein (2011) 'Genomics and Privacy: Implications of the New Reality of Closed Data for the Field', *PLoS Computational Biology* 7.12 (December 2011): e1002278.

Heemstra, H.E., S. van Weely, H.A. Büller, G.M.L. Hubert and R.L.A. de Vrueh (2009) 'Translation of Rare Disease Research into Orphan Drug Development: Disease Matters', *Drug Discovery Today* 14.23-24 (December 2009): 1166-73.

Human Genomics Strategy Group (2012) 'Building on Our Inheritance: Genomic Technology in Healthcare', www.dh.gov.uk/prod_consum_dh/groups/dh_digitalassets/@dh/@en/documents/digitalasset/dh_132382.pdf, accessed 12 December 2012.

Kanellopoulou, N. (2009) 'Advocacy Groups as Research Organizations: Novel Approaches in Research Governance', in C. Lyall, T. Papaioannou and J. Smith (eds.), *The Limits to Governance: The Challenge of Policy-Making for the New Life Sciences* (Farnham, UK: Ashgate).

Menko, F.H., M.A. van Steensel, S. Giraud, L. Friis-Hansen, S. Richard, S. Ungari, M. Nordenskjöld, T.V. Hansen, J. Solly, E.R. Maher, European BHD Consortium (2009) 'Birt-Hogg-Dubé Syndrome: Diagnosis and Management', *Lancet Oncology* 10.12 (December 2009): 1199-206.

Navlakha, S., and Z. Bar-Joseph (2011) 'Algorithms in Nature: The Convergence of Systems Biology and Computational Thinking', *Molecular Systems Biology* 8.7 (November 2011): 546.

Nickerson, M.L., M.B. Warren, J.R. Toro, V. Matrosova, G. Glenn, M.L. Turner, P. Duray, M. Merino, P. Choyke, C.P. Pavlovich, N. Sharma, M. Walther, D. Munroe, R. Hill, E. Maher, C. Greenberg, M.I. Lerman, W.M. Linehan, B. Zbar and L.S. Schmidt (2002) 'Mutations in a Novel Gene Lead to Kidney Tumors, Lung Wall Defects, and Benign Tumors of the Hair Follicle in Patients with the Birt-Hogg-Dubé Syndrome', *Cancer Cell* 2.2 (August 2002): 157-64.

Orman, M.A., F. Berthiaume, I.P. Androulakis and M.G. Ierapetritou (2011) 'Advanced Stoichiometric Analysis of Metabolic Networks of Mammalian Systems', *Critical Reviews in Biomedical Engineering* 39.6: 511-34.

Preston, R.S., A. Philp, T. Claessens, L. Gijezen, A.B. Dydensborg, E.A. Dunlop, K.T. Harper, T. Brinkhuizen, F.H. Menko, D.M. Davies, S.C. Land, A. Pause, K. Baar, M.A. van Steensel and A.R. Tee (2011) 'Absence of the Birt-Hogg-Dubé Gene Product is Associated with Increased Hypoxia-Inducible Factor Transcriptional Activity and a Loss of Metabolic Flexibility', *Oncogene* 10.30 (March 2011): 1159-73.

Shapin, S. (2008) *The Scientific Life: A Moral History of a Late Modern Vocation* (Chicago: University of Chicago Press).

Terry, S.F., P.F. Terry, K.A. Rauen, J. Uitto and L.G. Bercovitch (2007) 'Advocacy Groups as Research Organizations: The PXE International Example', *Nature Reviews Genetics* 8.2 (February 2007): 157-64.

Dr **John Solly** is Director of the Myrovlytis Trust (www.MyrovlytisTrust.org), a medical research charity that promotes research into rare genetic disorders. He previously worked at the management consultancy ZS Associates, advising clients in the biotech and pharmaceutical industries. John has a PhD in genetics from Cambridge University.

Galina Shyndriayeva was Communications and Administration Officer at the Myrovlytis Trust from 2010 to 2012. Holding degrees from Imperial College London and Harvard University, she is currently pursuing a PhD in the history of science, technology and medicine at Imperial College.

10

The BLACKSWAN Foundation for rare diseases

Olivier Menzel and Silvia Panigone

BLACKSWAN Foundation

We have been asked to share our experiences and projects on rare diseases from our two different perspectives and we thought it was a great opportunity to contribute to an increasing consciousness on rare disease conditions. In this chapter Dr Olivier Menzel, president and founder of BLACKSWAN Foundation, shares his personal experience and commitment on rare and orphan diseases from a research and community point of view while Dr Silvia Panigone, Board Member of BLACK-SWAN Foundation, describes her passion and commitment from a business and investment point of view.

My name is Olivier Menzel and I am a researcher. All of us are looking at and researching something. But I started as a scientist researcher. I spent more than 13 years in academic research, almost all of which involved working in the field of rare and orphan disease research. In fact, at 17 years old I was fascinated by Gregor Johann Mendel and his works on genetics and inheritance. This influenced my university studies. I studied biology and specialised in human genetics. During my Master's I realised how much we know and understand about the genetic mechanism and gene function from accidental changes in a genomic sequence (DNA deletions, duplications, chromosome translocations, frameshift mutations, etc.), which gave us a deeper understanding of the basic human genetic mechanisms. I also had the chance to participate in the extension of the Orphanet database[1] in Switzerland and I was shocked about how poorly rare and orphan diseases are known, even among healthcare specialists, and about the almost non-existent

---

1 www.orpha.net, accessed 12 December 2012.

therapeutic research for those diseases. As an idealistic academic researcher at that time it was unconceivable for me to 'use' those diseases to understand human genetics without pushing further the research in order to offer a cure to patients.

Nowadays, I still strongly believe that this lack of research is not fair. Furthermore, in 2006 I started to lead a laboratory focused on inborn liver metabolic diseases where we developed an interesting alternative to liver transplantation using an *ex vivo* gene therapy protocol. Paradoxically, by increasing the positive results towards a possible clinical application, the funding for supporting our research diminished. In six years I spent much more time trying to find financial support than working at the bench. And it was at this time that I started to be a different researcher, a grant researcher.

I was working on familial hypercholesterolemia[2] (prevalence of the homozygous form: one in a million births), which is permanent and isolated elevation in circulating cholesterol. I could not understand this difficulty in finding financial support because cholesterol is probably the most 'fashionable' subject for big pharmaceutical industry (approximately one in every six adults—16.3% of the US adult population—has high total cholesterol[3]) and the carriers who have one abnormal copy (heterozygous) of the familial hypercholesterolemia mutation are 1 in 500, which is four times more than the European definition of rare diseases prevalence (1 in 2,000).[4] The carriers have premature cardiovascular disease, even with a healthy lifestyle, around the age of 35 and about 50% of men will develop coronary artery disease before the age of 50.[5] Again, I could not understand the difficulty in finding financial support for a topic that could give and bring so many insights for a broader population than those with the particular rare disease.

After years of thinking and talking about it, eventually in 2010, I established the BLACKSWAN Foundation to support research on orphan and rare diseases.[6] Needless to say it was not easy, and it still is not. However, I have been witness to gestures of kindness and support from so many that, even though it is still early days for what I set forth to accomplish, I feel I have already gone a long way.

Rare diseases are not seen as a field for priority action by the medical community. Poor characterisation of the natural cause, pathologies and low numbers of cases make diagnosis difficult, often resulting in a real ordeal for patients and their families, who find themselves on a seemingly endless trek from one consultant to another. Rare diseases offer sufferers little hope of survival—and an even lower chance of leading a normal life. These diseases go hand in hand with discrimination, isolation and lack of understanding by others. Paradoxically the problem is aggravated by administrative and bureaucratic obstacles, as standards and norms cause these diseases to fall through the safety net.

2 Orpha number: ORPHA406
3 www.cdc.gov/cholesterol/facts.htm, accessed 12 December 2012.
4 ec.europa.eu/health/ph_threats/non_com/docs/rare_com_en.pdf, accessed 12 December 2012.
5 www.genetics.edu.au, accessed 12 December 2012.
6 www.blackswanfoundation.ch, accessed 12 December 2012.

There are already 8,000 rare diseases listed in the scientific literature and five new diseases are added each week. In other words, this means that some 6–8% of the world's population suffer from rare diseases: 470 million around the world and 500,000 in Switzerland.

An enormous effort is expended by national alliances and patient organisations in looking for grants, evidencing the lack of public and private financial support made available for research, a problem that the BLACKSWAN Foundation wishes to redress. The BLACKSWAN Foundation is an operating Swiss foundation, which organises and runs its own programmes worldwide. It is a grant-making organisation, and can act as a convening body as well.

Research on rare and orphan diseases is important because they can serve as a model for more common diseases and consequently help a large population. For research to be optimal, it is necessary that it is developed in collaboration with specialists from around the world, thereby including the greatest number of patients. This combined effort allows for an exchange of multidisciplinary expertise and best practices.

To motivate members of the industry to enter this small market, Regulation (EC) No 141/2000 of the European Parliament and of the Council of 16 December 1999 on orphan medicinal products[7] provides the opportunity to develop market 'niche', something of particular interest for small and medium-sized enterprises. Even though this policy has enabled the development of orphan drugs, most rare diseases are still without effective treatment. One of the main missions of the BLACKSWAN Foundation is to support translational and clinical research by allocating resources to investigators working on rare and orphan diseases. The idea is to increase the number of projects that have a strong therapeutic potential in order to maximise the chances that they will be rapidly accessible to patients. It is imperative to strengthen links between universities and industry to capitalise on the results of academic research by using them to develop new diagnostic and therapeutic tools.

In 2008, the first Rare Disease Day, 29 February, was proclaimed by EURORDIS,[8] the European alliance of rare disease patient organisations.

In February 2012 (29 February–2 March) the BLACKSWAN Foundation organised the first global symposium (The RE(ACT) Congress[9]) dedicated to research on orphan and rare diseases, which took place in Basel, Switzerland. The goal of this symposium was and will be to promote research on rare diseases, but also to increase awareness of the field by industry, the general public and policy-makers. Its name 'RE(ACT)' symbolises the need for rare disease patients and their families to react to present health industry approaches. Positively reinforced by the outcome of the RE(ACT) Congress, BLACKSWAN decided to reconvene it every two years.

7 ec.europa.eu/health/files/eudralex/vol-1/reg_2000_141/reg_2000_141_en.pdf, accessed 12 December 2012.
8 www.eurordis.org, accessed 12 December 2012.
9 www.react-congress.org, accessed 12 December 2012.

Following the RE(ACT) Congress event I had the idea to create the RE(ACT) Community[10] which consists of establishing a platform for research scientists so that if a patient wishes to verify the state of the art in terms of research development on any given disease, his or her enquiry need not be more than an email away. The principal aim of the creation of a RE(ACT) Community is to strengthen the synergies between people involved in rare and orphan diseases research in order to awaken general public consciousness about the achievements and goals of these researches, build international relationships and collaborations between researchers and intensify exchanges between researchers and other stakeholders (such as academic institutions, centres of expertise, pharmaceutical industries, patient organisations and policy-makers).

Moreover, the objective is to create a unique worldwide platform fostering exchange and collaboration on similar or new projects, identifying research projects, transferring know-how, finding expertise, discussing with key opinion leaders and optimising synergies between scientists and patient advocates with policy-makers and companies.

I believe that progress on information, diagnosis and care for patients suffering from rare disease relies on all stakeholders. Cures stem from science, yet the translation of scientific advances into benefits for patients requires international cooperation beyond the walls of the laboratory. Such initiatives aim to lift rare diseases from obscurity, destroying the veil of ignorance surrounding these too often life-threatening disorders.

In this context Silvia Panigone saw the opportunity to make a bridge between the research world and the financial world in a win–win situation:

I began my career as a molecular biologist focused on the oncology sector. After spending several years in research I then moved to industry where I had the opportunity to cover both operational and managerial positions that allowed me to acquire important experience in the entire drug development process including product positioning, development of new strategies and building up spin-off companies. I naturally moved to the business and investment sector, first as investment director and CSO in a venture investment firm and then as adviser for a private equity group of a Swiss bank.

What has changed from a few years ago when the rare diseases sector was neglected by industry and by investors? I am convinced that it is the right moment to set up an investment platform on orphan diseases thanks to the increased interest of the big pharmaceutical companies that are looking for new competitive solutions such as orphan drugs to enter the market in a short time with limited investments and with the potential to expand to larger indications. This is the main driver for venture capitalists and private investors that can see the pharmaceutical companies' appetite as a potential target for their investments.

From a scientific and clinical point of view, as extensively published, several rare diseases are characterised by symptoms that are common to other and better

10 www.react-community.org, accessed 12 December 2012.

known pathologies. Narcolepsy for example can be considered a disease model whose molecular mechanisms can be in some cases associated with other neurodegenerative and autoimmune disorders (such as multiple sclerosis). Looking at the molecular mechanisms behind a rare disease, novel therapeutic pathways can be explored even for diseases with an impact on a larger population. This fact opens the door for pharmaceutical intervention in ways that can help far larger numbers of patients.

During the last two years (2010–2012) we have seen an increased interest on the part of the pharmaceutical industry. In February 2010, GSK (Glaxo) announced it was setting up a standalone unit to develop and commercialise orphan drugs. In April 2011, Sanofi Aventis acquired Genzyme, maker of the orphan drugs, Myozyme, Ceredase and Fabrazyme. Shire, the UK's third largest pharmaceutical company by market capitalisation is maintaining rapid growth largely because of its specialisation in treatments for rare diseases. Revenue in the second quarter of 2012 rose 14% from a year earlier to US$1.2 billion, driven by a 43% rise in sales of the ADHD (attention deficit hyperactivity disorder, a rare disease) treatment, Vyvanse. In November 2011 Roche signed a licensing agreement with PTC. Under the terms of the agreement, Roche gains an exclusive worldwide licence for PTC's SMA programme, which includes three compounds in preclinical development targeting spinal muscular atrophy, a genetic muscle-weakening rare disease, for an overall deal value of US$490 million.

An interesting Life Science Venture Capital Survey was published in *Start-Up* (2011) and the results increased our confidence in the validity of this project. The Survey regards the disease areas that venture capitalists find more compelling (see Fig. 10.1) and according to the response a great number of market players are interested in entering the rare diseases arena.

Figure 10.1 **Which disease area do you find compelling?**
Source: *Start-Up* 2011

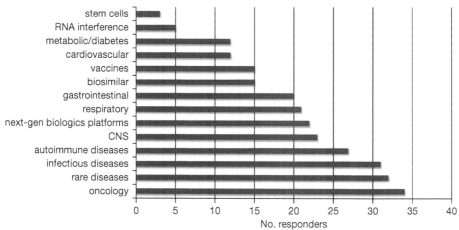

Table 10.1 **Diversified investment structure**

Vehicle	Closed End Fund
Asset under management	€50 million with a first closing at €30 million
Investment focus	Diagnostic tools and therapies in the orphan drug space at different development stages (up to phase II)
Portfolio companies	Diversified portfolio of approximately 15 investments

Based on these figures and other evidence, together with a few colleagues that embrace the same concept, I started working on and promoting a new financial platform that invests in rare diseases projects incorporated in start-up companies (with an industrial structure), where the investment is managed like a classical venture investment.

An adequately capitalised and diversified investment structure has been set and the governance structure is almost constituted (Table 10.1).

The fund managers, myself included, with my experience in life sciences venture investments, will deal with the screening, selection, due diligence and follow up of the investment opportunities (see Fig. 10.2).

A scientific advisory board driven by BLACKSWAN will be constituted to help in identifying the most promising projects.

The first step of defining the investment strategies, the fund team, structure and governance is almost finalised and we are currently in the fundraising phase supported by a financial adviser.

A global network of patient organisations, national diseases alliances, experts in pricing and reimbursement policies, is also being consolidated to support the initiative and a few potential programmes have been already identified as first target investments. We have also already started discussions with pharmaceutical companies interested in potential co-investments in specific opportunities whenever they fit their strategies.

Since we expect to have a high percentage of start-up companies, built up on university research programmes, appropriate management will be recruited to maximise the probability of success of the development and business plans. Each 'NewCo' can be financially supported to a stage at which proof of concept data are available to stimulate the appetite of a pharmaceutical company partner. The financial needs to reach such a stage are limited considering the reduced development timelines and the overall number of patients in the clinical trials. The investors can appreciate a relatively short holding period for each investment, forecasted to be 4–6 years, even when the start-up is at an early stage because of the reduced timelines to collect proof of concept clinical data on rare diseases populations.

The BLACKSWAN Foundation is supporting and promoting this initiative, helping in programme selection and understanding of the major clinical needs channelling through patient organisations and national diseases alliances. This initiative should have an important positive impact on patients and their families,

Figure 10.2 **Fund governance and investment process**

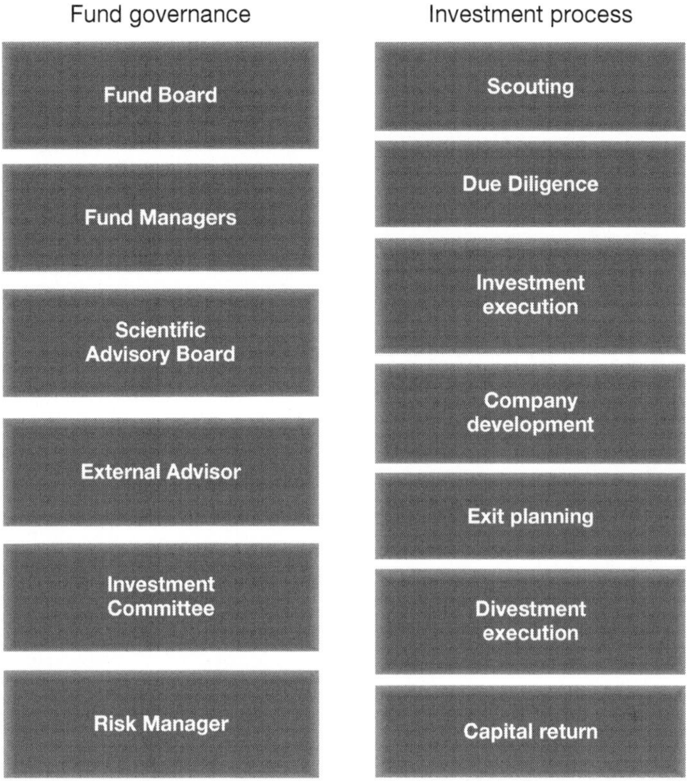

Fund governance	Investment process
Fund Board	Scouting
Fund Managers	Due Diligence
Scientific Advisory Board	Investment execution
External Advisor	Company development
Investment Committee	Exit planning
Risk Manager	Divestment execution
	Capital return

allowing the development of new diagnostic tools and new drugs to treat rare diseases patients.

Through the creation of these two platforms, RE(ACT) events and the investment vehicle, and thanks to the involvement of the four member groups (research scientists and clinicians, patient organisations, investors and pharmaceutical industry), we believe we are creating a win–win situation to help make available new medical solutions to rare disease patients while satisfying the needs of investors and of the market (pharmaceutical industry).

Reference

Start-Up (2011) 'START-UP's 2011 Life Science Venture Capital Survey: Biopharmaceutical Investors Let Some Sunshine In', *Start-Up: Emerging Medical Ventures*, 1 September 2011.

Dr **Olivier Menzel** graduated (BSc) in biology at the University of Geneva. He obtained his MSc in Medical Genetics at the Department of Genetic Medicine and Development in Geneva. During this tenure, he specialised in molecular and human genetics. Subsequently he moved to ISREC, the Swiss Institute for Experimental Cancer Research (EPFL) where he obtained his PhD. In December 2006, he joined the research laboratory of pediatric surgery at the University of Geneva Medical School, as Senior Research Assistant. He is supervising and working on the project of *ex vivo* gene therapy of rare metabolic liver diseases. In 2010 he founded the BLACKSWAN Foundation for supporting the research on orphan diseases. The Foundation is frequently referenced at the international level and linked to the most important stakeholders around Europe. In 2012 he organised the first International Congress on Research of Rare and Orphan Diseases: The RE(ACT) Congress. Based on the success of the congress, he realised the fundamental importance of having an international community, together with an online platform, of scientists working in the field of rare diseases in order to accelerate the accessibility to new therapeutic applications and to improve the quality of life of the patients. Therefore he created the RE(ACT) Community. He is a member of the board of ProRaris, the Swiss alliance of patient organisations.

Dr **Silvia Panigone** obtained her bachelor degree in Biological Sciences in 1996 and a PhD in Molecular and Cellular Oncology at the National Cancer Institute (INT), Milan (Italy) in collaboration with the Open University, London. She spent her first five years in academic research in Italy and the US and she then moved to Industry covering several roles from project leader of preclinical and clinical programmes, to Corporate Portfolio Manager & Business Development for R&D programmes (Bracco). She was in charge of the set up of two spin-off companies and she covered the role of Global Project Manager and Account Manager at Quintiles. She then moved to the finance sector as investment director in an venture firm (BSI Healthcapital, BSI/Generali group) where she was responsible for scouting, evaluation, due diligence and follow up of the investments, leading two investments, one in biotech and the other in medtech space. At present she is a board member of Globeimmune, Alphavax, Visioncare and SNC Holding, and co-director at Qualyst. She is currently an adviser of BSI SA bank, in the Merchant & Investment Banking department working on private equity projects. She is also Senior Director at XOVenture, a global cross-functional organisation of life science executives and experts. She is board member of BLACKSWAN Foundation and supportive member of the European Narcolepsy Network (EU-NN).

11
The rise and fall of Sanfilippo syndrome

Karen Aiach
LYSOGENE, France

11.1 *Ashes to Ashes*, David Bowie

Being told that one's child is going to suffer and die prematurely is the most tragic and bottomless experience in life. Feelings of devastation, ravage, desolation, solitude, rush through one's whole soul and body 24 hours a day. Life is silently ending up for one's child, oneself and the entire family. One feels that nothing will ever remain from all this but pain and void.

The tremendous metaphysical shock of diagnosis is often nurtured and reinforced as the major aspects of the disease are continuously ruminated. Deep anguish comes from the abstruse and hopeless information one constantly mulls over: 'neurodegenerative disease', 'severe, debilitating symptoms worsening over time', 'demyelination', 'chronic symptoms', 'life threatening condition', 'high unmet medical need'…not to mention unpronounceable words like 'mucopolysaccharidoses', 'alkaptonuria', 'glycosphingolipidoses', 'aspartylglucosaminuria', 'rhizomelic chondrodysplasia', '3-methylcrotonylglycinuria', 'glutaric aciduria type 1'…

However, whatever the technical meaning, parents know that behind the language, there is the inevitable decline and often loss of their child in the end. How then wouldn't they feel deprived of their intrinsic substance and roles, which are to protect and grow the children, accompany them during their adolescence and eventually bring them safely into adulthood? The question is then: 'what on earth should we do?'

11.2 *I'm Back*, Eminem

The day our baby daughter was diagnosed with Sanfilippo syndrome, a rare lethal disease, this disease was now to be her new and sole identity, we were told. We were torn apart.

After weeks of black hole and obscure inner fights, the bright side of our tempers gained the upper hand. Introduced by two guardian angels, Pierre and Yann, we started discovering an amazingly vivacious community—the rare diseases community—and some of its cutting edge patient advocacy groups. Knowing no frontier, these groups were striving for patient empowerment and making it happen. They were helping patients and their parents to gain more dignity than they had ever had before. When we got to know them, we came back to the world with more strength and motivation than ever. That was the beginning of our resilience process.

First, we discovered that families and patient advocacy groups were playing an increasingly instrumental role in this multi-stakeholder rare disease community. Not only were the patients and their families central players in care-giving and quality of life-ensuring activities. They were also committed to advancing public policy on medical research and health for rare diseases. And at that time, needless to say they had already won major battles…even if there is always a vast amount of work to do.

We also realised that patients and their families were essential players in research, not only as experts in the disease who can assist in developing projects, but also as participants or even leaders in the projects themselves.

As a consequence, we decided that our first mission was to understand as much as possible about Sanfilippo disease and its international research environment. We started our rare diseases- and more specifically lysosomal storage diseases-related 'education'. From PubMed pages to researchers' laboratories, from patient advocacy group meetings to hospital staffrooms, from PhDs to MDs, from Paris to Chappell Hill, Texas to Adelaide, we learnt and learnt again until we reached an unexpected and challenging conclusion: not enough would happen for our children from a mid-term therapeutic perspective, unless we took the initiative. Methods, motivation and money were missing. Our next decision was that we had to make it happen, and that we were going to do so in a way nobody had ever reasonably dreamed of: we would take the lead and set up a cutting edge therapeutic programme with the best-in-class partners, with an aim to effectively bring a first line investigational drug to Sanfilippo patients' bedsides.

11.3 *If I Can Make it There, I'll Make it Anywhere*, Frank Sinatra

Rare diseases (RDs) are defined as conditions affecting fewer than 200,000 patients for a given condition in the United States or less than 5 in 10,000 people in Europe.

Although any rare condition, by definition and taken individually, occurs infrequently in the general population, there are 8,000 or so rare diseases identified to date that affect millions of people in the world. Experts estimate that more than 60 million people are affected by an RD in the US and Europe alone.[1]

RDs are most often severely debilitating diseases associated with complex mixes of lifelong symptoms that lead to dramatically reduced life expectancies. Eighty per cent of orphan patients are children. In the illustrative case of Sanfilippo syndrome, an incurable lysosomal storage disease (LSD) with a heavy central nervous system involvement, patients do not usually live longer than their second decade.

At first glance, a patient affected with such a rare and severe disease should be perceived as unworthy of attention; obscure and unexplained conditions affecting only a few individuals worldwide should be perceived as structurally unattractive by pharmaceutical companies; and the belief that a drug could really be developed for a few children with highly complex conditions should be perceived as a utopia.

And well, there are objective reasons for that: the scientific, medical and ethical challenges to be faced in order to develop safe treatments for small and fragmented populations—and still more if these are paediatric ones—are considerable when compared with the perceived lack of commercial attractiveness they are associated with.

Developing drugs for RDs is an arduous task indeed, because of many considerable underlying factors.

Among others, the following realities have to be taken into consideration:

- For most diseases, pathophysiological mechanisms are only partly known, and epidemiological and biological data are insufficient

- Populations are small and often geographically scattered

- Disease-specific scientific and medical resources are scarce and scattered as well

- RDs are often severely debilitating and characterised by a complex mix of symptoms, making it difficult to determine biological and clinical end-points in order to assess the efficacy of treatments

- Patients are extremely vulnerable and often young, which raises concerns of protocol adherence and informed consent

- For the legitimate sake of safety and efficacy of (potential and/or approved) therapies, various regulations to be complied with (orphan-, paediatric- and advanced therapy medicinal product [ATMP] regulations for instance) are piling up in order to embrace the full complexity of human use of drugs

- Commercial attractiveness is perceived as lacking

- Business models can be challenging

1 www.eurordis.org, accessed 8 January 2013.

- Successful initiatives are still unknown to too many public and/or private investors
- Translational methods can be inadequate with respect to the challenges to be faced
- Funding is inadequate

Consequently, when new therapies emerge in the preclinical field, only outstanding work and skills can allow for a successful translation from animal proofs of concepts and laboratory benches to patient's bedsides. More than in any other areas, excellence should be the only rule.

Another fascinating consequence is that, paradoxically enough, the 'ultra-outsider' status of biotechnology-based orphan drugs is also what makes them unique pioneers:

- Patients to be treated are usually clearly identified
- Preclinical research is helped by the fact that most conditions are monogenic diseases[2]
- Unique physiological pathways involved in most rare diseases give them the status of 'model diseases' for most common conditions
- Regulatory requirements are meant to take into account the specificities of these drugs, even allowing for faster access to market in certain cases where unmet medical needs are extremely high and where market approval under exceptional circumstances can safely be envisaged
- Expertise is concentrated within dedicated scientific and clinical networks of excellence
- Patient advocacy groups interact more and more closely with the sponsors and other stakeholders (regulatory agencies, health technology assessment bodies) bringing added value all along the drug development process
- Multi-stakeholder processes are really at work, making it possible to bring value to each of them

Last but not least, thanks to the fact that they often target 'model diseases', orphan drugs are deemed to bring added value and therapies far beyond the boundaries of orphan diseases per se.

Our belief in this particular potential, together with a unique intrinsic patient-driven motivation, has been the pillar of our drug development project's inception and development and the creation of LYSOGENE, a gene therapy biotechnology company.

---

2 Monogenic diseases are single gene disorders resulting from a single mutated gene.

11.4 *Je Vois La Vie En Rose*, Edith Piaf

When we started the company, the momentum for orphan drugs was there. Until the early 1980s in effect, orphan diseases, paediatric or not, were completely ignored by health authorities, policy-makers and even by pharmaceutical companies. When governments were urged to design and enhance initiatives for rare diseases—mainly under the pressure of patient organisations such as NORD in the US or EURORDIS in Europe—things started to change. Years later, the implementation of the incentive-based orphan drug regulations in the US, in Europe and also in other regions, has had an undeniably positive impact in terms of stimulating research on rare diseases, scientific and medical innovation, as well as orphan drug discovery and development. This has had a global effect that is unanimously considered to be positive. In Europe alone, since the inception of the orphan drug regulation, approximately 60 new treatments for orphan diseases have received the centralised market approval, giving access to all Member States across the EU, and more than 600 experimental drugs have been designated as 'orphan'.

This blossoming of activities in orphan drug development has greatly contributed to the emergence of specialised biotech companies both in the US and Europe, stimulating employment and investment in innovation.

Additional regulations have been passed during the same period, such as paediatric regulations—applying to almost 80 per cent of orphan drugs—aiming at enhancing high quality and ethical paediatric biomedical research through an appropriate and stringent regulatory framework and policies on advanced therapies. These regulations have not been dictated by the need to develop orphan paediatric ATMPs; however, if you want to observe their effects, the latter are the best candidates because they fall under each of these policies concomitantly. From experience, the most blatant effect of those regulations on the drug development process we have seen until now is the pressing need to design and enforce a completely new body of best practices that can undoubtedly serve the whole pharmaceutical community.

11.5 LYSOGENE

LYSOGENE is now a clinical stage gene therapy company. It is developing a platform approach with a promising breakthrough to treat, and cure, life-threatening orphan diseases with a central nervous system (CNS) component that currently have few or no treatment options. The company's initial focus is on lysosomal storage diseases (LSDs) involving the CNS. LYSOGENE's first indication is for Sanfilippo syndrome type A (MPS-IIIA). It is developing a first-in-class gene therapy for MPS-IIIA, a rare genetic disorder. There are currently no treatment options for MPS-IIIA and most patients do not live beyond the second decade of life. The company's therapy, SAF-301, has successfully completed enrolment of its phase I/II clinical trials. Because of its 'genome', LYSOGENE will maintain the patient's quality of life as its key driver. To date, the company is run by its founder.

Karen Aiach is founding president and CEO of LYSOGENE, a clinical stage biotechnology company specialised in intracerebral gene delivery for the treatment of neurological diseases. In less than five years, Karen brought LYSOGENE's first product, SAF-301, into the clinic. SAF-301 is a gene therapy product aiming at treating a fatal lysosomal storage disease known as mucopolysaccharidosis type 3 or Sanfilippo Syndrome. Before creating LYSOGENE, Karen's entrepreneurial experience already included successfully founding and running a business consultancy specialised in the financial industry. Prior to that, Karen was a manager at Arthur Andersen where she began her career. At Andersen, she specialised in international M&A related transaction services for major tier one clients. From 2008 to 2009, Karen served as a Member of the Pediatric Committee of the European Medicine Agency established in accordance with the European Pediatric Regulation, as a patient representative. Karen has also been involved with several not-for-profit organisations engaged in advocacy and research in the field of rare diseases such as Alliance SANFILIPPO and EURORDIS, where she served on the board as treasurer from 2010 to 2011. Karen received her MS ('Grande Ecole') and MBA from ESSEC, France. She and her husband Gad reside in Paris, France, with their two children. Karen's involvement with biotechnology and advanced therapies stems from the diagnosis of her daughter with a fatal neurological orphan disease.

12

Lobbying for a national rare disease plan in the UK

Lessons for rare disease patient alliances

Stephen Nutt
Executive Officer, Rare Disease UK

This chapter examines the background to the campaign for a plan for rare diseases in the UK, and the establishment and role of Rare Disease UK (RDUK) in lobbying for a plan. RDUK's experience has been used to develop recommendations to inform other national alliances seeking to lobby their national governments to develop a rare disease plan. How recommendations would be applied in the particular circumstances of a particular alliance would of course vary, but nonetheless, it is hoped that the actions of RDUK can serve as a useful tool in informing the activity of others.

12.1 The European background to a plan for rare diseases

It was partly the recognition of a commonality of experience faced by people affected by rare diseases across Europe that the European Commission issued the 'Communication on rare diseases: Europe's challenges' in November 2008. The development of this Communication had been heavily informed by the European Rare Disease Task Force (RDTF), a multi-stakeholder group of experts from across the European Union (EU) which was established in January 2004 as part of the programme of Community action in the field of public health (2003–2008).[1]

The Communication recognised that the limited number of patients affected by each rare disease and scarce and fragmented knowledge and expertise made rare diseases an area of European added-value. Through cooperation, EU Member States could help ensure the most efficient utilisation of knowledge and expertise.

The Communication aimed:

> ...to be an integrated approach document, giving clear direction to present and future Community activities in the field of rare diseases in order to further improve the access and equity to prevention, diagnosis and treatment for patients suffering from a rare disease throughout the European Union.
> (European Commission 2008a: 2)

The broad objectives of the Communication were: to improve recognition and visibility of rare diseases; to develop European cooperation, coordination and regulation for rare diseases; and to support policies on rare diseases in Member States. It was the latter point which encompassed the recommendation that Member States of the EU develop national plans for rare diseases. This was reinforced by a proposal which accompanied the Communication for the Council of the European Union to issue a Recommendation to inform Member State plans or strategies on the issue (European Commission 2008b).

The Council of the European Union's 'Recommendation on an action in the field of rare diseases'[2] was adopted unanimously by each Member State in June 2009. According to the Recommendation, Member States should,

> elaborate and adopt a plan or strategy as soon as possible, preferably by the end of 2013 at the latest, aimed at guiding and structuring relevant actions in the field of rare diseases within the framework of their health and social systems.[3]

More specific actions proposed by the Recommendation related to:

- Ensuring that rare diseases are adequately coded and traceable in health information systems[4]

- Identifying needs and priorities for basic, clinical, translational and social research, and the inclusion in the rare disease plans or strategies of provisions aimed at fostering rare disease research to meet these needs[5]

---

1 Commission Decision 2004/192/EC.
2 eur-lex.europa.eu/LexUriServ/LexUriServ.do?uri=OJ:C:2009:151:0007:0010:EN:PDF, accessed 13 December 2012.
3 Council Recommendation s.1(a).
4 Council Recommendation s.2.
5 Council Recommendation s.3.

- Identifying centres of expertise for rare diseases and to consider supporting their creation[6]

- Gathering national expertise to support the sharing of this expertise across Europe[7]

- Empowering patient organisations including facilitating patient access to information on rare diseases[8]

The existence of the Council Recommendation, and its unanimous adoption by each of the EU's Member States was a significant milestone in European rare disease policy. Ensuring its implementation at the Council of Ministers meeting (which took place under the Czech Presidency) was by no means straightforward. Professor Milan Macek Jr, Chairman of the Institute of Biology and Medical Genetics in the Czech Republic, was a key adviser during the process. An OrphaNews (2009) article following the adoption on the Recommendation reported:

> Up to the final moment of adoption, the possibility of discord amongst the Council Ministers threatened to hinder the process. The challenge, commented Prof. Macek, lay in '…trying to reconcile the conflicting views on the role of government in regulating healthcare, together with balancing the principle of national "subsidiarity" with EU-wide principles in this area'. These differences, he explained, are a 'reflection of the rich cultural diversity across Europe'. He defined one principal challenge of the Council Ministers meeting as 'keeping the focus on the crucial elements of the Recommendation'.

Despite the achievement of ensuring the Recommendation was adopted unanimously and the significant milestones created by the Commission's Communication and Council Recommendation, a far greater challenge lay ahead in ensuring that each Member State developed and implemented plans or strategies for rare diseases as set out by the Recommendation. This was particularly true against the backdrop of the global financial crisis that had engulfed Member States with public spending subject to cuts and as austerity became the new watchword.

12.2 The impact of European policies in the UK

After the Council Recommendation was adopted, the impact it would have in the UK was uncertain for a number of reasons. Council of the European Union recommendations aim to influence policy in Member States; however, they are not binding, for example, in the way directives are. Although recommendations do carry

---

6 Council Recommendation s.4.
7 Council Recommendation s.5.
8 Council Recommendation s.6.

political weight it would be entirely possible for Member States, including the UK, to ignore the commitment made by adopting the Recommendation, or there was a danger that policy-makers might merely pay lip service to meeting its aims. This is a challenge for all patient organisations seeking to lobby their governments to implement national plans.

It was by no means certain that any meaningful action would be taken in the UK in response to a non-binding Recommendation, particularly in the field of health policy which is largely reserved for Member States. The position of the Department of Health in England was ambiguous in terms of whether there was any intention to develop a plan or a strategy for rare diseases. On 22 May 2009, the then Health Minister responsible for this area, Dawn Primarolo MP, wrote a letter to a Member of Parliament, Diane Abbott MP, which stated:

> Although we appreciate the needs of those people affected by rare medi-
> cal conditions, we currently have no plans to set up a national plan. We
> believe that the health and social care needs of those living with rare dis-
> eases should be met by local health bodies, which have the responsibility
> to commission services to meet all the needs of their local population.

It was a matter of concern that, less than three weeks before the Council of Min-isters' meeting on 9 June 2009, the possibility of developing a national plan did not seem an option. The belief that the needs of patients affected by rare diseases should be met by local health bodies was even more concerning, demonstrat-ing the low levels of awareness of the nature of rare diseases in the Department of Health. This is particularly so as specialised commissioning arrangements had been developed in England, recognition that the needs of patients affected by rare diseases cannot always be met by local health bodies.

Following a reshuffle of the Ministers at the Department of Health, Gillian Merron MP became the Minister responsible for this area of policy. After the Council meet-ing on 9 June, the Chair of Rare Disease UK wrote to the Minister to clarify the Department of Health's position following the adoption of the Recommendation. The response lacked any firm commitment to developing a national plan, but was nevertheless encouraging:

> We will be scoping out how we can ensure that the Recommendation's
> actions are imbedded into our systems across the UK with colleagues in
> the devolved administrations…please be rest assured that…[we] will be in
> touch later in the year to discuss how we can work with you to ensure that
> the Recommendation is effectively implemented across the UK.[9]

However, the same day, a letter was also sent to Edward Timpson MP which reverted to the position expressed by the Minister prior to the signing of the Rec-ommendation, which was that 'we currently have no plans to set up a national plan'

---

9 Letter from Gillian Merron MP to Alastair Kent dated 21 July 2009.

and a reiteration that the needs of people living with rare diseases could be met by local health bodies.

The situation was further complicated by the nature of the health system in the UK. The UK is considered as one Member State in the EU; however, there are four countries in the UK—England, Scotland, Wales and Northern Ireland—each with its own health ministers, governmental departments and increasingly different health service. For example, Northern Ireland is unique in the UK in having an integrated health and social care system; in England and Northern Ireland there is a split between purchasers of services (commissioners) and the providers of services, whereas Scotland and Wales abolished the purchaser/provider split after devolved powers over health policy were granted to the Scottish Parliament and the Welsh Assembly in 1999. In terms of commissioning and planning services for rare diseases, different commissioning bodies exist in each of the home nations, each with their own commissioning arrangements. Different bodies also exist in each nation to make decisions about whether or not a medicine should be funded; however, there are also overlaps in some respects. For example, Wales will follow the decisions of the National Institute of Care Excellence (NICE) in England; however, NICE generally does not appraise 'ultra-orphan' medicines, leaving Wales to make its own decisions through the All-Wales Medicines Strategy Group (AWMSG). To complicate matters further, some aspects of research governance policy is set for the UK at Westminster, whereas other aspects of research policy are set by the governments of each nation individually.

There was little precedent on how a European Recommendation on health policy, concerning a broad range of health and research issues relating to rare diseases, would be implemented in the UK, particularly given the diverse health systems. While there had been correspondence about the Recommendation between the different health departments, it was unclear to external observers to what extent the health departments in Scotland, Wales and Northern Ireland were engaged in the issue. It was not known whether (should a plan be developed) the plan would be a UK-wide plan, and if so, how the differences between the health systems would be incorporated, or whether each home nation would develop its own plans independently. The downside to the latter would be that collaboration is needed to provide the optimum level of service to patients with rare diseases and to utilise scarce expertise effectively, particularly considering the small populations of Northern Ireland, Wales and Scotland.

It was not until July 2010, almost a year after the Recommendation was signed, that the first public confirmation was made by the Department of Health in England that the UK would be developing a national plan, and that the plan was being developed collaboratively between each of the UK's home nations.[10] This

---

10 Parliamentary Under-Secretary of State, Anne Milton MP, in a response to a written parliamentary question from Ian Liddell-Grainger MP (13 July 2010 [7108]), www.publications
.parliament.uk/pa/cm201011/cmhansrd/cm100713/text/100713w0004.htm#1007141000479,
accessed 13 December 2012.

confirmation was particularly notable as, following the May 2010 general election, the Labour Party Government was ousted and replaced by a coalition between the Conservative Party and the Liberal Democrats. Although it was under the Labour Government that the Recommendation was signed, a confirmation was never received that a plan for rare diseases would be developed while that Government was in power. The commitment to developing a plan was subsequently reaffirmed by each of the devolved nations. This represented a significant milestone in the campaign for a rare disease plan in the UK.

How the commitment by the Conservative–Liberal Democrat Government was secured is discussed later on in the chapter.

12.3 Recommendation 1: Unite the stakeholder community for a stronger voice

Genetic Alliance UK (formerly the Genetic Interest Group) was founded in 1989. Owing to the large number of policy issues that were arising in the genetic field in the late 1980s, it became apparent that one voice was needed for all people affected by genetic conditions: 'There were many patient support groups, but little communication between them and most, entirely run by volunteers, could only handle the immediate concerns of their members' disorder and carried out no policy work' (Genetic Alliance UK 2006).

Genetic Alliance UK aims to improve the lives of people affected by genetic conditions by ensuring that high-quality services and information are available to all who need them.[11]

The organisation sets out to achieve this by raising awareness of genetic conditions and improving the quality of services and information available to patients and families; actively campaigning on issues of policy and practice to influence governments, policy-makers, industry and care providers such as the National Health Service; and by providing a united voice for all those affected by genetic conditions, to work together towards a common goal of making life better for patients and families at risk.

It is estimated that at least 80% of rare diseases are genetic in origin. As a result, Genetic Alliance UK has always had a strong interest in rare diseases and in advocating on behalf of patients and families affected by these diseases. To this end, the Director of Genetic Alliance UK sat on the RDTF discussed above, which was actively involved in drawing up the European Council Recommendation on rare diseases.

11 Genetic Alliance UK: mission statement, www.geneticalliance.org.uk/mission-statement.htm, accessed 3 January 2013.

With the increasing interest in rare diseases at a European level, Genetic Alliance UK spotted the window of opportunity to capitalise on this interest and to use it as a lever of change to improve rare disease services and facilitate research in the UK. Following discussions with key stakeholder groups, Genetic Alliance UK established a new organisation, Rare Disease UK (RDUK), which was launched in November 2008 to coincide with the European Commission's 'Communication on Rare Diseases'.

RDUK's tagline is 'the national alliance for people with rare diseases and all who support them'. The organisation was established to campaign for the development of a national plan for rare diseases in the UK, to shape the content of a national plan, and to ensure that a plan is implemented in practice. What was unique about RDUK was that it was a multi-stakeholder organisation, aimed at bringing together patient organisations, individual patients and carers, clinicians, health professionals, researchers and the pharmaceutical industry. Genetic Alliance UK had recognised that each of these groups had a strong interest in seeing improved care, information, treatment and support for patients affected by rare diseases as well as the need to facilitate and promote research in the field.

It is frequently asked why Genetic Alliance UK established a separate organisation to campaign for a rare disease plan, and did not undertake this activity under its own banner. The answer largely lies in the composition of the organisation; Genetic Alliance UK is an umbrella organisation representing over 150 patient organisations,[12] it is a charity and only charities or individual patients/carers can become a member. Although the organisation has always had a close relationship with a range of stakeholder groups, it ultimately represents patients and campaigns from a patient perspective. RDUK was established as a separate organisation in order to be able to effectively represent the views and interests of a broad stakeholder community. Despite being a multi-stakeholder organisation, patients' interests are the central tenet of RDUK.

The organisation does not have a separate legal identity; it is an unincorporated organisation and it is very much rooted in its parent organisation, Genetic Alliance UK. RDUK's activities are ultimately accountable to the Genetic Alliance UK Board of Trustees, comprising only patients and patient representatives.

RDUK has provided a vehicle for all stakeholders to act collaboratively and this has been one of its core strengths. By working together, it has been possible to demonstrate the strong weight of opinion behind developing a national plan for rare diseases. Rather than each stakeholder group acting in isolation, RDUK unites these to call for a common goal. One of the most notable features to come out of the process has been how little disagreement there has been between the different groups. Of course different groups have different priorities and there may be minor disagreement about the best way to achieve certain objectives, but there is a strong willingness and desire to work together to achieve the end goals. This was

12 As of the time of writing in August 2012.

demonstrated during the development of the report 'Improving Lives, Optimising Resources: A Vision for the UK Rare Disease Strategy' which is discussed below.

RDUK's work has been funded almost solely through unrestricted educational grants from the pharmaceutical industry. Another question that arises frequently is whether this has been problematic in terms of being considered a reputable organisation by policy-makers to convey patient's interests. In RDUK's experience, this has not been the case. As well as providing an important perspective in a multi-stakeholder organisation, industry support has enabled RDUK to conduct its programme of activity while offering free membership to other stakeholders, which is particularly important to enable the involvement of rare disease patient organisations which often operate with very limited resources. By August 2012, RDUK had amassed over 1,200 members which included 220 patient organisations, cementing its position as a powerful voice for the rare disease community.

To counter any negative perceptions which may arise from being entirely funded by industry, RDUK introduced a management committee made up of ten members[13] which is responsible for decision-making about RDUK's plans and activities. The committee has representatives from industry, but also representation from patient organisations, the research community, clinicians, health professionals and, within the committee, each of the UK's four home nations are represented. RDUK also operates a policy whereby each member company pays an equal amount, demonstrating that no one company has any greater say. RDUK complies with the Code of Practice for the Pharmaceutical Industry (ABPI 2012) which in Clause 23 sets out standards governing the relationship between patient organisations and pharmaceutical companies.

A secondary, but also important reason why Genetic Alliance UK established RDUK as a separate organisation was that it created a stronger brand. Genetic Alliance UK's membership includes patient organisations representing conditions which are not classed as rare. Moreover, as approximately 20% of rare diseases are not genetic, a campaign led under the banner of 'genetic' had the danger of making certain condition groups feel excluded or marginalised. RDUK created a strong brand identity and the sense that all stakeholders with an interest in rare diseases could buy in to the initiative.

12.4 Recommendation 2: Demonstrate the issues

One of the challenges of lobbying or campaigning on issues relating to rare diseases collectively as opposed to individual diseases is how little information or evidence is available to support arguments and to strengthen campaign messages. While in the early days of RDUK some organisations in the UK had produced evidence about

---

13 www.raredisease.org.uk/rduk-governance.htm, accessed 14 December 2012.

the impact of living with a rare disease on a patient and their family/carers, this tended to be very condition-focused, which although useful and extremely important, is difficult to translate into messages to represent rare diseases more broadly. Even information relating to specific conditions was, and still is, scarce. Much useful evidence had been produced at a European level, particularly by EURORDIS, the European Organisation for Rare Diseases, but this still left a gap in terms of UK-specific information.

This evidence gap was compounded by the fact that there are no official figures about how many people are actually affected by rare diseases in the UK. This information is not recorded, so it is impossible to calculate accurately, for example, how much rare diseases cost the health service. Nevertheless, it was important to demonstrate the scale of the issue of rare diseases. RDUK took the estimate arising from the European Commission that 1 in 17 people will be affected by a rare disease at some point in their lives which amounts to 3.5 million people in the UK. This message is reiterated in all of RDUK's communications along with the tagline 'collectively, rare diseases are not rare'. Emphasising how prevalent rare diseases are collectively and, accordingly, how they should be treated as a major health issue, has underpinned RDUK's campaigning activity.

Health campaigns are often led by patient organisations that can generate their own information and statistics to support these campaigns. Patient organisations representing rare disease patients are often small or entirely volunteer-led and lack the capacity to undertake this activity when their main objective is to provide support and information to patients, and for many rare diseases there are no patient organisations. Moreover, it is difficult to conduct a high-profile campaign around a disease which affects few people. This is in contrast to some of the major charities, representing generally more common conditions which can undertake research and formulate campaign messages as a result of this research. There is a very well-developed charity sector in the UK with a large number of these organisations carrying out lobbying and campaigning activity; many charities also have lobbying and campaigning teams who can work specifically on this.

Faced with a crowded health-lobbying field, it was vital that RDUK generated evidence to support its campaign messages if the issues affecting patients and families living with rare diseases were to be noticed by policy-makers. It was also important that these messages could reflect the commonality of the experience of people affected by rare diseases in order to have a greater impact. As a result RDUK set about producing a report which aimed to capture some of these experiences.

RDUK developed a wide-ranging survey covering topics including access to information and support, coordination of care, access to treatment, diagnosis and participation in research. The aim of the survey was to gain a better understanding of the issues faced by patients and families in accessing the services and support to be able to effectively communicate these to policy-makers.

Over the summer of 2010 a survey was distributed to members of RDUK, many of whom circulated it on to their own contacts. Nearly 600 responses were received representing 119 different rare diseases. Responses to the survey were split almost evenly between an individual with a rare condition and a family member/carer of a person with a rare condition.

The results of the survey highlighted obtaining a diagnosis of a rare disease as a significant area of concern. Without an accurate diagnosis patients and families cannot access effective treatment or manage their condition appropriately. Despite this, almost half (46 per cent) of patients with rare diseases had to wait over one year for a final diagnosis following the onset of symptoms. Of this number, one in five (20 per cent) had waited over five years and over one in ten (12 per cent) had waited over ten years. The results also reveal a striking inequality of experience with 26 per cent of respondents receiving a diagnosis within three months, whereas 36 per cent waited over two years.

Misdiagnosis was also revealed to be a significant factor in delayed diagnosis; 46 per cent of patients were initially incorrectly diagnosed and 30 per cent had received three or more misdiagnoses. Delays in diagnosis and misdiagnosis may involve multiple avoidable hospital appointments and patients receiving inappropriate treatments and tests. Not only is this an inefficient use of the resources of the health service, it can also lead to a deterioration of the condition while appropriate treatment and management of the condition is delayed. Many survey respondents reported the period prior to diagnosis as particularly distressing for both the patient and their family.

The findings of the survey highlighted a significant lack of support for rare disease patients with both their medical and non-medical needs. Only a third of respondents reported receiving sufficient support with their social needs; fewer still (29 per cent) felt that they receive sufficient psychological support. Less than a quarter (24 per cent) receive enough support with financial concerns. This is particularly problematic when considering that 61 per cent of those who care for someone with a rare disease reported that their role as a carer affected their ability to hold paid employment.

The survey highlighted how patients often struggled to access information about all aspects of living with, and managing, a rare condition. Over half of respondents (52 per cent) felt that they had not been given sufficient information on their condition following diagnosis. Even more worryingly, many respondents elaborated that they were given no information at all on diagnosis suggesting patients are left to their own initiative to find information on their condition even though good quality information about rare diseases can be difficult to find. Nearly two-thirds of patients (64 per cent) were not given details of the relevant patient support groups at the time of diagnosis, despite the fact that in RDUK's experience these organisations are a vital source of information and support; in the survey 52 per cent reported that patient organisations are the main source of information on their condition.

Most rare diseases affect multiple parts of the body and many different professionals often need to be involved in care and treatment. It is essential that there is good coordination and communication between all those involved. However, 75 per cent of respondents do not have a care coordinator. This aggravates a number of other problems experienced by patients and families as a result of poor coordination of care. Many problems were highlighted in the survey, including the following: each professional the patient comes into contact with looks at a specific aspect of the condition, but no one is concerned with the condition as a whole; patients or families have to repeatedly explain their condition to all those involved in their care because of a lack of knowledge about rare diseases; feelings of being lost in the healthcare system; patients' notes are lost or not passed on; patients and families have no one to go to with queries about their condition or care; and there is a lack of continuity of professionals involved in the care of the patient.

The results of the survey were highlighted in a report, 'Experiences of Rare Diseases: An Insight from Patients and Families' (Limb *et al.* 2010), which was launched in December 2010. Accompanying the survey results were case studies from 11 patients or family members about their experience of rare diseases to put the results of the survey into the context of the experience of real people. In the survey, free text boxes were included alongside many of the questions to allow respondent to elaborate on any of the issues should they wish to. This provided some powerful quotes which are used throughout the report to strengthen the messages.

Many of these findings confirmed what RDUK and Genetic Alliance UK had heard time and time again from patients anecdotally, but having statistics to reinforce some of these issues has been a key tool in ensuring that RDUK's messages are communicated effectively and has reinforced why a plan for rare diseases is needed in the UK to address these issues. One of the most important things the report demonstrated was that, despite the vast range of rare diseases, each with very different symptoms and prognoses, patients often face similar issues in accessing the services to meet their needs and, through this shared experience, it is possible to develop a plan for rare diseases to improve the experience of all patients.

The launch of the report provided the opportunity to gain media coverage to raise awareness of rare diseases. Obtaining media coverage to support the objective of securing a national plan for rare diseases in the UK can be difficult, but it is greatly aided by the launch of new 'newsworthy' findings.

While the 'Experiences of Rare Diseases' report continues to be valuable to help communicate the issues faced by patients, the majority of the respondents to the survey were based in England, which, even though the number of responses received were roughly proportionate to the population make-up of the UK,[14] weakens the message in the devolved nations. As a result, RDUK is conducting country-specific patient experience surveys in Scotland and Wales, the results of which will inform new reports which will be launched in 2013. In Northern Ireland, a survey conducted by the Patient and Client Council into patients' experiences of obtaining a diagnosis of a rare disease, highlighted many similar issues to the RDUK 'Experiences of Rare Diseases' report. The report 'Experience of Diagnosis: Views of Patients and Carers of Diagnosis of Rare Disease in Northern Ireland' (Patient

---

14 Of the respondents, 78 per cent lived in England, 12 per cent in Scotland, 6 per cent in Wales and 3 per cent in Northern Ireland.

and Client Council 2012) was launched on Rare Disease Day 2012, generating significant media attention in the country. This report demonstrated the value of country-specific, targeted information.

It is crucial to identify where some of the gaps in evidence are and to take steps to generate more evidence accordingly. Of course, many alliances will be operating with limited resources, so prioritisation of this activity is vital. In this respect RDUK identified supporting rare disease research as one of the potentially weaker areas of a national plan for rare diseases in the UK. To strengthen campaign messages around the importance of research into rare diseases, RDUK is currently conducting a review of how public and major funding bodies support research in this area. This review is not simply looking at how much funding is allocated to rare disease research, although this is of course an important consideration, but also whether there are any barriers preventing successful applications and how public and major funders promote opportunities in the area. A report outlining these findings will be launched in early 2013.

Another review currently being conducted by RDUK is looking at the value of care coordinators. The 'Experiences of Rare Diseases' report highlighted how important effective coordination of care is to improving patient experience. It is also generally accepted that, if a patient affected by a multi-system rare disease has a designated care coordinator, this leads to better health outcomes. Many care coordinator posts are funded by patient organisations, but these posts are vulnerable to financial pressures. Also, at a time where health service budgets are under pressure, care coordinator posts can be an easy target for cuts. To support RDUK's campaign for every patient with a chronic multi-system rare disease to have a designated care coordinator, RDUK is undertaking a review of the value of these posts, both to the patient and to the health service through improved efficiency and better patient outcomes. Given that the creation of these posts involves additional expenditure (although there is evidence that they save the health service money in the long term), strong campaign messages are needed to reinforce RDUK's calls.

12.5 Recommendation 3: Be clear about your asks

The Council of the European Union Recommendation gave some guidance about the content of national plans for rare diseases, but these were by no means comprehensive given that Member States would have to develop plans according to the specifics of their national health systems. It is unlikely that Member States would have accepted a highly prescriptive Recommendation outlining in detail the content of national plans. Given this lack of guidance, it is important that alliances seeking to lobby policy-makers to develop a rare disease plan are clear about what an effective plan for rare diseases should include. This is particularly so as those affected by or working in the field of rare diseases are the experts in terms of knowledge of the issues that need to be addressed and possible solutions.

When the Council Recommendation was signed, although RDUK had some idea of what an effective plan for rare diseases in the UK would need to include, it had by no means a comprehensive 'wish list' nor had it gathered the expertise and views of its membership on the issue in a systematic way. To be able to effectively communicate what the UK plan should look like to policy-makers, RDUK undertook its biggest piece of work to produce recommendations to inform the development of the national plan. Given the difficult financial climate at the time, it was crucial from the outset that any recommendations would have to be realistic and there was a strong focus on how resources could be used more efficiently. If additional expenditure was advocated, it should be emphasised how this could be offset by better health outcomes leading to improved efficiencies in the long run.

The process of developing recommendations for a rare disease plan began in mid-late 2009 and culminated in the launch of a report on Rare Disease Day in February 2011. The report, 'Improving Lives, Optimising Resources: A Vision for the UK Rare Disease Strategy' (Limb and Nutt 2011), sets out RDUK's comprehensive recommendations to inform a plan for rare diseases. The title reflects how an effective rare disease plan would not only lead to improved outcomes for patients, but also improved efficiencies within the NHS, a message which was received well by policy-makers. In the past, a significant public focus on rare diseases had been around orphan medicines which are often expensive. However, it was important to counter the perception that 'rare diseases equal expensive' as there will not be expensive interventions for the majority of rare diseases.

Alongside desk research and an extensive number of meetings and interviews with a broad range of stakeholders, in order to develop the report RDUK undertook a number of activities to gather evidence systematically. Central to the process were five multi-stakeholder working groups established by RDUK under the headings Coordination of Research; Prevention and Diagnosis; Commissioning and Planning; Patient Care, Information and Support; and Delivering Coordinated Care. Each of these working groups included representatives from a diverse range of backgrounds including patients/family members, representatives from patient organisations, researchers, clinicians, healthcare professionals, geneticists, pharmaceutical industry and commissioners.

Each group had approximately 10–12 members and a chair and was free to decide its own lines of inquiry; RDUK did, however, provide suggested terms of reference to each group, which they subsequently adapted to suit the needs of the group. RDUK also asked the working groups to consider a number of principles in developing recommendations. The first was that any recommendations developed should be responsive to changing patterns of NHS organisation. This proved to be particularly important following the massive reorganisation of the NHS in England following the election of the Conservative–Liberal Democrat Government in May 2010. Owing to the great uncertainty about what the new structures would look like, it was crucial that the recommendations were adaptable no matter how the NHS was arranged.

The second principle related to the existence of the four different health services in the UK. Given that the report aimed to cover the whole of the UK, recommendations should be relevant to all four home nations and adaptable to the different NHS structures in each. In recognition of the financial climate, recommendations should lead to a more efficient use of resources to maximise the health gain for patients with rare diseases, or where appropriate, the targeted use of resources for better outcomes.

The final principle that the working groups operated under was to make use of examples of good practice, both to ensure that current good practice is being optimally utilised and in order to provide models for new services. Examples of good practice also demonstrate that it is possible to provide high-quality services to patients affected by rare diseases, counter to the perceptions of many that it is simply 'too difficult' or 'too expensive'.

The working groups met over a period of a year. The approach of each working group was tailored to its particular needs; despite this the structure of the inquiry followed a broadly similar pattern: first, an assessment of the current situation was undertaken to identify needs; second, the groups developed initial solutions to the problem areas; third, examples of good practice were collected to act as models of service provision; and, finally, concrete recommendations were framed on the basis of the evidence gathered.

Midway through the process of developing the recommendations, a consultation document was produced outlining the initial recommendations of each working group. Aimed at stimulating further input, RDUK encouraged respondents to comment on the recommendations and issues identified, to elaborate on the recommendations with examples of good practice, to highlight problem areas and to suggest other solutions. The consultation was distributed to RDUK members and to other key stakeholders leading to 92 written responses from a range of different stakeholder groups and organisations.

Although there were members of the working groups professionally based across all four of the UK's home nations, RDUK was aware that there was not a representative from each devolved nation at each meeting. This could have led to a failure to take into account the increasingly divergent nature of the NHS and of health policy in each of the home nations when framing the recommendations. It was crucial not to overlook these differences.

In order to address the issue, three focus groups were held in Scotland, Wales and Northern Ireland. The focus groups broadly reviewed the recommendations highlighted in the consultation document, highlighting specific considerations or differences where appropriate. The focus groups comprised a range of stakeholders similar to the composition of the working groups as well as representation from the health departments of the devolved administrations.

The most striking outcome of the focus groups was that, while there are differences in the structures and organisations of each home nation and geographical considerations need to be taken into account, the needs of patients with rare diseases generally remain the same and the principles underlying our recommendations are applicable across the UK.

The European Project for Rare Diseases National Plans Development (EUROPLAN) was a three-year project of the European Commission's Programme of Community action in the field of Public Health (2003–2008), which began in April 2008. The ultimate aims of the project were to create guidance to aid the development of national plans/strategies for rare diseases, and to establish indicators to evaluate the impact of these plans/strategies. One of the work streams of the project involved organising conferences in 15 Member States to gather more information on the provision of services for rare diseases at a national level to inform the Commission in developing their final recommendations. RDUK was responsible for hosting the UK conference on 16 November 2010. With over 80 attendees, including representation from the health departments, the conference provided an opportunity to gather more valuable evidence to inform the recommendations outlined in the report (EUROPLAN 2010).

Additional evidence-gathering activities to inform the report included hosting a one-day workshop with the Association of Medical Research Charities (AMRC) to examine rare disease research and holding an afternoon of workshops relating to the plan at the Genetic Alliance UK 2010 Annual Conference. The evidence gathered from the 'Experiences of Rare Diseases' report was also used in the formation of recommendations for a rare disease plan. In total, 1,000 individuals and organisations contributed to the development of RDUK's recommendations.

The 'Improving Lives, Optimising Resources' report produced as a result of this work is the most comprehensive report on rare diseases ever produced in the UK. It outlines 27 broad recommendations and 89 specific recommendations to inform the UK rare disease plan.

Recommendations aimed at ensuring faster diagnosis and timely access to relevant care involves improving professionals' knowledge and awareness of rare diseases. It is recommended that this could be achieved through the development of an online 'portal' to reliable information, for example, and the inclusion of a module in rare diseases in medical training.

Other recommendations include ensuring the provision of ongoing patient-centred information on an individual's condition and how to manage it, including the provision of 'information prescriptions' for newly diagnosed patients. Closely related is the development of personalised care plans for patients setting out drug, therapy and follow up regimens ideally being linked to standard treatment guidelines for the condition.

As discussed previously RDUK advocates designating patients a care coordinator to oversee implementation of their care plan and to ensure all aspects of their care are brought together at the right time, are patient-centred, holistic and considerate of non-medical needs including social, psychological and financial needs.

A number of recommendations involve ensuring that commissioning and planning systems for rare disease services enable equitable access to services and treatments available in the UK. This includes the establishment of centres of excellence for clusters of diseases based on the needs and clinical features of conditions.

There are recommendations to ensure integration between specialised services and services delivered locally and to facilitate the dissemination of knowledge and information.

Recommendations relating to research include the provision of dedicated funding streams and the establishment of sustainable registries, while consideration is also given to how the research and development approval system in the UK has an adverse impact on research into rare diseases.

The 'Improving Lives' report was received by representatives of the health departments as it was launched at receptions in each of the UK's parliaments, and each health department confirmed that the recommendations would be taken into account in developing a plan for rare diseases in the UK.

As well as providing a blueprint for what RDUK hopes to achieve through a national plan, the process of developing the 'Improving Lives' report also allowed members to actively participate in and influence RDUK's work. The process of developing the recommendations helped to reinforce recommendations 1 and 2 of this chapter—to unite the stakeholder community and to demonstrate the issues—by working collaboratively to develop recommendations, it was possible to demonstrate that each stakeholder group was working to a common goal, which provided a powerful message to policy-makers. In addition, the process built on the 'Experiences of Rare Diseases' report by highlighting the issues facing both patients and professionals working in the field.

12.6 Recommendation 4: Involve patients in your lobbying activity

Of course the involvement of patients is of paramount importance in the activities of any organisation seeking to represent patients. However, there will be key points when it is particularly important to utilise the power of patient advocacy to achieve campaign objectives. A balance must be struck between enlisting your supporters and over-burdening your supporters. This is particularly so as patients with ill-health will not always be able to contribute actively and carers and family members will often already be busy with the demands of day-to-day care. Moreover, if there is a condition-specific patient organisation, a patient or carer may already have commitments to that organisation and any activity relating to the national rare disease alliance will be on top of this. As a result it is important to make it easy for people to get involved and enlist support when it will be most helpful to achieve campaign objectives.

There have been a number of key stages when RDUK has enlisted the support of patients and families to great effect. Two of these will be explored below to demonstrate the effect that patient advocacy can have.

The UK is split into 650 constituencies each represented by one Member of Parliament (MP) who is responsible for representing the interests of the people in their constituency (their constituents). Facilitating interaction between a patient/carer and their MP is an effective way to generate political pressure on the government. Scotland, Wales and Northern Ireland, as discussed above, have their own administrations responsible for health policy: the Scottish Parliament, Welsh Assembly and the Northern Ireland Assembly, respectively. In Scotland each person has eight MSPs (Members of the Scottish Parliament) who represent them (one constituency and seven regional); in Wales each person has five AMs (Assembly Members) who represent them (one constituency and four regional); and in Northern Ireland (which has multi-member constituencies) each person is represented by six MLAs (Members of the Legislative Assembly).

In order to facilitate interaction between patients and their elected representatives, RDUK conducts contact campaigns which encourage patients, carers and also other stakeholders to write to their elected representatives about a specific issue. RDUK draws up four template letters (one for England, Scotland, Wales and Northern Ireland) for members to adapt and send to their elected representative. A space is always left for a patient/carer to write briefly about their particular condition and experience. Alongside the contact politicians receive through their constituents, RDUK also contacts key politicians: for example, those who have been supportive in the past, those with an interest in the topic and members of key committees such as the health committee.

Such contact campaigns can be effective at times of change; this is illustrated by RDUK's contact campaign in the run up to the 2010 general election. The reader may recall that under the Labour Government which signed the Council Recommendation, a commitment was never made to developing a plan for rare diseases. In the run up to the election, it was apparent from the opinion polls and political commentary that there would be a change of governing party and Labour's 13 years in power would come to an end. It was also apparent that this, coupled with a number of MPs standing down, would lead to a massive turnover of MPs with an unprecedented number of new MPs to target to raise awareness of rare diseases and to gain support for a rare disease plan; in the event, predictions turned out to be accurate as there were 232 new MPs. Spotting the opportunity to influence policy in advance of the election, RDUK encouraged members to contact their local candidates in the election to ask for their support for a rare disease plan. RDUK advised members of those candidates most likely to win in the area to avoid members having to contact candidates with little chance of winning.

Following the election, the process was repeated; RDUK provided a template letter for members to adapt to send to their elected MP and targeted key new politicians with an interest in health policy. This process was successful in generating a body of supportive politicians and in generating political pressure on the new government to commit to developing a rare disease plan.

Another benefit arising from the election was that two out of the four new ministers in the Department of Health in England had experience of or interest in the field of rare diseases. One was Earl Howe, a member of the House of Lords, who prior to the election had chaired the Specialised Healthcare Alliance (SHCA), an alliance of patient organisations and pharmaceutical companies advocating specialised commissioning for rarer diseases. RDUK had also formed a relationship with Earl Howe given this interest and knowledge. Anne Milton MP was also appointed as a junior health minister. In the previous parliament, Ms Milton had chaired the All Party Parliamentary Group (APPG) on Rare Diseases for which RDUK had provided the secretariat, so she was also familiar with the issue of rare diseases.

Similar contact campaigns were conducted in Scotland, Wales and Northern Ireland in the lead up to, and following, the elections to the devolved parliaments in May 2011 which were successful in generating increased political support for a plan for rare diseases. This experience demonstrates that times of change can be successfully utilised to achieve campaign goals. Equally it is recommended that national alliances maintain a point of contact within their relevant health department. This has been crucial to ensure that the development of a national plan for rare diseases does not fall 'off the radar' of policy-makers. This can be difficult as frequent internal reorganisations can lead to responsibility being passed to different individuals, meaning that efforts made to build relationships can be wasted, but RDUK has endeavoured to meet with officials on a regular basis and to meet with new officials when they take over responsibility. Through this, RDUK had maintained a constructive ongoing relationship with each of the four health departments. Although this can take a certain amount of persistence in communication, it has been worthwhile.

The next example of when RDUK's members successfully applied pressure on the government was to ensure the public consultation on a UK rare disease plan was launched. It was originally indicated that a public consultation on a plan would be launched in the autumn of 2011. This was later postponed until the end of the year. As Christmas approached, there had been no news regarding the launch. RDUK decided against putting pressure on the health departments to launch the consultation prior to the end of the year. It was felt that it was preferable to allow the health departments sufficient time to prepare a good quality consultation document. Also, there was the danger that should the consultation be launched in the run up to Christmas, it would be more difficult for RDUK to raise awareness of the launch, and that the Christmas holiday period would lead to less time for people to respond.

At the beginning of 2012, there was still no news from the health departments about when the consultation on the rare disease plan would be launched. It was now over two and a half years since the Council Recommendation had been signed and little action had been taken by the UK's health departments. RDUK was mindful that international Rare Disease Day was approaching on 29 February. Spotting the opportunity to capitalise on this to ensure the launch of the consultation, RDUK instigated another contact campaign to get members to contact their local MP in England, or MSPs, AMs or MLAs in Scotland, Wales and Northern Ireland, respectively, to inform them of the upcoming Rare Disease Day and to ask for their support by writing to the relevant health minister to push for the timely launch of the consultation. There was a fantastic response from members which generated a significant number of letters from politicians to the health departments in each home nation. The consultation was duly launched for the mandatory 12 week public consultation period on Rare Disease Day.

Ensuring the launch of the consultation was not unproblematic. Owing to the difficulty of getting sign-off from four different health ministers, the launch could not be confirmed until mid-morning on Rare Disease Day itself, which hindered attempts to gain media coverage to a certain extent as the media could not be given advanced notification. Nevertheless, perhaps the most significant milestone to date had been achieved and the UK was another step closer to a national plan for rare diseases.

The other lesson to take from this is how Rare Disease Day can be a powerful tool to raise political awareness and for national alliances seeking to lobby their governments to achieve their campaign objectives. It is recommended that those approaching politicians have specific asks; in the above example, the ask was for politicians to write to the health minister, as this helps politicians who are supportive to channel this support effectively into a combined effort.

12.7 Recommendation 5: Facilitate the engagement of your members

RDUK had anticipated that the public consultation on the UK plan for rare diseases may not have been given the prominence that other health consultations are given. Moreover, given the very nature of rare diseases there was a danger that there would be fewer responses than would usually be received to such consultations. There are a number of reasons for this and a number of these have already been touched on.

As has been discussed already, patient organisations dealing with rare diseases are often small or entirely volunteer-led, most of which would have little, if any experience of policy work. This is in comparison to larger patient organisations, generally dealing with common conditions, which often have a policy officer, or even a policy team whose primary aim is to shape policy, including by responding to consultations. Individual patients or carers may have felt daunted by the prospect of responding to a government consultation, even though their perspective is invaluable, or without assistance and encouragement, individuals may not have believed it was appropriate for them to respond to a consultation.

Rare diseases attract far less media attention than common diseases meaning it was less likely that there would be media coverage to alert those who may be interested to the existence of the consultation. Equally, the health departments were less likely to actively promote the consultation than more 'vote winning' topics such as cancer and other major health conditions. Although there is an increasing amount of engagement from the Royal Colleges and professional bodies in rare diseases, there does tend to be less than for other health issues affecting such a vast number of people; therefore there may have been little awareness of the consultation among health professionals.

These are just some of the reasons why the total number of individuals and organisations participating in the consultation process on the plan may not have reflected the significance of rare diseases both in terms of individuals' experiences and the collective numbers of patients and impact on the health service. The knock-on effect of this could have been that health departments would continue not to view rare diseases as a priority which would have implications for the content of the plan and its successful implementation.

RDUK was disappointed with the efforts made by the health departments to publicise the launch of the consultation. RDUK was concerned that key stakeholders, particularly patient organisations had not been contacted directly to inform them about the opportunity to respond. Moreover, little effort was made to publicise the consultation. As an example, it is standard for public consultations to appear on governments' websites; after pressure from RDUK, it took two weeks for the consultation to even be included on the Scottish Parliament website and three weeks for the consultation to be included on the Welsh Government website. It was clear that RDUK would need to help promote the consultation and empower stakeholders to respond.

In the event, the consultation document was disappointing and RDUK regarded it as a missed opportunity by the health departments (Department of Health 2012). The consultation presented an overly optimistic account of the reality faced by most people living with a rare disease in the UK. Although there are examples of world-class services for patients and ground-breaking research taking place in the UK, in RDUK's experience, this is not the case for the majority of the over 6,000 rare diseases. The following passage from the consultation summarises well how the health departments had failed to grasp this issue:

> The United Kingdom can be proud of its record in treating people with rare disease. We have world-class research teams at the forefront of discovery and innovation in the treatment of rare disease. We have dedicated teams of clinicians and healthcare staff who provide care for complex conditions equal to the best available anywhere in the world, and we have strong patient organisations that powerfully articulate the needs and priorities of people with rare disease. However, there is always room for improvement.
> (Department of Health 2012: para 21)

While some of the sections of the consultation were stronger, for example, the sections dealing with diagnosis and centres of excellence, others were very weak, failing to acknowledge any issues and failing to suggest any new policy initiatives. The questions asked in the consultation also caused concern. Some questions seemed to actively divert responses away from the actual issues and there were some important issues, such as access to medicine, which were discussed but no questions were asked in order to invite comments.

Overall, the document was high on rhetoric but very light on detail and specific actions that will be taken as a result of the plan and there was little sense of the accountability for the delivery of the plan. Nevertheless, the existence of the consultation was an unprecedented opportunity for stakeholders to make their views known to policy-makers and RDUK was eager to ensure that stakeholders did in fact grasp this opportunity.

RDUK had anticipated the difficulties in raising awareness of the consultation and that the content of the consultation document may be disappointing. It light of this it had planned and sourced funding in advance from 12 pharmaceutical companies to conduct engagement activity designed to inform and empower people to respond to the public consultation. It was also designed to enable individuals and organisations to frame responses appropriately and with reference to the devolved administrations in the context of a UK strategy as it was an unusual situation for four health departments to be consulting on such a broad piece of health policy. It was vital to counteract the weakness of the consultation with a strong, unified response from the rare disease community.

Central to RDUK's engagement activity was the organisation of four one-day stakeholder engagement events. The aim of the stakeholder engagement events was to share viewpoints and debate the issues raised in the consultation, to encourage members and other stakeholders to think about how the consultation relates to them, to respond, and in turn to gather their views to inform RDUK's own responses. RDUK believed that in order to get the UK's health departments to take the issue of rare diseases seriously, and to influence a final plan which will improve access to treatment and care for those with rare diseases, both the quantity and quality of the responses received by the health departments was important. The events were designed not only to encourage stakeholders to respond, but also to produce good quality responses by helping attendees to think about what they would like to see in the final plan, to discuss issues with others and to hear expert opinions. To capture issues specific to each of the home nations separate events were held in Cardiff, London, Edinburgh and Belfast to discuss these specific issues.

Each event had presentations from invited expert guest speakers on the topics of 'diagnosis, prevention and screening', 'support and information', 'commissioning, planning and delivering coordinated care' and 'research'.[15] Presentations were followed by breakout discussions on each table which had a mix of stakeholders, including patients, representatives from patient organisations, healthcare professionals and representatives from industry. Facilitators on each table recorded the discussions, which were subsequently fed into RDUK's responses to the consultation.[16] Feedback was also gathered through forms distributed in delegate packs; the form asked for the three key things in each discussion area that delegates would like to see in the final rare disease plan.

The day finished with a session entitled 'getting your views across' where speakers with experience in policy and writing consultation responses gave delegates

15 The speakers' presentations can be downloaded at: www.raredisease.org.uk/consultation events.htm, accessed 13 December 2012.

16 RDUK's consultation responses are available at: www.raredisease.org.uk/consultation_ responses.htm, accessed 14 December 2012.

practical advice and tips on how best to respond to the consultation. The aim of this was to encourage those with little or no experience in responding to consultations to do so.

During the consultation period, RDUK also held four separate webinars (presentations delivered live over the Internet) aimed at each home nation. Providing the opportunity to view webinar recordings allowed those who may not be able to participate in the events during the day or working week to hear RDUK's views. This is particularly true for members who may be individual patients or small and/or volunteer organisations. The webinars could also be disseminated to others who may have an interest. Whereas the aim of the engagement events was to encourage attendees to consider the issues arising in the consultation document independently, the webinars outlined RDUK's views on the consultation. During the live webinars there was a chance for members to ask questions, but the presentations were also available to download and view at people's leisure to assist them in formulating their responses to the consultation.

RDUK also produced a series of supporting documents to assist people in responding to the consultation. The support materials available included a comparison document, which compared the recommendations for a rare disease plan in the 'Improving Lives, Optimising Resources' report to what was included in the consultation document. This was useful in guiding members about not only what was missing, but also what they could suggest should be included.

A practicalities document was produced with advice on how to respond to the consultation. This was particularly aimed at individuals and small organisations which did not have experience of responding to consultations; however, the document was also useful in terms of communicating how RDUK would be responding to the consultation. The consultation process itself was quite complicated. Many members had queries such as whether it was necessary to use the response form or how to communicate different messages to different health departments, so the document was useful to explain the process and guide members.

Finally, RDUK produced a frequently asked questions document. This covered key questions around the consultation process, the plan and how to respond, some of which were questions that were asked during the webinar discussions, others came from questions submitted by RDUK members.

Throughout the consultation process RDUK utilised social media such as Twitter and Facebook to raise awareness of the consultation, encourage responses and make stakeholders aware of its activities and materials.

RDUK is confident from the feedback gained from members that this activity was highly valuable in empowering and assisting members with their responses. The impact of this activity in terms of how it will shape the final plan is at this stage unknown, but hopefully a strong enough representation will have been made to the health departments to demonstrate that rare diseases are not a fringe issue and that an effective rare disease plan needs to be drawn up to make a real difference to patients and families.

12.8 Final recommendation: Don't give up

The reader will have, by now, ascertained that progress towards achieving a rare disease plan in the UK has been slow. It has taken a significant amount of time, energy and resources to get to the stage now, where a public consultation has been completed. RDUK hasn't yet achieved the goal of ensuring a national plan for rare diseases is in place, although significant progress has been made since June 2009, when there was no intent from any of the health departments to develop a national plan. In many ways, the most difficult stage still lies ahead: ensuring the effective implementation of the plan at a time when health budgets will continuously come under strain, not only because of the economic situation, but also because of an ageing population and as increasingly expensive interventions become available. RDUK's goal once the final plan is launched is to ensure and aid the implementation of the plan in practice in each of the UK's home nations. This may well require further lobbying for implementation plans in each of the home nations depending on how prescriptive the final plan is.

The development of rare disease plans across Europe and elsewhere should be seen as a process and not an event. It is very unlikely that once a plan is in place, all the issues facing patients affected by rare diseases today and in future will be addressed, no matter how good the plan is on paper. In the UK, RDUK sees the development of a national plan as an important stage in addressing the needs of patients affected by rare diseases in a systematic, strategic and holistic way. France is already on its second plan and it is likely that the process of developing new or updating existing plans will need to be repeated in all countries as technology advances and health systems change. As a result, national rare disease alliances must be prepared to continuously maintain pressure on their national authorities. It is for this reason that RDUK is advocating strongly around ensuring a designated team in each health department is accountable for delivering the rare disease plan and to ensure that there are in place timescales for delivery and outcome measures.

Although there will be times when progress will seem slow or non-existent, there may also be steps backwards; RDUK's final advice to other national alliances it to be persistent despite these frustrations. The idea of considering rare diseases as a whole in policy-making in the UK is relatively in its infancy compared with other major or common conditions, which have grabbed the attention of policy-makers. There are signs that times are changing. More and more interest is now being shown in rare diseases which is extremely encouraging. Whereas little interest or awareness was shown outside of the rare disease community previously, more and more rare diseases will feature in platforms for discussion of health policy. Many acknowledge that addressing some of the challenges rare diseases pose now will serve as a guide for the future as, increasingly, scientific advances will mean more 'common' diseases are broken down into rarer subsets.

As for many other rare disease alliances, RDUK works with a limited budget and limited staffing; the executive officer is the only full-time post working on RDUK. Nevertheless, it is hoped that the experience of RDUK, by working collaboratively, demonstrating the issues, being clear about asks and by involving and engaging members, demonstrates that it is possible to make progress and RDUK aims to ensure that this will continue.

References

ABPI (Association of the British Pharmaceutical Industry) (2012) 'The Code of Practice for the Pharmaceutical Industry Second 2012 Edition', www.abpi.org.uk/our-work/library/guidelines/Pages/code-2012.aspx, accessed 14 December 2012.

Department of Health (2012) 'Consultation on the United Kingdom Plan for Rare Diseases', www.dh.gov.uk/prod_consum_dh/groups/dh_digitalassets/@dh/@en/documents/digital asset/dh_132883.pdf, accessed 13 December 2012.

European Commission (2008a) 'Communication from the Commission of the European Parliament, the Council, the European Economic and Social Committee and the Committee of the Regions on Rare Diseases: Europe's Challenges', COM(2008) 679, ec.europa.eu/health/ph_threats/non_com/docs/rare_com_en.pdf, accessed 13 December 2012.

European Commission (2008b) 'Proposal for a Council Recommendation on a European Action in the Field of Rare Diseases', COM(2008) 726, ec.europa.eu/health/ph_threats/non_com/docs/rare_rec_en.pdf, accessed 13 December 2012.

EUROPLAN (2010) 'National Conference on Rare Diseases', full conference report, www.rare disease.org.uk/documents/europlan_uk_report_final2.pdf, accessed 13 December 2012.

Genetic Alliance UK (2006) 'History of Genetic Alliance UK', www.geneticalliance.org.uk/docs/historyofgig_final1006.pdf, accessed 13 December 2012.

Limb, L., and S. Nutt (2011) 'Improving Lives, Optimising Resources: A Vision for the UK Rare Disease Strategy', Rare Disease UK, www.raredisease.org.uk/documents/RD-UK-Strategy-Report.pdf, accessed 13 December 2012.

Limb, L., S. Nutt and A. Sen (2010) 'Experiences of Rare Diseases: An Insight from Patients and Families', Rare Disease UK, www.raredisease.org.uk/documents/RDUK-Family-Report.pdf, accessed 13 December 2012.

OrphaNews (2009) 'Editorial', 24 June 2009, www.orpha.net/actor/EuropaNews/2009/090624.html, accessed 13 December 2012.

Patient and Client Council (2012) 'Experience of Diagnosis: Views of Patients and Carers of Diagnosis of Rare Disease in Northern Ireland', www.patientclientcouncil.hscni.net/uploads/research/Experience_of_Diagnosis.pdf, accessed 13 December 2012.

Stephen Nutt is employed by Genetic Alliance UK, the national charity representing 150 patient organisations supporting all those affected by genetic conditions. Stephen's role is as Executive Officer for Rare Disease UK (RDUK), the UK multi-stakeholder alliance for people with rare diseases and all who support them, which was founded by Genetic Alliance UK. Stephen is responsible for developing and implementing RDUK's plan of political engagement activity as well as formulating RDUK's future strategy. His work spans public affairs, campaigns, policy and communications. Stephen previously worked in the Policy and Public Affairs Team at the National Autistic Society Cymru. Stephen has a degree in Law and an MA in Politics from the University of Manchester.

13

The global drug development process
What are the implications for rare diseases and where must we go?

Sharon F. Terry
Genetic Alliance, USA

with Jayson Swanson
University of Oslo, Sweden

13.1 Putting it in context: summary of global drug development opportunities and challenges

It is important to place the issues related to rare disease drug development in the context of all drug development. In one analysis, it has been suggested that the business model for even blockbuster drugs has not proven successful (Gilbert *et al.* 2003; *Lancet* 2011). Regardless of whether that is correct or not, it is clear that an industry that spent US$67.4 billion in 2010 (PhRMA 2012), a year in which 21 drugs were approved, is not a very effective one (Dooren 2010) from either a business or a human perspective. While rare disease advocates might rightfully complain about being 'orphaned' by the industry, thousands of common conditions see no treatment on the horizon either. In general, drug research and development productivity is declining as commercialisation costs rise. Payers and regulators have both more influence and more pressures. Finally, as early as ten years ago it was projected that '...shorter exclusivity periods have driven up the average cost per successful launch to $1.7 billion and reduced average expected returns on new investment to the unsustainable level of 5%' (Gilbert *et al.* 2003). More recent analysis suggests that return on investment for the average new chemical entity is barely 6–8% (Sharma 2010). As many patents expire in the next five years, generics will compete with name brands, and pipelines will dry up, causing prospects to look even more dismal.

13.1.1 Complexity of human biology

The underlying reason for this lacklustre performance is in part the complexity of human biology. A great deal of serendipity is at play in the arena of drug discovery. Even when drugs are discovered and are effective, such as aspirin, the mechanism of action is rarely well understood. While this is supported by traditional methods of basic science, it is not especially effective in accelerating the drug discovery and development process. Understanding biology in a systematic way, with the goal of creating therapies, will provide better methods for discovery and development. Rare diseases are therefore not so 'special' in their lack of available treatments—and perhaps they even fare better in recent years than 'common' conditions in relative number of approved therapies. Of the 35 drugs approved by the US Food and Drug Administration (FDA) in 2011, 10 were for rare diseases (FDA 2011).

13.1.2 Culture

Culture in the biomedical research arena plays an enormous role in both the lack of productivity and the focus on common conditions as well. One of the most articulate spokespersons for this, Aled Edwards, describes this well in a paper entitled 'Too Many Roads Not Taken' (Edwards *et al.* 2011). His thesis is that the current research model promotes research on limited, well-characterised proteins and disincentivises researchers from looking at novel proteins, even those connected to disease.

> Why the reluctance to work on the unknown? As the Nobel-prizewinning biochemist Roger Kornberg put it, scientists are wont to 'fondle their problems': they have a natural tendency to dig deeper into their areas of expertise. Plus, funding and peer review systems are risk-averse; funders and reviewers alike are less willing to support research on unstudied proteins, for which it is often harder to explain the rationale and significance. Moreover, the time frames associated with academic promotion and training encourage researchers to focus on systems that are likely to generate results rapidly, and for which research infrastructure and methods are already available.

Rare disease research won't generate rapid results, nor are infrastructure or methods readily available.

Rare disease drug discovery resides in this difficult morass, and is then only further complicated by small cohorts that make it difficult to characterise the disease and create adequate trial size. Heterogeneity in disease pathophysiology plagues rare conditions, although it affects common ones as well. Finally, because of the small audience for a product, there is limited investment as a consequence of the lack of business models for discovery and development.

13.1.3 Regulatory issues

Regulatory agencies such as United States Food and Drug Administration, Health Canada and the European Medicines Agency examine the safety and efficacy of potential therapies. They try to be sure that a drug is, first, safe to take and, second, that it does what the sponsor (the company or organisation bringing the drug forward) says it will. For common conditions, there are large pools of people on which to test the drug. These large pools provide ample numbers of participants to characterise a disease: defining its effect on the body and characterising its progression. This allows something called validated biomarkers. These are measures of effectiveness for a drug that have been tested to be correct. For example, a biomarker for a cancer might be the size of the tumour. The tumour can be measured and tracked in many individuals so that its typical progression can be described. Then, when a drug is tried, one can again measure many tumours, usually in a double blind study, a study in which neither the patient nor the clinician knows whether they are being given a drug or a placebo. Then the change in the tumour size is measured throughout the trial and a decision made as to the efficacy of the drug. In rare conditions, biomarkers are hard to discover, and then often the biomarkers cannot be validated, because there are too few people with the condition.

A good example is the rare genetic disease pseudoxanthoma elasticum (PXE). A protein primarily expressed in the liver neglects to shuttle something out of the cell and causes this disease. This in turn causes mineralisation of the membrane behind the eye, the mid-dermis of the skin, and the mid-laminar layer of the mid-sized arteries. Though there is a registry of more than 4,000 individuals with the condition, the disease expression and progression is highly variable and no cohort has been followed carefully and long enough to quantify a reasonable biomarker. Thus a measure that works for one person might not be reasonable for another. One could use the mineralisation of Bruch's membrane, or decreased elasticity in the skin, but these are difficult to measure in a replicable way. Therefore it is very difficult to tell if a drug is effective when the disease progression is not well known and there are few tangible, scientifically agreed on measures.

Even if a validated biomarker is available, it is difficult to get a large enough pool of people for studies to have high enough 'power'. This means the statistical analysis done on the data accumulated in the trial is reasonable enough to accept as evidence for the effectiveness of the drug.

Because of these challenges, regulatory agencies in some countries have taken steps to incentivise rare disease drug development. These include, but are not limited to, extended market exclusivity, tax incentives, fast track/pre-approval and fee waivers. Extended market exclusivity means that a manufacturer can be the only one to market a treatment for a particular disease for longer than is usually given. Fast track and pre-approvals refer to unique mechanisms to move more quickly to approval, skipping some of the usual steps. Fee waivers either reduce or eliminate the large fee that sponsors pay to apply for drug approval.

These measures are sometimes offered to alleviate regulatory challenges: for example, the concerns related to trial size. As described in the example above, the development of drugs for rare diseases is impeded by much smaller cohort sizes than those available and used for traditional pre-approval clinical trials. These 'low power' trials lead to questions of safety and effectiveness when evaluating data for approval. When held to the same standards as ordinary drugs, as they often are, the efficacy rate must be higher in order to retain statistical significance. Some have called for even greater regulatory flexibility to incentivise and accelerate approvals (*Nature* 2010). As biomedical research progresses and various incentives are used to interest companies and academic research groups in rare disease research, regulatory agencies hope to see more applications with data from small clinical trials. This will thrust regulators into the uncomfortable position of ascertaining safety and efficacy with less than optimal data.

Despite the concerns over population and related sample sizes, some therapies are able to overcome these and other barriers. An example of this is pegademase bovine (Adagen). The treatment was approved for use by individuals suffering from severe combined immunodeficiency syndrome (SCID). At the time of approval, only 14 diagnosed cases existed in the US, and 8 of those were used for clinical trials. In this particular case the circumstances were ideal: a PhD candidate was particularly interested in the compound, the treatment was 100% effective and a historical control was used, meaning the standard against which the drug was measured was data from the past. Many regulatory approvals from numerous institutional review boards representing equally numerous hospitals were required and the study actively utilised the involvement of an even greater number of institutions than those requiring clearance. This case additionally benefited from the fact that the country in which they were seeking approval was the same as where the study and trials were taking place (Haffner 2006). This serendipity was likely an exceptional case. Is it fair to ask that more drugs be approved with greater flexibility? It is clear that the number of people helped would rise exponentially if additional allowances were made for the unique challenges of rare diseases.

In addition to the sample/population size concerns, some regulations could potentially affect safety, affordability and in part consequential accessibility. The patent and market exclusivity incentives could have unforeseen consequences on costs. The fast track/pre-approval provisions and more relaxed clinical trial regulations could, retrospectively in the years to come, prove to be detrimental or harmful. Unfortunately, time is the only true indicator of these possibilities.

13.2 Advances in recent years and how they affect rare disease drug development

13.2.1 Genetics

13.2.1.1 Human genome project

The human genome project (HGP) formally began in 1990 (US DoE 2011). It was a 13-year, international effort coordinated by the National Institutes of Health and the US Department of Energy. The project was originally planned to last 15 years, but rapid technological advances accelerated the completion date to 2003. The project provided a great boon to rare diseases, since it aimed at and achieved identification of all of the genes in the human genome, mutations in thousands of which lead to rare diseases. The information was made instantly public, which began a culture change with regard to data sharing in biomedical research that is essential to rare diseases. Further, the project integrated the study of ethical, legal and social issues into the work. In this context, some issues critical to rare diseases were studied. For example, because a rare disease affects a limited number of individuals, these individuals can be more easily identified and privacy might be of concern (Rubinstein *et al*. 2010). On the other hand, individuals with a rare disease are often ready to accept more risk and will eschew privacy for the opportunity to be involved in clinical trials and the potential for treatment. In short, there would be no path to rare disease treatment without the human genome sequence. However, this is only a starting point. In the words of Francis Collins, the leader of the HGP,

> It's a history book—a narrative of the journey of our species through time. It's a shop manual, with an incredibly detailed blueprint for building every human cell. And it's a transformative textbook of medicine, with insights that will give health care providers immense new powers to treat, prevent and cure disease.
>
> (National Human Genome Research Institute 2011)

Eric Lander, of the Broad Institute said:

> We've opened a box here that has got a huge amount of valuable information. It is the key to understanding disease and in the long run to curing disease. But having opened it, we're also going to be very uncomfortable with that information for some time to come.
>
> (Krulwich 2001)

Understanding the relationships between genes and disease signs and symptoms (phenotypes) is an important next step. Some of these associations are quite easy to establish, but the variable expressivity of the disease does not help in discerning the result of the genetic effect on various cells or organs. Other associations are harder to find, but new tools such as whole genome sequencing are accelerating the discovery of clinically relevant variants that can inform clinical care (Lupski *et al*. 2010).

13.2.1.2 Whole genome sequencing

Genetic technologies, the tools that are critical to these discoveries, are enabling discovery in novel ways at a rapid rate. These technologies have become more accessible because they have rapidly decreased in cost. Figure 13.1 illustrates this dramatic decrease in costs over time. As these technologies become less expensive, they are applied to more people in more situations. Thus, as many genomes are sequenced and analysed, more information about variation in the human genome is available. These large projects, such as the Personal Genome Project that maps variation and associates clinical information with it in a public forum, are accelerating the discovery of variation that will also accelerate discovery for rare diseases. The National Institutes of Health in the US is funding a 1000 Genomes Project to discover, genotype and provide accurate haplotype information on all forms of human DNA polymorphism in multiple human populations (Xue *et al.* 2010). The Wellcome Trust has a project to create the first ever CNV (copy number variation) map.[1]

Figure 13.1 **Cost per genome rapidly decreasing**
Source: Wetterstrand 2012; Courtesy of National Human Genome Research Institute

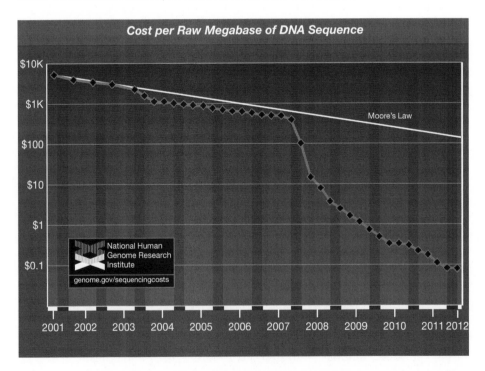

1 'Copy number variation—the gain or loss of large chunks of DNA sequence—has been revealed as a major factor in human variation and disease' (www.wellcome.ac.uk/Funding/Biomedical-science/Funded-projects/Research-profiles/WTDV029749.htm, accessed 17 December 2012).

In addition to discovering and mapping variation, whole genome sequencing (WGS) will also create cheaper diagnostics. This in turn will allow the development of larger cohorts, even for rare diseases, since some individuals previously undiagnosed will be discovered. Milder forms of diseases will also be discovered. If many people are having their genomes mapped, then more variation will be catalogued, and the 'needles in a haystack' that rare diseases are today, will be catalogued and more readily discoverable (Ng *et al*. 2010). At the present time, those building cohorts for rare disease drug discovery are limited to traditional pathways. Disease advocacy organisations (DAO) and clinician/researchers look for these affected individuals in clinics, specialists' offices and via various Internet groups and search engines. This leads to finding only some of the individuals affected by a condition, and certainly to finding those with moderate to severe disease more often than those with mild disease. This results in an incomplete characterisation of the disease. Imagine a day when many individuals engaged in WGS and carriers and affected individuals all across the spectrum of disease are identified and well characterised.

Genomic sequencing is dramatically improving our understanding of the genetic basis of rare diseases and emerging technologies are making whole genome sequencing a viable diagnostic tool for the future. Technologies such as nanopore and fluorophore (single molecule, real-time: SMRT) are arising as potential methods for accomplishing high throughput whole genome sequencing. Nanopore technology has seen interest at a variety of commercial and academic levels as it becomes a more promising tool for reading DNA sequences (Ingelman-Sundberg and Rodriguez-Antona 2005; Eid *et al*. 2009). One company is working on a device the size of a thumb drive on which one would put a drop of blood, plug it into a computer USB drive and read one's genome.

In addition to WGS, exome sequencing is being used as a cheaper and more efficient alternative. This approach selectively sequences the coding regions of the genome in order to identify monogenic variations responsible for Mendelian disorders.

Although exome sequencing is proving to be promising from a cost and proficiency standpoint, it is likely to not give as complete a picture as one would hope. This is because it is becoming increasingly clear that many diseases are caused by rare mutations in multiple genes (McClellan and King 2010). This becomes problematic from a molecular perspective as exome sequencing works to identify monogenic variations when diseases are proving to be much more genetically heterogeneous than initially understood.

The complexity of modifier genes also has an effect on whole genome sequencing. These are genes which modify, or alter, another gene. Genome wide studies for modifier genes are limited because of lack of samples; as whole genomic sequencing becomes more widely practised, these studies can move forward. Following the guidelines that have been proposed for reproducing genotype–phenotype relationships has proven to be very difficult because of the non-existence of sufficiently sized samples with identical phenotypic data that are frequently encountered when searching for genetic modifiers (Genin *et al*. 2008).

13.2.2 Stratified medicine and pharmacogenomics

Stratified, or personalised, medicine and rare diseases have an interesting relationship. As more nuanced understanding of variation stratifies common conditions, there will be many rare subsets of those diseases. This means one might be examining a cancer or diabetes, and when one analyses the affected individuals on the level of the genome, these diseases are probably many diseases called by a single catch-all name. Characterising these subsets will have all of the challenges of rare diseases. Rare diseases might in fact be easier models of disease since the main cause of the disease is usually a single gene, though it is quite probable that other genes and certainly environment have an effect.

Stratified medicine challenges the traditional drug development paradigm because it creates smaller cohorts and reduces the power of studies. The emerging science of pharmacogenomics is an example. Pharmacogenomics examines the inherited variations in genes that influence drug response and explores ways these variations can be used to predict whether someone will have a good response to a drug, a bad response to a drug, or no response at all (NCBI 2004). At the present time, when someone has a common condition, diabetes or arthritis for example, drugs are prescribed and whether they are effective or not is somewhat hit or miss dependent on many factors. In the new age of pharmacogenomics, it is possible to tailor or target some treatments based on genotypes, and thus treat disease more effectively. At this point, one might ask, 'What does this have to do with rare diseases?'

Here is the connection. Regulatory agencies are accustomed to approving treatments based on trials with substantial numbers of participants, called high-powered studies. Blockbuster drugs were traditionally developed in large trials of thousands of individuals. These drugs were then prescribed for everyone. One can think of pain relievers such as ibuprofen or acetaminophen; they are advertised to relieve pain for anyone and everyone. If one polls a group of individuals, however, one will find that some people have preferences as to which drug to take, based in part on the effectiveness of the drug and its side-effects. When drugs are developed for smaller subsets of disease, thousands of individuals might not be appropriate for the trial. New methods for clinical trials have to be developed and tested. Sometimes these are called 'N of 1', or low power, trials. Various groups around the globe have begun to address the problem of 'N of 1' trials and all of the challenges they present.

13.2.3 Drug repurposing

Potential therapies often fail during the clinical trial process. This is part of what adds to the enormous costs of drug development. Sometimes, testing these drugs on smaller subsets of individuals could allow previously failed drugs to be used safely and effectively on these subsets of patients (Hamburg and Collins 2010). This is because the initial promise of the drug may have been in a subset of individuals with the disease. This is especially meaningful for rare diseases because drugs that have failed or been shelved through lack of effectiveness or efficiency for common conditions might be able to be repurposed for rare diseases.

The attitudes and goals of repurposing drugs have changed substantially. Up until recently, drug repurposing and repositioning happened mostly by serendipity. Now, intentional strategies are undertaken. Some researchers are examining molecular pathways instead of the traditional routes of investigation. Most approaches ultimately focus on reducing 'risk'—the potential that the drug might fail and the investment be lost. These advances have been heartily promoted by some creative public–private partnerships, including those between patient support groups and government incentives (Muthyala 2011).

Many public–private partnerships and initiatives between big pharma, biotech/speciality pharma, DAOs and government have a long-term goal of integrating academic efforts and others into collaborative repositioning efforts. A number of these ventures already exist. The National Center for Advancing Translational Sciences (NCATS) at the National Institutes of Health (NIH) has formed a special research division for 'rescuing and repurposing drugs'. They espouse:

> Drug rescue and repurposing are two such (sic) strategies. Drug 'rescue' refers to research involving small molecules and biologics whose development was abandoned before they could be approved by the U.S. Food and Drug Administration (FDA). 'Repurposing' refers to studying small molecules and biologics approved to treat a disease or condition to see if they are safe and effective for treating other diseases.
>
> (NIH NCATS 2012)

This division launched an initiative called Discovering New Therapeutic Uses for Existing Molecules in early 2012 in the hope of bringing together and speeding up efforts for repurposing. Another project, NCGC (NIH Chemical Genomics Center) Pharmaceutical Collection (NPC), has brought together the collaborative repurposing missions of NCGC and the NIH's Translating Rare and Neglected Diseases (TRND). At the same time the US FDA has created a comprehensive collection of products that have received orphan status designation and are already market-approved for the treatment of other diseases along with known molecular targets called the Rare Disease and Repurposing Database (RDRD). This database is intended to further enable repurposing efforts and increase release rate for new products. The NIH has also been involved in another project through its Clinical and Translational Science Award (CTSA) consortium. The CTSA Pharmaceutical Assets Portal project was initiated by the group of universities linked by the CTSA which 'aims to facilitate industry–academic collaborations for discovery of new indications for compounds no longer being developed by pharmaceutical companies, through eliminating barriers to access such compounds' (Marusina *et al.* 2011). Though much has been done to spur repurposing efforts both publically and privately as well as through collaborations between the two, further incentives are necessary to speed up the process and deliver more treatments to patients in need more quickly.

Of course, because TRND will probably identify subtypes of common conditions as described above, common conditions could benefit from TRND and thus encourage future funding. This could lead to new therapies, either through the development of targeted drugs or through the repurposing of abandoned or failed drugs by identifying subgroups of patients likely to benefit from them.

13.2.4 Registries and biobanks

For the purposes of this discussion, a registry is a collection of clinical data and a biobank is a collection of biological samples, such as DNA, blood and/or tissue. In many cases, the word biobank is used to describe all of it.

In an interview by OrphaNews Europe, Dr Carla E.M. Hollak discussed the importance of post-marketing drug registries and their unique characteristics (OrphaNews 2011). Challenges include fragmentation of data and the lack of collaboration between centres. Dr Hollak suggested that disease registries may be more advantageous than drug registries for the rare disease community. There seems to be growing interest in this once controversial idea.

13.2.4.1 Disease advocacy organisations run biobanks

Building large cohorts is the only pathway to strong correlations between the tremendous amount of variation in the genome, the effects of environment and lifestyle and the health and disease of individuals. Francis Collins, director of the National Institutes of Health, has asked the nation, via numerous presentations to national advisory councils, to consider a national patient-centred research network to this end (Collins 2012). It will take leadership from the top and the demand of the consumer from the bottom.

New information technology tools and even improvements in freezer and liquid nitrogen technologies have made the banking of biological samples and clinical information much easier and less expensive. There are still thousands of disconnects in a mess that does not approximate the system it must become to be useful, but it is vastly improved from the early days. The advocacy organisation for the disease pseudoxanthoma elasticum (PXE), PXE International, created the first completely lay-owned and managed biobank and registry in 1995. The word biobank was not really part of scientific discussions, let alone found in common vocabulary. There were no standards, no recommended minimum data sets, and no inexpensive solutions to keeping samples at minus 80°C. There was not even consensus on protocols for extracting DNA and archiving it. Added to the technical challenges, PXE International was strongly discouraged from creating the biobank by many leaders in the research community, claiming this was no place for advocates. Other advocates also weighed in, recommending that PXE International support patients and leave research to the researchers. Despite this naysaying, the biobank formed the basis for all research PXE International has conducted; it has encouraged and operationalised data sharing, and accelerated discoveries (Terry and Boyd 2001;

Bercovitch *et al.* 2003, 2004, 2005; Terry *et al.* 2007). The word biobank is now a fairly readily recognised word (only in small part because of PXE International), and the associated concept is often discussed as a critical element in the suite of tools necessary to discover and develop drugs.

When the Genetic Alliance Registry and BioBank was established in 2003, it was built on the PXE International biobank infrastructure.[2] It allows cross-disease shared infrastructure in a cooperative format subscribed to by DAOs, iteratively improving as needed by the member groups. DAO involvement in registries and biobanks is a boon for this needed resource. While other entities, such as NIH or pharmaceutical companies, fund these registries, they often do so for only a limited amount of time. Once the funding runs out, or the clinical trial for which the registry was established is over, the registry either languishes or is abandoned. DAOs have a long-term commitment to the community affected by the disease and are not usually project based or time limited in that commitment.

A new option that offers individuals affected by rare diseases and not affiliated with a DAO the option of contributing their own data has been created. This registry option can be found at Disease InfoSearch.[3] Data can be shared with the DAO and other entities that would further research on the disease if the individual permits this by determining their preferences. Or, the individual can make all of their data open access. Privacy solutions such as that offered by Private Access make open sharing possible, all the while honouring an individual's preferences (Shelton 2011).

Many DAOs are also creating registries and biobanks, or are at least active in trying to sustain them. Of 124 disease advocacy organisations (DAO) surveyed in 2011, 45% had supported a research registry or biobank (Landy *et al.* 2012).

13.2.4.2 Nation-based biobanks

Several nations have established national biobanks. These include Iceland, Estonia and the UK, among others. These biobanks are attempting to associate large amounts of clinical data with genotypic data and thereby create large registries of potentially useful information. Some nations are more ideally suited to these than others. This is because the nation has had electronic clinical records for a long time, or it is a small and somewhat homogeneous nation. There are naysayers for these projects as well, often saying that what is learned in these very homogeneous populations will not be readily applicable to more heterogeneous populations or other racial and/or ethnic groups. In some cases, such as the UK Biobank, concern was expressed that the populace would not voluntarily participate to a sufficient degree to make the project worthwhile. This has not been the case and participation is robust. The goal of recruiting half a million participants was reached in just three years and the funder, the Wellcome Trust and several of the government agencies

2 www.biobank.org, accessed 18 December 2012.
3 www.diseaseinfosearch.org, accessed 18 December 2012.

in the UK, opened the registry and biobank to researchers to analyse the data in early 2012.

Rare Disease-HUB is a biospecimens/biorepositories resource managed by the Office of Rare Diseases Research (ORDR) at the National Institutes of Health.[4] The website provides a searchable database to help researchers find biospecimens collected and stored by domestic and international biorepositories. Although RD-HUB focuses on rare diseases, common diseases are included in the resource. RD-HUB can assist investigators and others to locate and identify specific biospecimens, and facilitate sharing of material and information. RD-HUB includes a convenient list of fields required for entering biorepository data.

13.2.4.3 Hybrid models

The Global Rare Disease Patient Registry and Data Repository (GRDR) was established by the Office of Rare Diseases Research,[5] an organisational component of the National Center for Advancing Translational Sciences,[6] National Institutes of Health (NIH), in 2012. It recognised the importance of DAOs in establishing and maintaining registries. Using an application processes, it chose a small number of DAOs (half without registries and half with) and is guiding them through inviting their membership to fill out some registry questions which the ORDR has determined to be common data elements. Several DAOs have been chosen to invite their members to contribute to this online open access registry, in a two-year pilot project. It is hoped that the funding will remain available beyond the pilot phase of this project.

13.2.5 Social media and the resulting long tail networks

Social media has transformed at least the developed world with arguably the greatest social changes it has witnessed. This has had enormous impact on rare diseases. Needles in haystacks, the individuals affected by rare diseases, are much easier to find and connect in networks using social media. Tools such as the Internet, Facebook and Twitter have ushered in the era of the 'long tail'. This phrase was originally used to describe the kind of selling that happens on Amazon or Ebay—large numbers of unique items—rather than the older more traditional method of 'big box' selling—large numbers of relatively few items (Anderson 2006). Music, books and even a variety of rare objects are readily available in a long tail selling strategy. Now if that concept is applied to rare diseases, one can see that common conditions are like the big box sales, and rare conditions are like the long tail offerings. In an age that catalogues the long tail well in many sectors, it was just a matter of time before

---

4 RD-HUB, biospecimens.ordr.info.nih.gov, accessed 18 December 2012.
5 ORDR, rarediseases.info.nih.gov, accessed 18 December 2012.
6 NCATS, www.ncats.nih.gov, accessed 18 December 2012.

the long tail in rare diseases was robust enough to be seen. Thus both the diseases and the people affected by them have tools that easily link them to each other.

Genetic Alliance combined crowdsourcing with long tail aggregation long before it was fashionable. It created Disease InfoSearch: a crowdsourced tool for giving individuals all over the globe the information they needed. Crowdsourced because Genetic Alliance believes that only the true experts in each disease, the DAO, can offer quality credible current information. And long tail, because, using this method, Genetic Alliance has been able to amass information on all 6,000+ rare conditions that is kept up to date on a regular basis, at least every six months and as often as the DAO wishes. This then becomes an even more important tool as the long tail era matures. More about that in Section 13.5 on the future vision.

13.3 Advantages to studying rare diseases

Despite the many challenges associated with researching and finding treatments for rare diseases, there are some advantages to studying them. Sequencing the human genome, and subsequently understanding which genes are associated with the approximately 6,000 rare conditions, certainly provides a solid starting point for discovery. These genes are usually highly penetrant, potentially creating an opportunity for strong genotype–phenotype correlations, or at least fairly certain definitive diagnosis. However, expressivity in monogenic diseases is highly variable, probably because of environmental effects and other genes that make up the background of the individual and/or modify the primary gene. Often those affected with the condition are aggregated by non-profit DAOs, and are therefore somewhat more accessible. Further, individuals and families affected by rare conditions are probably more likely to participate in clinical trials since it is the only pathway to benefit for them, and though no data is available, most likely exceed the 3–5% participation rate in common cancer trials, for example (NCI 2002; Peppercorn *et al.* 2004; Baquet *et al.* 2006; Stead *et al.* 2011).

Incentives for rare disease drug development are also provided by governments, as well as support from the FDA and EU Commission in special protocols. The 1983 Orphan Drug Act in the USA and the European Union's (EU), Regulation (EC) No 141/2000, in which pharmaceuticals developed to treat rare diseases are referred to as 'orphan medicinal products', have provided incentives to companies. One study of policies and orphan drug incentives worldwide along with the challenges faced by the pharmaceutical companies, concluded that, 'Although there may still be challenges ahead for the pharmaceutical industry, orphan drugs seem to offer the key to recovery and stability within the market'. It documented advances in orphan drug approval, the various drugs in the orphan drug pipeline, and the future prospects for orphan drugs and diseases (Sharma 2010). More recent studies have indicated that there is an economically viable strategy for research and development on rare diseases.

13.3.1 Rare disease drug development: Successes and failures

Despite the varied incentives and bright horizons for the development of rare disease therapies that have led to and will continue to lead to noted successes, the market has been marked by its fair share of failures. Limited information specific to successes about companies in the rare disease drug market can be found in the press or peer-reviewed papers. Their own public and web presence is also difficult to navigate for indications, and the failures even harder to find. This seems to be a testament to the black box nature of the industry.

13.3.2 Common is rare?

In a twist brought about by the advent of genetics and stratified medicine, the dichotomy between common and rare diseases is simplistic and has perhaps been overemphasised. A number of thought leaders in the biomedical research arena now acknowledge that 'common genetic variants conferring large effects are not routinely found by association studies, and rare genetic variants are gaining credibility as important contributors to common diseases' (Burns and Chakravarti 2011). Further, the rare variants present in the genome are collectively common (Church 2011).

Pharmacogenomics, if successful, will change patient care. As such every patient's 'disease' is rare. As discovery becomes more rational and targeted, clinical trial cohorts will become smaller, and drugs that may have been blockbusters in prior years will be useful to only a small group of patients, a number that may fall within the definition of a rare disease. There will certainly be policy questions as these convergences occur. When this author suggested as early as 2006 in various presentations and interviews (Fernandez and Weijer 2006) that common is rare, and rare is common, there was a great deal of push back to protect the sacred space of 'rare'. This is a hard won space, and one that was necessary to protect with strong boundary walls and moats in a different age. When Abbey Meyers bravely marched into the rare disease space, founded the National Organization for Rare Disorders (Putkowski 2010), co-founded with Joan Weiss and others Genetic Alliance (founded as the Alliance of Genetic Support Groups) (Weiss 1989), and fought for the Orphan Drug Act, a strong distinct identity was critical to laying the foundation for today. The time for separation and distinction based on 'body count' is over. The science and the business call us to collaboration, commons and network coordination.

13.4 The players

13.4.1 Advocates have held the space for about 50 years

Disease advocacy organisations largely came into being to provide support and education for individuals and families with rare diseases, as was also the case for many common conditions. Many of these organisations modelled themselves after Alcoholics Anonymous, which was established in 1935.

As individuals became more activist, some of this activism was based on the disability rights movement and the influence on research and policy by HIV/AIDS and breast cancer groups (Stockdale and Terry 2002). For the most part, these groups focused on policy and support. This was true in most countries, especially in Germany (Moeller *et al.* 2006) and Japan (Oka 1994) where the self-help groups became locally active and supported the people with disease. It was also noted that, much like clinical trials, not everyone with a genetic condition becomes involved with an advocacy organisation. Several studies have noted that it is often white and middle-class individuals who become involved in advocacy and support, thus leaving out others that both need the support and are critical to an understanding of the disease (Rapp 2000).

In the 1990s, American DAOs in particular began to be involved in research. The dawning of the genetic era provided DAOs with more rational targets for discovery. As genes were discovered, these foundations began to recruit academic scientists, and eventually companies, to work on the specific disease of interest. As described above, DAOs became involved in biobanks and registries in the 1990s. Many other DAOs soared ahead in terms of both money raised and number of projects in the pipeline and became models for other foundations to follow. These included the Progeria Research Foundation, Cystic Fibrosis Foundation and Multiple Myeloma Research Foundation, to name just a few.

It became obvious in the 21st century that the role of the DAO simply supporting individuals with the condition, or assisting researchers, was evolving to one of active engagement and even initiating and leading research. As described above, a study of 124 DAOs (62% of those approached) showed that, between 2009 and 2011, 91% of them participated in the recruitment of research subjects, 75% collected research data, 56% provided researchers with advice on study design, and as reported above, 45% supported a research registry or biobank (Landy *et al.* 2012). This is certainly a dramatic increase from even 10 years before.

13.4.2 Pharma's race to the long tail

Technology, as described above, is making exploration into the 'long tail' much easier. This long tail, the place where more people reside, albeit with rarer and rarer conditions, is being fleshed out before our eyes, as common diseases are stratified. With mounting evidence of the convergence of common and rare diseases, and the fact that '68% of respondents [industry executives] believe that the current pharmaceutical model is broken and needs significant repair' (Aguirre *et al.* 2005), pharma companies are turning to rare disease discovery and development out of business necessity. Major companies are creating or acquiring rare disease divisions, including Pfizer, GlaxoSmithKline (GSK), Roche, Novartis and Sanofi. GSK was the first big pharma company to set up a special rare disease division in February 2010 and before that in 2009, entered into collaborative efforts with both Prosensa and JCR Pharma for various orphan disease objectives. After GSK's February launch, Pfizer followed with the debut of its rare disease business unit in June of the same year. Roche, though without an official division, uses its subsidiary, Genentech, for focusing on development of rare disease drugs. Roche has also recently collaborated with Biogen Idec in a successful venture resulting in the approval of a rare disease therapy in April 2011. Also in 2011, Sanofi acquired Genzyme, one of the top companies focused on rare diseases. Novartis, also without a specially defined division specific to rare disease drugs, has set up various business matrices such as Novartis Institutes for BioMedical Research (NIBR) to cater to the rare disease drug market (LaMattina 2012). Novartis is also aware that, in addition to the advantages listed above, with the sunset of the blockbuster model, revenues for rare disease treatments can be substantial if the annual treatment costs are high enough. Table 13.1 lays out some of these pharmaceutical company forays into rare diseases.

A new study has shown that orphan drugs have the potential to generate as much lifetime revenue as drugs used for more common health conditions (Meekings *et al.* 2012). For example, often cited as the prime example of long-term commitment to individuals with rare diseases, Genzyme markets a drug called Cerezyme for the treatment of a rare disease, Gaucher disease. Cerezyme is an extremely effective treatment, and is also extremely expensive with annual treatment costs as high as US$300,000/patient. Cerezyme's 2010 sales were over US$700 million, which is a substantial number for any drug. It is not yet known if the acquisition of Genzyme by Sanofi will alter a key ingredient of Genzyme's success: authentic engagement with the community of affected individuals, and with the DAOs that represent them. It remains to be seen if other companies understand the critical nature of working with these communities. In fact, analysts have predicted that Sanofi will become the largest pharmaceutical company, measured in revenue, by the end of 2012 (McConaghie 2012).

Table 13.1 **Pharmaceutical companies' rare disease divisions**

Company	Rare disease division		Name	Established or acquired	Previous or current collaborations
	Yes	No			
GlaxoSmithKline (GSK)	×			February 2010	Prosensa (2009), JCR Pharma (2009)
Pfizer	×			June 2010	
Roche		×	Genentech*	March 2009	Biogen Idec
Sanofi		×	Genzyme**	February 2011	
Genzyme			Rare Disease Business Unit		
Novartis		×	Novartis Institutes for BioMedical Research (NIBR)*		

* Not an official specialised division of the company, but rather operating as a subsidiary or business matrix
** Company acquisition, now subsidiary responsible for rare disease

13.4.3 Academia steps up

Academia is also formally making a commitment to getting on the rare disease bandwagon. Universities such as Notre Dame, University of Birmingham, the Keck Graduate Institute and University of Minnesota have established programmes or departments in rare diseases, while many others throughout the world are engaged in thousands of research projects, networks and collaborations dedicated to rare diseases. Several networks of universities are worth noting. The Rare Disease Clinical Research Network, established in 2002, currently consists of 19 Rare Diseases Clinical Research Consortia in addition to a Data Management Coordinating Center (DMCC) studying approximately 90 rare diseases at more than 97 academic institutions with several hundred investigators in the United States and in other countries (NIH 2010). Another network that focuses on rare disease is the National Laboratory Network for Rare Diseases (Zonno and Terry 2009). Laboratories engaged in rare disease testing voluntarily created this network, with support from the Office of Rare Disease Research, NIH. Both academic and commercial labs felt it was important to share reference samples and variation in order to serve patients better.

13.4.4 Government-supported initiatives

A number of efforts spearheaded by various national governments have focused attention on rare diseases. These include, for example, the establishment of the aforementioned Office of Rare Disease Research at the National Institutes of Health in the USA in 1993, the French National Plan for Rare Diseases established in 2004, the European Commission Communication and Proposal for a European Council Recommendation on Rare Diseases of 2008, and the UK plan on rare diseases, published for consultation on Rare Disease Day, 29 February 2012. The NIH office has become part of the recently established National Center for Accelerating Translational Science (NCATS), and is part of an overall emphasis on accelerating the kind of science that is needed to discover more treatments for all conditions, rare included. The aforementioned TRND, which has moved into this new centre, focuses on more than the repurposing work described above. It has partnered with a number of other agencies, including DAOs, to discover novel targets for rare and neglected diseases.

The European Commission's 7th Framework Programme call for applications has in recent years included specific calls for rare diseases. These particularly encourage research on the translational end of the spectrum and also collaborative efforts that transcend a single disease. The community eagerly awaits further calls.

Recently the EU and US spearheaded a global effort called the International Rare Disease Research Consortium (IRDiRC) (Baxter and Terry 2011; Abbott 2011). Begun in 2011, its goal is to establish 200 new therapies and the means to diagnose most rare diseases by 2020. The consortium is composed of funding entities, usually at the level of national governments. These entities must invest a minimum of US$10 million over five years in research programmes contributing toward the IRDiRC's objectives. Umbrella organisations for DAOs, including EURORDIS (a patient-driven organisation comprising DAOs from 48 countries, based in France), the National Organization for Rare Disorders and Genetic Alliance, have seats on the interim executive committee in a non-voting capacity. There are many workgroups with more than one hundred individuals working on this international coordinated effort for rare diseases. It is certainly good to put a stake in the sand and create a challenging goal. Much work must be done, and done quickly, to achieve the goal.

Europe's largest public–private partnership, a collaborative effort in Europe between the EU and the European Federation of Pharmaceutical Industries and Associations (EFPIA), called the Innovative Medicines Initiative (IMI), aimed at increasing the development safety and speed of new pharmaceuticals, has also been successful in the rare disease drug realm. The main aim of IMI is to address the bottlenecks in current drug development processes rather than the direct development of new drugs (Ragan 2009).

13.4.5 The public has a role too

Beyond, and sometimes without any awareness of, formal involvement in DAOs, the public is now finding tools to contribute to the discovery of therapies, in both the common and the rare disease arena. Certainly it is not only DAOs that can use long tail technologies and crowdsourcing to their benefit; the public can as well. Some of these are experiments in crowdsourcing led by companies that give individuals the power to report various signs and symptoms and compare them with others, such as PatientsLikeMe and 23andMe.[7] Others are taking this a step further and putting the controls in the hands of the individuals, whether it is the control of their data and where it is used, in projects such as PrivateAccess[8] and the Portable Legal Consent,[9] or actually determining what questions should be asked and how the ensuing clinical trial should be done, as is enabled by Genomera.[10] As time goes on, there will be more of these tools created to manage the influx of information necessary, and to organise the data. While not specifically designed for rare diseases, and almost agnostic to the distinction, these tools will undoubtedly be used for rare diseases. This is already apparent in the work of both PatientsLikeMe on amyotrophic lateral sclerosis (ALS), the disease from which the founders' brother died and the inspiration for PatientsLikeMe (Wicks *et al.* 2010), and 23andMe, which has initiated a number of rare disease efforts.

7 www.patientslikeme.com, www.23andme.com, accessed 18 December 2012.
8 www.privateaccess.com, accessed 18 December 2012.
9 See www.weconsent.us, accessed 18 December 2012.
10 www.genomera.com, accessed 18 December 2012.

13.5 Where must we go?

This final section describes Genetic Alliance's vision of the future. Predicting the future is not for the faint of heart. Authentic and meaningful engagement in creating a better future means taking responsibility for that future. Therefore, this section will offer our perspective at Genetic Alliance integral with our obligation to work towards this vision.

Buckminster Fuller, the American systems theorist, architect, engineer, author, designer, inventor and futurist, said: 'You never change things by fighting existing reality. To change something, build a new model that makes the existing model obsolete'. This is very true for rare disease drug development. Drug development, as we know it today, is a failed model. Applying that failed model to rare diseases is not useful nor will it be successful. This is the time, and the perfect opportunity, to build the new model. Change occurs when the conditions are right. It occurs when the risk of staying with the status quo outweighs the risk of trying something new, something unproven. It is often difficult to see that tipping point from the safety of the familiar. Even the dysfunctional familiar does not seem so bad, because it is familiar. If we look into the eyes of the men, women and children dying from rare diseases, are we inclined to be cautious, competitive, tentative and staid in our approach? I think we are not as long as that gaze is held, but then when it is broken we forget that if we are not bold beyond the current systems, we will not succeed.

In prior ages, particularly the recent industrial age, based on scarce materials such as wood and steel, it was important to compete. It was critical to set up an us-against-them system. After all, commodities were limited, projects were sequential and process had to be controlled (Table 13.2). We have not, in drug development, explored what it means to take advantage of the abundant raw material we now use to create products—information. What does it mean to build a model in the information age of openness, collaboration, organic and simultaneous advances? This is a time when we should be testing new ideas, rapidly learning from both successes and failures, and not repeating elements of the old systems that have failed

Table 13.2 **Comparison of industrial and information ages**

Industrial age (old)	Information age (new)
Control means of production	Open means of production
Based on scarcity	Based on abundance
Hierarchical/Command and control	Network/Collaboration
Linear/Sequential	Organic
Win/Lose	Win/Win
Materials	Information

repeatedly. Rare diseases have both the most to gain and the most to lose. They make a fertile ground for some productive and accelerated experiments.

13.5.1 We must be boundary-less

In this information age, we must not defend our borders. They worked in a time of scarcity, but are inappropriate now. There are those who claim this is still a time of scarcity; there is little money to go around. I think if we fight for the small pools of money, we waste precious resources that could be spent on imagining new organisational structures. In a networked age, why do we think the structures we set up 50 years ago, before networks were imagined, would work? What if we threw open our borders, our boundaries, our databases and our coffers and created new organic entities? What would those look like? How would we know they were right?

First, we can look at ourselves. Examine our fears, my fears, in not worrying about my organisation, my company, my agency's success. In those fears, I come face to face with the impediments to success, for others and me. I begin to understand how I am more concerned about my disease, my idea, my stuff, than I am about succeeding.

It is both simple and hard. I am afraid to write in this chapter what I think, because you, the reader, will undoubtedly think I have either forgotten an important thing, misrepresented something or that I am nuts. And if you think I am nuts, then I lose your respect, and my reputation suffers. This calls me to ask why I am worried about your respect and my reputation, juxtaposed with the pending blindness of my children, the fragility of Sam or Ashley, the suffering of Anna, or the passing of Michael. In that light, I find courage, and know that if I have a vision, it is not arrogance to put it forth, and it is not humility to keep it quiet. If I have a vision, I have a responsibility to share it, and to risk letting it out into the world. I risk losing my credibility, and perhaps I shall, but if it is a stepping stone to the new models we all need, then why would I not let you step on it? Why not set it free to be remodelled until it is right and productive?

In 2010, I published a paper about earmarking for specific disease and how we need to put an end to them: 'Accelerate Medical Breakthroughs by Ending Disease Earmarks' (Terry 2010). I asked that we:

> ...step into the future as real collaborators building an infrastructure and a process that accelerates medical research overall, faster than what any organisation or agency can do alone. Let's consider the health of our children, our families and our communities as our first priority and our organisations and agencies as the tools to get there.

Imagine the progress we could achieve working together as though each of our successes was the responsibility of the other, and each of our challenges shared as well? I believe we can try this quickly and easily, and build new economic models to sustain it at the same time. Other industries have seen this succeed, even as they decried the fall of the boundaries they thought were essential to their existence. In other words, let's move a good deal of our intellectual property—our ideas, our foundations, our information, our samples—into the precompetitive space. Let's recognise all of it for what it is, simply the raw materials on which we can build solutions.

13.5.1.1 Universal cross-disease registries: Registries for All

The boundaries we have set up around disease can be considered everything from arbitrary to ridiculous. In a linear age, when one could only consider one disease at a time, if that, there was a need to split off and isolate diseases. There was a concerted effort to find constellations of symptoms, name them something (usually very esoteric names of researchers or no longer relevant symptoms) and find the gene responsible for the condition. It was thought that this approach would yield great results. Instead, we have some energetic advocates decrying the hype associated with finding genes and thinking that the job was just about done. We now know, 10, 20, 30 years after the discovery of the gene for cystic fibrosis, sickle cell trait and Huntington's disease, that we do not have a clear model for finding pathways to treatments and therapies. One shining light is the speed at which a therapy for Hutchinson-Gilford Progeria was discovered, a testimony to the power of parents, and to advocacy participation in research and partnership building (Gordon *et al.* 2012).

In this new age of networks, there is a network sensibility about disease as well. Systems biology is a conceptual framework that takes into consideration the 'network' of biology in complex systems such as the human. It presupposes that non-linear and emergent dynamics and behaviour, interlopers and context, must all be studied, and that anything in isolation will not elucidate the true reality. It relies heavily on mathematical and computational models and '*in silico*' experiments, to generate hypotheses. It ties the theory and the experimentation together in an iterative loop (Khatri *et al.* 2012). Systems biology allows cross-disciplinary fertilisation to occur and can accelerate the development of therapeutic intervention. Lee Hood uses the term P4 as integral to systems biology: predictive, preventive, personalised and participatory (Hood and Friend 2011; Tian *et al.* 2012). We are of course most interested in participatory science and believe that above all it will accelerate the science we so desperately need.

To take advantage of the emerging connections in pathways and networks of diseases, it is critical that cross-disease registries and biobanks are developed. These entities should be built on interoperable infrastructures with common nomenclature and standards. There are substantial efforts under way internationally (Rath *et al.* 2012). Genetic Alliance created Registries for All (www.reg4 all.org), a cross-disease platform that will be essential in the work of understanding health and disease, to allow individuals and organisations to aggregate both common data elements and disease-specific information on an interoperable platform.

13.5.1.2 Free data; let it thrive in the commons

There are many who have both thought about and written more eloquently than I about sharing data freely in a commons. And individuals, such as Stephen Friend, of Sage Bionetworks, have established such commons, in the form of tools such as Synapse that provide structures in which even participant-level clinical trial data can be shared. In an interview, Friend said:

> We are considering projects that will bring together hundreds of patients to collect information about the deep molecular characteristics of their diseases, along with all the information about which molecular charac-teristics respond to which existing therapies. We hope this will allow us to detect molecular classifications that can get the right drug to the right patient. Thus, patients can start to see themselves as active agents in their own treatments, an evolution toward being self-responsible citizens. This will be 'the democratisation of medicine'.
>
> (Paul and Clay 2011)

When data is freed to mingle in new ways, new results will emerge. New associa-tions of data, in structures that allow an intelligent intermingling, will provide critical insights.

Bernard Munos, founder of InnoThink Center for Research in Biomedical Inno-vation believes that drug development for rare diseases has improved tremen-dously in past years. While this is encouraging, Munos emphasises that 87% of rare diseases are not actively researched and there is much work to be done and it should be done in the commons (Munos 2010). In order for innovation to flour-ish, we need to tap the knowledge of patients and physicians, attract more scien-tists, stimulate new knowledge and pursue empirical approaches that can deliver treatments even in the absence of complete knowledge. Data in the commons with the eyes of many, from many stakeholder groups, will provide the basis for these empirical approaches.

Genetic Alliance established Registries for All (Reg4ALL) to catalyse a struc-ture for data to be collected and aggregated from ordinary people empowered to reclaim their health, and have a say in their own healing. I see Reg4ALL as a struc-ture that gives individuals the tools they need to share data and biological samples. It also provides novel governance structures to allow the complete participation of the citizen scientists, in a meaningful way (Winickoff 2008). It provides for cultur-ally sensitive and empowering policy and practice. It becomes a vehicle for ena-bling boundary-less-ness in both the data and in the organisations that can make meaningful use of the data. This cannot be proprietary information any longer. This information belongs to the human family, and with the right vehicles in place to protect privacy and respect variation in levels of comfort with sharing different kinds of information, trust can be the basis for significant scientific advancement (Anderson and Edwards 2010).

13.5.1.3 New advocacy

In the prior industrial age, advocacy took on a certain shape and quality. It had to scream to be heard. It had to claw its way in. It made remarkable strides in the form of strong women such as Abbey Meyers, the founder of the National Organization for Rare Disorders, and Mary Lasker, a philanthropist who worked tirelessly on behalf of health, particularly for the National Institutes of Health. Advocacy for rare diseases was often modelled on what common conditions were doing. Women with breast cancer chained themselves to the gates of Genentech to accelerate trials in Herceptin (Bazell 1998). Men with AIDS declared they should take charge of their lives in the early 1980s, engaged in non-violent civil disobedience and changed the national agenda, especially the research agenda. These were the tools of a win–lose era. We declared war on diseases, we were the 'squeaky wheels that got the grease', we became militant and it worked. In the networked era, advocacy must take on a new form.

Some of this is practical. Because we are all able to declare multiple affinities in the form of belonging to Facebook groups, Google+ hangouts, and others, we are not inclined to join organisations with the loyalty we once had. As individuals and communities, we find ways to belong to multiple entities and get what we need from a custom mash-up of those groups. This will impact rare disease advocacy organisations negatively if we continue to depend on affected individuals to join us and declare loyalty, particularly in the form of membership dues. We can no longer think of our membership in a proprietary way. Our 'members' float in and out of our groups, across many groups for different needs, and have those needs met in multiple ways. Some of them create their own solutions, seemingly in competition with our organisations. If advocacy embraces networks, multiple affinities and shared allegiances, then it will thrive. It will, however, look completely different from the way it does today. It is not sustainable in the current bricks and mortar, my-donor-list-is-my-ticket-to-sustainability, manner.

Advocates were inventive when they created the current structures. Moms (and some Dads) sat in their kitchens and said, 'we can do anything the big foundations are doing. We will emulate them, and we will modify their structures slightly where necessary'. Hundreds of 'mom and pop' foundations were born the 1980s and 1990s in kitchens and neighbourhoods. Some are thriving; many are working hard to stay alive. Some are closing down. The ones that are really thriving today, however, are largely online virtual communities that are not depending on regular member contributions for their livelihood. Two examples of these are i[2]y and PatientsLikeMe.[11]

---

11 I'm Too Young for This! Cancer Foundation, www.stupidcancer.org, accessed 18 December 2012.

Every chance I get, I ask a room filled with hundreds of advocates: 'If you were the mastermind for structuring the translational research that is needed today for each of the 6,000+ rare diseases, would you create 6,000+ disease foundations, boards of directors, secretaries and book-keeping systems (to name just a few practical components)?' They always say, no, they would not create this structure. Back to Buckminster Fuller: it is time to create that new model to make the old one obsolete. Even today's funders of advocacy and support are looking for collaborations, partnerships and novel new structures.

So what does new advocacy look like? I don't know, and were I to claim I did, or to aim at a certain model, I would box it in and reduce its effectiveness. If I claimed to know, I would not be taking the principles of crowdsourcing, open access and learning systems seriously. To quote Jamie Heywood at a recent Sage Bionetworks Congress: 'I may not solve your problem, but we might!' (Heywood 2012). I believe that to answer the question, all stakeholders must make this question a priority. And not for the sake of advocacy, but for the sake of the object of the advocacy. Part of the problem with disease advocacy today is its focus on sustaining itself as a goal, rather than on the disease.

I think it will take being very open to new thinkers in this space and others. It will take the shape of so many other entities in the new networked age. It will have no rigid boundaries; it will be person-centric; it will not depend on information being proprietary. It will be flexible, open, systems-focused and find value in connecting things, rather than siloing them. It will encourage leadership from the bottom, the top and the sides, and most essentially, from outside. It will boldly focus on the task at hand. It will sunset, die, morph and be recreated as needed. It will allow an expiration date to be stamped on it, and celebrate the next emergent model.

13.5.2 Networks: This time as NETS

In the same way as networks of organisations and people will be critical to accelerating rare disease drug discovery, so will networks in the structure of science. Navigating the Ecosystem of Translational Science (NETS) (Fig. 13.2) offers a networked view of drug development (Baxter *et al.* 2013). After many interviews, salons and meetings with CEOs of biotech and pharma companies, academic researchers, government agencies and advocates, Genetic Alliance assembled NETS. It is a response to the idea that drug development overall is a pipeline, i.e. a linear activity. The map we have created contains 'neighbourhoods' that allow activities to be carried on simultaneously in synergistic and connected ways. This more accurately portrays the intensely interconnected system that is needed to move towards therapies. It is often said that the incentives are misaligned in drug development (Munos and Chin 2009). In the linear system that is depicted most frequently, the handoffs are problematic. In addition, the incentives to continue to work on the same problems and just go deeper (Edwards *et al.* 2011) are enormous, and risk-taking is generally not rewarded. In the networked model, the neighbourhoods could determine what structures would work best for them, all the while

Figure 13.2 **Navigating the Ecosystem of Translational Science (NETS)**

Source: Baxter *et al.* 2013: 171

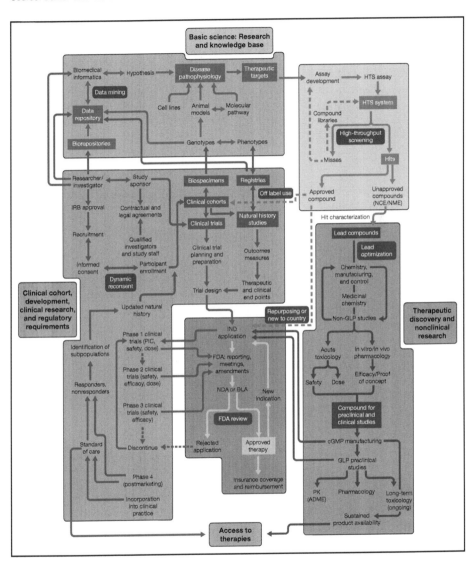

keeping their eyes on the prize, on why they exist and look for the best paths to creating the quickest and safest therapies.

13.5.3 Rapid experimentation

Experimentation must also change. Many of the elements of that change for common conditions have been written about extensively. They are even more important for rare diseases. A few brave souls are taking steps toward experimenting with the experiments of adaptive clinical trials (Chow and Chang 2008), first-in-human studies (EMEA 2007), surrogate end-points (Lesko and Atkinson 2001), retrospective prospective studies, dynamic regulatory systems, and global harmonisation for better worldwide coordination. Further, the negative results of studies must be fed into the system in order to prevent enormous waste of resources through redundant experiments (Gupta and Stopfer 2011). In its report from the workshop on the Learning Healthcare System (Olsen *et al.* 2007), the Institute of Medicine (IOM) asked these questions:

- 'Should we continue to call the RCT the 'gold standard'? Although clearly useful and necessary in some circumstances, does this designation over-promise?'

- 'What do we need to do to better characterise the range of alternatives to RCTs and the applications and implications for each?'

- 'What constitutes evidence, and how does it vary by circumstance?'

- 'How much of evidence development and evidence application will ultimately fall outside of even a fully interoperable and universally adopted electronic health record (EHR)? What are the boundaries of a technical approach to improving care?'

These questions and concepts must be considered in the rare disease context. Again, from an IOM report of a study, *Rare Diseases and Orphan Products: Accelerating Research and Development* (Field and Boat 2010).

> In addition, it is sometimes stated that FDA inappropriately requires two phase III, randomized, placebo-controlled, double-blind trials to support orphan drug approvals. Analyses of recent approval records for orphan drugs, however, show that a substantial proportion did not require two phase III trials. Some have been approved on the basis of phase II trials, and at least one approval has been based on a small historical case series.
>
> At the same time, agency staff have identified a number of problems with studies that sponsors have submitted. These include delayed toxicology studies; inadequate characterisation of chemical compounds; lack of natural history studies to characterise the disease process; poor use of early-phase studies (e.g. safety, dosing) to guide the design of phase III studies; inadequate trial design (including lack of a formal protocol, well-defined question, adequate controls, validated biomarkers, and appropriate surrogate measures), and lack of advance communication with FDA about the adequacy of clinical trial plans. Given the scarce resources available for rare diseases research and orphan product development, it is particularly unfortunate for these resources to be used ineffectively.

The study offered a number of detailed recommendations that should not be left for a top-down approach. There should be a people's workshop or flash mob convened to determine what should be taken forward with some rapidity and urgency.

13.5.4 Citizen scientists

Perhaps the greatest catalyst to rare disease therapeutic development will come from the consumer movement producing citizen scientists. Some of these in the past have been somewhat traditional advocates (Solovitch 2001). But in more recent times, ordinary folks have the tools to do what they need to build support, create networks and even do drug development in their kitchen (Marcus 2011) and create their own clinical trials (Swan 2012). A consumer movement in health will probably be the way rare disease drug development is accelerated. The intense power of crowdsourcing, across the long tail, will give individuals tools to reclaim their health. Once we all do that, there will be no holding back the free sharing of information and data. There will be an onslaught of inventive ways of overcoming the challenges that rare diseases pose. We will not need the gatekeepers of old in the form of advocacy leadership, and we will find our voice.

13.6 The system reflects the actions of those who make it up: Leadership

In conclusion, it was thought in prior years that heroics were called for in order to make a difference. But in this networked age, we now know that what's at stake for ourselves, our children and grandchildren, our communities, and the world is our seamlessly working together for health without regard for what we win or how we look. This knowing is not always conscious, but *it is present* within us. Opening space together to explore this is an opportunity to discover it, declare it and do something about it with others of like mind and heart.

This requires an investment of our very self, our ideas, our hopes and dreams, our passions, and our responsibility for acting on them. Discuss, debate, conceive novel partnerships, and emerge transformed and transforming—creating new systems that solve old problems, forging new relationships that empower action, and inspiring ourselves and others to rise above the limitations that used to constrain us.

If we are to discover treatments and therapies for those suffering from rare diseases, we must be as bold as these diseases. They literally take life and limb of millions of individuals around the globe. We cannot walk in trodden paths and hope to succeed in solving the complex problems that underlie their suffering. We must ask ourselves how we can maintain the tempered urgency necessary to apply ourselves in novel ways without fear. We cannot concern ourselves with traditional measures of success—money, prestige, tenure, promotion, acclaim, a solid bottom line or sustainability. If we pause for a moment at every new step, at every challenge and opportunity, and ask: 'How can we make the most of this? What holds me back from really taking this to where it needs to go? How can I free myself and the system I embody?' Then we will make a difference. What are we waiting for?

References

Abbott, A. (2011) 'Rare-Disease Project has Global Ambitions', *Nature* 472: 17.

Aguirre, D., L. Howell, D. Kletter and G. Neilson (2005) *A Global Check-up: Diagnosing the Health of Today's Organizations* (McLean, VA: Booz Allen Hamilton).

Anderson, C. (2006) *The Long Tail: Why the Future of Business Is Selling Less of More* (New York: Hyperion).

Anderson, N., and K. Edwards (2010) 'Building a Chain of Trust: Using Policy and Practice to Enhance Trustworthy Clinical Data Discovery and Sharing', in *Proceedings of the 2010 Workshop on Governance of Technology, Information and Policies, Austin, Texas*, ACM, pp. 15-20.

Baquet, C.R., C.P. Mullins and S.I. Mishra (2006) 'Recruitment and Participation in Clinical Trials: Sociodemographic, Rural/Urban, and Health Care Access Predictors', *Cancer Detection and Prevention* 30: 24-33.

Baxter, K., and S.F. Terry (2011) 'International Rare Disease Research Consortium Commits to Aggressive Goals', *Genetic Testing and Molecular Biomarkers* 15: 465.

Baxter, K., E. Horn, N. Gal-Edd, K. Zonno, J. O'Leary, P.F. Terry and S.F. Terry (2013) 'An End to the Myth: There is no drug development pipeline', *Science Translational Medicine* 5 (February 2013): 171; doi: 10.1126/scitranslmed.3003505.

Bazell, R. (1998) *HER-2: The Making of Herceptin, a Revolutionary Treatment for Breast Cancer* (New York: Random House).

Bercovitch, L., B. Schepps, S. Koelliker, C. Magro, S. Terry and M. Lebwohl (2003) 'Mammographic Findings in Pseudoxanthoma Elasticum', *Journal of the American Academy of Dermatology* 48: 359-66.

Bercovitch, L., T. Leroux, S. Terry and M.A. Weinstock (2004) 'Pregnancy and Obstetrical Outcomes in Pseudoxanthoma Elasticum', *British Journal of Dermatology* 151: 1011-18.

Bercovitch, R.S., J.A. Januario, S.F. Terry, K. Boekelheide, A.D. Podis, D.E. Dupuy and L.G. Bercovitch (2005) 'Testicular Microlithiasis in Association with Pseudoxanthoma Elasticum', *Radiology* 237: 550-54.

Burns, K.H., and A. Chakravarti (2011) 'Massively Parallel Rare Disease Genetics', *Genome Medicine* 3: 29.

Chow, S.C., and M. Chang (2008) 'Adaptive Design Methods in Clinical Trials: A Review', *Orphanet Journal of Rare Diseases* 3: 11.

Church, G.M. (2011) 'New Technologies for Integrating Genomic, Environmental and Trait Data', *Journal of Clinical Sleep Medicine* 7: S43-44.

Collins, F.S. (2012) 'A Vision for a National Patient-Centered Research Network', *National Workshop to Advance the Use of Electronic Data in Patient-Centered Outcomes Research, Palo Alto, CA*.

Dooren, J.C. (2010) 'New Drug Approvals Slipped in 2010', *Wall Street Journal*, 31 December 2010 (online.wsj.com/article/SB10001424052748704543004576052170335871018.html).

Edwards, A.M., R. Isserlin, G.D. Bader, S.V. Frye, T.M. Willson and F.H. Yu (2011) 'Too Many Roads Not Taken', *Nature* 470: 163-65.

Eid, J., A. Fehr, J. Gray, K. Luong, J. Lyle, G. Otto, P. Peluso, D. Rank, P. Baybayan, B. Bettman, A. Bibillo, K. Bjornson, B. Chaudhuri, F. Christians, R. Cicero, S. Clark, R. Dalal, A. Dewinter, J. Dixon, M. Foquet, A. Gaertner, P. Hardenbol, C. Heiner, K. Hester, D. Holden, G. Kearns, X. Kong, R. Kuse, Y. Lacroix, S. Lin, P. Lundquist, C. Ma, P. Marks, M. Maxham, D. Murphy, I. Park, T. Pham, M. Phillips, J. Roy, R. Sebra, G. Shen, J. Sorenson, A. Tomaney, K. Travers, M. Trulson, J. Vieceli, J. Wegener, D. Wu, A. Yang, D. Zaccarin, P. Zhao, F. Zhong, J. Korlach and S. Turner (2009) 'Real-time DNA Sequencing from Single Polymerase Molecules', *Science* 323: 133-38.

EMEA (2007) *Guideline on Requirements for First-in-Man Clinical Trials for Potential High-Risk Medicinal Products* (London: EMEA).

FDA (2011) 'FDA: 35 Innovative New Drugs Approved in Fiscal Year 2011', News Release 3 November 2011, www.fda.gov/newsevents/newsroom/pressannouncements/ucm278383 .htm, accessed 8 January 2013.

Fernandez, C.V., and C. Weijer (2006) 'Obligations in Offering to Disclose Genetic Research Results', *The American Journal of Bioethics: AJOB* 6: 44-46; author reply W10-42.

Field, M.J. and T.F. Boat (eds.) (2010) *Rare Diseases and Orphan Products: Accelerating Research and Development* (Washington, DC: National Academy of Sciences).

Genin, E., J. Feingold and F. Clerget-Darpoux (2008) 'Identifying Modifier Genes of Monogenic Disease: Strategies and Difficulties', *Human Genetics* 124: 357-68.

Gilbert, J., P. Henske and A. Singh (2003) 'Rebuilding Big Pharma's Business Model', *In Vivo: The Business and Medicine Report* 21.10 (November 2003).

Gordon, L.B., M.E. Kleinman, D.T. Miller, D.S. Neuberg, A. Giobbie-Hurder, M. Gerhard-Herman, L.B. Smoot, C.M. Gordon, R. Cleveland, B.D. Snyder, B. Fligor, W.R. Bishop, P. Statkevich, A. Regen, A. Sonis, S. Riley, C. Ploski, A. Correia, N. Quinn, N.J. Ullrich, A. Nazarian, M.G. Liang, S.Y. Huh, A. Schwartzman and M.W. Kieran (2012) 'Clinical Trial of a Farnesyltransferase Inhibitor in Children with Hutchinson-Gilford Progeria Syndrome', *Proceedings of the National Academy of Sciences USA* 109.41: 16666-71 (doi: 10.1073/pnas.1202529109).

Gupta, N., and M. Stopfer (2011) 'Negative Results Need Airing Too', *Nature* 470: 39.

Haffner, M.E. (2006) 'Adopting Orphan Drugs: Two Dozen Years of Treating Rare Diseases', *New England Journal of Medicine* 354: 445-47.

Hamburg, M.A., and F.S. Collins (2010) 'The Path to Personalized Medicine', *New England Journal of Medicine* 363: 301-04.

Heywood, J. (2012) 'We Might Know How to Solve the Problem', Sage Bionetworks Commons Congress 2012, fora.tv/2012/04/21/Discovery_20_-_We_Might_Know_How_to_Solve_the_Problem, accessed 8 January 2013.

Hood, L., and S.H. Friend (2011) 'Predictive, Personalized, Preventive, Participatory (P4) Cancer Medicine', *Nature Reviews Clinical Oncology* 8: 184-87.

Ingelman-Sundberg, M., and C. Rodriguez-Antona (2005) 'Pharmacogenetics of Drug-Metabolizing Enzymes: Implications for a Safer and More Effective Drug Therapy', *Philosophical Transactions of the Royal Society of London B Biological Sciences* 360: 1563-70.

Khatri, P., M. Sirota and A.J. Butte (2012) 'Ten Years of Pathway Analysis: Current Approaches and Outstanding Challenges', *PLoS Computational Biology* 8: e1002375.

Krulwich, R. (2001) 'Cracking the Code of Life', PBS television show, 17 April 2001, www.pbs .org/wgbh/nova/body/cracking-the-code-of-life.html, accessed 8 January 2013.

LaMattina, J. (2012) 'How Committed is Big Pharma to Rare Diseases?' *Forbes*, 2 May 2012.

Landy, D.C., M.A. Brinich, M.E. Colten, E.J. Horn, S.F. Terry and R.R. Sharp (2012) 'How Disease Advocacy Organizations Participate in Clinical Research: A Survey of Genetic Organizations', *Genetics in Medicine* 14: 223-28.

Lesko, L.J., and A.J. Atkinson, Jr (2001) 'Use of Biomarkers and Surrogate Endpoints in Drug Development and Regulatory Decision Making: Criteria, Validation, Strategies', *Annual Review of Pharmacology and Toxicology* 41: 347-66.

Lupski, J.R., J.G. Reid, C. Gonzaga-Jauregui, D. Rio Deiros, D.C. Chen, L. Nazareth, M. Bainbridge, H. Dinh, C. Jing, D.A. Wheeler, A.L. McGuire, F. Zhang, P. Stankiewicz, J.J. Halperin, C. Yang, C. Gehman, D. Guo, R.K. Irikat, W. Tom, N.J. Fantin, D.M. Muzny and R.A. Gibbs (2010) 'Whole-Genome Sequencing in a Patient with Charcot-Marie-Tooth Neuropathy', *New England Journal of Medicine* 362: 1181-91.

Marcus, A.D. (2011) 'Citizen Scientists', *Wall Street Journal*, 3 December 2011: C1-2.

Marusina, K., D.J. Welsch, L. Rose, D. Brock and N. Bahr (2011) 'The CTSA Pharmaceutical Assets Portal: A Public-Private Partnership Model for Drug Repositioning', *Drug Discovery Today Therapeutic Strategies* 8: 77-83.

McClellan, J., and M.C. King (2010) 'Genetic Heterogeneity in Human Disease', *Cell* 141: 210-17.

McConaghie, A. (2012) 'Rare Diseases: Pharma's New Frontier', Pharmafile, www.pharmafile .com/news/171918/rare-diseases-pharma-s-new-frontier, accessed 8 January 2013.

Meekings, K.N., C.S. Williams and J.E. Arrowsmith (2012) 'Orphan Drug Development: An Economically Viable Strategy for Biopharma R&D', *Drug Discovery Today* 17: 660-64.

Moeller, M.P., K.R. White and L. Shisler (2006) 'Primary Care Physicians' Knowledge, Attitudes, and Practices Related to Newborn Hearing Screening', *Pediatrics* 118: 1357-70.

Munos, B. (2010) 'Can Open-Source Drug R&D Repower Pharmaceutical Innovation?' *Clinical Pharmacology and Therapeutics* 87: 534-36.

Munos, B.H., and W.W. Chin (2009) 'A Call for Sharing: Adapting Pharmaceutical Research to New Realities', *Science Translational Medicine* 1: 9cm8.

Muthyala, R. (2011) 'Orphan/Rare Drug Discovery through Drug Repositioning', *Drug Discovery Today: Therapeutic Strategies* 8: 71-76.

National Human Genome Research Institute (2011) 'An Overview of the Human Genome Project', www.genome.gov/12011238, accessed 8 January 2013.

Nature (2010) 'Editorial: The needs of the few', *Nature* 466: 160.

NCBI (National Center for Biotechnology Information) (2004) *Just the Facts: A Basic Introduction to the Science Underlying NCBI Resources* (Bethesda, MD: NCBI, US National Library of Medicine, www.ncbi.nlm.nih.gov/About/primer/pharm.html).

NCI (National Cancer Institute) (2002) *Cancer Clinical Trials: The Basic Workbook* (Bethesda, MD: National Cancer Institute).

Ng, S.B., K.J. Buckingham, C. Lee, A.W. Bigham, H.K. Tabor, K.M. Dent, C.D. Huff, P.T. Shannon, E.W. Jabs, D.A. Nickerson, J. Shendure and M.J. Bamshad (2010) 'Exome Sequencing Identifies the Cause of a Mendelian Disorder', *Nature Genetics* 42: 30-35.

NIH (National Institutes for Health) (2010) 'Rare Diseases Clinical Research Network', NIH Fact Sheet, report.nih.gov/nihfactsheets/ViewFactSheet.aspx?csid=126, accessed 8 January 2013.

NIH NCATS (National Center for Advancing Translational Sciences) (2012) *Rescuing and Repurposing Drugs* (Bethesda, MD: NIH, www.ncats.nih.gov/research/reengineering/ rescue-repurpose/rescue-repurpose.html).

Oka, T. (1994) 'Self-Help Groups in Japan: Trends and Traditions', in T.B.F. Lavoie and B. Gidron (ed.), *Self-Help and Mutual Aid Groups: International and Multicultural Perspectives* (New York: Haworth Press): 69-95.

Olsen, L.A., D. Aisner and J.M. McGinnis (eds.) (2007) *The Learning Healthcare System: Workshop Summary* (Washington, DC: National Academy of Sciences).

OrphaNews (2011) 'Disease-based Registries for Rare Disorders', 11 May 2011, www.orpha .net/actor/EuropaNews/2011/110511.html, accessed 8 January 2013.

Paul, R., and A. Clay (2011) 'An Open Source Approach to Medical Research', Stanford Social Innovation Review, www.ssireview.org/blog/entry/interview_an_open_source_ approach_to_medical_research, accessed 8 January 2013.

Peppercorn, J.M., J.C. Weeks, E.F. Cook and S. Joffe (2004) 'Comparison of Outcomes in Cancer Patients Treated Within and Outside Clinical Trials: Conceptual Framework and Structured Review', *Lancet* 363: 263-70.

PhRMA (2012) *About the Pharmaceutical Sector* (Washington, DC: PhRMA).

Putkowski, S. (2010) 'National Organization for Rare Disorders (NORD): Providing Advocacy for People with Rare Disorders', *NASN School Nurse* 25: 38-41.

Ragan, I. (2009) *An Update on the Innovative Medicines Initiative and its Implications for the 3Rs* (London: National Centre for the Replacement, Refinement and Reduction of Animals in Research).

Rapp, R. (2000) *Testing Women, Testing the Fetus: The Social Impact of Amniocentesis in America* (London: Taylor & Francis).

Rath, A., A. Olry, F. Dhombres, M.M. Brandt, B. Urbero and S. Ayme (2012) 'Representation of Rare Diseases in Health Information Systems: The Orphanet Approach to Serve a Wide Range of End Users', *Human Mutation* 33: 803-808.

Rubinstein, Y.R., S.C. Groft, R. Bartek, K. Brown, R.A. Christensen, E. Collier, A. Farber, J. Farmer, J.H. Ferguson, C.B. Forrest, N.C. Lockhart, K.R. McCurdy, H. Moore, G.B. Pollen, R. Richesson, V.R. Miller, S. Hull and J. Vaught (2010) 'Creating a Global Rare Disease Patient Registry Linked to a Rare Diseases Biorepository Database: Rare Disease-HUB (RD-HUB)', *Contemporary Clinical Trials* 31: 394-404.

Sharma, A. (2010) 'Orphan Drug: Development Trends and Strategies', *Journal of Pharmacy and Bioallied Sciences* 2: 290-99.

Shelton, R.H. (2011) 'Electronic Consent Channels: Preserving Patient Privacy without Handcuffing Researchers', *Science Translational Medicine* 3: 69cm64.

Solovitch, S. (2001) 'The Citizen Scientists', *Wired Magazine* 9.09 (June 2001).

Stead, M., D. Cameron, N. Lester, M. Parmar, R. Haward, R. Kaplan, T. Maughan, R. Wilson, H. Campbell, R. Hamilton, D. Stewart, L. O'Toole, D. Kerr, V. Potts, R. Moser, J. Darbyshire, P. Selby and National Cancer Research Networks across the UK (2011) 'Strengthening Clinical Cancer Research in the United Kingdom', *British Journal of Cancer* 104: 1529-34.

Stockdale, A., and S.F. Terry (2002) 'Advocacy Groups and the New Genetics', in J. Alper, C. Ard and A. Asch (eds.), *The Double-Edged Helix* (Baltimore, MD: The Johns Hopkins University Press): 80-101.

Swan, M. (2012) 'Crowdsourced Health Research Studies: An Important Emerging Complement to Clinical Trials in the Public Health Research Ecosystem', *Journal of Medical Internet Research* 14: e46.

Terry, S. (2010) 'Accelerate Medical Breakthroughs by Ending Disease Earmarks', *Nature Reviews Genetics* 11: 310-11.

Terry, S.F., and C.D. Boyd (2001) 'Researching the Biology of PXE: Partnering in the Process', *American Journal of Medical Genetics* 106: 177-84.

Terry, S.F., P.F. Terry, K.A. Rauen, J. Uitto and L.G. Bercovitch (2007) 'Advocacy Groups as Research Organizations: The PXE International Example', *Nature Reviews Genetics* 8: 157-64.

The Lancet (2011) 'Lessons from Lipitor and the Broken Blockbuster Drug Model', *The Lancet* 378: 1976.

Tian, Q., N.D. Price and L. Hood (2012) 'Systems Cancer Medicine: Towards Realization of Predictive, Preventive, Personalized and Participatory (P4) Medicine', *Journal of Internal Medicine* 271: 111-21.

US Department of Energy Office of Science (2011) 'About the Human Genome Project', www.ornl.gov/sci/techresources/Human_Genome/project/about.shtml, accessed 8 January 2013.

Weiss, J.O. (1989) 'Genetic Support Groups: A Continuum of Genetic Services', *Women Health* 15: 37-53.

Wetterstrand, K. (2012) *DNA Sequencing Costs: Data from the NHGRI Large-Scale Genome Sequencing Program* (Bethesda, MD: National Human Genome Institute).

Wicks, P., M. Massagli, J. Frost, C. Brownstein, S. Okun, T. Vaughan, R. Bradley and J. Heywood (2010) 'Sharing Health Data for Better Outcomes on PatientsLikeMe', *Journal of Medical Internet Research* 12: e19.

Winickoff, D.E. (2008) *From Benefit Sharing to Power Sharing: Partnership Governance in Population Genomics Research* (Faculty Working Papers; Berkeley, CA: JSP/Center for the Study of Law and Society).

Xue, Y., R.A. Cartwright, D. Altshuler, J. Kebbel, P. Kokko-Gonzales and D.A. Nickerson (2010) 'A Map of Human Genome Variation from Population-Scale Sequencing', *Nature* 467: 1061-73 (doi: 10.1038/nature09534).

Zonno, K.D., and S.F. Terry (2009) 'Collaboration: The Foundation for Success in Rare Disease Genetic Test Development', *Genetic Testing and Molecular Biomarkers* 13: 553-54.

Sharon F. Terry is President and CEO of Genetic Alliance, a network of more than 10,000 organisations, of which 1,200 are disease advocacy organisations. Genetic Alliance enables individuals, families and communities to reclaim their health and become full participants in translational research and services. She is the founding CEO of PXE International, a research advocacy organisation for the genetic condition pseudoxanthoma elasticum (PXE). As co-discoverer of the gene associated with PXE, she holds the patent for ABCC6 to act as its steward and has assigned her rights to the foundation. She developed a diagnostic test and conducts clinical trials. Terry is also a co-founder of the Genetic Alliance Registry and Biobank. She is the author of more than 90 peer-reviewed articles. In her focus at the forefront of consumer participation in genetics research, services and policy, she serves in a leadership role on many of the major international and national organisations, including the Institute of Medicine Science and Policy Board, the IOM Roundtable on Translating Genomic-Based Research for Health, the National Coalition for Health Professional Education in Genetics Board, the International Rare Disease Research Consortium Interim Executive Committee and as a member of the Board of Instigators for InvokeHealth! She is on the editorial boards of several journals. She was instrumental in the passage of the Genetic Information Nondiscrimination Act. In 2005, she received an honorary doctorate from Iona College for her work in community engagement; the first Patient Service Award from the UNC Institute for Pharmacogenomics and Individualized Therapy in 2007; the Research!America Distinguished Organization Advocacy Award in 2009; and the Clinical Research Forum and Foundation's Annual Award for Leadership in Public Advocacy in 2011. In 2012, she became an honorary professor of Hebei United University in China, and also received the Facing Our Risk of Cancer Empowered (FORCE) Spirit of Empowerment Award. She is a fellow of the Ashoka fellowship of social entrepreneurs.

Jayson Swanson is a 2011 graduate of Luther College in Decorah, Iowa, with degrees in biology and business management where he was also an NCAA All-American in wrestling. He is currently a graduate student pursuing a double degree Master's in Health economics, policy and management (MPhil) from the University of Oslo, Norway, and in international health and social management (MA) from Management Center Innsbruck, Austria. His hopes are to pursue a career in policy, management or clinical practice. Most recently he served as the chief blogger/editor for MCI at the 2012 European Health Forum Gastein in Austria.

Conclusion

Are fundamental diseases the answer?

The world of rare diseases has changed significantly in the past two decades. As the contributors to this book have shown, much remains to be done. Identifying patients, moving ahead with the science, developing new drugs, building international registries and reference networks—all these activities take time and money. As many of the contributors have emphasised, a key problem is the lack of awareness and interest in rare diseases. Yet, as again has been shown, rare diseases play a role that goes far beyond the diseases themselves.

It has been known for centuries that the study of extreme and rare diseases is fundamental for understanding common diseases. Dr William Harvey, the 17th-century physician who discovered circulation in 1657, said:

> Nature is nowhere accustomed more openly to display her secret mysteries than in cases where she shows traces of her workings apart from the beaten path; nor is there any better way to advance the proper practice of medicine than to give our minds to the discovery of the usual law of nature by the careful investigation of cases of rarer forms of disease.

Two hundred and fifty years later, Sir Archibald Garrod, who first identified alkaptonuria as an inherited disease in 1901, made a similar statement: 'The study of nature's experiments is of special value; and many lessons which rare maladies can teach could hardly be learned in other ways'.

More recently, Dr Francis Collins, Director of the National Institutes of Health, said that 'what we learn from rare disorders often has profound consequences for our understanding of more common conditions'. Professor Doris Zallen, a member of NORD's Medical Advisory Committee, said on 3 October 2012 that:

> rare diseases, because they often have a singular genetic basis, present unique scientific opportunities for discovering and understanding gene

action without the confounding factors that characterize the common disorders (factors such as contributions from multiple genes, environmental influences, diet, smoking and other life-style choices). The study of rare diseases has already provided fundamental understandings of genetic systems, biochemical pathways, and DNA-repair mechanisms that have helped elucidate the basis of and improve treatments for common diseases.

So why aren't more researchers studying rare diseases as a way of unlocking the secrets of human biology and finding new treatments for common diseases? Why aren't government funding bodies such as the Medical Research Council in the UK devoting large sums of money to this research? Why are they continuing to focus on the same scientific approaches and the same common diseases, but with fewer and fewer results?

A major problem is the term 'rare disease' itself. 'Rare' has connotations of not being important, or being quirky, not affecting many people. With that understanding of rare diseases, it's hardly surprising that they are low on everyone's agenda.

That's why Tony Hall and I have set up a new foundation called Findacure, which will focus on what we call 'fundamental diseases'—rare and extreme diseases that are fundamental to understanding human biology and common diseases. We believe that by investing in research into these fundamental diseases, we will unlock new insights and discover potential treatments for chronic conditions from which so many people suffer. We will raise funds on a scale big enough to support global research, patient help, drug development and public awareness programmes. The drug development will take place through Findacure's non-profit social enterprise, Findacure Development, which aims to develop medicines for fundamental diseases and to sell them to the health service at an affordable price in order to take the strain off health budgets and make more treatments available for more people.

If you'd like to join us in this journey, please go to www.findacure.org.uk or email nick@findacure.org.uk.

Nick Sireau

Index

6-minute walk test   31
23andMe   248
1000 Genomes Project   236

Abbott, Diane   210
Access   40–1
   early market access   37, 103–7
   expanded access   36–7
   market access   109
   pre-approval access systems   34
Action Duchenne   26
Adagen   234
ADHD (attention deficit hyperactivity
      disorder)   197
Advocacy organisations *see* Disease advocacy
      organisations; Parents/caregivers
      organisations; Patient groups/
      organisations
AFM (Association Française contre les
      Myopathies)   27
AKU Society   1–2, 3–4, 44, 48–56, 83, 108
   drug repositioning strategy   138–9
   international societies   49
   partnerships   53–6
   patient identification campaign   49–50,
      55, 58
   raising awareness   60
   research initiative   50–3
Alkaptonuria (AKU)   1–2, 3, 17, 35, 44–5, 80
   academia and   53, 54
   animal models   50, 51, 53, 80–1, 139
   centres of excellence   58–60
   clinical centres   53, 54–5

commencing treatment   52–3
costs of treatment   58–60
diagnosis   1, 45, 57–8
drug repositioning   138–9
effects on the body   51–3, 80
enzyme therapy   134–8
funding research   56–7
in vitro models   50, 53
incidence/prevalence   43, 83
international network   53–6
mouse models   51, 80–1, 135, 139
natural history   51–3
nitisinone *see* Nitisinone
ochronosis   50–1, 52, 53, 54, 55, 57, 80, 81,
      82, 83, 84
osteoarthritis and   3, 17, 45, 51, 54, 57, 58
public awareness   60
research   1, 50–3, 56–7, 60
Severity Score Index (AKUSSI)   53, 81
tetrad of features   45, 58
see also AKU Society
All-Wales Medicines Strategy Group
      (AWMSG)   211
Alzheimer's disease   119, 120, 140, 142–3
Amgen   93
Amyotrophic lateral sclerosis (ALS)   248
Angiogenesis   123
Animal models   31
   AKU   50, 51, 53, 80–1, 139
Animal trials   116
   see also Pre-clinical trials
Annual treatment costs *see* Treatment costs
Antibiotic resistance   128

Antibiotics
  as neuroprotective agents   127
Antimalarials   129
Antimicrobials   128
Antisense oligonucleotides (AONs)   27, 32
Approval *see* Regulatory approval
Ashoka   2
Autosomal dominant monogenic
  conditions   179
Autosomal recessive disorders   80
  see also Alkaptonuria
Awareness of rare diseases *see* Public
  awareness

BAMARA project   172
Belgium   94–5
Biobanks   240–2, 245
Biogen Idec   246
BioMarin   28
Biomarkers   81, 99, 233
Biotherapeutics   130
BioVista   142
Birt-Hogg-Dubé Syndrome (BHD)   5, 179–91
  research *see* Myrovlytis Trust
Bisphosphonates   3
BLACKSWAN Foundation   2, 5, 193–9
Breast cancer   39, 123, 245, 253
Businesses/companies
  drug repositioning   139–43
  partnerships   28, 38, 55–6

Cancer   119, 123, 142, 233
  breast cancer   39, 123, 245, 253
  innovative drugs   107
  rare cancers   130
  research   14, 57
  treatment   17–18, 39
Catlin, Nick   26
Ceftriaxone   127
Centres of excellence/expertise   35–6, 161,
  209, 221–2, 226
  AKU research   58–60
  funding   163
  reference networks   166, 167
Centro Nazionale Malattie Rare (Istituto
  Superiore di Sanità)   13
Charge coupled device (CCD) cameras   116
Charley's Fund   26, 27
Chemistry, manufacturing and control
  (CMC)   117
Chlorophyll   46
Clinical trials   31–2
  approval *see* Regulatory approval
  biomarkers   81, 99, 233

challenges in design   79–84
drug repositioning   122
end-points   28, 31, 48, 53, 80–3, 94, 99,
  100, 203
global   18
in vivo testing   117
nitisinone   47–8, 53, 55, 80–4, 138
phases   117
pivotal trial stage   66–7, 99–100, 101
randomised controlled trials (RCTs)   31–2,
  40, 81, 83–4, 99, 256
regulatory dialogue   101–3
sample/population size   18, 66, 234, 244
small/single pivotal trial   66–7
surrogate end-points   67, 68, 80–3, 94, 99,
  104, 256
tax incentives   90
toxicity testing   117
see also Pre-clinical trials
Collins, Dr Francis   17, 263
Combinatorial chemistry   115
Committee for Medicinal Products
  for Human Use (CHMP)   89
Common diseases   114–15
  funding research into   57
  rare diseases as special
    forms of   3, 17, 244
Complex molecules   32
Compound libraries   123–4, 125–7
Copy number variation (CNV)   236
Costs *see* Drug development; Treatment costs
Craig, Michael   58
Crowley, John   26
Cudos   55
Cure Duchenne   26, 27
Cyclodextrin   108
Cystic fibrosis   39

Databases of patients *see* Patient registries
Definitions of rare/orphan diseases   114,
  202–3
Developing countries   115
Diagnosis
  AKU   1, 45, 57–8
  diagnostic infrastructure   34–5
  difficulties/delays   30, 34, 57–8, 194, 216
  lack of information and   216
  misdiagnosis   57–8, 216
Disease advocacy organisations (DAOs)   243,
  244–5, 246
  biobanks   240–1, 245
  registries   242, 245
  see also Parents/caregivers organisations;
    Patient groups/organisations

Disease InfoSearch   241, 243
DNA sequencing   34, 236, 237
    see also Genome sequencing
Drug development   4, 62–85
    academia   53, 54, 247
    accelerated development   39–40
    advantages to studying rare
        diseases   243–4
    biologicals   32
    citizen scientists   257
    clinical superiority   64, 65
    combinatorial chemistry   115
    complexity of human biology   232
    costs   33–4, 69, 117–18
    culture and   232–3
    drug discovery technologies   115–16
    European Union   89–92, 94–7
    expanded access   36–7
    freeing data   252–3
    functional outcome parameters   31
    global process   231–57
    high content screening (HCS)   116
    high throughput screening (HTS)   115–16,
        119, 120
    hurdles in   29–34
    incentives   62–5, 89–90, 234, 243
    issues   31
    leadership   257
    manufacturing challenges   32
    market exclusivity   64–5, 90, 91, 234
    misconceptions   65–9
    NETS   254–5
    OMPD *see* Orphan medicinal product
        designation
    preclinical models   30–1
    pricing   33–4
    rapid experimentation   255–6
    rare/orphan diseases/drugs   62–85, 89–97,
        129–33, 203–4
    rarity of the disease   30
    recent advances   235–43
    regulatory issues   233–4
    regulatory pathways   32–3
    reimbursement *see* Reimbursement
    return on investment   9, 15, 75, 76,
        77, 232
    risks   118–20
    role of patient   108
    similar medicinal products   65
    stages of development   116–17
    standards of care   37–8
    timescale   30, 115
    trials *see* Clinical trials
    United States   89–94

Drug Information Association   11
Drug repositioning/repurposing   4, 114–43,
        238–40
    AKU   138–9
    antibiotics as neuroprotective agents   127
    antimicrobials   128
    biotherapeutics   130
    businesses/companies   139–43
    compound libraries   123–4, 125–7
    database mining   124–5, 239
    definition   120
    enzyme replacement therapy (ERT)   131–2
    intellectual property issues   125
    know mechanism-new indication   122
    known compound-new target   121
    for neglected diseases   127–8
    NF-kB inhibitors   126–7
    parasiticides   128–9
    pharmacological chaperones   132–3
    principles   121–5
    screening small libraries   125–7
    small molecule drugs   123, 132–3
    as strategy   120–1
Drug trials *see* Clinical trials; Pre-clinical trials
Duchenne muscular dystrophy   26, 27, 29, 31,
        35, 39, 41
    registries   156–7
Duchenne Parent Project NL   26, 27
DuchenneConnect   156–7
Duloxetine   122, 139
Dutch Steering Group for Rare Diseases   23

Early access   37, 103–7
EC Regulation on Orphan Medicinal Products
        (141/2000)   63, 70, 87, 94, 95–6, 195, 243
Eli Lilly   119, 130, 139
Emerging markets   29, 122
Enzyme replacement therapy (ERT)   32, 131–2
    AKU   134–8
    Pompe disease   23–4
Epidemiological indices *see* Incidence/
        prevalence of rare diseases
Erectile dysfunction   122
EU Rare Disease Patient Solidarity   12
European BHD Consortium (EBC)   184
European Medicines
        Agency (EMA)   24, 32–3
    conditional approval   68–9, 84
    early market access   104–7
    expedited approval   67–8
    OMPD   69–79, 89, 90–1
    patient organisation involvement   168–9
    pivotal trials   66
    regulatory dialogue   101–3

European Network for Epidemiological and Public Health Data Collection on Rare Diseases 13
European Organisation for Rare Diseases (EURORDIS) 63, 130, 195, 205, 215, 248
  ERNs 163, 168, 169, 171
  online communities 168
  public awareness initiatives 8, 10, 11, 12–13
European Platform for Rare Disease Registries (EPIRARE) 172
European Porphyria Network (EPNET) 166
European Project for Rare Diseases National Plans Development (EUROPLAN) 221
European Rare Disease Awareness Week 12
European Rare Disease Task Force (RDTF) 208, 212
European reference networks (ERNs) 4–5, 159–75
  clinician cooperation 169–70
  conflict resolution 170
  decision-making 165–6
  dissemination 173–4
  governance structure 164–5
  identifying expertise 167–8
  legal framework 161–2
  main activities 163–4
  membership criteria 166–7
  objectives 163
  outcome indicators 172–3
  patient registries 163, 169, 170, 172, 173
  sources of finance 162–3
  sustainability 171–2
  team working 169–70
  telemedicine/tele-expertise 170–1
European Screening Port (ESP) 123
European Union Committee of Experts on Rare Diseases (EUCERD) 162
EuroWilson 167
Exon skipping 27
Expanded access 36–7

Findacure 264
FindAKUreproject 50
Fluorescence-based image analysis 116
Food and Drug Administration (FDA) 7–8, 11, 13, 32–3, 117, 127
  Center for Drug Evaluation and Research (CDER) 10
  conditional approval 68–9
  early market access 103–4
  expedited approval 67
  Office of Orphan Medicinal Products (OOMP) 92
  OMPD 70–9, 90–4

  pivotal trials 66
  regulatory dialogue 101
Food and Drug Administration Safety and Innovation Act 10
Founder effect 54
Friend, Stephen 252
Fuller, Buckminster 249, 254
Fumarylacetoacetic acid hydrolase 47
Functional outcome parameters 31
Funding 5, 18
  AKU research 56–7
  centralised 38
  centres of excellence 58
  investors see Investors
  patient organisations 27
  venture capital 27, 89, 108, 196, 197
  see also Reimbursement
Furlong, Pat 26

Garrod, Sir Archibald 44, 136, 263
Gateway diseases 17
Gaucher disease 28, 35, 131, 246
Gene therapy 32, 108
Genentech 93, 245
Genetic Alliance 2, 243, 248, 249
  NETS 254–5
  Registries for All 251–2
Genetic Alliance Registry and BioBank 241
Genetic Alliance UK 2, 11, 212–14
  RDUK see Rare Disease UK
Genome sequencing 5, 178, 235, 243
  whole genome sequencing (WGS) 236–7
  see also DNA sequencing
Genzyme 22–4, 28, 29, 32, 35, 93, 131, 197, 246
GlaxoSmithKline (GSK) 3, 29, 39, 88, 101, 128, 197, 245, 246
Global Rare Diseases Patient Registry and Data Repository (GRDR) 155–6, 172, 242
Glutamate 127
Glycogen 23
Government
  awareness of rare diseases 15
  initiatives 9, 247–8
Gregory, Robert 1, 48

Harvey, William 263
Health technology assessment (HTA) 69
Herceptin 253
Heywood, Jamie 254
High content screening (HCS) 116
High throughput screening (HTS) 115–16, 119, 120

HIV/AIDS 92, 106, 107, 245
H.M. Pharma 143
Hollak, Dr Carla E.M. 240
Homogentisate 1,2-dioxygenase (HGD) 44, 51, 80
Homogentisic acid (HGA) 44–5, 47, 51, 55, 80, 81
Hôpital Necker Enfants Maladies 49, 54, 55
Howard Hughes Medical Institute 178
HT-1 (tyrosinaemia type I) 47, 80
Human genome project 5, 34, 178, 235
Hypercholesterolemia 3, 194
Hypophosphatasia 3

Ibuprofen 121, 238
ICI 46, 47
In vitro models 50, 53
In vivo testing 117
Incidence/prevalence of rare diseases 2–3, 13, 30, 176, 194, 195, 215
    AKU 43, 83
    orphan drug designation and 30, 76, 91
Individualised medicine 39
Industry *see* Businesses/companies
Infantile Refsum disease 30
Innovative Medicines Initiative (IMI) 137, 248
International Conference on Rare Diseases & Orphan Drugs (ICORD) 12
International Rare Disease Day 11, 19, 195, 224–5, 247
International Rare Diseases Research Consortium (IRDiRC) 11, 12, 172, 247–8
Investors 9, 17, 196, 197–9
    awareness of rare diseases 14, 15
    venture capital 27, 89, 108, 196, 197
    see also Venture capital
Itraconzale 123

Johns Hopkins Clinical Compound Library (JHCCL) 123
Joint replacements 45, 47, 58

Kidney disorders 189–90
    see also Birt-Hogg-Dubé Syndrome
Kornberg, Roger 232

LAM Foundation 182
Lasker, Mary 253
Leishmanicidals 129
Liddell-Grainger, Ian 211
Limb girdle muscular dystrophy 30
Lobbying for UK national rare disease plan
    contact campaigns 223–4
    demonstrating the issues 214–18

developing recommendations 218–22
engagement of members 225–8
European background 207–9
impact of European policies 209–12
patient involvement 222–5
RDUK lobbying campaign 207–30
survey 215–17
uniting stakeholders 212–14
working groups 219–20
see also National rare disease plans; Rare Disease UK
Lumophore Ltd 138–9
LYSOGENE 5, 108, 204, 205–6
Lysosomal storage diseases (LSDs) 32, 131–2, 202, 203, 205
    see also Sanfilippo syndrome

Malaria 129
Manufacturing challenges 32
Market access 109
Market exclusivity 64–5, 90, 91, 234
Marketing authorisation
    conditional 106–7
    early market access 103–7
Max Planck Society 178
Medicines Healthcare Products Regulatory Agency (MHRA) 117
Melior Discovery 142
Merron, Gillian 210
Messenger RNA (mRNA) 27
Meyers, Abbey 7–8, 9, 13, 253
Miller, Paul and Debra 26
Milton, Anne 211, 224
Misdiagnosis 57–8, 216
    see also Diagnosis
Mouse models 51, 80–1, 135, 139
Mucopolysaccharide storage (MPS) disorders 35
Mucopolysaccharidosis IIIA 108
Multiple Myeloma Research Foundation (MMRF) 182
Muscular dystrophy
    limb girdle 30
    telethon 16
    see also Duchenne muscular dystrophy
Myrovlytis Trust 2, 5, 176–91
    annual BHD Symposium 185
    creation 176–80
    formation of research community 183–6
    funding 180
    managing research 182–3
    online resources 186–8
    as research hub 180–2

N-acetylglutamate synthase (NAGS) deficiency 133
Narcolepsy 197
National alliances 12–13
National biobanks 241–2
National Institute of Care Excellence (NICE) 211
National Institutes of Health (NIH) 17, 124, 177, 181
1000 Genomes Project 236
AKU research 1, 2, 46, 47, 53
drug repositioning 239
GRDR 155–6, 172, 242
public awareness initiatives 11
National Organization for Rare Disorders (NORD) 2, 3, 62, 66–7, 108, 138, 205, 248, 253
public awareness initiative 8, 10–11
vision statement 19
National rare disease plans 172
EUROPLAN 221
France 94, 172, 247
UK *see* Lobbying for UK national rare disease plan
Natural history studies 18, 28, 31, 32
Navigating the Ecosystem of Translational Science (NETS) 254–5
NEPHIRD 13
New chemical entities (NCEs) 116, 117
New drug application (NDA) 117
New molecular entities (NMEs) 116
NF-kB inhibitors 126–7
Niemann-Pick type C 108
Nitisinone 3–4, 44, 46–8, 51, 108, 135
clinical trials 47–8, 53, 55, 80–4, 138
Nordic Bioscience 55
Novartis 88, 101, 245, 246
Numbers of rare diseases *see* Incidence/prevalence of rare diseases

Ochronosis 50–1, 52, 53, 54, 55, 57, 80, 81, 82, 83, 84
Online/virtual communities 11, 23, 38, 168, 253
Organon 22
Orlistat 129
Orphan diseases
rare diseases distinguished 129–30
use of term 2–3, 8
Orphan Drug Act 1983 8, 28, 62, 66, 90, 95, 96, 243
Orphan medicinal product designation (OMPD) 30
application to FDA/EMA 90–2

European Medicines Agency 69–79, 89, 90–1
prevalence criterion 30, 76, 91
seriousness criterion 91
significance criterion 91
United States 70–9, 92–4
US and Europe compared 70–3
see also Regulatory approval
Orphanet 30, 108, 167, 193
Osteoarthritis 3, 17, 45, 51, 54, 57, 58

Pan-European Patient Network for Information on Rare Diseases and Orphan Drugs 12
Parent Project Muscular Dystrophy 26, 156
Parents/caregivers organisations 35, 202
advocacy 26
AKU *see* AKU Society
see also Disease advocacy organisations
Parkinson's disease 121, 140, 142
Partnerships 28, 38
Patent cliff 29
Patent expiration 29, 114, 119, 139
Patient groups/organisations 9, 25, 26, 28, 35, 108, 202, 205, 216
AKU patients *see* AKU Society
ERNs 168–9
funding 27, 28
information/knowledge 41
online/virtual communities 11, 23, 38, 168, 253
partnerships 28, 38
setting-up 60
see also Disease advocacy organisations
Patient registries 4, 31, 32, 36, 150–7, 240, 242, 245, 251–2
AKU patients 83
BHD patients 184
consent and privacy issues 153–4
DuchenneConnect case study 156–7
EPIRARE 172
ERNs 163, 169, 170, 172, 173
GRDR case study 155–6
institutional review board (IRB) approval 154
patient self-reporting 153–4, 156–7
patient/family participation 152
PatientCrossroads 157
physician-entered 153–4
Registries for All 251–2
security issues 154
sustainability 172
PatientCrossroads 2, 4, 157
Patients' Consensus on Preferred Policy Scenarios for Rare Diseases (POLKA) 13

PatientsLikeMe   248, 253
Pegademase bovine   234
Personal Genome Project   236
Personalised medicine   39
Pfizer   29, 88, 101, 128, 245
Pharmacogenomics   238, 244
Pharmacological chaperones   132–3
PharmaKure   142–3
Pharming   23, 24
Phenylketonuria (PKU)   133
Placebos *see* randomised controlled trials
POLKA   13
Pompe disease   23–4, 26, 30, 35, 133
Porphyria   166
Postcode pharmacy   25, 38
Pre-approval access systems   34
Pre-clinical models   30–1
Pre-clinical trials   116, 135, 136, 140
    see also Animal trials; Clinical trials
Prevalence of rare diseases *see* Incidence/
    prevalence of rare diseases
Primarolo, Dawn   210
PROMISCUOUS   124
Prosensa   2, 3, 26–9, 35, 39
Protein Technologies   2, 54, 135–6
Pseudoxanthoma elasticum (PXE)   233, 240
PSR Group   55
Public awareness   3, 7–20, 60
    AKU   60
    the audiences   14–16
    benefits   14
    efforts to increase   10–13
    EURORDIS   10, 11, 12–13, 109
    general public   16
    healthcare professionals   15, 18, 19, 22
    how to increase   18–20
    ICORD   12
    IRDiRC   11, 12
    meetings   11–12
    the messages   16–18
    need to enhance   13–14
    NEPHIRD   13
    NORD   8, 10–11
    online communities   11, 23
    Rare Disease Day   11, 19, 195, 224–5, 247
Pulmonary arterial hypertension (PAH)   92
PXE International   240–1

Randomised controlled trials (RCTs)   31–2, 40,
    81, 83–4, 99, 256
Ranganath, Dr Lakshminarayan   2, 48
Rare Disease Act 2002   130
Rare Disease Clinical Research Network   247
Rare Disease Day   11, 19, 195, 224–5, 247

Rare Disease-HUB (RD-HUB)   242
Rare Disease UK (RDUK)   5, 11, 57
    'Experiences of Rare Diseases' report
        217–18, 221, 222
    funding   214
    Improving Lives, Optimising Resources:
        A Vision for the UK Rare Disease
        Strategy   11, 214, 219
    lobbying for national rare disease
        plan   207–30
    objectives   213
RD-Connect   172
(RE)ACT Community   196
(RE)ACT Congresses   5, 195
Reference networks *see* European reference
    networks
Registries *see* Patient registries
Registries for All   251–2
Regulatory approval   4, 24, 87–109, 233–4
    accelerated approval   103–7
    conditional approval   68–9, 84, 105
    early market access   37, 103–7
    European Union   97–103
    expedited procedures   67–8
    legislation   89–92
    numbers approved   93, 95–7, 115, 119, 232
    pathways   32–3
    pivotal clinical trial stage   66–7, 99–100, 101
    regulatory dialogue   101–3
    size/experience of company   100–1
    successful/non-successful approvals
        compared   97–103
    United States   92–4, 96, 97–103
    see also Orphan medicinal product
        designation
Reimbursement   24–5, 33, 40, 89
    drug development costs   33–4, 69, 117–18
    postcode pharmacy   25, 38
    see also Funding
Repurposing of drugs *see* Drug repositioning/
    repurposing
RNA (ribonucleic acid) modulation   26, 27
Roche   142, 197, 245–6

Sanfilippo syndrome   5, 201–6
    type A (MPS-IIIA)   108, 205
Sanofi Aventis   139, 197, 245, 246
Schmorl's stain   50
Schoneveld van der Linde, Maryze   23–4, 25
Schoneveld van der Linde, Tanneke   25
Screening programmes for prenatal/
    newborn   34
Seckler, Benjamin and Tracey   26
Seroxat   120

Severe combined immunodeficiency
    syndrome (SCID) 234
Shire 28, 197
Small and medium-sized enterprises
    (SMEs) 64, 87, 88, 100, 101
Small molecule drugs 132–3
Social entrepreneurship 2–3
Social media 19, 31, 187–8, 228,
    242–3, 253
SOM Biotech 140
Sosei 142
Standards of care 37–8
Statins 3
Stratified medicine 238
Stress urinary incontinence (SIU) 122
Swedish Orphan Biovitrum International
    (Sobi) 55

Tau Therapeutics 142
Telemedicine/tele-expertise 170–1
Telethons 16, 19
Timpson, Edward 210
TKT 28

Treatment costs 25, 33, 40
  AKU 58–60
  price of orphan drugs 69
Trypanocidals 128–9
Tyrosinaemia type I (HT-1) 47, 80
Tyrosine metabolism 46–7, 80

Van Ommon, Gert-Jan 27
Venture capital 27, 89, 108, 196, 197
Viagra 121, 122
Virtual communities *see* Online/virtual
    communities
Vroom, Elizabeth 26

Wellcome Trust 138, 178, 236, 241
Whole genome sequencing (WGS) 236–7
Wilson's disease 167
World Health Organisation (WHO) 127

X-linked spastic paraplegia type 16 30

Zallen, Doris 263–4
Zyprexa 119